Soldiers of Perón

SOLDIERS OF PERON
Argentina's Montoneros

Richard Gillespie

CLARENDON PRESS · OXFORD
1982

Oxford University Press, Walton Street, Oxford OX2 6DP
London Glasgow New York Toronto
Delhi Bombay Calcutta Madras Karachi
Kuala Lumpur Singapore Hong Kong Tokyo
Nairobi Dar es Salaam Cape Town
Melbourne Auckland
and associates in
Beirut Berlin Ibadan Mexico City Nicosia

Published in the United States by
Oxford University Press, New York

All rights reserved. No part of this publication may be reproduced, stored in a retrieval system, or transmitted, in any form or by any means, electronic, mechanical, photocopying, recording, or otherwise, without the prior permission of Oxford University Press

© Richard Gillespie 1982

British Library Cataloguing in Publication Data
Gillespie, Richard
Soldiers of Perón.
1. Montoneros   2. Argentine — Politics and
government — 1955-
I. Title
322.4'2'0982   JL3698.M/
ISBN 0-19-821131-7

Library of Congress Cataloging in Publication Data
Gillespie, Richard, 1952-
Soldiers of Perón — Argentina's Montoneros.
Bibliography: p.
Includes index.
1. Argentina — Politics and government — 1955-
2. Peronism.   3. Guerrillas — Argentina.   I. Title.
F2849.2.G47 1982   982'063   82-8054
ISBN 0-19-821131-7   AACR2

Typeset by Hope Services (Abingdon)
Printed in Great Britain
at the University Press, Oxford
by Eric Buckley
Printer to the University

Preface

Urban guerrilla warfare, especially when waged in an acutely-polarized and blood-stained society such as that of contemporary Argentina, has attracted the commentaries of an undue number both of apologists and of detractors. Neither hagiography nor demonology has benefited noticeably from their efforts, which have not always culminated in valid observations concerning the instrumental effects of this form of warfare. In offering this critical history of Latin America's foremost urban guerrilla force to date, I attempt to examine the ambitions and impact of insurrectional violence without depicting its combatants as either saints or sinners. The prevalent images of guerrillas as either 'heroic freedom fighters' or 'bloodthirsty terrorists' are rejected as inappropriate.

At no time during the 1970s did the Montoneros appear capable of leading a popular revolution or of seizing State power by military means: indeed, they themselves classified much of that decade as phases of 'defensive' struggle. Their relevance lies not in political triumph, but rather in their serving as an illustration of both the potential and the limitations of a strategy which numerous left-wing and national liberation movements have experimented with in recent years. No account of the Montonero experience would be complete, however, if it merely discussed the trials and tribulations of an organization of urban guerrillas. The Montoneros started out as such, but rapidly developed into a radical nationalist movement which, when permitted openly and legally to mobilize political support, did so and did so impressively. Tens and even hundreds of thousands of Argentines rallied behind their banners in the heady months of 1973-4. Thus, in addition to illuminating the obscure reality of the guerrilla underworld, this study examines the Montoneros as political performers whose influence upon Argentine political life in general and evolving Peronism in particular has been substantial.

The first two chapters, which analyse the historical and ideological background to the emergence of the Montoneros, provide some of the clues as to why they rather than other contemporaneous guerrilla forces achieved pre-eminence. Chapters three to six look at the political and military initiatives taken by the Montoneros in four distinct periods: the last three years of the 1966-73 military regime; the 1973-4 Presidencies of Héctor Cámpora and Juan Domingo Perón; the considerably less popular 1974-6 administration of María Estela Martínez de Perón, Argentina's first woman president; and, finally, the first five years of the military regime installed in March 1976 and originally headed by General Jorge Rafael Videla.

Much of the material upon which this work is based was assembled during the course of a sixteen-month research visit to Buenos Aires in 1975-6, its first elaboration being my doctoral thesis, 'The Peronist Left' (University of Liverpool, 1979), but a number of interviews since 1976, along with the acquisition of recent guerrilla publications and documents, permit the present work to span the whole of the 1970s. The basic kinds of sources utilized are: Argentine daily newspapers and weekly news magazines; Montonero political magazines and those produced by other political tendencies; public and internal guerrilla documents; published Montonero interviews; personal interviews with Montonero members and sympathizers, as well as with critical journalists, academics, and authors; and books pertaining to the Peronist Left and Argentine political history.

Few abbreviations denoting source material are used lest they be confused with the initials and acronyms representing the scores of political, guerrilla, and trade union organizations that intervened in the late Argentine imbroglio, a list of which appears at the start of the book, with a glossary of Spanish terms towards the end. Names of organizations have generally been Anglicized in the text itself, though the initials of the more important organizations appear in Spanish, especially where a whole section refers to them.

A number of people and institutions provided indispensable assistance during the preparation of this book. In particular, Dr Walter Little of the University of Liverpool deserves recognition as an excellent doctoral research supervisor who dispensed criticism and blandishment in fair measure, while always being a source of stimulating ideas. Among those who kindly examined draft chapters, Alan Angell of St. Antony's

College, Oxford, is to be thanked for his trenchant comments and positive suggestions. From 1974-7, the Social Science Research Council generously allocated me a research studentship, without which the original investigation could not have been carried out. In addition, both the Department of Political Theory and Institutions in the University of Liverpool and the Department of Politics in the University of Newcastle upon Tyne, and above all St. John's College, Oxford, are to be thanked for providing me with facilities during the research and writing phases of the project.

Unfortunately I am not able to mention by name many Argentines who helped me in innumerable ways, even though some now temporarily reside in exile. They include academics, lawyers, militants, and personal friends who helped me to establish contact with those able to assist me in my work. Given the present political climate within Argentina and the apparent ease with which Argentine dissidents living abroad have been kidnapped, never to reappear, identifying them might well amount to the conferment of a death sentence. Their contribution was absolutely essential, whether it took the form of personal interviews, informal but informed discussions, the supply of illicit political material, or introductions to further contacts. Apart from the considerable time which they invested in my undertaking, I would like to express my thanks to them for the risks which they took and the confidence which they placed in me.

Richard Gillespie
1981

Contents

Abbreviations	xi
Map of Argentina	xviii

1. Antecedents 1
   Developments within Argentine nationalism 6
   The Peronist phenomenon 17
   Post-1955 political instability 26
   The emergence of the Peronist Left 29

2. Montonero Origins 47
   Nationalism, Catholicism, and the proto-Montoneros 47
   Radicalization in the late 1960s 60
   Montonero Peronism 70
   Urban guerrilla theory and the appeal of armed struggle 75
   Preparing for warfare 82

3. For the Return of Perón 89
   (1970-1973)
   Early operations and political definitions 89
   Relations with Perón and other guerrilla organizations 103
   The nature and effects of Montonero activity 110
   Guerrilla losses and the cult of the martyr 116
   Promotion of the Peronist Youth 119

4. Coming up for Air 123
   (1973-1974)
   The return of Peronism and the advance of the
   Peronist Left 123
   Limitations of the Revolutionary Tendency 136
   Perón attacks the Montoneros 144
   The Triple A and the Rightist offensive 153
   The failure of the *movimientista* strategy 159

5. The Return to Arms 164
   (1974-1976)
   Guerrilla attacks on the labour bureaucracy 167

x   *Contents*

    The attempt to build a Montonero Army   174
    A new phase of armed struggle   183
        'Montonero justice'   184
        Communications problems and the growth of militarism   190
        Raising the level of warfare   193
    Political initiatives through the *Auténticos*   205
    The cost of involvement   215
    A coup approaches   223

6. The Retreat from Argentina (1976-1981)   227
    The Videla regime   227
    The Montonero response: 'active defence'   232
    Reorganization, rethinking, and the growth of internal dissent   239
    The use of 'State terrorism' to eradicate 'subversion'   244
    The Montonero emigration   252
    A disastrous attempted return   262
    The Montonero decline   266

Glossary of Spanish Terms   272

Appendices
A: Splits and Mergers in Montonero and PRT-ERP Development   275
B: Montonero Organizational Structures   277

Bibliography   281

Index   295

Abbreviations

(i) Argentine Organizations

AAA	*Alianza Anticomunista Argentina* (Argentine Anti-Communist Alliance: The Triple A)
AB	*Asociación Bancaria* (Bank Employees Association)
AC	*Acción Católica* (Catholic Action)
AE	*Agrupación Evita* (Evita Group)
ANDE	*Asociación Nacional de Estudiantes de Derecho* (National Law Students Association)
APA	*Agrupación del Peronismo Auténtico* (Authentic Peronist Group)
APR	*Alianza Popular Revolucionaria* (Revolutionary Popular Alliance)
ATE	*Asociación de Trabajadores del Estado* (State Workers Association)
CAR	*Corriente Argentina Revolucionaria* (Argentine Revolutionary Current)
C de O	*Comando de Organización* (Organizational Command)
CGE	*Confederación General Económica* (General Economic Confederation)
CGT	*Confederación General del Trabajo* (General Labour Confederation)
CGTA	*Confederación General del Trabajo de los Argentinos* (General Labour Confederation of the Argentines)
CGT-R	*Confederación General del Trabajo en la Resistencia* (General Labour Confederation in the Resistance)
CGU	*Confederación General Universitaria* (General University Confederation)
CNFC	*Consejo Nacional de Federaciones y Centros* (National Council of Federations and Centres)
CNT	*Comisión Nacional de Trabajo* (National Labour Commission)
CNU	*Concentración Nacional Universitaria* (National University Concentration)

Abbreviations

CPL	*Comandos Populares de Liberación* (Popular Liberation Commands)
CSP	*Comando/Consejo Superior Peronista* (Peronist Superior Command/Council)
CUTA	*Conducción Unica de Trabajadores Argentinos* (United Leadership of Argentine Workers)
EGP	*Ejército Guerrillero del Pueblo* (People's Guerrilla Army)
EM	*Ejército Montonero* (Montonero Army)
ENR	*Ejército Nacional Revolucionario* (National Revolutionary Army)
ERP	*Ejército Revolucionario del Pueblo* (People's Revolutionary Army)
FAL	*Fuerzas Armadas de Liberación* (Armed Liberation Forces)
FAP	*Fuerzas Armadas Peronistas* (Peronist Armed Forces)
FAR	*Fuerzas Armadas Revolucionarias* (Revolutionary Armed Forces)
FEN	*Frente Estudiantil Nacional* (National Student Front)
FGB	*Federación Gráfica Bonaerense* (Buenos Aires Printers Federation)
FIP	*Frente de Izquierda Popular* (Popular Left Front)
FM	*Franja Morada* (*Alfonsinista* Radicals' student group)
FORJA	*Fuerza de Orientación Radical de la Joven Argentina* (Radical Orientation Force of the Argentine Youth)
FOTIA	*Federación de Obreros Tucumanos de la Industria de Azúcar* (Federation of Tucumán Sugar Industry Workers)
FRECILINA	*Frente Cívico de Liberación Nacional* (Civic Front of National Liberation)
FREJULI	*Frente Justicialista de Liberación* (Justicialist Liberation Front)
FRIP	*Frente Revolucionario Indoamericanista Popular* (Indo-American Popular Revolutionary Front)
FUA	*Federación Universitaria Argentina* (Argentine

Abbreviations xiii

	University Federation)
GNR	*Guardia Nacionalista Restauradora* (Restorationist Nationalist Guard)
JAEN	*Juventud Argentina por la Emancipación Nacional* (Argentine Youth for National Emancipation)
JCR	*Junta de Coordinación Revolucionaria* (Revolutionary Coordinating Council)
JEC	*Juventud Estudiantil Católica* (Catholic Student Youth)
JOC	*Juventud Obrera Católica* (Catholic Working Youth)
JP	*Juventud Peronista* (Peronist Youth)
JPA	*Juventudes Políticas Argentinas* (Argentine Political Youth)
JPM	*Juventud Peronista Montonera* (Montonero Peronist Youth)
JPRA	*Juventud Peronista de la República Argentina* (Peronist Youth of the Argentine Republic)
JRP	*Juventud Revolucionaria Peronista* (Peronist Revolutionary Youth)
JSP	*Juventud Sindical Peronista* (Peronist Trade Union Youth)
JTP	*Juventud Trabajadora Peronista* (Peronist Working Youth)
JUC	*Juventud Universitaria Católica* (Catholic University Youth)
JUP	*Juventud Universitaria Peronista* (Peronist University Youth)
M-17	*Montoneros 17 de Octubre* (Montoneros 17th October)
MID	*Movimiento de Integración y Desarrollo* (Movement of Integration and Development)
MIP	*Movimiento de Inquilinos Peronistas* (Peronist Tenants Movement)
MJP	*Movimiento de la Juventud Peronista* (Peronist Youth Movement)
MNR	*Movimiento Nacional Reformista* (National Reformist Movement)
MNRT	*Movimiento Nacionalista Revolucionario Tacuara* (Tacuara Revolutionary Nationalist Movement)

MOR	*Movimiento de Orientación Reformista* (Movement of Reformist Orientation)
MPA	*Movimiento Peronista Auténtico* (Authentic Peronist Movement)
MPM	*Movimiento Peronista Montonero* (Montonero Peronist Movement)
MRP	*Movimiento Revolucionario Peronista* (Revolutionary Peronist Movement)
MVP	*Movimiento de Villeros Peronistas* (Peronist Shanty-Town Dwellers Movement)
OAP	*Organizaciones Armadas Peronistas* (Peronist Armed Organizations)
OCPO	*Organización Comunista Poder Obrero* (Workers Power Communist Organization)
OLA	*Organización para la Liberación de Argentina* (Argentine Liberation Organization)
OPM	*Organización Político-Militar* (Montonero Politico-Military Organization)
PA	*Partido Auténtico* (Authentic Party)
PB	*Peronismo de Base* (Rank-and-File Peronism)
PCA	*Partido Comunista de la Argentina* (Argentine Communist Party)
PCR	*Partido Comunista Revolucionario* (Revolutionary Communist Party)
PI	*Partido Intransigente* (Intransigent Party)
PJ	*Partido Justicialista* (Justicialist Party)
PM	*Partido Montonero* (Montonero Party)
PPA	*Partido Peronista Auténtico* (Authentic Peronist Party)
PRC	*Partido Revolucionario Cristiano* (Revolutionary Christian Party)
PRT	*Partido Revolucionario de los Trabajadores* (Workers Revolutionary Party)
PSA	*Partido Socialista Argentino* (Argentine Socialist Party)
PSRN	*Partido Socialista de la Revolución Nacional* (Socialist Party of the National Revolution)
PST	*Partido Socialista de los Trabajadores* (Socialist Workers Party)
SITRAC	*Sindicato de Trabajadores de Concord* (Concord Workers Union, Córdoba)

SITRAM	*Sindicato de Trabajadores de Materfer* (Materfer Workers Union, Córdoba)
62 De Pie	*62 De Pie Junto a Perón* (62 on Foot with Perón)
SMATA	*Sindicato de Mecánicos y Afines del Transporte Automotor* (Car Workers Union)
SUD	*Sindicato Universitario de Derecho* (University Law Union)
TEA	*Tropas Especiales de Agitación* (Special Agitational Troops)
TEI	*Tropas Especiales de Infantería* (Special Infantry Troops)
TP	*Tercera Posición* (Third Position)
Triple A	See AAA
UCR	*Unión Cívica Radical* (Radical Civic Union)
UCRI	*Unión Cívica Radical Intransigente* (Intransigent Radical Civic Union)
UCRP	*Unión Cívica Radical del Pueblo* (People's Radical Civic Union)
UDELPA	*Unión del Pueblo Adelante* (Popular Advance Union)
UES	*Unión de Estudiantes Secundarios* (Secondary Students Union)
UNE	*Unión Nacional de Estudiantes* (National Union of Students)
UNES	*Unión Nacionalista de Estudiantes Secundarios* (Secondary Students Nationalist Union)
UOCRA	*Unión Obrera de la Construcción de la República Argentina* (Construction Workers Union of the Argentine Republic)
UOM	*Unión Obrera Metalúrgica* (Metalworkers Union)
UTA	*Unión Tranviarios Automotor* (Transport Workers Union)
VC	*Vanguardia Comunista* (Communist Vanguard)
VR	*Vanguardia Revolucionaria* (Revolutionary Vanguard)

(ii) Non-Argentine Organizations

ELN	*Ejército de Liberación Nacional* (National Liberation Army, Bolivia)

xvi *Abbreviations*

ETA	*Euzkadi Ta Askatasuna* (Basque Homeland and Freedom)
FAI-CNT	*Federación Anarquista Ibérica-Confederación Nacional del Trabajo* (Iberian Anarchist Federation-National Labour Confederation, Spain)
FSLN	*Frente Sandinista de Liberación Nacional* (Sandinista National Liberation Front, Nicaragua)
MIR	*Movimiento de Izquierda Revolucionaria* (Movement of the Revolutionary Left, Chile)
MLN(T)	*Movimiento de Liberación Nacional, Tupamaros* (Tupamaro National Liberation Movement, Uruguay)
PLO	Palestine Liberation Organization
PSOE	*Partido Socialista Obrero Español* (Spanish Socialist Workers Party)
ZANU	Zimbabwe African National Union

(iii) Miscellaneous

CONINTES	*Conmoción Interna del Estado* (Frondizi's provisions for use against civil disturbances and insurgency)
ESMA	*Escuela de Mecánica de la Armada* (Navy Engineering School, a secret detention centre after the 1976 coup)
GAN	*Gran Acuerdo Nacional* (Lanusse's Great National Agreement scheme)

(iv) Sources

CICSO	*Centro de Investigaciones en Ciencias Sociales* (Social Science Research Centre, Buenos Aires)
NACLA	North American Congress on Latin America
OAS	Organization of American States

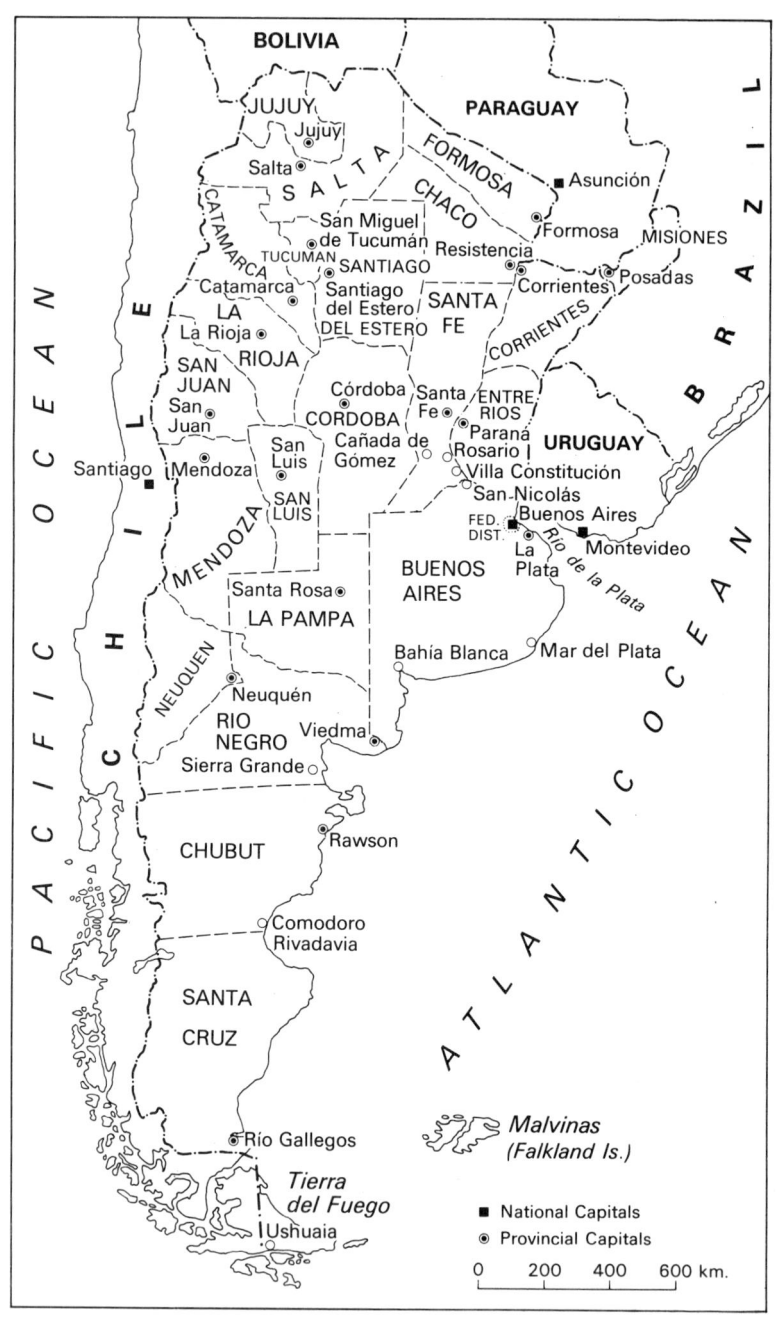

Argentina
Source: James R. Scobie, *Argentina: A City and Nation* (USA: OUP, 1971), p. 9.

1
Antecedents

'We are not in the least the enemies of capital, and the future will show that we have been its true defenders.'
— Juan D. Perón, 21 October 1946[1]

'Peaceful co-existence between oppressed and oppressive classes is impossible. We have set ourselves the fundamental task of triumphing over the exploiters, even if they are infiltrated in our own political movement.'
— Juan D. Perón, 20 October 1965[2]

Long before the appearance of the modern urban guerrilla, and indeed more than a century before Peronism arrived on the political scene, *montoneros* made their presence felt in Argentina, that illusory 'land of silver'. They were the rural plebeian horsemen, the *gauchos*, who followed the nation's early-nineteenth-century Independence heroes in their quest for emancipation from decadent Spain's final colonial hold on their country. Yet though autonomy was asserted in 1810 and political independence declared in 1816, Argentina's dependent integration into the world economy was gradually strengthened, not weakened. Juan Manuel de Rosas, the first *caudillo* to impose a semblance of national authority (1835–52), took some faltering steps in the direction of a nationally-based development strategy, but was eventually defeated by General Urquiza, Governor of the Province of Entre Ríos, at the Battle of Caseros. Subsequently, the consolidation of political power in the hands of an 'oligarchy' of landowners and merchants linked primarily to British interests proceeded apace with British commercial and financial expansionism and the growing dominance of the port-city of Buenos Aires over the nation.[3] By the end of the century the land was

[1] Perón, quoted in José Luis Romero, *A History of Argentine Political Thought* (California: Stanford University Press, 1963), p. 254.
[2] Idem, 'Mensaje a la Juventud', reproduced in *Militancia*, no. 11 (23 August 1973), p. 49. Unless otherwise stated, all the Spanish-titled newspapers, journals, and political magazines cited in this book are Buenos Aires publications.
[3] Perhaps the most useful introduction to diverse aspects of Argentine life and history available in English is James Scobie, *Argentina: A City and a Nation*, 2nd edition (USA: OUP, 1971).

2 Antecedents

being referred to as 'British Argentina'; by 1916 its financial dependence on British capital was sufficiently pronounced for it to merit a special mention in Lenin's work on imperialism.[4] But the surging, centralizing, unitarian tide of the middle decades of the last century was resisted, heroically if hopelessly. And the Federal forces of the Interior who so staunchly defended provincial autonomy again went by that name which now began to embed itself into national-popular folklore: *montoneros*.

The mid-nineteenth-century rebellions arose out of genuine popular discontent, but were channelled by the local *caudillos* of La Rioja and Entre Ríos into the defence of archaic provincial structures. Their leading personalities — Angel Vicente Peñaloza, Felipe Varela, and Ricardo López Jordán — counted with the support of Chilecito miners, impoverished by mine closures, and artisans ruined by foreign competition, but lacked a viable economic order to counterpose to that of the dominant landowners and commerical concerns linked to Britain and other external metropoli.[5] Socially, these provincial movements, finally suppressed at Alcaracito in 1876 with the capture of López Jordán, involved the subordination of the landless *gaucho* to the landed *caudillo*, and their historical contribution to the nationalism of the following century was to be one which encouraged the subordination of the lower classes to popular, but generally authoritarian, nationalist elite figures.

Buenos Aires became the undisputed capital of Argentina in 1880. That same year, in his inaugural speech to Congress, General Roca depicted the rapidly-increasing influx of foreign capital, labour, technology, and ideas as agents of 'progress' and 'civilization', sweeping away a barbarian past:

> Anyone who has attentively followed the progress of this country has been able to notice, as you Honourable Gentlemen know, the profound economic, social and political revolution that the iron road and the telegraph bring as they penetrate the Interior. National unity has been assured by these powerful agents of civilization; they have conquered and exterminated the spirit of the *montonera*....[6]

---

[4] V. I. Lenin, *Imperialism, the Highest Stage of Capitalism* (1916), 15th printing (Moscow: Progress Publishers, 1970), pp. 82-3.

[5] David Viñas, *De los montoneros a los anarquistas*, vol. 1 of *Rebeliones populares argentinas* (Buenos Aires: Carlos Pérez Editor, 1971), pp. 15-148.

[6] Quoted in Romero, p. 172. A *montonera* was a band of *montoneros*.

This was the voice of the victorious oligarchy, proud of its Liberal 1853 Constitution, brim-full of confidence and optimism. It had coined the term *montonero* purposefully to denigrate the 'wild' horsemen of the now-vanquished irregular armies: in Liberal oligarchic eyes, they were merely a *montón*, a rabble, unenlightened by any appreciation of the European cultural heritage. True, the dominant classes soon had fresh problems to face, especially the threatening but necessary arrival of immigrant labourers. Both the beginnings of industrial development after 1880, mainly catering for the needs of the agro-export economy, and the grossly underpopulated state of the country[7] demanded their presence, yet with these strangers from Italy, Spain, and other lands came organizational experience and transfusions of support for the ideas of anarchism and syndicalism, socialism and communism. Nevertheless, for decades even the ghosts of the *montoneros* seemed to have been, in Roca's word, 'exterminated'. The agro-export model — whereby the Argentine economy specialized in meat, grain, hides, and other products suggested by the ecology of the country — appeared to be the guarantor of continuing growth and untold prosperity. Even the demands of the middle classes, expressed by the Radical Party (UCR) and largely political in character, given such propitious circumstances, were satisfied without major structural dislocation: the 1912 Sáenz Peña Law of universal male suffrage, the admission to office of the elected Radical Governments of 1916-30, and the highly progressive University Reform of 1918, while important middle-class achievements, did not herald an anti-oligarchic social revolution.[8]

[7] The population of Argentina, territorially the world's eighth largest nation, was still only 7,885,237 in 1914 (having been 1,830,214 in 1869 and 3,956,060 in 1895), of whom 29.9 per cent were foreigners and 410, 201 were employed in industry. Romero, p. 169; Oscar Cornblit, 'European Immigrants in Argentine Industry and Politics', in Claudio Veliz (ed), *The Politics of Conformity in Latin America* (USA: OUP, 1970), pp. 221-48.

[8] It has been shown that during the 1916-30 period of Radical Government 60 per cent of the bills presented to Congress favouring livestock producers were introduced by the Radicals. See Peter H. Smith, 'Los radicales argentinos y la defensa de los intereses ganaderos, 1916-30', *Desarrollo Económico*, vol. 7, no. 25 (April-June 1967), pp. 795-829. On this period, see especially David Rock, 'Machine Politics in Buenos Aires and the Argentine Radical Party, 1912-1930', *Journal of Latin American Studies*, vol. 4, no. 2 (November 1972), pp. 233-74; and 'Radical Populism and the Conservative Elite, 1912-1930' in Rock (ed),

4   *Antecedents*

Argentina's model of dependent development, of development in unequal, subordinate association with British and other foreign capital, enjoyed a public acceptance that was challenged by individual nationalists but not by schools of thought. It took the onset of the world depression for the frailty of the model to be exposed, and for *montoneros* to reappear, if only at first through the revisionist historiography of the 1930s. As the prices of traditional Argentine exports and their volume fell, Radicalism languished, devoid of antidotes. The now almost-senile President Hipólito Yrigoyen was bundled out of office in September 1930 by an army whose mission was to apply austerity measures and authoritarian controls to Argentine society. And if the corporatist hopes of the right-wing nationalist General Uriburu were thwarted in 1932, they were only, in the form of President Justo and his successors, to give way to a Conservatism which was in no way democratic. Elections were rigged, fraud practised, and anarchists and Communists, even Socialists and Radicals, suffered the attentions of the new Special Section of the Federal Police. This was Argentina's *década infame*, her infamous decade.

In broadly similar fashion to, though to a far greater extent than, the way in which the First World War had stimulated Argentine manufacturing, the latest international crisis now catalysed a far-reaching process of import-substitutive industrialization. But Argentina's dependent status was underlined by the 1933 Roca-Runciman Pact and its 1936 extension: to avoid the loss of her remaining exports to Britain to Commonwealth supply rivals, Argentina was obliged to authorize deeply humiliating commercial concessions, including an end to local bus services which competed with the British transport network of Buenos Aires. With additional impetus provided by the rise of the radical Right in Italy, Germany, and Spain, and the continuing influence of right-wing French authors like Charles Maurras, literary nationalism flourished. In seeking a solution to the national crisis or justifications for authoritarian rule, many writers looked into

---

Argentina in the Twentieth Century (London: Duckworth, 1975), pp. 66-87. On the University Reform, see Richard J. Walter, *Student Politics in Argentina* (USA: Basic Books, 1968), pp. 23-62.

the past for inspiration, and whether they exalted the golden Hispanic Age of yesteryear or turned their pens to the rehabilitation of Rosas, their historical revisionism was marked by a sharp rejection of European Liberal conceptions. It counterposed Hispanicism to Anglo-Argentine linkage, monarchism and aristocracy to liberal democracy, Catholicism to secularism; the masses were distrusted, unless regimented behind a strong *caudillo*, and political and economic liberalism were blamed for the world crisis and the flagrant corruption characteristic of Yrigoyen's second (1928-30) administration.[9]

The historical revisionism of the 1930s was not short of internal contradictions: it presented itself as Argentine nationalism yet drew much of its inspiration from abroad; it was an anti-intellectual movement composed of intellectuals; it proclaimed the foundation of a new historiographic school while refusing to indulge in serious historical investigation; and it extolled elitism, though it was itself shunned by most oligarchs. An idealized, dusted-down Rosas was recalled from the past to serve as a standard against which other historic figures and forces were judged, quite irrespective of differing socio-economic circumstances and the march of time. It is therefore with considerable justification that historical revisionism has been dismissed as 'an exercise in retrospective militancy.'[10]

Since several of its more prominent figures were either of oligarchic origin or were middle-class intellectuals forced into economic dependence as bureaucrats of the oligarchic regime of the day,[11] it is hardly surprising that the nationalism of the 1930s was predominantly reactionary. In practice its ideas were mirrored by the para-military activities of Uriburu's Civic Legion (*Legión Cívica*), whose early 1930s violence against the Left and labour unions evoked memories of the strike-breaking Argentine Patriotic League (*Liga Patriótica Argentina*) of 1919-21.[12] The *rosistas* had no sympathies for

[9] On Argentine right-wing nationalism, see Juan José Hernández Arregui, *La formación de la conciencia nacional*, 3rd ed. (Buenos Aires: Editorial Plus Ultra, 1973), pp. 165-281.
[10] Tulio Halperin Donghi, *El revisionismo histórico argentino* (Buenos Aires: Siglo XXI Argentina Editores, 1971), p. 79.
[11] Hernández Arregui, op. cit.
[12] For a who's who of Argentine right-wing nationalist organizations, see Ray Josephs, *Argentine Diary* (London: Gollancz, 1945), pp. 265-71.

the popular struggles of the past as such, yet they did shape future popular nationalist writing in three fundamental ways. One was through their emphasis upon a Nation versus Imperialism dichotomy as straddling the axis of Argentina's national identity and dilemma. In other words, often in highly idealistic terms, the 'National Question' was posed, if not coherently answered. Secondly, historical revisionism bore forward the culture of *caudillo* politics, of the strong leader paternalistically directing an uninformed but patriotic mass. And thirdly, the primacy of politics was asserted, at least implicitly, either through a total neglect of social and economic history or through their subordination to political history.

DEVELOPMENTS WITHIN ARGENTINE NATIONALISM

Without departing from its fundamental historiographical moorings, revisionism underwent significant changes in the 1940s when confronted with the rise of Peronism.[13] Here was a movement which was indisputably national, authoritarian in government, and rhetorically anti-imperialist, but at the same time a popular-based protagonist of sweeping social change: it dispensed welfare benefits, substantially increased labour's share of national income, promoted the growth of mighty trade unions, enfranchised women, and, though no agrarian revolution was attempted, both the official anti-oligarchic rhetoric and the transfer of income from the rural to the industrial sector alienated traditionalists. Under Peronist auspices, Argentina developed into a semi-industrialized country of some sixteen million people, 63 per cent of them urbanites, according to the 1947 Census.[14]

What troubled the reactionary nationalists was not so much the industrial modernization commitments of the rebel officers who seized power in June 1943, and it was certainly not the domestic authoritarianism which matched the new regime's declared sympathies for the Axis powers in the international arena. Their alarm arose from the fact that

---

[13] On the rise of Peronism, see Walter Little, 'The Popular Origins of Peronism', in Rock (ed), *Argentina*, pp. 162-78; and Rodolfo Puiggrós, *El peronismo: sus causas* (Buenos Aires: Ediciones Cepe, 1969).

[14] Scobie, p. 304.

Antecedents 7

within the regime successively headed by Generals Rawson, Ramírez, and Farrell, Colonel Juan Domingo Perón was using his relatively humble initial posting as president of the National Labour Department (soon to become the Secretariat of Labour and Social Welfare) to build an independent power base among the scorned 'lower classes'. Perón was virtually alone in recognizing that, with labour hitherto poorly organized and politically divided, with the industrial workforce expanding and high wartime export earnings permitting a progressive redistribution of income, the way was open for the construction of a new popular movement, bolstered by and controlled from the State but acclaimed by the workers as their own political expression. His reciprocation of benefits for labour backing, capitalizing upon the needs and aspirations of a long-neglected and frequently-repressed working class, was not slow in producing results. When on 9 October 1945 he was dismissed as Vice-President and detained by rival officers opposed to his strategy, the trade unionists whom he had favoured repaid their debts by agitating for his release, and secured it by organizing a vociferous workers' convergence upon *Plaza de Mayo* in the centre of Buenos Aires on 17 October. To the elitist nationalists, this subversive spectacle smacked of anarchy and revolution, and their fears appeared to be confirmed when Perón went into the ensuing February 1946 elections as the presidential candidate of not only Radical Party dissidents but also of a Labour Party which on paper denounced national as well as foreign capital. It was little consolation for these nationalists that Perón's election-winning campaign was able to emphasize national sovereignty as the key issue, US Ambassador Spruille Braden having actively intervened on behalf of the opposing Democratic Union coalition.[15]

The turbulent events of these three years obliged nationalists to surrender the shields of the past and define themselves in relation to contemporary Argentine realities. This made a

[15] In the 1946 presidential elections, the Peronists won 52.40 per cent of the vote, as opposed to 42.51 per cent for the rival *Unión Demfocrática* — an alliance of Radicals, Conservatives, Socialists, Communists, landowners, and businessmen, backed by the US government, all of whom characterized Peronism as a form of fascism. For electoral data, see Darío Canton, *Elecciones y partidos políticos en la Argentina* (Buenos Aires: Siglo XXI Argentina Editores, 1973), p. 272.

deep division in their ranks inevitable. While some, notably Julio Irazusta,[16] refused to sponsor the new movement, others, such as Ernesto Palacio, fervently endorsed it, seeing Peronism as the force to provide nationalism with a mass base. Many of the sympathetic nationalists withdrew their patronage when Perón fell into disfavour with the Church over matters such as the 1954 legalization of divorce, but those who stayed on increasingly found themselves in the company of popular nationalists whose routes to Peronism had originated either within Radicalism or on the Left, and both of these ideological shifts contributed to the eventual emergence of the Peronist Left.

Peronism incorporated from the Radical Party a good number of careerists whose guiding ambition was to recover Congressional seats or party or ministerial positions, but it also attracted *Sabattinistas*[17] who were later further radicalized such as Juan José Hernández Arregui, and, more decisively, it won over many members of the Radical Orientation Force of the Argentine Youth (FORJA). The latter was a militant nationalist organization of Radical 'young turks' founded by Arturo Jauretche in 1935,[18] ten years before he and most of the *forjistas* transferred their allegiances to Peronsim. FORJA was a middle-class intellectual force within the Radical Party which challenged the 'deviations' of party leaders from national-popular principles, but which saw itself and the party as historically redundant when Peronism appeared on the scene, prepared to assimilate many Radical ideas. What the *forjistas* contributed to Peronism, apart from democratic counterweights to authoritarianism, were the so-called 'Three Banners of Justicialism', the three unifying principles of Perón's movement: political sovereignty, economic independence, and social justice. A decade before the banners were raised by Perón, Jauretche, himself influenced

[16] For his critique of Peronism, condemned for leading a social rather than a national revolution, see Irazusta, *Perón y la crisis argentina* (Buenos Aires: Editorial Huemul, 1966), especially his homage to Luis Dellepiane, pp. 241-3.
[17] Based in pre-industrial Córdoba, *Sabattinista* Radicalism was the most nationalistic UCR tendency of the 1940s.
[18] On FORJA and Jauretche, see Miguel Angel Scenna, *FORJA: una aventura argentina*, 2 vols. (Buenos Aires: Ediciones La Bastilla, 1972); Arturo Jauretche, *FORJA y la década infame* (Buenos Aires: A. Peña Lillo Editor, 1962); and Ernesto Goldar, *Jauretche* (Buenos Aires: Cuadernos de Crisis 17, 1975).

by Hipólito Yrigoyen, Manuel Ugarte, and Haya de la Torre, had written that 'economic emancipation and social justice will be the indispensable counterparts of political independence'.[19] Banal as such statements may seem, it should be recognized that most national-popular movements have deliberately opted for this kind of ideological vagueness, so as to maximize their appeal to diverse classes, social forces, and political currents.[20]

Along with FORJA recruits, a number of individuals and small groups of erstwhile Socialist, Communist, and Trotskyist affiliation responded positively to Perón's overtures. Most Socialists and Communists, however, did not. Under the influence of European Social Democracy, Soviet Stalinism, and Argentine Liberalism, both parties, once the Nazis had invaded the USSR, characterized the Second World War as one between democracy and Fascism; then, faced with the authoritarian methods of the 1943-6 military regime and its refusal to enter the Allied camp until the Axis powers were doomed, Peronism, in part an offshoot of that regime, came to be branded by the traditional Left as a fascist movement. This was in spite of the fact that Perón, as Labour Secretary, had bestowed unquestionable material favours upon the growing working class: apart from well-publicized wage rises, existing labour legislation was enforced for the first time, recognized unions were provided with a legal right to engage in political activity, and workers were able to enjoy cheap housing, a rent freeze, food and transport price ceilings, a shorter working week, greater job security, holidays with pay, annual bonuses, and pensions.

Socialist and Communist reactions against Peronism were of course sharpened by the way in which most of the trade unions in which they had been influential had either been taken over or suppressed by Perón's supporters; officially-sponsored parallel unions had been created to lure workers away from recalcitrant established union leaderships, and dozens of Socialists and Communists languished in prisons. The fact remained, however, that Perón had granted labour

[19] Jauretche, quoted in Hernández Arregui, p. 307.
[20] Cf. The *San Min Chu I* (Three Principles of the People) outlined by Chinese nationalist leader Sun Yat-sen in 1905: nationalism, people's democracy, people's livelihood.

more in two years than the Socialists had managed in almost fifty years of pursuing a parliamentary strategy. Moreover as President, while intolerant of independent labour organization, Perón continued to boost working-class living standards during his first three years in office. Between 1943–9, the real wages of industrial workers rose by 50–60 per cent, and between 1946–9, in sharp contrast to European fascist experiences, labour's share in national income rose from 40.1 to 49 per cent.[21] Under these circumstances, for the Left to dismiss Perón's supporters, including the mass of workers, as *peronazis*[22] was not only unjust but also politically suicidal.

Yet some dissidents swam against the hostile traditional Left tide. Rodolfo Puiggrós travelled the lonely road from the Communist Party to Peronism in the mid-1940s, and in 1954 Enrique Dickmann broke with his Socialist colleagues to establish the small, pro-Peronist, Socialist Party of the National Revolution (PSRN). People of Trotskyist persuasion, such as Jorge Abelardo Ramos and Enrique Rivera, also arrived at a positive evaluation of Peronism, grounded upon its national, industrial, and social achievements. Collectively they, along with ex-*forjistas* and other popular nationalists, eventually became known as the National Left (*Izquierda Nacional*), a term whose paternity was claimed in 1957 by Hernández Arregui,[23] though the PSRN had used 'For a New National and Latin American Left' as its main slogan two years earlier.[24] Hernández Arregui was the one, however, to define 'National Left' in the context of the underdeveloped world as signifying:

general theory applied to a concrete national case, which analyses the national-defensive and revolutionary contents of the economy, history, and culture in the light of Marxism (seen as a method of interpreting reality, and taking into account primarily the peculiarities

---

[21] Carlos F. Díaz Alejandro, *Exchange-Rate Devaluation in a Semi-Industrialized Country. The Experience of Argentina 1955–1961* (USA: MIT Press, 1965), p. 110; and D. Rock, 'The Survival of Peronism', in Rock (ed), *Argentina*, p. 187.

[22] The Communist Party response to the events of 17 October 1945 was a 21 October manifesto which ended: 'PERON IS THE NUMBER ONE ENEMY OF THE ARGENTINE PEOPLE' (Puiggrós, p. 172). For the party's attitude to early Peronism, see Victorio Codovilla, *Batir al nazi-peronismo para abrir una era de libertad y progreso* (Buenos Aires: Editorial Anteo, 1946).

[23] Hernández Arregui, p. 475, footnote.

[24] Jorge Enea Spilimbergo, *El socialismo en la Argentina*, 2 vols., 2nd ed. (Buenos Aires: Ediciones Octubre, 1974), vol. 2, p. 101.

Antecedents 11

and development of each country) and which combines such a theoretical analysis with the practical struggle of the masses against imperialism at national, Latin American, and world levels, and in that order.[25]

Rejecting subordination to any international revolutionary party or centre, the National Left insisted that the theory and strategy of the Argentine socialist revolution had to emerge out of analyses of Argentine society rather than from studies of international capitalism or of external revolutionary successes. Its authors,[26] though heterogenous as a group, contributed greatly to the changing face of Peronism in the late 1960s and early 1970s by together making the idea of a Peronist Left *thinkable*, and thus helping to reorientate the Left, if not the Left parties, towards the national-popular movement. For coming to terms with post-war national reality meant coming to terms with the Peronist identity of the overwhelming majority of workers.

An essential precondition for the reconciliation of socialism with nationalism was a questioning of the credentials of those who had traditionally claimed to represent these trends. Thus

[25] Hernández Arregui, p. 475.
[26] Several of the authors made practical contributions to Montonero development. In the late 1960s both Jauretche and Hernández Arregui participated in regular discussions with Montonero founders including Mario Firmenich. Jauretche was appointed to run the University of Buenos Aires publishing department (EUDEBA) in 1973, but died at the age of seventy-two in May 1974. His nephew, Ernesto, became a leading Montonero before joining a breakaway group early in 1980. Hernández Arregui, like Jauretche, died a natural death during the last, 1973-6, period of Peronist rule. Puiggrós, from being a Communist Party leader in the 1940s, became the Montonero-supported trustee rector of the University of Buenos Aires in May-October 1973 before siding unequivocally with the organization two years later. In 1977 he became the First Secretary of the Professionals, Intellectuals, and Artists' Branch of the Montonero Peronist Movement (MPM), and remained so until his death in November 1980 from heart failure in Havana. Ramos was highly unpopular among the Montoneros due to his equation of urban guerrilla warfare with 'individual terrorism' and *blanquism*. Nevertheless, his popular history of Argentina [*Revolución y contrarevolución en la Argentina*, 5 vols., 5th ed. (Buenos Aires: Editorial Plus Ultra, 1973)] was widely read in university circles, and contributed to a positive re-evaluation of Peronism on the part of many students. Ramos's party, the Popular Left Front (FIP), sought to support Peronism from a position of critical independence. In March 1973, it polled almost 70,000 votes when standing its own candidates; in September 1973, its nominal vote soared to 889,000 in the presidential election, though many of those votes were undoubtedly a result of voters' confusion when presented, this time, with an opportunity to vote for Perón on a FIP ticket. For Ramos's criticisms of guerrilla warfare and the FIP line on Peronism, see his *La era del bonapartismo, 1943-1973* (Buenos Aires: Editorial Plus Ultra, 1973), especially pp. 297-309.

12 Antecedents

the seminal work of this school, written by Hernández Arregui in 1958-9, was offered precisely as a critique of 'the Argentine Left, which lacks national consciousness, and right-wing nationalism, which possesses national consciousness but which lacks a love of the people'.[27] In this and other National Left volumes, the traditional Left was declaimed for its preoccupation with immediate labour needs or implementation of party lines decided upon in Moscow, to the neglect of the anti-imperialist struggle of dependent Argentina.[28] The Socialist Party, founded by Juan B. Justo and others in 1896, had consistently upheld free trade principles which, while in the short term offering cheaper, better-quality goods than a protectionist policy, aligned the party with the forces of traditional agro-exporting Argentina.[29] Meanwhile the Communist Party (PCA), founded in 1920, had adjusted its 'line' in accordance with all the twists and turns of Stalinist foreign policy, thereby putting Soviet 'national' interests before those of Argentina and her working population. The party had even promoted strike-breaking activities during the Second World War in an effort to keep the allied war effort provisioned.

Despite their reactionary politics, the right-wing nationalists of the 1930s were treated by the National Left with relatively greater respect, the latter having been earned by their bequest of the revisionist approach to history. In its more idealistic expressions, historical revisionism had merely knocked equestrian oligarchic heroes off their plinths and had shattered

[27] *La formación*, p. 19. Other highly influential works by this author were *Imperialismo y cultura* (Buenos Aires: Editorial Plus Ultra, 1973), *Nacionalismo y liberación* (Buenos Aires: Ediciones Corregidor, 1973), and *¿Qué es el ser nacional?* (Buenos Aires: Editorial Plus Ultra, 1973) – all 3rd editions.

[28] The principal critiques are Spilimbergo, op. cit.; Ramos, *Historia del stalinismo en la Argentina* (Buenos Aires: Editorial Rancagua, 1974); and Puiggrós, *Las izquierdas y el problema nacional* (Buenos Aires: Ediciones Cepe, 1973).

[29] Though many criticisms of the Socialists' lack of economic nationalism are valid, they tend to mislead by implying that real alternatives were open to the party earlier in the century. Richard Walter [*The Socialist Party of Argentina, 1890-1930* (USA: University of Texas at Austin, 1977), pp. 227-33] argues that no party claiming to represent working-class interests could have adopted the high-tariff policies of employers' organizations such as the Argentine Industrial Union (UIA); and has moreover reminded critics that the Socialists provided Perón with much of his social programme. Researched replies to National Left attacks on the Socialists are also to be found in Emilio Corbière's 1975-6 articles in *Cuestionario*.

Liberal myths, only to offer nationalist heroes and myths as alternatives.[30] Now, however, certain attempts were made to relate imperium-nation conflicts to internal class structures, the list of approved national *caudillos* was extended to include the popularly-elected Yrigoyen and Perón, and the plebeian aspect of the nineteenth-century rebellions — their *montonero* content — began to attract more attention, albeit of a highly romantic nature. Nevertheless the nation-imperialism dichotomy remained supreme, above considerations of class differentiation. Hence more weight was attached by the National Left to Yrigoyen's 1920s oil nationalization programme than to his government's complicity in the bloody repression of striking workers by the Army and Rightist squads organized by employers during Argentina's *Semana Trágica* of January 1919.[31] On numerous occasions the National Left showed itself to be more National than Left, and not least in its evaluation of Peronism.

Since the National Left's aim was to redirect the Left towards Peronism, and because much of their readership was inevitably constituted by a university-based, middle-class clientele, noted for its hostility towards early Peronism, there was a strong tendency for the desire to justify and legitimize to greatly exceed any readiness to criticize the 1946–55 record of Peronism in office. Perhaps their most important contribution to radicalization and 'peronization' among the middle classes was a negative one: their rejection of the Liberal equation of Peronism with Fascism. It had to be admitted that Perón had praised Mussolini and that, in the name of corporatism, the Peronist State had been intolerant of independent labour unions and politics; but, more tellingly, it could be demonstrated that labour had benefited materially under Peronism, that pluralist structures and electoral practices had persisted alongside corporatist features, and that Perón, far from being ideologically-motivated, had an eminently pragmatic commitment to national development.

---

[30] Occasionally nationalists and Liberals perpetuated the same myths. Several writers of both schools saw Perón's power base as mainly constituted by workers of provincial origin, isolated from the traditional labour movement: the 'dualist' thesis, refuted in Little, op. cit.

[31] On the event itself, see David Rock, 'Lucha civil en la Argentina Semana Trágica de enero de 1919', *Desarrollo Económico*, vol. 11, no. 42 (July 1971), pp. 165–215.

On the other hand the National Left laid themselves open to criticism for offering a view of Peronism which overstated its radical significance and promise. It was presented as an anti-oligarchic, anti-imperialist movement based chiefly on the industrial classes, part of the middle classes, and a nationalist wing of the military; and although the talk was of 'national revolution' and 'national liberation', most National Left authors implicitly represented Peronism as having undertaken, during the 1940s, a path of national-democratic revolution which, though primarily favouring a 'national bourgeoisie', merited left-wing support as a progressive development in an underdeveloped country. For Hernández Arregui, Peronism was the vehicle of the Nation doing battle with Imperialism; for Puiggrós and Ramos compatibility with this historical-revisionist dichotomy was to be found in the notion that a stage of national-democratic revolution (embracing anti-imperialist tasks, agrarian reform, and so on) had to precede a socialist revolutionary process, whether these two stages were seen as being temporally divorced and distinct or as telescoped together in a 'permanent revolution'.[32]

Four principal objections may be raised against such views. First, while it is true that Peronism's industrial-promotion and pro-labour measures transformed the face of Argentina, the origins of its development strategy lay in the 1930s when not only manufacturers but also an oligarchic sector favoured import-substitutive industrialization as a response to the Depression.[33] Second, although Peronism embodied the political will to implement national-popular policies, it did enjoy exceptionally propitious financial circumstances, wartime credits and high post-war international prices for Argentine exports facilitating the simultaneous achievement

[32] To some extent, the differences between Puiggrós and Ramos, between a stages approach to revolution and one stressing the indivisibility of national and social revolutionary tasks, were echoes of the Third International dispute between Stalin and Trotsky in the late 1920s. However, as time passed, Ramos increasingly abandoned Trotskyism in practice. In 1975, in the face of probable military intervention against the right-wing Peronist Government of Isabel Perón, Ramos and the FIP called not only for the defence of democratic institutions but also for support for Isabel. See *Izquierda Nacional*, no. 39 (September 1975), p. 4.

[33] On the industrialization process, see Eduardo F. Jorge, *Industria y concentración económica* (Buenos Aires: Siglo XXI Argentina Editores, 1971); and Miguel Murmis & Juan Carlos Portantiero, *Estudios sobre los orígenes del peronismo*, vol. 1 (Buenos Aires: Siglo XXI Argentina Editores, 1971).

of industrial growth and progressive income redistribution. Third, for most of Perón's 1946-55 years as President foreign capital was not aggressively endeavouring to penetrate or retain a decisive stake in Argentina's economy:[34] the 'golden' Peronist years of the late 1940s coincided with British needs to cut her losses abroad following a costly war, and preceded the successful efforts by US-based and other multi-national corporations to acquire a decisive presence in the more dynamic sectors of the country's economy. Finally, though a major shift in income from the rural to the industrial sector occurred under Peronist auspices the traditional structure of land ownership remained unchallenged: the oligarchy, obliged to sell its products cheaply to the State (to demand far higher prices internationally and thus help finance industrial expansion), was antagonized but not destroyed. Along with disaffected entrepreneurs and the middle classes, with Western approval, it was therefore able to mount a successful challenge to Peronism in 1955, culminating in the *Revolución Libertadora* of 16 September.

Despite the 1955 defeat and the fact that only labour had stuck solidly with Perón to the last, National Left writers retained national-revolutionary expectations of all the sectors of the Peronist Movement — including a purportedly-progressive wing of the Army — right into the 1970s. Those of traditional Left origin, such as Puiggrós, did however attempt to draw some lessons from early Peronism's demise and concluded that, whereas an anti-oligarchic, anti-imperialist alliance of the 'national bourgeoisie', middle classes, and working class was still viable, a national liberation front of this kind would require working-class hegemony and a guiding revolutionary theory if it were to prosper once again.[35] Others, including Ramos, meanwhile recognized that no bourgeoisie, whether 'national' or not, would submit itself to a workers' leadership or embrace a revolutionary theory; nevertheless, they maintained that a sector of the industrial bourgeoisie still had a capacity for anti-imperialist struggle

---

[34] A Central Bank report of 1940 stated that the British Government had expressed the wish that Argentina should consider the purchase of the English railways operating there. See Leopoldo Portnoy, *Análisis crítico de la economía* (Buenos Aires: Fondo de Cultura Económica, 1961), p. 143.

[35] Puiggrós, *El proletariado en la revolución nacional* (Buenos Aires: Editorial Sudestado, 1968), *passim*.

and that it was the duty of the Left to support this force, from a position of independence, until it faltered. What they all took insufficient cognizance of was the major decline after 1955 of the 'national' industrialists, increasingly confined to small- and medium-sized enterprises, vis-à-vis foreign concerns. The stake of foreign enterprise in industrial production grew from 8 to 40 per cent between 1955 and 1972, with US capital accounting for 70 per cent of new direct foreign investment in the decade from 1959-69.[36] Among the leading 25 companies, the number of national firms fell from 16 in 1957 to 8 by 1966.[37] All this weakened not only the local industrialists' potential for economic nationalism — especially in a decade of economic woe such as the 1970s — but also its capacity for a harmonious partnership with labour. For national entrepreneurs to improve their economic standing against that of the foreign monopolies, they may for political reasons have needed labour, and indeed a national alliance, as crucial buttresses, yet economic reality dictated that labour sacrifices rather than labour gains were essential preconditions for raising investment levels and generating national capitalist growth.

The intellectual and political message of the National Left was one which by 1973, when Peronism returned to power after eighteen years of resistance and opposition, had led many of its youthful recipients to expect the advent of a vibrant process of national development and radical reform led by a progressive and even revolutionary Perón. After originating specifically in order to rehabilitate Peronism in the eyes of its critics the National Left evolved from a defence of Peronism to an accommodation which envisaged no real political alternative to it.[38] Though famous for charging the

[36] North American Congress on Latin America (NACLA), *Argentina in the Hour of the Furnaces* (USA: NACLA, 1975), p. 24.

[37] Jorge Niosi, *Los empresarios y el estado argentino, 1955-1969* (Buenos Aires: Siglo XXI Argentina Editores, 1974), p. 215.

[38] Hernández Arregui, for example, continued to back official Peronism even after its right wing became totally dominant at governmental level, following the death of Perón in July 1974. In response to the latter event Hernández Arregui changed the name of his political magazine from *Peronismo y Socialismo* to *Peronismo y Liberación*, called for a postponement of internal Peronist feuding between partisans of independent capitalism and of socialism, and maintained that 'the mandate of the hour is not in this particular dramatic moment of Argentine history to quarrel over scholastic words...' ['Aclaración sobre el cambio de nombre de nuestra revista',*Peronismo y Liberación*, no. 1 (August 1974), p. 5].

traditional Left with having been a left-wing shield of the oligarchic order, the National Left thus left itself open to accusations of being a left-wing shield of 'national bourgeois' interests.

THE PERONIST PHENOMENON

Through most of its exegetists Peronism has presented itself to the world as a national-popular movement, as an anti-imperialist, anti-oligarchic force of a peculiarly Argentine variety.[39] Once qualifications of the above nature have been made, the general self-cultivated image, if something of a caricature, is not totally misleading. When it came to economic strategy what really passed for 'anti-imperialism' during the 1946-55 years were purchases of foreign interests, including the railways, gasworks, and telephone system, at prices which absorbed 45 per cent of Argentina's post-war foreign exchange;[40] later, under the 1973-6 Peronist Governments, it consisted of initial efforts to diversify the country's trading relations, plus timid nationalization measures that were partially reversed in 1975.[41] Nonetheless, anti-imperialism was certainly present in the official doctrine of *Justicialismo* and as an often-vague and variously-defined, yet highly-emotive and generically-unifying, orientation shared by all the Peronist Movement's principal social and political components. Indeed, apart from personalities and symbols, it has been historically the only unifying theme with which the mass of Peronists could identify. Of the Three Banners of Justicialism, social justice always proved more controversial than political sovereignty and economic independence when Peronists of different shades and classes came together, especially once the economic boom of the 1940s had subsided.

[39] For useful guides to the numerous interpretations of Peronism, see Ernesto Laclau, 'Peronism and Revolution', *Latin American Review of Books* (London and Leeds), no. 1 (1973), pp. 117-30; and Carlos S. Fayt, *La naturaleza del peronismo* (Buenos Aires: Viracocha, 1967). For general political background reading on the post-1943 period, see Félix Luna, *De Perón a Lanusse, 1943/1973* (Buenos Aires: Editorial Planeta Argentina, 1973); Rock (ed), *Argentina*; and Donald C. Hodges, *Argentina, 1943-1976* (USA: University of New Mexico Press, 1976).
[40] Scobie, p. 235.
[41] See Edward S. Milenky, *Argentina's Foreign Policies* (USA: Westview Press, 1978), especially pp. 114-19.

Apart from these banners Peronism's meagre ideological baggage contained just two key notions: the 'Third Position' and the 'Organized Community'. The former represented a repudiation of the so-called 'two imperialisms', Yankee and Soviet, and purported to be 'as distinct from one of the dominant imperialisms of that time as from the other'.[42] It was presented as an attempt to exploit antagonisms between the Great Powers so as to permit Argentina to pursue an independent course at home and internationally. In practice, however, concessions were made to US oil interests as the economy declined during the early 1950s, and several diplomatic moves left the country distinctly closer to the USA than to the USSR.[43] The Third Position supposedly occupied by Justicialism laid claim, moreover, to philosophical equidistance from both idealism and materialism and, in terms of socio-economic models, counterposed itself equally to capitalism and communism: 'neither the exploitation of man in the name of capital nor in the name of the State'.[44] The Organized Community was one designed to avoid the excesses of both models: the existence of private property was guaranteed, with the proviso that it fulfilled a social function; on the other hand, the State was to intervene to ensure that 'society will be harmonious, free of discord, neither dominated by materialism nor a state of fantasy'.[45] Conflict between labour and capital, it was asserted, could be vanquished by means of 'the tutelage of authority and justice which emanate from the State'.[46] Of course successes in this field proved increasingly difficult to repeat as the early 1950s progressed and the economy lurched towards a series of destructive crises:[47] evidence of the fact that success for policies favouring

[42] Perón, interview in Enrique Pavón Pereyra, *Perón tal como es* (Buenos Aires: Editorial Macacha Güemes, 1973), p. 225.

[43] See Fernando Nadra, *Perón hoy y ayer, 1971–1943* (Buenos Aires: Editorial Polémica, 1972), pp. 79–81.

[44] Juan D. Perón, *Doctrina peronista*, 2nd ed. (Buenos Aires: Ediciones Macacha Güemes, 1973), p. 241.

[45] Idem, *La comunidad organizada* (Buenos Aires: Ediciones Cepe, 1974), p. 111. On the Organized Community, see also Rodolfo Terragno, *Los 400 días de Perón* (Buenos Aires: Ediciones de la Flor, 1974), pp. 65–9.

[46] Perón, 28 June 1944, quoted in Milciades Peña, *El peronismo, selección de documentos para la historia* (Buenos Aires: Ediciones Fichas, 1973), p. 99.

[47] See Díaz Alejandro, op. cit., *passim*; idem, *Essays in the Economic History of the Argentine Republic* (USA: Yale, 1970); Guido Di Tella and Manuel Zymel-

both sides of industry simultaneously depended far more on the general economic climate than upon the intrinsic merits of Justicialism.

The Peronist Movement has traditionally consisted of three Branches or *Ramas*: a Political Branch (generally bearing the name 'Peronist' or 'Justicialist' Party, depending on the period), which served as a dispenser of patronage when in office and as the electoral instrument of the Movement; a Feminine Branch, originally led by Perón's second wife María Eva Duarte (Evita), which impressively mobilized the female vote for the 1951 elections,[48] following the enfranchisement of women in 1947; and a Labour Branch — at first, during the 1946-55 period, synonymous with the General Labour Confederation (CGT), then from 1957 represented by the 62 Organizations, but still overwhelmingly dominant within the broader labour movement. A *de facto* Youth Branch, founded chiefly by left-wing Peronist militants, was to join the other three Branches in 1971-4, but was never institutionalized.[49]

Many commentators have been guilty of allowing the problem of how Peronism should be characterized to be dominated exclusively by the controversies over its political and social identity, thus attaching no importance to Peronism's status as a *movement*. In emphasizing this latter feature, attention is drawn not only to Peronism's composition being one of vertically-integrated classes and social forces, in contrast to the horizontal class base of many parties, but also to the fact that membership was more a question of identification than of affiliation. To be a *peronista* did not necessarily

---

man, *Las etapas del desarrollo económico argentino* (Buenos Aires: EUDEBA, 1967); and Aldo Ferrer *et al.*, *Los planes de estabilización en la Argentina* (Buenos Aires: Paidós, 1969).

[48] The Peronist vote rose from 52.40 per cent in 1946 to 62.49 per cent of the total vote in the 1951 presidential and vice-presidential elections. See Canton, pp. 272-3.

[49] The first Peronist Youth (JP) was formed at the end of 1957 and included Gustavo Rearte, Envar El Kadri, Jorge Rulli, Héctor Espina, and Carlos Caride. However, its development was stunted by the imprisonment of its leaders in the early 1960s and then, when they were amnestied in 1963, by a split giving rise to Rearte's Peronist Revolutionary Youth (JRP) and the far less radical Peronist Youth Movement (MJP) led by El Kadri. For more details, see R.H.C. Gillespie, 'The Peronist Left', unpublished Ph.D. thesis, University of Liverpool, 1979, pp. 175-88.

imply regular political activity, and formal affiliation procedures, except in fulfillment of electoral registration requirements, were generally alien to the Movement. Membership of the Movement was a question of identification with Perón and with the Argentina of Perón, and, after 1955, not just as a memory of previous golden years but through appreciation of the stark contrast between that past and what ensured: the crises, draconian political and economic measures, and what many saw as a 'surrender to imperialism' of vital areas of economic activity, which characterized the 1955-73 interregnum. Peronism penetrated the class-consciousness of millions of workers who, as the industrial work-force grew spectacularly, became aware of themselves as a class, and for the first time felt valued as workers, contemporaneously with their acclamation of Peronism and integration by it. In other words, Peronism developed at the level of a social, as well as a political, movement, and it was this which provided so much of its vitality, dynamism, and spontaneity, if also its organic weakness. This political force was to prove far more resilient, when faced with post-1955 attempts to stifle and suppress it, than would have been the case had the cumbersome Peronist Party been its axis.

Prevailing characterizations of Peronism tend to portray it either in sociological terms as a class alliance or in political terms as some kind of a national movement. The limitations of the former approach are several.[50] First, class membership of the Peronist 'alliance' has altered considerably over the years. During the early years Peronism drew its support from among local industrialists, part of the middle classes, and from the working class, yet by 1955 non-proletarian sponsorship had been far more seriously eroded than was the case with labour backing; there were then eighteen years during which labour was the principal bastion of the Movement, with entrepreneurs mainly conspicuous by their absence; and, later, the final years of the 1966-73 military regime witnessed mounting support among the university-based middle classes (students, intellectuals, professionals) and from local businessmen associated with the General Economic Confederation

---

[50] Though infused with Peronist mythology, José Pablo Feinmann, *El peronismo y la primacia de la política* (Buenos Aires: Editorial Cimarrón, 1974) is an interesting antidote to the class-reductionist approach to Peronism.

(CGE). Second, institutions have often been as important as classes in constituting Peronism's bases of support, whether one examines the early institutional support emanating from the Church and military or the permanent loyalty of the major trade unions. Even the latter organizations are irreducible to a class: when Army rivals briefly jailed Perón in 1945, the general strike and labour mobilization which ensured his release occurred on that historic 17 October, a day before the date set by the CGT;[51] and again in mid-1975, when labour repudiated the economic strategy of the Government of María Estela Martínez (Perón's third wife), a *de facto* general strike paralysed economic activity days before it was officially 'called' by the CGT leadership. Third, class characterizations of Peronism frequently result in a total neglect of crucial facets of the history of Peronism on the grounds that they are of 'secondary' importance: a case in point here is the rejuvenescence which the arrival of the university sectors brought to the Movement, something that has relevance not only to the early 1970s dynamism of Peronism's revolutionary wing but also to any understanding of why so many Peronist Left creeds were distinguishable by their naivety.

To label the Peronist phenomenon, as many critics have, an expression of bourgeois nationalism or a class alliance led by a national bourgeoisie is clearly inadequate. A considerable number of Argentine entrepreneurs opposed Peronism for its improvement of working-class living standards or for its authoritarianism; and of those who did back it, the approval of most was conditional, informed with opportunism, and thus withdrawn well in advance of the anti-Peronist military takeovers of 1955 and 1976. Peronism's cheap-credit policies certainly benefited local industrialists, but among the latter there were many who considered their new economic advantages to be outweighed by the accompanying rise in regimented, yet nevertheless substantial, union power. As industry developed, attracting rural migrants to work in expanding labour-intensive enterprises, as public-sector employees became automatically registered as unionists, trade-union membership grew from 440,000 in 1941 to 1.5 million in 1947 and 3 million by1951;[52] and though unions

[51] See Puiggrós, *El Peronismo*, pp. 164-72.
[52] Murmis and Portantiero, pp. 77-9.

became thoroughly dependent upon State patronage, their representatives established themselves for the first time as a real presence in ministries, embassies, and in Congress. Whatever advantages Peronism offered capitalists in the way of an integrated union movement which accepted inter-class cooperation, these were more than counterbalanced, when economic decline set in, by the financial costs of that integration. Moreover, when in the early 1950s and again in the mid-1970s Peronist governments attempted to introduce austerity measures and boost productivity in response to economic crises, the latent strength of labour within the Movement moderated the impact of such efforts, leaving many industrialists ready to applaud military intervention.

While it is true that real wage levels fell during the early 1950s, general working-class living standards remained well above those of the pre-1943 years; and though economic deterioration led to strikes, these did not represent a conscious political challenge to the Peronist regime.[53] The weakness of the immediate labour reaction to the September 1955 *golpe*[54] indicated a degree of disenchantment as well as the stultifying bureaucratization of the unions, yet no viable political alternatives to Peronism were perceived by the mass of workers. The working-class component continued to be, as Perón himself acknowledged, the historic 'backbone' of his Movement. At no time was labour's devotion to Peronism monolithic: apart from the 1940s attempts by some unions to defend their independence vis-à-vis the State, and various transitory efforts after 1955 to develop independent economistic labour groupings, Perón's authority was questioned as shop stewards committees and combative rank-and-file coordinating bodies led by revolutionary Peronists and Marxist militants grew in the late 1960s and early 1970s. Nevertheless, the great majority of workers continued to offer Perón stalwart loyalty throughout the 1955–73 years of opposition. This fidelity was a product not only of labour progressing under Peronist tutelage, but also of the contrast between that experience and that which followed: after the brief military presidency of Lonardi, General Pedro Eugenio

---

[53] Little, pp. 175–6.
[54] On Perón's fall, see Julio Godio, *La caída de Perón* (Buenos Aires: Granica Editor, 1973).

Aramburu's 1955-8 regime unleashed a major offensive against the workers, involving the military takeover of the CGT, mass arrests, cuts in labour's share in national income, and — guaranteeing Aramburu lasting Peronist enmity — the confiscation and expatriation of the corpse of Eva Perón.[55] In attempting to defend and reassert their political and economic rights, it was the workers who most consistently raised the demand for the return of Perón and, with bans and proscriptions nullifying most constitutional initiatives, who demonstrated a readiness to resort to direct and even violent action. Most of their struggles were devoid of anticapitalist overtones, yet nevertheless threatened 'the system': for workers to fight for comparable conditions to those which they had enjoyed under Perón, given the subsequent setting of economic stagnation, seemed revolutionary and was certainly right at the centre of Argentina's post-1955 political instability. Revolutionary Peronist John William Cooke had the destabilizing power of labour rebelliousness in mind when he declared that 'Peronism is the curse of bourgeois politics in this country'.[56]

Peronism can no more be characterized as a movement of the working class, however, than as one of the national bourgeoisie. Perón, though obliged to live in exile from 1955, retained ultimate control over the Peronist and labour movements by use of thirteen consecutive 'delegates' or representatives; and his sponsorship of labour was more manipulative than supportive. He had discovered the potential of labour as a power base while himself Labour and Welfare Secretary in the 1943-6 military government; had courted and won labour allies by authorizing rights and conditions which workers had never previously experienced; and had been rewarded for his efforts with the labour mobilization of 17 October 1945 and labour votes of 24 February 1946. But far from being an altruistic champion of the working class Perón's overtures in its direction were firmly within the *caudillo* tradition. Rosas, having noted that previous rulers had 'scorned the lower classes', once pointed out the authoritarian

[55] On this period, see Clara Budeisky, *El retorno oligárquico, 1955-1958* (Buenos Aires: Schapire Editor, 1973); and Rock, 'The Survival'.
[56] John William Cooke, 'La revolución y el peronismo' (1967), in his *La lucha por la liberación nacional*, 2nd ed. (Buenos Aires: Granica Editor, 1973), p. 81.

benefits to be derived from posing as a standard-bearer of the poor: 'I believe it is important to establish a major influence over this class to contain it and direct it, and I have acquired this influence. I am a *gaucho* among *gauchos*. I talk as they do. I protect them. I am their attorney. I care for their interests'.[57] With Evita acting as his intermediary, prior to her early death in 1952, Perón assumed the same style, while also displaying alarm at disorder and betraying a fear of the masses when not doctrinally and institutionally controlled: 'It is useless to give an inorganic and anarchic mass a leader', he remarked on one occasion, 'They will string him up.'[58]

Perón was never prepared to entertain the idea of the working class organizing itself independently of his Movement's vertical structures, as some *laborista* leaders such as Cipriano Reyes were to find to their cost when in the late 1940s they resisted integration into the official Peronist Party.[59] And well after being abandoned by most of his entrepreneurial backers in the mid-1950s, the Peronist leader continued to preach State-arbitrated and State-imposed class conciliation, and firmly vetoed all proposals to establish a defensive trade union militia. Though he was to claim repeatedly that his failure to put up a real fight in September 1955 had been to avoid bloodshed, while in Paraguay conceding his first interview since his fall from power a tired Perón released the scared thought, 'just think what would have happened if I had handed arms from the arsenals over to the workers ready to grasp them . . .'[60]

Thus Peronism, when a characterization of its historical status is required, cannot be presented as a specific class alliance or solely in class terms: its social composition fluctuated and

[57] Rosas, quoted in John Barnes, *Eva Perón* (Glasgow: Fontana, 1978), pp. 7-8.
[58] Perón, quoted in W. Little, 'Party and State in Peronist Argentina, 1945-1955', *Hispanic American Historical Review*, vol. 53, no. 4 (November 1973), p. 655.
[59] Reyes was jailed in 1948 after several attempts on his life. For a view of the grimmer side of life in Peronist Argentina, see Mary Main, *Evita: The Woman with the Whip* (GB: Corgi, 1977), pp. 212-21.
[60] Perón, quoted in *El Día* (Montevideo), 5 October 1955; reproduced in Enrique Rivera, *Peronismo y frondizismo* (Buenos Aires: Editorial Patria Grande, 1958), pp. 84-92. Cooke later commented: 'all the posthumous laments about workers militias for me are just speculative fantasies. Because one cannot arm the working class in order to defend your regime and the next day tell workers: fine, my son, hand back the arms and go and produce surplus value for the bosses'. See his *Apuntes para la militancia* (Buenos Aires: Schapire Editor, 1973), p. 102.

no single class exercised continuous hegemony over the Movement. Looked at generically it is most useful and least misleading to regard Peronism as simply a multi-sectoral, national-popular movement whose social integrants have varied in accordance with how different classes, social sectors, and institutions have perceived their interests in relation to a national-popular line in different, evolving, political and economic circumstances. Of course that 'national-popular line', embodying policies of independent national development and social reform, has always embraced sub-currents, been marked by dissidence, and in recent years has seen conflict between sharply-polarized extremes of Left and Right. Yet all attempts at shifting the centre of gravity of the Movement to either ideological pole have ended in failure. Neither the Peronist Right, in the ascendancy at governmental level in 1974-6, nor the Peronist Left, when it broke with the mainstream of the Movement in 1974, managed to reconstruct a viable national-popular alliance around its own ideological axis. The Movement remained for the most part welded to broadly nationalist and reformist ideas which assumed that industrial cooperation and polyclass progress were possible if actively encouraged by an interventionist State.

To see Peronism in this light does not involve acceptance of the historical revisionists' elevation of nation-imperialism dichotomies above class evaluation. It means only that neither dimension should be ignored: the 'National Question' cannot be usefully posed in isolation from analysis of the class components of the nation involved, any more than class interests can be defined without some reference to Argentine dependency and national-popular political responses to it. While Peronism is not amenable to crude, one dimensional variants of class analysis, analyses of class composition and interests in different periods of its history are indispensable to any understanding of what national-popular politics have signified at one time or another, and of the behaviour and potential of Peronism at different stages of its history. As will be seen, what was termed *Justicialismo* by early Peronist officialdom had to be dressed up by the early 1970s as *socialismo nacional.*

POST-1955 POLITICAL INSTABILITY

Following the 1955 *golpe*, and throughout the subsequent eighteen years of political exclusion, Peronist organizational strength lay fundamentally in the labour movement. There were several attempts, especially under Presidents Frondizi (1958-62) and Onganía (1966-70), to integrate labour sectors and Peronist elements via conciliatory leaders of 'participationist' and 'neo-Peronist' trends into new governing frameworks, but each ended in failure: Peronism, on account of its continuing labour presence, was simply incompatible with regimes unable to satisfy the material needs and aspirations of the working class for any significant length of time.[61] The crises of a sluggish economy contributed decisively to political instability, for though Argentina's economic fortunes did not plummet unremittingly, the mini-booms were far too short-lived and fragile to sustain the political fortunes of governments seeking national reconciliation or at least social order. Major fluctuations in income distribution, stagnation, stop-go syndromes, and bouts of hyper-inflation 'spawned a Hobbesian world of strife and competition, as different groups stuggled to maintain their real incomes'.[62]

Argentina's recent reputation for political instability is one which outsiders have found difficult to reconcile with her abundance in natural resources and substantial cultural achievements. High levels of urbanization and literacy combined with the industrial advance under Perón (mainly in the field of light industry) blinded many observers to those features of the old Argentina which remained as obstacles to further development. Above all, economic growth was hampered by the survival of traditional attitudes and structures in the countryside, still the vital source of export earnings needed to finance the imports required by industry, yet incapable of generating sufficient foreign exchange to permit regular industrial expansion. By the 1960s agricultural exports were still accounting for 85-90 per cent of the country's foreign exchange earnings,[63] but the level of exportation was distinctly disappointing. With world prices

---

[61] On the post-1955 history of Peronism, see Angel Cairo, *Peronismo claves* (Buenos Aires: Centro de Estudios Aporte, 1975), pp. 9-68; and Ernesto González, *Qué fue y qué es el peronismo* (Buenos Aires: Ediciones Pluma, 1974).
[62] Rock, *Argentina*, p. 195.   [63] Scobie, p. 241.

for manufactures and capital goods continuing to rise and export prices for primary goods tending to fall, recurrent balance of payments crises, the main brake on growth since 1948, critically disrupted economic progress.

One of Peronism's legacies had been to boost consumption and consumer expectations well beyond its development of the productive infrastructure of the country. An antiquated transportation system, insufficient fuel and energy sources, and the absence of a steel industry were inherited as industrial challenges by the post-1955 regimes,[64] yet while differing degrees of success were achieved in these areas, the cardinal problem of anachronistic agrarian structures received only cosmetic treatment. Land ownership remained highly concentrated and agricultural techniques on many of the huge *latifundios* fell way behind those of competitors in Australia, Canada, and the USA. The agrarian bougeoisie, owners of 74 per cent of all arable land (around 1970), continued to attract the popular appellation of 'oligarchy', just 1800 people and companies possessing a combined land area the size of Italy, Belgium, Holland, and Denmark.[65] While small farmers generally lacked sufficient land, credit, and equipment to prosper, the big landowners persisted with their traditional under-utilization of land, often preferring to invest in sectors where immediate returns were higher. The pampas region, heartland of Argentina's agricultural wealth, accounted for some 60 per cent of the nation's agriculture and 80 per cent of cattle production, but only 38 per cent of the land there was cultivated.[66] Pastoral usage and traditional extensive farming methods continued to predominate. Government efforts to stimulate the agrarian sector, although in some cases achieving greater productivity, failed to raise productive volumes sufficiently. Indeed, it remained a standard practice of the agrarian magnates to withdraw land from production so as to control supply levels and thereby manipulate prices. The annual growth rates of this sector during the 1960s were under 2 per cent — an

[64] Ibid., pp. 238-46.
[65] Mariano Lesseps and Lucia Traveler, *Argentina: un país entregado* (Madrid: Castellote Editor, 1978), p. 105.
[66] Eugenio Gastiazoro, *Argentina hoy. Latifundio, dependencia y estructura de clases*, 3rd ed. (Buenos Aires: Ediciones Pueblo, 1975), p. 21.

amount totally inadequate to the country's rate of demographic growth and the needs of the rest of the economy.[67]

The reasons why agrarian backwardness has been allowed (along with other factors) to bridle national development stem from the pattern of industrialization. Under both Perón and Onganía the interests of the major agrarian producers were clearly subordinated to industrial concerns, but Argentina has never experienced a genuine industrial revolution. As has been noted, industrialization was supported by a sector of the oligarchy in the 1930s, and the import-substituting development strategy continued by Perón during the following decade involved the exploitation of agriculture for national purposes rather than an inevitably disruptive agrarian revolution. Since then, though the theme has still to be properly examined, writers have pointed to the way in which conflicts between agrarian and industrial interests have been significantly mitigated by a whole web of relationships, ranging from marital ties to the practice of major landowners and industrialists of diversifying their interests and investing, often for purely speculative purposes, in each other's sectors.[68]

Within the Argentine Left the agrarian situation has tended to produce one of two responses: whereas revolutionary nationalists and much of the traditional Left have focused upon the theoretical industrial-agrarian contradiction, often mistaking the agrarian bourgeoisie for a feudal class and envisaging a role for the industrial bourgeoisie in an anti-oligarchic revolution,[69] the more revolutionary Marxist groups, while recognizing the existence of intra-bourgeois conflicts, have attached greater importance to the community of interests shared by the bourgeoisie (agrarian, industrial, commercial, financial) as a whole, and have insisted that any assault upon anachronistic rural structures could succeed only if forming part of a broader offensive against capital in general.

Whatever solutions were proposed the key problem was apparent to most development-minded Argentines: continued dependence for economic growth upon an agrarian sector which, apart from being subject to climatic vagaries, clearly

[67] Scobie, p. 245; Lesseps and Traveler, p. 106.
[68] Lesseps and Traveler, p. 108.
[69] See Laclau, 'Peronism and Revolution'.

lacked the export capacity to pay for the costs of developing heavy industry and at the same time to finance the social expenditures demanded by a powerful labour movement. Rather than antagonize the landowners, governments proved readier to curb domestic consumption when attempting to boost exports, yet onslaughts on popular living standards could never be consolidated — not only due to labour resilience, but also because competition between the legal political forces involved some in attempts to mobilize mass support through promises of short-term material gains and a more equitable income distribution. The mix was inherently unstable and many observers became quite fatalistic about the relentless cyclical pattern of economic crises, which no government was capable of interrupting or surviving. During the eighteen-year proscription of Peronism, Argentina knew eight different presidents, of whom three were civilians (Frondizi, Guido, Illia) and five were generals (Lonardi, Aramburu, Onganía, Levingston, and Lanusse).

THE EMERGENCE OF THE PERONIST LEFT

It was during these years that Peronism acquired its left wing, not through 'entrism' practised by the largely still-hostile non-Peronist Left,[70] but through the radicalization of Peronist activists and the radicalization and original 'peronization' of youths who in some cases had looked first to right-wing and Catholic nationalism for inspiration. The emergence and growth of left-wing tendencies within Peronism were irregular rather than steady. Before 1955 John William Cooke and those who identified with his political review *De Frente*[71] were militant with regard to the methods which they advocated for the defence of the Peronist regime and also differed from more conciliatory sectors in the fervour of their nationalism. But the Peronist Left, taken to comprise all those Peronists positing socialism and popular sovereignty as goals,

---

[70] The only non-Peronist Left group to strongly orientate its work towards Peronist workers was the tiny *Palabra Obrera*, an organization of Trotskyist origin which in the late 1950s and early 1960s brought out a bulletin of the same name, presented as an organ of 'revolutionary workers' Peronism'.

[71] *De Frente* appeared in March 1954 and ran to eighty-five issues before being banned in October 1955. No. 85 reported Cooke's arrest.

did not really emerge until the late 1950s, when Arturo Frondizi's Intransigent Radical (UCRI) Government, elected with the indispensable aid of Peronist votes, replaced the harsh regime of General Aramburu. It then flourished briefly during the early 1960s and crystallized into a revolutionary tendency in 1963-4, only to decline in the mid-1960s before re-emerging vigorously in the late 1960s and early 1970s as the Peronist Youth (JP) grew and 'special formations' embarked upon urban guerrilla campaigns.

Peronist Left vicissitudes in the mid-1960s were possibly influenced by a temporary amelioration of working-class hardship[72] and were certainly affected by the early repressive impact of the 1966 military takeover which brought Onganía to power. However, one would not wish to overstate the irregularity of the Peronist Left developmental chart, for the apparent vivacity of this tendency in the first half of the 1960s was partially illusory. The 'first revolutionary tendency' of Peronism, which attained momentary cohesion in 1964 with the founding of the Revolutionary Peronist Movement (MRP), was in fact an alliance between revolutionaries, centrists, and reformists. Its basic documents, drawn up principally by revolutionary Peronist Gustavo Rearte, and *Compañero*,[73] its weekly paper edited by Mario Valotta, were anti-capitalist in implication if not to the letter. Really, though, as Rearte himself later acknowledged, these only faithfully represented the outlook of the MRP's small, youthful revolutionary wing, composed mainly of Rearte's own Peronist Revolutionary Youth (JRP) and Armando Jaime's Peronist Youth of Salta (Province).[74]

Nevertheless the publications issued by the early Peronist Left help to explain the process of radicalization that affected Peronism in the 1960s and 1970s, in which numerous factors intervened. First there was the general decline in workers' living standards after 1955 amidst recurrent economic crises. Real wages in 1963 were 15 per cent below 1958

[72] Certainly the share of wages and salaries in Argentine GNP rose at this time. See Mónica Peralta Ramos, *Etapas de acumulación y alianzas de clases en la Argentina (1930-1970)* (Buenos Aires: Siglo XXI Argentina Editores, 1972), p. 150.

[73] There were seventy-seven issues of *Compañero*, June 1963-February 1965.

[74] For the MRP founding documents and Rearte's explanation of the MRP's failure, see the special supplement to *En Lucha*, no. 18 (September 1974).

levels;[75] the share of wages and salaries, as opposed to capital, in the Argentine GNP descended from 43 per cent in 1955 to around 35 per cent by 1972.[76] Only a small minority of activists regarded the country's economic problems as structural rather than conjunctural, but for them the efficiency of capitalism was brought into question and they began to add monopoly industrial capital to imperialism and the oligarchy as a foe of the Peronist Movement and working class.

Most workers remained far more interested in trade-union issues than in socialist politics, and to that extent they can be described as 'economistic', though theirs was an 'economism' very much linked to the Peronist political model and very much bound up with the fundamental political demand for the return of Perón. That there was not greater labour radicalization after 1955 was in part owing to the fact that Argentina's economic decline was not constant but rather interspersed with short spurts of growth: the latter encouraged the belief that progress could still come without fundamental structural changes and all the sacrifices and upheavals that would be involved in attempts to bring such a transformation about. At the same time, while the union base of the Movement in these years was a guarantor of durability, it was also (contrary to anarcho-syndicalist dreams of revolutionary general strikes) something which militated in favour of 'economistic' campaigns and against a revolutionary approach to national problems. To be effective the unions needed to incorporate as many workers as possible and their leaders were well aware that political definitions, other than the widely-endorsed call for a Peronist restoration, were as divisive as economic programmes could be cohesive. Moreover, neither the traditional Left's hostility towards Peronism nor the growing heterogeneity in labour circumstances during the 1960s facilitated the advent of a socialist working-class consciousness.[77]

Many left-wing observers and activists deluded themselves into optimism by equating high levels of economistic militancy with labour being ready for revolutionary politics. In fact labour militancy was not even sustained over economic issues

[75] Rock, *Argentina*, p. 205.
[76] NACLA, op. cit., p. 28.
[77] On this, see Peralta Ramos, pp. 58–63 & 163–70.

but pursued an irregular path not dissimilar to that ventured along by the Peronist Left. There were initially four years of struggle to regain control of the unions and resist economic decline — the famous 1955-9 period of the *Resistencia Peronista*; then came three years of comparative passivity following a series of crushing labour defeats in 1959.[78] Another upsurge occurred in 1963-4,[79] but here again there was a mid-1960s slump in labour struggles before industrial militancy again became visibly important in the late 1960s and early 1970s.

A second crucial factor in the emergence of radical Peronist organizations was the experience of Arturo Frondizi's 1958-62 Government. In return for decisively supporting Frondizi's UCRI party in the 1958 election, the Peronists were conceded a general amnesty, a new Law of Professional Associations (providing for a national reorganization of the labour movement), and a 60 per cent wage rise. But the promised 'normalization' of the CGT, taken over by the military regime in 1955, was delayed until 1961 and the (as it transpired, abortive) legalization of the Peronist Party until 1962. Frondizi reneged on his nationalistic statements of intent made before and during 1958 by signing contracts with eight foreign oil companies, and by denationalizing *Frigorífico Lisandro de la Torre* in 1959 — the latter sparking off an attempted 'revolutionary general strike', led by Sebastián Borro and John William Cooke, in January.[80] Faced with growing labour opposition and violent resistance activities, the UCRI leader bowed to military pressures and brought in first a state of siege and then, in 1960, the CONINTES (*Conmoción Interna del Estado*) Plan. Under it, those accused

---

[78] Five million days were lost in strikes in 1956, over 3.6m in 1957, over 6m in 1958, and over 11m in 1959, but only 1.5m days were lost in 1960 and 1961, and only 268,000 in 1962. See Daniel James, 'Power and Politics in Peronist Trade Unions', *Journal of Interamerican Studies and World Affairs*, vol. 20, no. 1 (February 1978), pp. 21-2. On the labour history of this period, see also Santiago Senén González, *El sindicalismo después de Perón* (Buenos Aires: Editorial Galerna, 1971).

[79] In 1964, the CGT launched a 'Plan of Struggle' which involved the occupation of some 11,000 workplaces by almost 4 million workers. See Peralta Ramos, p. 166.

[80] See 'El Lisandro de la Torre del 59: bastión de Resistencia Peronista', interview with Sebastián Borro, *Peronismo y Liberación*, no. 1 (August 1974), pp. 97-102.

of terrorism were subjected to military jurisdiction, Berisso, La Plata, and Ensenada were declared military zones, unions were hit by *intervenciones*,[81] and strikers were arrested.

Peronists felt betrayed by Frondizi, though he enjoyed little room for manoeuvre. Jostled between contending military and Peronist pressures, Frondizi was obliged, in order to retain office, to both placate and 'betray' the Peronist Movement. Yet he could not do enough to satisfy Peronist demands without being deposed by military *gorilas*, nor could he become a military puppet without provoking an angry popular reaction. The economic health of the country was far too poor for him to be able to dispense lasting favours to the workers — and thus facilitate the co-option of Peronist labour leaders — without damaging the interests of those industrialists who were his major backers. Foreign investment was seen, both now and again under Onganía, as the key to development, a means of regenerating the economy and moving towards self-sufficiency in basic goods without resorting to vast public spending; but it was bound to take years before this *desarrollista* strategy could bear fruit (if it were ever to), and to Peronists it all smacked of a 'sell-out' to imperialism.

Frondizi's project eventually collapsed because Peronism remained intransigent in its demands and refused to abandon its aspiration for what was anathema to the military command: the return of Perón, which they feared Frondizi, out of venality or weakness, might engineer or connive at. Pressures to legalize Peronism, emanating from most of the civilian political forces and even an apparently-reformed General Aramburu, became too strong to resist. The Peronists were thus authorized to compete in the 1962 elections for provincial governors, and did far too well for nervous military chiefs to permit ratification of the results. Frondizi's *Unión Cívica Radical Intransigente* triumphed in ten provinces plus the Federal Capital, but neo-Peronists won control of four provinces (five if one includes Jujuy, where they successfully

---

[81] Intervención here refers to the government's sending in of trustees to take over the running of unions, but can also refer to the government appointment of a trustee (*interventor*) to take charge of a province or university. Under the 1973–6 Peronist administrations, national union leaders were also empowered to take over the management of dissident unions and regional union bodies.

backed a Christian Democrat) and official *peronista* candidates won in five provinces, including the decisive Province of Buenos Aires where militant trade unionist and future Montonero ally Andrés Framini was elected Governor. By annulling the election results and deposing Frondizi, the military fulfilled Perón's prediction: 'If we lose, we win nothing. And if we win, we lose everything'[82] — but nevertheless bring final discredit to the *frondizista* alternative to Peronism. Frustrated in their efforts to succeed by constitutional means in 1962, then proscribed for the 1963 elections (which brought Arturo Illia and the Popular Radicals to power with only one-quarter of the electorate behind them), many Peronists now saw their only option as direct action: in most cases, solely to oblige power-holders to permit them to exploit constitutional mechanisms; some, however, because far more radical conclusions had been drawn from the Frondizi experience, especially with regard to the passage of industrialists out of the national-popular camp and into that of the enemy. As a *Compañero* editorial saw it:

> The timid bourgeoisie is no threat to the oligarchic structures which must be destroyed urgently; it only aspires to become a junior partner in the share-out [of national wealth with imperialism]. Its sole motive in seeking popular support is to use it as a bargaining counter, only to sacrifice the people's interests and those of the nation later on if that becomes necessary in order to safeguard its own interests.[83]

In other words, the 'national bourgeoisie' was now regarded as more bourgeois than national.

A third radicalizing factor was the need for militant Peronists to define their loyalties more precisely as Vandorism, the conciliatory trade union tendency associated with Augusto Vandor, became dominant within the CGT. As the 1960s progressed, the *burocracia sindical* increasingly sought a place for the labour movement, or at least its leaders, within non-Peronist orders, instead of a return of Peronism and Perón to power. There was a reformist response to this development provided by recently-displaced union leaders and non-strategic union sections which participated in the MRP and then, in 1965-6, in the *62 De Pie Junto a Perón*, a union

---

[82] See Luna, pp. 137-43.
[83] 'Falsa opción', *Compañero*, no. 1 (7 June 1963), p. 1.

coordinator established to oppose the Vandorist-dominated 62 Organizations and led by José Alonso. But the rise of the Vandorist bureaucracy appears too to have exercised a revolutionizing effect on some young militant leaders of small unions, who now began to see the limitations of trade union struggle as erstwhile *compañeros* like Vandor ostentatiously renounced class warfare. Cases in point here were Gustavo Rearte, elected to lead the Federation of Soap and Perfume Workers at the age of 25, and Jorge Di Pasquale, also in his twenties when chosen to lead the Association of Pharmaceutical Workers.

Fourth, Argentina like the rest of Latin America felt the impact of the Cuban Revolution. Ironically, initial jubilation over the 1959 overthrow of the Batista dictatorship had come from the confirmed anti-Peronists, who viewed the rebel victory as a Caribbean version of their own 1955 deposition of Perón. Former Vice-President, Admiral Rojas, one of the right-wing architects of the *Revolución Libertadora*, had immediately hailed Castro's success as 'a triumph which will bring joy not only to Argentina, but also to all America and all the free world'.[84] This reactionary support rapidly dissipated as the Cuban revolutionary process became more profound, yet Peronist hostility, in line with the traditional anti-Communism of the Movement, remained widespread for years. Even a militant labour leader like Andrés Framini rejected the 'strange ideologies' emanating from Cuba in the early 1960s.[85]

John William Cooke, who owed his name to Irish forefathers, was until his death in 1968 the leading exponent of the minority viewpoint that sought to identify *peronismo* with *fidelismo*. Born in 1920, a *forjista* in his youth, then a deputy in the first Peronist-controlled Congress, Cooke stood out early on as a result of his nationalist ardour, but subsequently moved distinctly to the Left.[86] His major political role was played out after the 1955 coup, when Perón appointed him as his delegate in Argentina and as leader of the *Resistencia* — roles which he was only able fully to perform after

[84] Reported in the *Buenos Aires Herald*, 3 January 1959.
[85] Ibid., 25 March 1962.
[86] For an analysis of Cooke's ideological development, see my 'The Peronist Left', pp. 16–78.

his escape, in the company of Héctor Cámpora and others, from Río Gallegos prison in southern Argentina to Punta Arenas, Chile, in March 1957. As resistance commander, though not one unchallenged by Peronist politicians, Cooke encouraged two forms of struggle above all others: industrial campaigns, including the major late 1958 oil workers' strike which he personally intervened in; and the direct action, sabotage, and propaganda activities of small *comando* units, at times independently, at others in support of labour struggles.[87] With Borro, he placed himself at the head of the 1959 Lisandro de la Torre strike, seeking to transform it into a revolutionary general strike, but was jailed by Frondizi and ditched by Perón when the strike eventually was broken.

For the remainder of his life Cooke's influence was primarily ideological. Permitted to leave Argentina in 1960, he was not to return until President Illia's 1963 amnesty enabled him to do so. Those three years, spent in Cuba, greatly affected his political writing. Cooke now began to maintain, with the industrialists' desertion of Peronism and the experience of the Cuban Revolution in mind, that anti-imperialist undertakings could not be pursued without simultaneously waging war on capitalism in the underdeveloped world. Appealing to Perón to side unequivocally with the infant Peronist Left, he wrote: 'Nowadays nobody thinks that national liberation can be achieved without social revolution and therefore the struggle is also [one] by the poor against the rich...[88] Since national liberation is indivisible from

[87] *Comando* activities were characterized by much spontaneity and improvisation, and were hardly coordinated. They nevertheless expressed the feeling that violence was necessary to secure a Peronist restoration. According to one estimate ['Los guerrilleros', *Confirmado*, no. 402 (18-24 December 1975), pp. 20-5], there were 7,000 bomb explosions in 1956-7 — more than during the Algerian independence struggle. However, elsewhere ['Terrorismo y antiterrorismo', *Confirmado*, no. 411 (August 1976), pp. 14-19] the same magazine claimed that between 1956-61, resistance groups were responsible for 1022 explosions of petards and other devices; 104 cases of arson against public buildings, industrial plant, and railway wagons; and 440 attacks of various kinds (obstruction of railway tracks, attacks on policemen, etc.). On the *Resistencia*, see 'Apuntes para una historia de la resistencia y del peronismo revolucionario', six supplements to *En Lucha*, nos. 13-18 (December 1973-September 1974); and the memoirs of Juan M. Vigo, *¡La vida por Perón!* (Buenos Aires: A Peña Lillo, 1973).

[88] Cooke, letter to Perón of 24 July 1961, *Correspondencia Perón-Cooke*, 2 vols., 2nd ed. (Buenos Aires: Granica Editor, 1973), vol. 2, p. 203.

social revolution, there is no bourgeois nationalism',[89] for the bourgeoisie's objective was to 'privatize the lucre and socialize the sacrifices'.[90]

Cooke's position was contradictory, for while he urged working-class leadership of the Peronist Movement, he clearly expected Peronism to retain a multi-class character for some time and often wrote as if bourgeois Peronists would subordinate themselves, suicidally, to a revolutionary workers' leadership. There was also a lot of wishful thinking behind his contentions that a 'dialectical relationship' existed between Peronism and Castroism as 'national variations of the continental revolutionary struggle';[91] and that Perón, along with the working class, was a revolutionary who should disavow the reformist bureaucracy which had 'usurped' the local leadership of the Movement. For a long time, Cooke retained the hope that Perón would take up Fidel Castro's offer of hospitality in Havana. He wrote at length, providing ten arguments as to why Perón should shift his 'revolutionary' base to Cuba,[92] but his leader only responded with evasions.

In spite of his shortcomings Cooke's unification of the objectives of national liberation and social revolution became a hallmark of the most revolutionary strains of Peronist Left thought. His message was essentially that Peronism's proletarian base provided the Movement with a revolutionary potential, the realization of which would involve its left-wing and combative labour sectors in an internal struggle against the bureaucratic local Peronist leadership, for the latter in general accepted the values and conventional strategies of the dominant social system. Moreover Cooke, echoing sentiments which went right back to the late nineteenth century origins of Argentine Radicalism, insisted that Peronism would prosper through intransigence rather than compromise. Resisting all efforts to reach a political accommodation with non-Peronist forces, Cooke looked to direct action – the general strike, insurrection, guerrilla warfare – as the only

---

[89] Idem, *El peronismo y el golpe de estado (informe a las bases del movimiento)* (Buenos Aires: Ediciones Acción Revolucionaria Peronista, 1966), p. 38. Also published under the name *Peronismo y revolución* (Buenos Aires: Granica Editor, 1971).
[90] Ibid., p. 98.
[91] Letter of 18 October 1962, *Correspondencia*, vol. 2, p. 262.
[92] Ibid., pp. 261–90; and letter of 27 January 1965, ibid., pp. 324–38.

38 *Antecedents*

means of overcoming the post-1966 stalemate between a military regime 'unable to stabilize itself but with sufficient material power to survive, and a mass movement powerful enough to submit it to constant harassment but not to overthrow it'.[93]

Cuban influence was also evident in the 1959-60 attempt to launch a rural guerrilla movement, commonly known as the *Uturuncos*, in the provinces of Tucumán and Santiago del Estero; and it was present within the MRP. Héctor Villalón, who as Perón's delegate sent a message of support to the MRP founding congress in 1964, was, until accused by the Cubans of embezzling their money, also a dealer in Cuban tobacco and reputedly a representative of Fidel Castro. Meanwhile, beyond Peronism, both Angel Bengochea's faction of the initially-Trotskyist Workers' Word (*Palabra Obrera*) tendency and Jorge Ricardo Masetti's People's Guerrilla Army (EGP) rural guerrilla *foco* in Salta Province were, to different extents, persuaded to undertake armed struggles during the early 1960s by the Cuban argument of revolutionary success.

Finally Perón's own gestures and pronouncements after 1955 assisted the rise of the Peronist Left. It was not until the mid-1960s that the radical rhetoric which so delighted his more combative devotees entered the official Peronist lexicon; then Perón reformulated his Third Position so as to associate it with liberation struggles against colonialism and neo-colonialism in the Third World, while claiming for Justicialism and himself credit as their harbingers.[94] Simultaneously, Perón applauded the Sino-Soviet split, appreciating it as a blow to the 'international dogmatic socialism' of the Soviet Union, and envisaging it as part of a world trend towards the emergence of diverse varieties of *socialismo nacional*.[95] But what did Perón's new catch-phrase mean? Certainly very different things to different kinds of Peronist. While the Peronist Right interpreted it as National Socialism, a blood brother of Nazism and Fascism, the Peronist Left equated it with a 'national' road to socialism, understood as

[93] Cooke, *Apuntes*, p. 29.
[94] See Perón, *La hora de los pueblos* (Buenos Aires: Editorial Norte, 1968), p. 162; and Pavón Pereyra, pp. 55-6.
[95] See Nadra, p. 16; and Feinmann, pp. 226-30.

Antecedents   39

a system of economic socialization and popular power respectful of specific national conditions and traditions. As supportive evidence, the ultra-Right were able to cite a passage in *La hora de los pueblos* in which Perón had argued that the Allied defeat of Germany and Italy eliminated 'all momentary possibilities of a *socialismo nacional*',[96] and a January 1969 statement to the effect that, during his 1937 trip to Italy, Perón had encountered 'the first *socialismo nacional* to appear in the world'.[97] Yet the Left could refer to many more apparent indications of Perón having undergone a dramatic revolutionary metamorphosis in exile: he publicly commended the rebel French students in May 1968, claimed that 'if I were Chinese, I would be a Maoist',[98] and declared that 'the solution is to liberate the country in the way Fidel freed his'.[99]

Perón's exploitation of *socialismo nacional* was deliberately ambiguous and extensive. When pressed to state precisely why *Justicialismo* deserved socialist accreditation, his only answer was that 'it pivots on social justice';[100] and indeed, if one examines all of the ways in which the Peronist leader applied his new doctrinal label, the only common theme is that each regime and movement offered as an example preached social justice — whether they pursued it or not. Within the covers of a single volume, one could discover a Perón proclaiming: 'The reign of the bourgeoisie over the world has ended. The government of the people begins', as well as a Perón clearly seeking elite patronage. Amidst the quasi-revolutionary bombast were images of Argentina heading towards an abyss, with Perón looming up providentially as the one man who could 'pacify the Argentine population', implement a 'national solution', and preside over a 'national reconstruction' programme based in part upon hard work (West Germany being presented as an example).[101] Claiming

[96] Op. cit., p. 174.
[97] Perón, quoted in Félix Luna, *El 45*, 7th ed. (Buenos Aires: Editorial Sudamericana, 1975), p. 58.
[98] See Perón's letter of 10 December 1969 to Hernández Arregui, and a November 1972 interview, both republished in *Peronismo y socialismo*, no. 1 (September 1973), pp. 31-4.
[99] Perón, quoted in the *Buenos Aires Herald*, 7 July 1970.
[100] Perón, quoted in Pavón Pereyra, p. 336.
[101] Perón, *La hora*, pp. 19, 43 and 132.

that his policies 'made sure that communism never became a problem in our country',[102] Perón on occasions carefully cultivated an image as a fireman of revolutions.

The credibility of both the revolutionary and the reactionary Perón rested upon the readiness of many of those associated with the Peronist Left and Right to believe that his overtures to political foes and class enemies were merely tactical ploys, devised to strengthen the national movement by attracting new supporters, neutralizing other sectors, and isolating the 1966-73 military regime. Any doubts that the mainstream Peronist Left harboured over the authenticity of Perón's purported conversion to socialism — which he presented as just a doctrinal updating, adapting Justicialism to the modern world — were soon cast aside when Peronist Youth militants and combatants of the 'special formations' received communications specifically addressed to their aspirations. In these Perón now appeared to admit that he had been wrong to yield so easily in 1955, given the amount of popular suffering which had ensued.[103] Moreover he encouraged young activists to believe that they would soon inherit the leadership of his Movement through a *transvasamiento generacional*, or generational rejuvenation of its structures. Feigning humility and revolutionary ardour, the old man, who had been sixty-years-old when deposed, claimed that he hoped he could still be of some use to 'the wonderful youth we have and who will, sooner or later, take up our banners and, we hope, will carry them forward to victory'.[104]

Perón not only authorized revolutionary warfare — he flattered its combatants in ways which few could resist. His praise for the urban guerrillas of the Peronist 'special formations' was totally unreserved. 'We have a marvellous youth [section] which every day unequivocally demonstrates its capacity and greatness.... I have absolute faith in our lads who have learnt how to die for their ideals', Perón wrote in a 1971 'Message to the Youth'. Besides eulogies, the combatants were awarded full tactical independence, owing to the impracticality of direction from Madrid, and

---

[102] Perón, interview in *Primera Plana*, 7 September 1971.

[103] See, for example, Perón's statements reported in the *Buenos Aires Herald* of 23 April 1969 and 7 July 1970.

[104] Ibid., 16 February 1972.

were promised 'gradual preponderance as the violent struggle develops'.[105] While conferring great legitimacy upon the Peronist guerrillas of the late 1960s and early 1970s, these statements were regarded by the fighters as tantamount to a revolutionary definition on the part of Perón. As far as they were concerned the decisive, though not single, factor involved in determining who was a revolutionary and who was not was the method employed in the pursuit of goals. The traditional Left had spoken about socialism for decades but had achieved little. All sorts of left-wing political and ideological formulae had been applied with negligible success. Now, during the late 1960s, faced with a military regime which seemingly ruled out all possibilities of Peronism returning to power by legal and constitutional means, direct armed action was postulated as the only effective means of toppling that regime, and hence the only means which true revolutionaries would adopt. In the bellicose words of the Montonero Luis Losada, radical Peronists held that 'The only orthodoxy is combat'.[106]

Although the Peronist Left was strengthened by Perón's endorsement, the main beneficiary of the relationship was Perón himself. It guaranteed him the naive loyalty of most of the Left Peronists, including the Montoneros, while those revolutionary Peronists who did see through Perón's stratagems often felt that they might be turned to the advantage of the Left, regardless of his intent. Ingenuousness abounded, yet one can understand why Perón suddenly became so acceptable to radical opinion. No member of the Peronist or non-Peronist Left had yet provided a comprehensive history of post-1955 Peronist politics, which might have encouraged a more critical attitude to be taken to Perón; and most of the Peronist Left, whether late-comers to the Movement or not, were far too young to recall what Peronist Argentina had been like before 1955. They heard taped messages from Perón urging as much violence as they could manage,[107] and most assumed him to be a revolutionary;

[105] 'Perón habla a la juventud', *Cristianismo y Revolución*, no. 29 (June 1971), pp. 8–10.
[106] Interview in *Córdoba* newspaper, 20 February 1971.
[107] This had been one of Perón's exhortations ever since the 1955 coup: 'The more violent we are the better', he had written in a 3 November 1956 letter to Cooke [*Correspondencia*, vol. 1, p. 35].

they saw Peronist workers repeatedly paralysing the economy, mounting large demonstrations, and in places even erecting barricades to fight soldiers at the end of the 1960s, and assumed them to be revolutionary — with Peronism, their political identity, and Perón, their political leader, revolutionary by implication.

There was plenty of 'circumstantial evidence' available to support the contention that Peronism indeed merited revolutionary status. A historical analysis of Perón's political behaviour would nevertheless have revealed him to have always been remarkably adept at pragmatically bowing to the Left, Right, or Centre whenever one particular line served his overall aim of a Peronist restoration; and that such gestures in no way negated his traditional beliefs in national development, class conciliation, and a semi-corporatist 'organized community'. What has frequently been misleadingly termed Perón's 'pendular strategy' (implying alternate swings towards the Left and Right) was actually a judicious policy of acquiring the broadest possible political and social support as could be achieved behind national liberation banners, but at times placing his own immense personal authority behind whatever part of the Movement was tactically best suited to exploit a specific political situation. Occasionally, the leader's great political weight would also be placed behind 'rebel' factions when a dominant clique threatened to assert too much independence or to alter the multi-class character of the Movement.

Perhaps the clearest example of Perón's highly successful opportunism is provided by the brief history of the MRP. On 5 August 1964 two thousand delegates[108] at the founding congress of the Revolutionary Peronist Movement heard a message from Villalón conveying Perón's blessings. It seemed to many observers that Perón was siding finally with the more radical wing of his Movement, when in reality he merely regarded the MRP as a means of putting a spoke in the wheel of advancing Vandorism. And, if only temporarily, Perón's resort to a 'revolutionary threat' to bring the Vandorists to heel worked: alarmed by his sponsorship of the MRP and fearful of being outflanked on the Left, Vandor and his

[108] '5 de agosto: jornada histórica', *Compañero*, no. 59 (11 August 1964), p. 1.

Antecedents   43

colleagues (Iturbe, Parodi, and Carvalli) immediately flew off to make their peace with Perón. On 25 August 1964 they returned triumphant from Madrid and gleefully presented Peronist Superior Command (CSP) resolutions signed by Perón to the press. These confirmed the Justicialist Party as the sole political organization of the Peronist Movement, ratified the CSP as the tactical leadership within Argentina, and described Alberto Iturbe as Perón's delegate. Their function was further 'to proscribe the Revolutionary Peronist Movement, set up under the inspiration of Héctor Villalón, who does not belong to this Command nor to the Peronist Movement, and also its mouthpiece, the weekly *Compañero*.'[109]

In this way Perón in 1964 aborted the left-wing embryo before it could take on flesh and muscle. His disavowal of the MRP immediately brought its latent internal contradictions to breaking point: in the name of loyalty and orthodoxy, the reformists, including most of the trade unionists, abandoned the MRP virtually overnight. A conference organized by its revolutionary rump in February 1965 attracted only 118 delegates[110] and served as little more than an index of the impact of Perón's disclaimer. He had only promoted the MRP while it had served his immediate purposes. Later, when the Vandorists attempted at the 1965 Avellaneda Congress to 'don long trousers'[111] and proclaim the coming of 'Peronism without Perón', the exiled leader looked to more solid labour counterweights to Vandorism. Faced with the implicit threat of something akin to the British Labour Party being constructed by the Vandorist union leaders on the foundations of the Peronist Movement, Perón threw his weight, again with considerable but not lasting success, behind José Alonso and other displaced and marginal trade unionists who formed the *62 De Pie*.

Later still, when the Vandorists showed themselves happy to wheel and deal with the personnel of General Onganía's regime, Perón encouraged the March 1968 emergence of the

[109] *La Razón*, 25 August 1964.
[110] Gustavo Rearte, 'La única respuesta válida', *Compañero*, no. 77 (2nd fortnight of February 1965), p. 3.
[111] One of the slogans of the Congress was 'Now we've got long trousers'. See Peralta Ramos, p. 167.

'rebel' CGT of the Argentines (CGTA) by warmly receiving its future leader, Raimundo Ongaro, in Madrid a month earlier. Once more though, as soon as the Vandorist 'participationists' had been given their warning, as soon as they had been reminded that they were nothing without Perón, the experiment was called off for fear that it might get out of hand and alienate potential bourgeois backers. Hence, Bernardo Alberte, one of Perón's most left-wing delegates, was sacked and replaced by the more conservative Jerónimo Remorino when the dissolution of the CGTA and the CGT's reunification were ordered from Madrid at the end of 1968.[112] By this time, however, it was not so easy for Perón to control the fortunes of revolutionary and militant Peronists. He could still tap their support, but the tap was now much easier to turn on than to turn off: most CGTA activists ignored Perón's orders to disband, and when trade union reunification was achieved in 1970 it was mainly because the CGTA had been destroyed by repressive governmental measures, introduced under the pretext of the June 1969 assassination of Augusto T. Vandor.[113]

Right up to 1973 Perón nevertheless managed to avoid the damaging loss of his left-wing forces, among which two trends were increasingly discernible. The more revolutionary tendency, associated with the names of Cooke, Rearte, Di Pasquale, Ongaro, and Jaime, certainly took note of Perón's machiavellianism. In one of his last writings Cooke finally criticized Perón, describing him as 'the main asset of bourgeois-democratic politics in Argentina', yet acknowledging the continuing strength of his charisma, he being the symbol of 'the only period in which the worker was happy'.[114] Rearte, on the other hand, though he had suffered as much as anybody as a result of a Perón U-turn, considered it politic to keep quiet about the MRP experience for much longer. He realized that an open break with Perón in the mid-1960s

[112] See 'Mayo 69: Cordobazo', *En Lucha*, no. 16 (June 1974), p. 6. Bernardo Alberte's revolutionary stance was synthesized in the dichotomies, 'Dictatorship or Revolution' and 'Imperialist bourgeois dictatorial regime or revolutionary people's government', which appeared in his paper *Con Todo*, no. 0 (September 1968), p. 3.

[113] This and other cases of guerrilla assassinations of union leaders are discussed in the first part of Chapter 5.

[114] Cooke, 'La revolución y el peronismo', pp. 50–1 and 92.

would have led to the instant collapse of the fragile bridges which revolutionaries were establishing between themselves and the organized labour movement. Moreover, though the MRP affair had highlighted Perón's opportunism, it had also shown his willingness to let the Peronist 'hard line' develop. Rearte now knew that Perón's encouragement of the MRP had been merely tactical, but he also perceived that Perón had political differences with Vandor which could be exploited by the Left. Whereas the Vandorist project aimed 'to transform the Movement into a political party to represent the workers under the existing regime', Perón's return and the implementation of his 'own capitalist project' required a change of regime.[115] Vandor's integrationist-participationist schemes demanded the destruction of the Movement's radical flank; Perón's strategy called for both a 'hard' and a 'soft' line, the revolutionary and the bureaucratic.

In recognition of Perón's deliberate strategic ambiguity, revolutionary Peronists concentrated their efforts more and more on the building of militant rank-and-file organizations, motivated by the eventual aim of linking them into an 'independent alternative of the working class'. Yet labour support for these *alternativistas* was far too slender for them to disclaim the mantle of Perón. His authority being so great, it seemed prudent to make no great fuss about his manoeuvres, but rather to use his quasi-revolutionary rhetoric and gestures in order to justify and make more acceptable their own ideas and activities. There was no naivety on their part. They may be accused (and were by the non-Peronist Left) of having aided the survival of Peronist mythology, of having fuelled workers' illusions in Perón's ability to solve their economic problems, and of not having themselves resolved a fundamental contradiction between their short-term tactic (support for a 'revolutionary' Perón) and their long-term strategy (the creation of a revolutionary party based on the workers). But they were in an unenviable position for revolutionaries: the options facing them were political compromise or the political wilderness.

The less radical but far more numerous Peronist Left

[115] Rearte, 'Por que fracasó el MRP', supplement to *En Lucha*, no. 18 (September 1974), p. 3. Cooke died in September 1968, a victim of cancer at the age of forty-seven; Rearte died of leukaemia in July 1973, aged forty.

tendency, which the Montoneros came to lead, could not be accused prior to 1973 of political compromise, for it had no conception of any 'independent alternative' whatsoever. Its militants' faith in Perón's revolutionism was absolutely sincere, rooted in his sanction of armed struggle, in their own youthful lack of political experience, and in some cases, as will be seen, it was also a guilty reaction against their own anti-Peronist backgrounds. Most were middle class, and more favourably disposed towards class alliances than class struggles, even if on paper those alliances were to be constructed in the name of *socialismo nacional*. They became known as *movimientistas* because they regarded the Peronist Movement as basically a revolutionary class alliance, standing for national liberation and social revolution. Their impression of both pre- and post-1955 Peronist history was coloured by romanticism and flawed by all the myths which the Peronist Movement had to offer. Not for one moment did the young soldiers of Perón suspect that they might be doing battle for an unfaithful general.

2
Montonero Origins

> 'They do not know Peronism from within. They know anti-Peronism from within.'[1]

The Montoneros arrived on the Argentine political scene during some of the stormiest years of social conflict ever experienced by their country. Founded two years after the 1966 usurpation of power by General Juan Carlos Onganía and the Armed Forces, they devoted two years to preparatory training and the accumulation of resources before announcing their existence to the world in May 1970. Less is known about the 1968-70 phase than about any other period of Montonero history, yet those years of anonymity, as well as those immediately preceding them, were of fundamental importance in the shaping of the organization's political physiognomy.

NATIONALISM, CATHOLICISM, AND THE PROTO-MONTONEROS

An initial glance at the political backgrounds of prominent early Montoneros presents the observer with an enigma: many of the young men and women who took up arms in the late 1960s and early 1970s in pursuit of popular nationalist and socialist ideals had gained their political baptism in branches of the traditionally-conservative Catholic Action (AC); some had even started out in the Falange-inspired Tacuara; very few originated on the Left, and hardly any began their political lives as Peronists. Later they were to paint a retrospective self-portrait which presented the birth of their organization as a synthesis of Peronist and Guevarist currents.[2] The portrayal was ideologically ahistorical, but highly revealing nevertheless: its rationale was that the

---
[1] Padre Hernán Benítez, 'Causas y responsables de la "ejecución" de Aramburu', *Cristianismo y Revolución*, no. 25 (September 1970), pp. 5-11.
[2] 'Informe del Consejo Nacional del Partido Montonero, septiembre de 1977', *Boletín Interno*, no. 4 (nd), pp. 1-2.

Montoneros set out to fuse urban guerrilla warfare, an adaption of Che Guevara's *foco* theory,[3] with the popular struggles of the Peronist Movement, in other words to unify vanguard and mass activity. They thus characterized themselves in a manner which emphasized strategies and methods rather than political and ideological definitions and, in passing, through omission, sought to obscure the fact that most Montonero pioneers were initially anything but revolutionaries.

Although the Montoneros were subsequently to benefit from the incorporation of individuals and organizations of erstwhile Guevarist political identity, their genesis owed most to developments within Argentine nationalism and Catholicism. Founding members Fernando Abal Medina and Carlos Gustavo Ramus had in the early 1960s, as fourteen-year-olds, both participated in the violently right-wing Tacuara. And youths who later joined the Montoneros and filled senior positions were also involved: the young Rodolfo Galimberti, future Peronist Youth leader, hung around its fringes, while Dardo Cabo led an equally right-wing, but pro-Peronist, Catholic nationalist breakaway group called the New Argentina Movement, before his imprisonment in 1966.

Tacuara held great romantic appeal for boisterous youths of Catholic upbringing. Formed by activists of the Secondary Students Nationalist Union (UNES) after the 1955 military coup, its lineage went back through the nationalist organizations of the 1940s to the *Legión Cívica* of the 1930s and the *Liga Patriótica* of 1919.[4] Tacuara's novelty lay in its fascination with Spanish *falangismo*, but like its Argentine predecessors it stressed the values of courage, sacrifice,

---

[3] The theory of the *foco*, or *foquismo* (subscribed to by *foquistas*), though originally elaborated with rural warfare in mind, contends that revolutionaries should begin to wage armed struggle even if some of the 'conditions' for a successful revolution are not yet present in their country; that guerrilla activities help to create such conditions; and that, by exploiting the classical guerrilla advantages of mobility, flexibility, and surprise, small armed nuclei can develop into popular revolutionary armies, capable of defeating regular armies. See Régis Debray, *Revolution in the Revolution?* (Harmondsworth: Penguin, 1968); and Che Guevara, *Guerrilla Warfare* (Harmondsworth: Penguin, 1969).

'Guevarist', when used in this book as a *political* label, refers to pro-Cuban, non-Peronist forces which define themselves as 'Marxist-Leninist' and engage in armed struggle.

[4] See Marysa Navarro Gerassi, *Los nacionalistas* (Buenos Aires: Editorial Jorge Alvarez, 1968).

violence, and struggle, and went in for direct action, uniforms, and ceremonies in a big way. The *tacuaristas* habitually wore the Maltese Cross in their lapels and would put on uniforms for secret initiation rites in the darkest recesses of the Chacarita cemetery in Buenos Aires. Thanks to police and military contacts, they possessed small arms from the start, and even when not engaged in attacks on Jewish schoolchildren carried coshes and knuckle-dusters with them. Training exercises, combined with open-air banquets and folkloric discussion, were held at a Paraná Delta country house owned by the family of leader Alberto Ezcurra, whose family tree linked him directly to Uriburu, author of the right-wing nationalist coup of 1930, and indirectly to Rosas. Partly because several members belonged to eminent or at least 'respectable' families, and in part owing to its virulent anti-communism, the early Tacuara enjoyed great immunity from police attention. At its height in the late 1950s, when Tacuara mobilized hundreds of students in defence of the status of Catholic educational institutions, it was said that activists rarely spent more than twenty-four hours in police custody and that policemen drew back from photographing detainees for fear of dismissal.[5]

During the early 1960s Tacuara controlled the University Law Union (SUD), but by then was already beginning to disintegrate into various offshoots. As a result of the entry of youths of Peronist parentage and a growing recognition on the part of one faction that nationalists had to come to terms with the vitality of labour's support for Peronism, a left-wing Tacuara tendency gradually emerged and took the name of the Tacuara Revolutionary Nationalist Movement (MNRT) in 1962.[6] Disappointed with the empty nationalist rhetoric of the post-1955 governments, they had initially looked to Peronism simply for the realization of the Falangist

[5] On Tacuara and its offshoots, see especially Horacio Salas, 'La ideología de la violencia', *Discusión*, no. 15 (3-16 April 1975), pp. 14-17; and Rogelio García Lupo, 'Diálogo con los jóvenes fascistas', in his *La rebelión de los generales* (Buenos Aires: Proceso Ediciones, 1962), pp. 71-8.

[6] Radicalization within Tacuara may also have had something to do with the lower-middle-class circumstances of the new recruits to an organization whose original leaders, at least, were of bourgeois extraction. A good number of the new *tacuaristas* of the early 1960s were still students at university or night school but had to work, usually as employees, to finance their studies. See García Lupo, pp. 72-3.

idea of *sindicalismo nacional*. 'In the face of Liberal indifference and the Marxist negation', Tacuara had advocated 'the National Syndicalist State, which will replace the Liberal regime [and] be an authentic State based on the unions.'[7] Now, whereas the nationalism of the hard-line anti-Peronists remained reactionary, authoritarian, Catholic, and largely foreign-inspired, that of the emergent faction became more secular and identified its nationalist, pro-labour stance with the Peronist cause.

Led by José Luis Nell and 'Joe' Baxter (a law student of English descent), the MNRT forged links with the Peronist Youth, Left organizations, and a few trade unions, and dismissed right-wing Tacuara splinters such as the Restorationist Nationalist Guard (GNR) as 'those who think that the battle for Argentine sovereignty was fought in the Berlin Chancellery in 1945'.[8] In turn, the GNR claimed that Tacuara had been taken over by 'Fidelism, Trotskyism, and atheism', and asserted that 'ultra-hierarchy is necessary in order to distinguish qualities'.[9]

Later characterized as the 'young Peronists who wanted to fight',[10] the MNRT, as a former member recalled, 'read everything subversive and clandestine – even OAS stuff – the political ideology did not matter. There was a lot of infantilism and romanticism'. Their literary commitment derived primarily from a desire to learn how to conduct a guerrilla struggle, yet most of the literature which they devoured, much of it from Cuba and Algeria, also imparted left-wing ideas.[11] Nevertheless, the MNRT was not unambiguously left wing: one faction, led briefly by Ezcurra[12] and apparently including Galimberti, embraced Peronism but remained hostile to Marxism; the other, associated with Nell, took up Marxism as a method of analysis, declared that

[7] 'Tacuara juega a la milicia revolucionaria', *Che*, no. 15 (2 June 1961), pp. 10–11.
[8] Baxter, quoted in Salas, p. 17.
[9] *Guardia Restauradora Nacionalista* declarations, quoted in Navarro Gerassi, p. 228, and Salas, p. 16.
[10] García Lupo, p. 73.
[11] Personal interview with a former MNRT member, Buenos Aires, October 1976.
[12] Ezcurra, a seminarist prior to the creation of Tacuara, returned to his old vocation by entering the Paraná seminary in 1964. He was ordained in December 1971.

there could be no national liberation without social revolution, and saw the working class as the revolutionary vanguard.[13] On 29 August 1963 it was the latter faction which mounted Argentina's first real urban guerrilla operation, though the target they chose indicated the ambiguity of even their radicalism.[14] Using a hired ambulance, they drove up to the Bank Employees Union Clinic, shot dead two guards, wounded a policeman, and then escaped with the clinic's 100,000 dollar payroll. The MNRT's organizational infrastructure was too primitive, however, and its political support far too limited for it to withstand the police hunt which ensued. The guerrilla nucleus was destroyed in 1964 through the arrest of half its members, though Nell himself managed to stage a spectacular one-man escape from the Buenos Aires Law Courts.

After a visit to China Nell was reunited with other MNRT survivors in Montevideo at the end of 1965, and most of them, after contributing to the political and military development of the Tupamaros,[15] went on to play important roles in the structuring and strengthening of Argentina's own modern urban guerrilla forces a few years later. Joe Baxter, who had fought in Vietnam, lent his military expertise to the non-Peronist People's Revolutionary Army (ERP), and reputedly participated in its March–April 1971 kidnapping and 'execution' of Fiat boss Oberdan Sallustro before himself dying in the July 1973 Orly air crash at the age of thirty-two. Jorge Caffatti began a prison sentence for the 1963 raid, but later escaped twice, joined the Peronist Armed Forces

---

[13] Their basic documents were the 'Reportaje al Movimiento N. Revolucionario Tacuara', *Compañero*, no. 63 (8 September 1964), p. 4; and 'MNRT: Violencia revolucionaria' (1 May 1964), *Militancia*, no. 6 (19 July 1973), pp. 35–8.

[14] The seizure of a trade union clinic payroll hardly enhanced MNRT chances of working-class approbation. According to press reports, this target was chosen purely because Gustavo Posse, who was only a sympathizer of the organization, learnt of the movement of the payroll money and passed the information on to an MNRT friend in return for a share in the takings. For accounts of this *Operación Rosaura*, see *La Razón*, 25 March 1964 (police report); *Ocurrió*, no. 54 (1 April 1964), pp. 12–14; & Carlos A. Arbelos and Alfredo M. Roca, *Los muchachos peronistas* (Madrid: Emiliano Escolar Editor, 1981), p. 56. The latter, written by veteran militants, provides valuable internal accounts of the earliest urban guerrilla efforts, and includes anecdotic references to pioneers such as Nell, Baxter, Caffatti, Espina, and Ibarra.

[15] See ibid., pp. 87–117; and James Kohl and John Litt, *Urban Guerrilla Warfare in Latin America* (USA: MIT Press, 1974), pp. 185–7.

(FAP), and helped to propagate the idea of organizing rank-and-file groups of Peronist workers in opposition to Peronism's bourgeois and bureaucratic elements. Finally Nell himself was to exercise a politico-military influence within the Montoneros, before joining the more orthodox *Leal* (Loyalist) Peronist tendency early in 1974. The fact that the leading cadres of the MNRT went on to intervene influentially in three politically-distinct armed organizations is indicative of their lack of conceptual unity back in 1963-4, when the most solid cementing link between them was provided by the method of the urban guerrilla. Their ideological progress towards the Left was not unimportant, but it must be emphasized that a penchant for violent direct action, developing into an urban guerrilla commitment, was the only constant, apart from nationalism, in the evolution of those Montoneros who started out on the Right. Even their own comrades were to admit that the early intervention of Abal Medina and Ramus in the ultra-Right Tacuara had shown their desire for action to have been stronger than their ideological motivation.[16]

Those who took a violent path during the 1960s were very much aware of the way in which constitutional efforts to bring about change had been repeatedly frustrated. By the end of the decade, they could look back upon the military veto of the 1962 election results, the proscription of Peronism in 1963, and the 1966 seizure of power by generals intent upon a lengthy spell in power. More and more people began to concur with Perón's maxim, 'against brute force, only intelligently-applied force can be effective'.[17] Yet acceptance of armed struggle and the flourishing of left-wing and popular expressions of nationalism could never have occurred on the scale which they did without that wind of change which blew so forcefully through the Catholic Church during the same decade. In a country where 90 per cent of the population are baptized and 70 per cent reach the stage of First Communion,[18] radical Catholic ideas crucially undermined the

[16] '7 de setiembre — Día del Montonero', *El Descamisado*, no. 17 (11 September 1973), pp. 5-8.
[17] Perón, quoted in MNRT, 'Violencia revolucionaria'.
[18] Padre Carlos Mugica, *Peronismo y cristianismo* (Buenos Aires: Editorial Merlin, 1973), p. 81.

conservative hold of Church leaders over many thousands of Argentine youths. They bred concern for social problems and change, legitimized revolutionary action, and pointed many in the direction of the Peronist Movement. Indeed, for the handful of Catholics who constituted the Montonero core of 1968, these ideas were the single most important element in their radicalization.

The diffusion of radical Catholic theses was not of course a phenomenon peculiar to Argentina. Though Father Carlos Mugica propagated them and Juan García Elorrio further developed them, much of the impetus came from the Vatican and from the example set by the martyred Colombian guerrilla-priest, Camilo Torres. Mindful of the existence of over one-third of its followers in Latin America and fearful of the loss of the impoverished millions to the rival attraction of atheistic Marxism, the Vatican began to concern itself more with the lot of the poor from the late 1950s, and especially during the 1960s papacies of John XXIII and Paul VI. In recognition of the growing participation of Catholics in popular class struggles, dialogue with Marxists became acceptable to Rome. John XXIII in *Pacem in terris* (1963) even went so far as to comment that Marxism contained 'good elements, worthy of approval'.[19]

The Second Vatican Council and the documents which issued from it formalized the new orientation. Poverty, injustice, and exploitation were condemned as results of man's greed for power and wealth; Christians were urged, in the name of love for their fellow men, to struggle for equality. The new message found one of its most radical expressions at the Council in 1965, when Patriarch Maximos IV declared that 'true socialism is a full Christian life that involves a just sharing of goods and fundamental equality'.[20] Pope Paul VI's proclamation of *Populorum progressio*, the most important synthesis of the ideas of Vatican II, appeared two years later. It attacked inequality, the profit motive, racism, and the selfishness of the richer nations, but was not entirely clear on how these sins were to be vanquished:

---

[19] Quoted in John Gerassi (ed), *Revolutionary Priest* (Harmondsworth: Penguin, 1973), p. 17.
[20] Quoted in Dorothy Day (ed), *Camilo Torres: Priest and Revolutionary* (London: Sheed and Ward, 1968), p. 16.

violence was ruled out, 'save where there is manifest long-standing tyranny which would do damage to fundamental personal rights and dangerous harm to the common good of the country'.[21] Conscious of the presence of 'exploiters' among its brethren, the Vatican equivocated in this way for fear of the Catholic Church becoming exclusively a 'Church of the Poor'. *Populorum progressio* could be and was interpreted by some as implying that tyranny was not solely a matter of repressive political regimes but also of social systems which dehumanize and maintain the existence of widespread poverty, with this justifying the violence of the oppressed of the Third World. For others, however, 'manifest long-standing tyranny' was restricted to the political variant, with their interpretation providing a justification for non-involvement in revolutionary movements and only timid opposition to young dictatorships.

Worker-priests were active in Argentina prior to the proclamation of *Populorum progressio*, foreshadowing in practice some of the ideas of the Vatican II documents by working among the poor and sharing their experiences. The movement only became overtly political with the creation of the Third World Priests Movement (*Movimiento de Sacerdotes para el Tercer Mundo*) in 1967, heralded by a Third World Bishops' document which referred to socialism in highly positive terms: 'The Church can only rejoice at seeing the appearance among humanity of another social system which is less alien to the ethics of the prophets and the Gospel.' It was 'less alien' of course than capitalism, which was firmly condemned for its 'evil' characteristics of subjecting man to the economy and subordinating social to economic values.[22]

That document soon received the sponsorship of nearly one thousand Latin American priests, who submitted a manifesto to the Medellín Conference of the Latin American Episcopate in Colombia in 1968. The manifesto differentiated between the 'unjust violence of the oppressors' and the 'just violence of the oppressed', a distinction only entertained up to a point by the Church leaders present at Medellín. While blaming institutionalized violence and unjust social structures

---

[21] Quoted in J. Gerassi, p. 45.
[22] Quoted in Mugica, p. 89.

for Latin America's major problems, they categorically opposed the idea of armed revolution ('generally, it engenders new injustices')[23] and criticized Marxism as well as liberal capitalism on the grounds that 'both militate against the dignity of the human person'.[24] Nevertheless, the more radical pronouncements voiced at Medellín fuelled the theological revolution which swept through broad sectors of the Catholic Church during the 1960s, and its impact upon young people was particularly strong in Argentina.

Radical theology was imparted to the Montonero embryo by two men whose different attitudes towards violence reflected a general dilemma for Catholic radicals. Juan García Elorrio adopted Camilo Torres's view that 'revolution is not only permitted but is obligatory for all Christians who see in it the most effective way of making possible a greater love for all men',[25] adding that it would be 'at times necessarily violent because some hearts are so callous'.[26] Carlos Mugica, on the other hand, typified a more generally-accepted view in rejecting the participation of priests in armed revolutionary struggles and in stating, 'I am prepared to be killed but I am not prepared to kill'.[27]

Mugica, a member of the Jesuit Order and Third World Priests Movement, became a Peronist at the age of twenty-six. The key to his conversion was a feeling of intense guilt over the Church's support for the 1955 overthrow of Perón, coupled with the realization that this had led many working people, with good reason, to identify the Church with the oligarchy and oppressive post-1955 regimes. His sense of guilt, which was to find parallels in feelings of vicarious guilt felt by student late-comers to Peronism over the anti-Peronism of their predecessors,[28] helps to explain why he adopted an exceedingly naive attitude towards Peronism when he entered the popular camp. Mugica's acceptance of Perón's claim

[23] Quoted in J. Gerassi, p. 49.
[24] Quoted in Peter Strafford, 'The Church of Change', *The Times* (London), 2 December 1977.
[25] Camilo Torres, 'A Message to Christians' (3 August 1965), in Day (ed), pp. 72-4.
[26] García Elorrio, *Cristianismo y Revolución*, no. 1 (September 1966), p. 23.
[27] Mugica, quoted in Mario Eduardo Firmenich, 'Nuestras diferencias políticas', *El Peronista*, no. 5 (21 May 1974), pp. 4-8.
[28] Mugica, p. 84. For signs of student feelings of guilt, cf. JUP, 'El peronismo y la universidad', *Envido*, no. 9 (May 1973), pp. 54-61.

about his government 'only doing what the people wanted' stemmed from a desire to get closer to the ordinary people, faith in their allegiance to Perón, and an assumption that such a popular-based movement as Peronism had at least to possess socialist potential. His socialist sympathies were compatible with support for Peronism owing to his belief that the Argentine revolution had to proceed first through a 'liberation' stage before it embarked upon socialist tasks; and Peronism had, he believed, initiated this kind of process in 1945.[29]

It was around 1964 that Mugica came into contact with the ex-*tacuaristas*, Fernando Abal Medina and Carlos Gustavo Ramus, as well as Mario Eduardo Firmenich. At that time these three future Montonero founders were pupils at the National School of Buenos Aires and active together in the Catholic Student Youth (JEC), a branch of Catholic Action. Mugica became the school branch's spiritual advisor and it was he who, according to Firmenich, 'taught us that Christianity was impossible without love for the poor, for those persecuted for defending justice and for fighting against injustice'.[30] Early on he apparently claimed that Christ had come into the world to bring the sword rather than peace, and that this sword was directed against the exploiters of man and violators of human dignity; later, however, he was to reject this interpretation of the biblical passage, arguing that it was not a call to arms but a warning by Christ to his followers that they might be persecuted.[31]

The message preached by Mugica would not have made such an impression on the trio had he not attempted to put it into practice. On several occasions, he took his three young devotees to work with him among the shanty-town dwellers of Retiro, in Buenos Aires. Firmenich and Ramus also accompanied him on a trip to Tartagal, Santa Fe, in February 1966 in order to work with the poor and preach the new ideas of the Church. These experiences of evangelical social work combined with the inspiration of Camilo Torres to lead the missioners to conclude that 'the basic problem was

[29] Mugica, pp. 35 and 55.
[30] Firmenich, 'Mi afecto y agradecimiento al Padre Carlos Mugica', *El Peronista*, no. 5, op. cit.
[31] Mugica, pp. 16 and 66.

political and the solution was political revolution'.[32] But in 1967 the group parted company. Though Mugica had reputedly advocated the machine-gun as the only solution while in Tartagal, he now rejected guerrilla warfare as incompatible with the example of Christ. He remained a priest and condemned violence, except in cases where it was employed by the mass of the people when denied other possibilities of expression. Abal Medina, Ramus, and Firmenich, on the other hand, began to prepare to wage armed struggle, considering it a legitimate response to institutionalized violence. They broke with their lay Catholic organizations and went underground in the same year, with Firmenich sacrificing his studies as an engineering student and his position as President of the JEC.

In establishing the Camilo Torres Command in 1967, the three became comrades of Juan García Elorrio. The Command, committed to Peronism, socialism, and armed struggle, was merely a stepping stone *en route* to the creation of the Montonero organization a year later, and its only publicized feat took place on May Day 1967, when García Elorrio and two others broke up a mass attended by General Onganía in the Metropolitan Cathedral of Buenos Aires. Their intention was to expose the institutional Church as a defender of the military regime, and a call was made for revolutionary struggle against the government.

García Elorrio's collaboration with the proto-Montoneros was brief but his influence was great. Before being killed by a car in 1970 he more than any other individual reconciled radical Catholics to violent politics. The son of upper-middle-class parents of the Catholic Right, he passed through the San Isidro seminary before renouncing his priesthood training at the age of twenty-one. Through a trip to Cuba, dialogue with Marxists in the Faculty of Philosophy and Letters (University of Buenos Aires) in 1965, and meetings with Cooke, he eventually became a revolutionary Peronist.[33] The end product of his political evolution was the review *Cristianismo y Revolución* (*Christianity and Revolution*), which appeared for the first time in September 1966. It was

---

[32] Firmenich, 'Mi afecto'.

[33] 'Juan García Elorrio' (Obituary), *Cristianismo y Revolución*, no. 28 (April 1971), p. 23.

designed to expose Onganía's attempts to justify his regime on the basis of Christian ideas: on 31 November 1969, the military president consecrated the Argentine nation to the 'protection and divine invocation of the immaculate heart of Mary'.[34]

Taking as its watchword the maxims of Torres and Guevara — 'The duty of every Catholic is to be a revolutionary; The duty of every revolutionary is to make the revolution' — *Cristianismo y Revolución* became a decisive force in the radicalization of the 400 Argentine priests and the handful of bishops who backed the Third World Priests Movement. Very few directly assisted the guerrillas or condoned their activities, but many, while working for peace, refused to condemn them publicly, calling instead for a questioning of the system that engendered their violence. Parish priests took part in the workers' struggles of the late 1960s to prevent sugar mill closures in Tucumán Province, and in the popular risings of 1969. An indication of their localized success was seen in July 1969 when the transfer of a radical priest by the Catholic Church led to a twenty-four-hour protest strike and mass demonstrations in Cañada de Gómez, Santa Fe.[35]

For the Montoneros García Elorrio's publicism strengthened their *tercermundismo*, their sympathy for the oppressed and their identification with the national liberation struggles of the Third World. It also provided them with an eschatological outlook. The glorification of militants who had heroically sacrificed their lives for the downtrodden, in the form of homages published in his review, helped prepare the young radicals for a politico-military struggle which would in all probability claim their lives. Quite apart from being assured of heavenly solace, the future fallen were promised life after death among the people for whom they fought. Referring to the deaths of Camilo Torres and Paz Zamora (a Catholic killed while fighting for the Bolivian National Liberation Army — ELN), the review claimed: 'They will live for ever in the rifle of that anonymous guerrilla who fights everywhere in Latin America, in the rebel machete

---

[34] *Buenos Aires Herald*, 1 December 1969.
[35] Ibid., 24 July 1969.

of the peasants, or in the avenging fire of miners' dynamite.'[36] Furthermore the publication spread the idea, brilliantly dramatized in Camus's *Les Justes*,[37] that being an agent of violence was not so wrongful, and was indeed in a sense legitimate, if one were prepared to sacrifice one's own life as a result of undertaking armed struggle. For a Christian, there is no greater proof of love than giving one's life for others — and what higher form of expiation?

Other prominent early Montoneros whose radicalization took place in Catholic organizations were Emilio Angel Maza, a medical student at Córdoba's Catholic University and leader of the *Integralista* youth centre there; José Sabino Navarro and Jorge Gustavo Rossi, who both started out in the Catholic Young Workers (JOC) collateral of Catholic Action; and Carlos Capuano Martínez, who began his political life in the JEC. Through its commitment to social justice and the popular cause, radical Catholicism drew many youths towards the Peronist Movement. Like Mugica, a lot came with guilt-ridden consciences over their previous anti-Peronism, and now embraced Peronism with the zeal of reformed sinners. In seeking to adopt the standpoint of the masses, a good many echoed the sentiments of García Elorrio when explaining his own radicalization: 'I had to fight *with* the slaves, the people, as *they* fought, not as an elitist teacher who tells them what is good and what is evil and then goes back to his study to read Saint Augustine, but as a genuine participant, *with* them not *for* them, in their misery, their failings, their violence ... Either I fought or I was a phony.'[38] The irony was, of course, that many of those who at least overcame their nominal political estrangement from Peronism were nothing if not elitist in embarking upon revolutionary warfare. The launching of the urban guerrillas was an initiative 'from above', the decision of small groups of militants rather than a response to widespread popular demand; and though the combatants were to be eulogized by Perón and to enjoy considerable popular sympathy during the early 1970s, they were never to be able to eliminate the

---

[36] *Cristianismo y Revolución*, no. 28 (April 1971), p. 81.
[37] Albert Camus, *The Just* (English translation, Harmondsworth: Penguin, 1970).
[38] García Elorrio, interview with John Gerassi, in Gerassi, pp. 41-2.

traces of their elitist origins, never able to transform the 'special formations' of the Peronist Movement into a truly popular army. To say that what ensued became a civil war between two fractions of the middle classes, with the working class merely spectating, would be to exaggerate, yet such a sociological caricature is distinctly closer to the reality than was the scenario of popular war aspired to by the Montoneros.

RADICALIZATION IN THE LATE 1960s

Developments within nationalism and Catholicism were, then, decisive elements in the radicalization and 'peronization' of the original core, the proto-Montoneros. Yet they were not the only guerrilla group born in 1968: the Peronist Armed Forces appeared and the decisive break from Trotskyist ranks of those shortly to create the People's Revolutionary Army also occurred that year.[39] Other armed nuclei emerged around the same time. Above all, though, the 1960s was a decade when a whole generation of young Argentines was affected by disillusionment with and disaffection from the political system — both in its ostensibly constitutional form under the Radical Governments of Frondizi and Illia, and in its bastardized form under Onganía. Only if one appreciates this more general spread of alienation and rebelliousness can one understand why the Montoneros and their

[39] The ERP's genealogy (illustrated in Appendix A) stretches back to the early 1960s, when a pro-guerrilla faction led by Angel Bengochea emerged within the Trotskyist *Palabra Obrera*. The would-be guerrillas formed themselves into the *Comando Buenos Aires*, originally intended as an urban support force for Masetti's EGP in Salta; but they perished when their arsenal blew up in a *Calle Posadas* apartment house in 1964. Nevertheless, when *Palabra Obrera* merged with a group from Santiago del Estero (the FRIP) to become the Workers' Revolutionary Party (PRT) in 1965, Bengochea's line was carried forward by the PRT's *El Combatiente* wing, led by Luis Pujals and Mario Roberto Santucho. The decisive break with Trotskyism came at the 1968 PRT Congress, for although the pro-guerrilla tendency retained formal links with the international Trotskyist movement until 1973, Guevara rather than Trotsky became its principal mentor. Armed operations began in 1969 and the following year the ERP was founded as the armed wing of the PRT. The other, *La Verdad*, wing of the PRT, led by Nahuel Moreno, came together with Juan Carlos Coral's left-wing Argentine Socialist Party (PSA) to form the Socialist Workers Party (PST) in 1972. The PST attracted 73,796 votes (0.62 per cent of the poll) in the March 1973 general election, and 181,474 (1.52 per cent) votes in the presidential election of the following September. On the ERP, see my 'Armed Struggle in Argentina', *New Scholar* (California), forthcoming.

fellow fighters were to be favoured by so many recruits and sympathizers, making them a considerable foe of the military regime, a guerrilla movement and, briefly, a mass political force.

Peronism benefited more from this alienation than from its own historical achievements, validating Perón's mouthing of the Spanish refrain, 'Detrás de mí vendrán, los que bueno me harán'[40] (After I have gone, those who replace me will make me seem good). Frondizi had disappointed hopeful nationalists, had been unable consistently to impose his will when pressurized by the military, and had eventually been overthrown by the Army for allowing Peronism to reveal its electoral popularity. Illia's Government, although today recalled with nostalgia by many as marking the least repressive triennium in post-war Argentine history, lacked both direction and legitimacy, and proved devoid of solutions when recession set in again in 1966. The deposition of each government, while executed by the military, reminded Argentines of the durability and forcefulness of Peronism, exhibited at the polls in 1962, in the industrial action of 1964, and in most forecasts of what the Movement might achieve in the mid-term elections scheduled for March 1967.

The crucial experience, however, for most of those who later rallied to the Montonero cause was that of the 1966–70 *Onganiato*. It undermined the labour support for conciliatory Vandorism, opening the way for limited but significant working-class radicalization, and it also had a pronounced effect among the middle classes — especially upon the students, employees, and professional people who predominated, sociologically, in subsequent press references to slain guerrillas, in Montonero obituaries, and indeed in all of the literature providing evidence of the Montoneros' social composition and constituency.[41] Onganía's economic design, officially pursued in the name of an 'Argentine Revolution', was soon interpreted as an attempt to consolidate the hegemony of big industrial and financial monopolies associated with foreign capital, at the expense of the rural bourgeoisie and the popular sectors.[42] In the hands of Economy Minister

[40] Perón, interview in Pavón Pereyra, p. 327.
[41] For details, see my 'The Peronist Left', pp. 509–13.
[42] See Oscar Braun, *El capitalismo argentino en crisis* (Buenos Aires: Siglo XXI Argentina Editores, 1973); and Peralta Ramos.

Adalbert Krieger Vasena, the plan produced shifts in national income from the agrarian to the industrial sector, from small capital to large, and from wage and salary earners to owners of capital. By 1971, sixty-six of the leading 120 companies were owned or controlled by foreign interests, and a further eighteen were clearly linked to them.[43] Nationalism was stimulated and many young nationalists, viewing the post-Peronist trend of the 'national bourgeoisie' losing ground to an expansionist 'international bourgeoisie', questioned whether national development was compatible with the continued existence of capitalism in Argentina. National capital, hit hard by Krieger Vasena's 40 per cent devaluation, just could not compete with the technologically-superior monopolies. Bankruptcies rose from 1,647 in 1968 to 2,982 in 1970; other 'national' firms entered into dependent relationships with foreign concerns.[44]

However, though the impact of neo-liberal economic policies enhanced the attraction of nationalist alternatives, it is very doubtful whether economic deprivation was a major factor in middle-class radicalization in this period. Certainly, there was a long-term tendency towards relative decline, with (as has already been demonstrated) the share of wages and salaries as a percentage of GNP falling since the 1950s, yet in the late 1960s it was the workers who bore the brunt of this decline. While their living standards were depressed through a wage freeze, inflation, the main concern of the middle classes, dropped below 10 per cent[45] — 'less than nothing' by modern Argentine standards. State employees, numbering about 1.4m by 1970, were affected by the 'rationalization' of State enterprises, but though employment levels here fell by 3 per cent in the late 1960s, the axe hacked at certain sectors — especially the railways — far more than at others.[46]

The radicalization from which the Montoneros benefited owed far more to political and cultural than social and economic factors. For the middle classes, Onganía's coup represented more than a loss of political representation. It signified a violent attack on what they had traditionally

[43] NACLA, pp. 29-35. [44] Ibid., pp. 23-4.
[45] See Scobie, pp. 243-5.
[46] CICSO, *Los asalariados. Composición social y orientaciones organizativas* (Buenos Aires: Centro de Investigaciones en Ciencias Sociales, nd), pp. 223-4.

regarded as their preserves, even during the infamous decade of the 1930s: the universities and the world of culture in general. Congress, provincial legislatures, and the political parties were dissolved; the leading satirical magazine, *Tía Vicenta*, was closed for portraying the mustachioed Onganía as a walrus on its cover; sales of the radical Uruguayan review, *Marcha*, were banned; and characters such as Police Inspector Luis Margaride, appointed as the 'moral guardian' of the City of Buenos Aires, campaigned against mini-skirts and ill-lit night-clubs. Above all, so far as students were concerned, the eight national universities were 'intervened' and their autonomy crushed. In theory a drive against 'communist infiltration', in practice an assault on academic freedom and an attempt to reform higher education in the interests of the dominant economic groups, Onganía's onslaught did much to push middle-class youth into the national-popular opposition camp.[47] Student political activity was banned and their right to participate, along with academics and alumni, in the traditional tripartite system of university administration was rescinded. Now, they lacked even the token representation of the earlier Peronist period. Aggrieved academics, perhaps as many as 3,000 and including some of Argentina's most eminent scholars, resigned and left the country in droves; students protested and were mercilessly beaten.

On 29 July 1966, a month after the Rightist coup, the 'Night of the Long Sticks' made a deep impression on student attitudes. Mounted Federal Policemen galloped into the University of Buenos Aires, ordered students and lecturers alike to leave, used their clubs and truncheons with indiscriminate ferocity on those who refused, and finally carried off hundreds of detainees. Sixty students ended up in hospital.[48] In retrospect, compared with repression under the Videla regime, it was not a particularly nightmarish event, but for years the students involved retained vivid memories of that night when they were the 'victims' of brutal philistinism.

---

[47] See Peter G. Snow, *Political Forces in Argentina* (USA: Praeger, 1979), pp. 132-4; and Joan Monahan, 'I agreed to teach but not to be a gaoler', *Times Higher Education Supplement* (London), 11 February 1977, p. 10.

[48] On the *Noche de los bastones largos*, see Gregorio Selser, *El Onganiato: la espada y el hisopo*, vol. 1 (Buenos Aires: Carlos Samonta Editor, 1973), pp. 117-28.

Two months later, the Córdoba Police presented the forces of protest with their first martyr by mortally wounding Santiago Pampillón during a student demonstration; but two years later the more resistant of the malcontents, backed by the radical intelligentsia, were already making determined efforts to overcome their strategic impotence by establishing bonds of solidarity with militant labour organizations.

Although in 1966 the academic community had been the only vociferous group to object to Onganía from the start,[49] by 1968 most popular spokesmen had disabused themselves of vague ideas that Illia's departure might represent a change for the better. Vandor and other participationist union leaders continued to negotiate with the new regime, but their failure to prevail against Krieger Vasena soon enhanced the appeal of more militant labour leaders and strategies, especially in the smaller unions and regions. Growing militancy rapidly found expression through the CGT of the Argentines, the 1968-9 'rebel' labour faction led by the revolutionary Catholic printers' leader, Raimundo Ongaro. On May Day 1968, it declared that 'property must only exist for the benefit of society' and issued a combative call for action and struggle from below against the regime and monopolies. 'The CGT of the Argentines does not offer workers an easy road, a pleasing outlook, another lie', the CGTA manifesto warned, 'it offers each person a battle station'. Calling for the recovery of 'freedom and social justice' and for 'the exercise of power to be returned to the people', the rebel confederation declared that 'the struggle against the monopolies and all forms of foreign penetration is the natural mission of the working class'. The main thrust of this *sindicalismo de liberación* resided in direct workers' action and rank-and-file anti-bureaucratic revolt in the Vandorist unions, though such emphasis was qualified by CGTA backing for 'each national

---

[49] Not only the union leadership and entrepreneurs but also Perón hoped that the 1966 coup would produce a change for the better. Perón's initial 'wait and see' attitude when Onganía, a 'good solder', seized power, was based in part upon Onganía's reputation as a constitutionalist, acquired during the *Azul* v. *Colorado* intra-military conflict of 1962. It was three months before Perón characterized the new regime as *gorila* and 'reactionary'. See Nadra, p. 84; and Andrew Graham-Yooll, *Tiempo de tragedia* (Buenos Aires: Ediciones de la Flor, 1972), p. 30.

company opposing a foreign company'[50] and, with greater practical implications, by endeavours to develop a popular alliance resting upon a worker-student axis.

Ongaro himself promoted student-worker coordination by receiving the leaders of fourteen student groups at a Printers Union holiday camp in June 1968 to discuss anti-regime activities. *CGTA*, the rebels' paper, edited behind the scenes by the future leading Montonero, Rodolfo Walsh, nurtured the alliance. Strengthened by joint involvement in demonstrations and street battles with the police, its high-point came in May 1969 with the anticipated but largely-spontaneous *Cordobazo*: a fusion of student protest with generally more economically-motivated labour discontent in the underprivileged cities of the Interior.[51] The run-up to the explosion began in mid-month when students of the University of the North-East took to the streets of Corrientes to demonstrate against food price rises of 537 per cent, following the privatization of their canteen. Juan José Cabral, a student of nineteen, was killed, four other students were wounded, and a further twenty were injured when policemen answered their protests with firearms. Thereafter, a student-worker protest movement, enjoying considerable middle-class sympathy, arose in other major cities, as manifestations of solidarity with the Corrientes victims merged with the denunciation of local and national grievances. Rioting spread, students and trade unionists confronted armed police and soldiers with stones and molotovs, and labour unrest became so forceful that even the Vandorist labour leaders were obliged to endorse the climactic general strike of 30 May 1969. Two days of street fighting in Córdoba, during which

[50] CGT de los Argentinos, 'Mensaje a los trabajadores y al pueblo', 1 May 1968, in Raimundo Ongaro, *Sólo el pueblo salvará al pueblo* (Buenos Aires: Editorial de las Bases, 1970), pp. 27–40.

[51] On the *Cordobazo*, see Beba Balvé et al., *Lucha de calles, lucha de clases* (Buenos Aires: Ediciones de la Rosa Blindada, 1973); Francisco J. Delich, *Crisis y protesta social. Córdoba 1969–1973* (Buenos Aires: Siglo XXI Argentina Editores, 1974); Oscar Moreno, *Contradicciones, conflictos y movimientos sociales en la problemática urbano-regional* (Caracas: CENDES, 1979); Ernesto Laclau, 'Argentina – Imperialist Strategy and the May Crisis', *New Left Review* (London), no. 62 (July–August 1970), pp. 3–21; Carlos Tagle Achával, 'Córdoba: de Cabrera al Cordobazo', *Todo es Historia*, no. 75 (July 1973), pp. 102–29; 'El Cordobazo', *Polémica*, no. 15 (July 1972); and 'Córdoba rebelde', *Transformaciones en la historia presente*, no. 23 (September 1974).

barricades were erected, bonfires lit, and areas of the city seized by protestors, were bloodily brought to an end by the Armed Forces. A death toll of fourteen remained a bloodstain on the events.

Nevertheless the provincial revolt and successful strike spelled the beginning of the end for the *Onganiato*. Its key men, Krieger Vasena and Interior Minister Guillermo Borda, lost their posts ten days later (the former to José Dagnino Pastore the latter to Brig. Gen. Francisco Imaz), and more pressure was put on the regime at the end of June — this time in Buenos Aires, a mere spectator of the *Cordobazo*. CGTA initiatives to organize a strike and rally in protest against a visit by US presidential envoy, Nelson Rockefeller, ended in more violence: Emilio Jáuregui, former JRP militant and press secretary of the Press Workers Union before its 1966 *intervención*, was shot dead by a policeman near *Plaza Once*. Five thousand mourners who joined his funeral procession were attacked by the security forces. Also in the metropolis, the Revolutionary Armed Forces (FAR) firebombed fifteen Minimax supermarkets owned by the Rockefeller family, while elsewhere the visit sparked other displays of anti-imperialist sentiment: bombs exploded in Rosario, Mendoza, and Paraná; Córdoba University was closed by student protests; a thousand students demonstrated in Rosario. Thanks partly to the assassination of Vandor on 30 June 1969 by pre-Montoneros (on which more later), Onganía managed to cling to power for a further year,[52] but now even many of his erstwhile backers were alarmed at the social response to his policies. Military officialdom was rapidly rent by disputes between pro-regime corporatists and 'liberal' critics who looked to Aramburu and then Lanusse for leadership; and for the critics, a return to civilian rule became an imperative means of defusing the mounting pressures for radical change.

Peronization and radicalization, in evidence in many of the

[52] Onganía used Vandor's assassination as a pretext for outlawing the CGTA, taking over all the unions which supported a CGTA strike call, declaring a state of siege, and imposing martial law. Hundreds of workers and students were jailed, and Ongaro, charged with responsibility for Vandor's death, was deprived of his liberty for the rest of the year. It was the sixth time that he had been detained that year, the harassment being designed to prevent his participation in strikes and meetings.

slogans voiced and targets chosen in the course of these turbulent events, can also be traced at the level of student organizations and professional bodies. By the early 1960s, Communist activists had become dominant within the university federations, but this indicated the political fragmentation of the student movement rather than the political sympathies of most of the 150,000-plus students.[53] Moreover, orthodox Communist influence was being increasingly undermined by the appeal of *fidelismo*. Peronism, still anathema to most students, was only present at this time in the form of a few hundred right-wing nationalists based mainly in the Buenos Aires Law Faculty. There, they operated as shock troops, as often as not doing battle with more extreme, anti-Peronist nationalists. In June 1962, a meeting organized by the Peronist Youth and General University Confederation (CGU) to mark the sixth anniversary of the 1956 Peronist military rising was violently attacked by ultra-Right *tacuaristas*; as a result, one of the defenders, Carlos Caride, despite protestations of his innocence, spent the next four years in prison for the killing of Norma Melena. Later, Caride, Envar El Kadri, and others identified with the National Law Students Association (ANDE) would help found the FAP; Grassi Susini, leader of the University Law Union (SUD), had a rather different destiny: under the last Peronist Government, he become San Juan's Chief of Police.

Towards the end of 1962 the replacement of the CGU by the Peronist University Youth (JUP) represented a leftward shift which, though small-scale, paralleled the developments within Tacuara. By 1964, when the JUP held an MNRT-applauded National Congress, it possessed groups in five University of Buenos Aires faculties and islets of support elsewhere. The Peronist University Youth anticipated its pro-Montonero namesake of 1973-6 in stating that its mission was to bring 'to the lecture halls of the Liberal, oligarchic, and *cipaya* University, a combative Peronist presence – i.e. a national and revolutionary presence. The *raison d'être* of such a presence is the need to link the student struggle in a concrete manner to the struggle of the working people'.[54] But it was

[53] See Walter, *Student Politics*, pp. 172-4.
[54] On the JUP's strength and political orientation, see *Compañero*, nos. 47 (19 May 1964) and 49 (2 June 1964).

only with the Onganía coup and the new regime's ban on existing political groups in the universities that radical Peronist organizations began to flourish, offering as they did the most obvious opportunities for semi-clandestine struggle in conjunction with Peronist labour. Here, the most important were the National Student Front (FEN), led by Roberto Grabois, and the National Union of Students (UNE), founded by progressive Social-Christians, nationalists, and Peronists, though Rodolfo Galimberti also created his Argentine Youth for National Emancipation (JAEN) while at university in 1967. As the Argentine University Federation (FUA — founded in 1918) declined, over-preoccupied with purely university issues, the FEN and UNE offered students a mass political option. Declaring itself 'nationalist, revolutionary, anti-imperialist, and in support of revolutionary Peronism', the FEN endorsed the May Day manifesto of the CGT of the Argentines in 1968, and probably played the more important role of the two before post-*Cordobazo* arrests deprived it of leadership.[55]

Other radical developments, in part an outgrowth of student militancy, affected professional bodies, most after a short time-lag.[56] The flood of liberal and socialist resignations provoked by Onganía's university onslaught created a vacuum which, though largely filled by personnel sympathetic to the regime, also enabled popular nationalists to secure academic posts. Within the Faculty of Philosophy and Letters, the so-called *cátedras nacionales* appeared with student support, occupied by people like Juan Pablo Franco and Fernando

[55] The political differences between the FEN and UNE were clarified when representatives of each were interviewed by *Panorama* magazine in 1969. Asked about the student revolt, Grabois (FEN) said: 'The movement must not exhaust itself in the University, for it is the workers who form the axis around which the struggle is unified. In the long term, through a worker-student united front, a new type of power will emerge in Argentina: *socialismo nacional*, which only violence can achieve.' UNE spokesman Julio Bárbaro exhibited a more populist orientation: 'As far as the youngsters who are now taking to the streets are concerned, their historical fathers are Federalism, Yrigoyenism, and Peronism. Marcuse and Marx don't come into it. The people alone are the historic axis of emancipation' [from Horacio González Trejo, *Argentina: tiempo de violencia* (Buenos Aires: Carlos Pérez Editor, 1969), pp. 100–5]. Of course the real fathers of most were anti- or non-Peronists.

[56] Information about developments within the professional bodies derives from interviews in late 1980 with a former member of the *Asociación Gremial de Abogados*, whose identity cannot be made known.

Alvarez, who for a while sided with the *movimientista* Peronist Left. More surprising divisons took place in other professions whose associations had traditionally been conservative and elitist. Dissidents broke from the Argentine Psycho-analytical Association to join the Argentine Psychiatry Federation in the early 1970s, and the latter, significantly, held its first training course in the Printers Union headquarters. Members of the Argentine Plastic Arts Association began to organize street exhibitions of their work, rather than submit them to the prestigious but elitist *Salón Nacional*. A Peronist list even stood in Argentine Engineering Centre elections, but lost.

Above all the radicalization affected the legal profession. Several lawyers lent their services to Ongaro's CGT of the Argentines and soon came to the notice of the police death squad, a unit active since the early 1960s but hitherto largely concerned with murdering common criminals.[57] In the Federal Capital lawyers had previously belonged to the reactionary, oligarchic *Colegio de Abogados* or the liberal *Asociación de Abogados de Buenos Aires*, and it was the latter which called a strike when left-wing lawyer Néstor Martins, along with a client who went to his aid, was kidnapped on 16 December 1970. Neither victim reappeared. The radicals did not organize themselves independently, though, until after the abduction of lawyer and Revolutionary Armed Forces leader, Roberto Quieto, in July 1971. Those from the *Asociación* who successfully took up his defence, obliging the police to legalize the detention, created the *Asociación Gremial de Abogados*, which went on to represent political prisoners and denounce repression in general. By August 1972, when it held its 'Néstor Martins National Meeting of Lawyers', the new body counted with 350 adherents, and membership reached 400 lawyers by 1973.[58] They served as a crucial link between clandestine and semi-legal opposition to the regime, some even as conduits between guerrilla prisoners and their organizations outside, but all were highly exposed themselves and many paid a terrible price for their

[57] On the death squad, see Andrew Graham-Yooll, *Tiempo de violencia* (Buenos Aires: Granica Editor, 1973), Appendix IV, pp. 125–60.

[58] See Mario Kestelboim, 'Una experiencia de militancia: la Asociación Gremial de Abogados', *Peronismo y Socialismo*, no. 1 (September 1973), pp. 87-9.

activities. Several were later assassinated (like CGTA and PB lawyer José Antonio Pastor Deleroni and FAR lawyer Rodolfo Ortega Peña) or forced into exile (like Ortega Peña's partner, Eduardo Duhalde) by the Right; dozens of former members, including Mario Hernández, were picked up by uniformed men after the March 1976 coup and never seen again.[59]

The radicalization process of the late 1960s and early 1970s, more often than not accompanied by 'peronization', was thus quite extensive, most directly a product of political and cultural factors, and greatly stimulated by the authoritarianism of the military regime — a regime whose repressive methods were at times brutal, always unsophisticated, but never efficient. For many, Peronism was perceived merely as a popular alternative; tens of thousands, however, came to take Perón's radical rhetoric at face value and embrace Peronism as a genuinely revolutionary alternative. Their naivety, their readiness to accept the Movement's myths, was not merely a matter of youthful romanticism but of the need of people from liberal or reactionary backgrounds to *prove themselves* as Peronists. It was their way of atoning for the past, their way of establishing their credentials in a Movement which has always emphasized loyalty to the leader and doctrinal orthodoxy as virtues. At the same time it should be remembered that those of Montonero orientation were defining or re-defining themselves within the confines of a long-standing strain of Argentine political culture, and that which was arguably the most authentically national and Latin American: they conformed to the tendency to support and trust personalities rather than policies, leaders rather than organizations; and they shared in their political methods the individualism of an immigrant society, and the preparedness to use violent direct action to achieve political objectives, especially when the political force of anti-Peronism rested primarily upon the armed force of the Argentine military.

MONTONERO PERONISM

In drawing together radical Catholicism, nationalism, and

[59] In April 1978 a report issued by the International Commission of Jurists stated that twenty-three judges and lawyers had been killed in Argentina during the previous four years, that forty-one had disappeared, that 109 were or had been detained, and that many had fled (*The Times*, 18 April 1978).

Peronism into a populistic expression of socialism, the Montoneros brought together a whole wealth of historical legitimacy into something which attracted civilians of diverse political denominations: Catholic militants, popular nationalists, authoritarian but populistic nationalists, recruits from the traditional Left, combative Peronists. The original group contained no outstanding theoretician, yet its very pragmatism was as often a source of strength as of weakness in the early years, facilitating tactical flexibility and the forging of political alliances. Emphases differed: some members saw the goal as a national variant of socialism; others envisaged it as a socialist form of national revolution. All, however, saw the 'principal contradiction' affecting Argentina in terms of imperialism versus the nation, and the latter's interests as represented by a popular but multi-class alliance. Indeed, due to their relegation of class struggle to a secondary plane and their devotion to a leader who had in power sponsored class harmonization, it can be said that the Montoneros were less 'leftist' to the extent that they were Peronist, and vice versa. They presented their organization as a champion of the people, *el pueblo*, because they were not working class themselves; and, rather than seek the 'workers state' aspired to by the non-Peronist revolutionary Left, their central commitments were to national development, social justice, and 'popular power'. Vague in their notions of what *socialismo nacional* signified, some agreed with José Pablo Feinmann that it and Justicialism were 'equivalent concepts'; that it was not some new 4th Banner of Justicialism but 'the most profound synthesis of the political project which has animated Peronism since its origins'.[60] Others, concurring with Juan Pablo Franco and Fernando Alvarez, did not project *socialismo nacional* so forcibly back into the 1940s, and instead asserted the proletarianization, dialectical development, and social darwinization of Peronism since 1955.[61] All, though, created a Perón in their own image and proved more willing

[60] Feinmann, pp. 185 and 229.

[61] Juan Pablo Franco and Fernando Alvarez, 'Peronismo: antecedentes y gobierno', *Cuadernos de Antropología 3er. Mundo*, no. 1 (June 1972); and Franco, 'Notas para una historia del peronismo', supplement to *Envido*, no. 3 (June 1971). For a critique of these authors, see Blas Manuel Alberti, *Peronismo, burocracia y burguesía nacional* (Buenos Aires: Ediciones Rancagua, 1974), pp. 41–90.

to listen to rhetoric than study political history.

As would-be revolutionaries, the Montoneros' most damaging illusion was that Peronism was a specifically Argentine revolutionary movement, owing its dynamism to an intimate bond between Perón and the masses. Perón's monologues addressed to his followers at mass rallies in *Plaza de Mayo* were ingenuously imagined to have formed part of a symbiotic dialogue: 'Perón spoke with the workers, explaining to them the principal problems of the fatherland, and listened to the masses' proposals and desires.'[62] If at times Perón had appeared weak or made tactical mistakes, if the Peronist process had run into crisis in the early 1950s, it was largely, in Montonero minds, because the revolutionary darling of the Peronist Left, the nexus binding Perón and the masses together, had died in 1952. Their *evitismo*, their acceptance of the Eva Perón cult, extended even to believing the claim that she, not the union leaders, deserved the credit for the big 17 October 1945 mobilization which ensured Perón's release from detention — a claim belied by all historical investigation of the event.[63]

Evita's posthumous reputation was greatly enhanced by the fact that her political career coincided with the 'golden years' of Peronism. She was associated with the general benefits made possible by the late 1940s economic boom, especially the handouts to the poor from her *Fundación Eva Perón*. Allegations that she had invested *Fundación* money in her vast wardrobe were dismissed as slanders spread by an embittered Radical Party. But it was her diatribes against the oligarchy and impassioned denunciations of social injustice which really endeared her to the Peronist Left. She preached death to the oligarchs: 'With or without bloodshed, the race of oligarchs, exploiters of man, will undoubtedly die this century';[64] and she also provided the Left with ammunition

---

[62] Franco and Alvarez, p. 94.

[63] Eva Perón, in her *La razón de mi vida* (Buenos Aires: Editorial Relevo, 1973), p. 36, claimed that she went from door to door, appealing for help. The myths were propagated through books such as Juan José Sebrelli, *Eva Perón: ¿aventurera o militante?* (Buenos Aires: Editorial Siglo Veinte, 1966). For researched accounts of the event, see Luna, *El 45*, especially pp. 340-1; and Juan Carlos Torre, 'La CGT y el 17 de octubre de 1945', *Todo es Historia*, no. 105 (February 1976), pp. 70-90.

[64] *La razón de mi vida*, p. 154.

for use in their battle against the Peronist Right and Vandorist bureaucracy: 'I am more afraid of the oligarchy within than the one we defeated on October 17th', Eva wrote. She warned against 'the Pilots within our cause', and maintained that 'the official who uses his station to serve himself is an oligarch. He does not serve the people but his own vanity, pride, egoism, and ambition'.[65]

Yet these same personality traits speak out from under the cover of that false humility which permeated Eva Perón's writings. She presented herself as 'only a humble woman', but the message was that she was really a modest heroine whose whole life was bound up with the popular cause, a saintly figure who had dedicated her life to 'serve my people, my fatherland, and Perón'.[66] Her hatred of the oligarchs, who snubbed her throughout her short life, was undoubtedly sincere, but many of her postures were hypocritical. She adopted a plebeian self-image, true only to her origins, yet loved to dress in the most glamorous minks and expensive jewellery, weakly explaining to her *descamisados*, 'I am taking the jewels from the oligarchs for you ... one day you'll inherit the whole collection'[67] — but it was invariably 'one day' or during 'this century', not right now. She posed as a dedicated and selfless servant of Perón and his people, yet her career as the 'greatest social climber since Cinderella'[68] involved the acquisition of an ever-expanding bureaucratic empire. And she set herself up as a revolutionary, as a banner of the proletariat, yet had no qualms about visiting fascist Spain, receiving the Grand Cross of Isabel the Catholic from Franco, and reciprocating Falangist salutes at reception rallies during her 1947 Rainbow Tour.

The Montoneros, however, upon 'discovering the people', were only too ready to share their adoration of her, to embrace the myth of Evita the jacobin, for their desire for acceptance by Peronists over-rode their critical faculties. For them, she was a symbol of combativity, the woman who had tried to create a 'workers militia' in the early 1950s. She had

---

[65] Eva Perón, *Historia del peronismo* (Buenos Aires: Editorial Freeland, 1971), pp. 36 and 79.
[66] *La razón de mi vida*, pp. 113–14.
[67] Eva Perón, quoted in Barnes, p. 126.
[68] Tim Rice, lyrics of the rock opera *Evita*, 1976.

made an arms deal with the Dutch Royal Family for its munitioning: 5,000 .45 pistols were ordered, of which only 100 were distributed before the plan was shelved. In fact, its membership was to have included junior Army officers as well as trade union contingents, and it was to have been essentially a defence mechanism for activation only when a military coup seemed likely. Nevertheless, the Montonero Dardo Cabo (who derived his knowledge of it from his father, the trade union leader Armando Cabo) was to compare it with 'the Cubans' armed defence scheme',[69] failing to differentiate between what was to be defended in each case. If Perón had vetoed the plan in 1952, this could be understood in terms of Army pressures on him, an unfavourable balance of forces, and so on; if the exiled leader who was telling the Montoneros to hit the regime until it fell[70] had been fêted by notorious dictators — Alfredo Stroessner in Paraguay, Marcos Pérez Jiménez in Venezuela, Rafael Trujillo in the Dominican Republic, and Francisco Franco, Generalissimo of the Armies of Land, Sea, and Air, by the Grace of God[71] — well, one had to remember that Perón had been a military man, and so was 'naturally' predisposed to friendship with other military men.[72] After years of isolation from the working people of Argentina, the middle-class militants now accepted Peronist mythology lock, stock, and barrel, for whatever criticisms had been raised against the Peróns, they could not believe that the people's unwavering faith in them could be misplaced. Hence

[69] Dardo Cabo, 'La milicia peronista', *La Causa Peronista*, no. 4 (30 July 1974), p. 29. See also his 'La lucha interna en el movimiento peronista: 1945-1955', *Nuevo Hombre*, no. 8 (8-14 September 1971), pp. 8-9.

[70] Letter of Perón to the Montoneros, reported in the *Buenos Aires Herald*, 22 December 1971.

[71] The only other country to provide Perón with hospitality during his 1955-73 exile was Panama. There in 1956 he met his third wife, María Estela Martínez (Isabel), thirty-five years younger than he and working as a night club dancer in the Happy Land Bar. Its manager was Raúl Lastiri (provisional President of Argentina, July-October 1973), the son-in-law of José López Rega, who himself later became Perón's private secretary in Madrid, Social Welfare Minister 1973-5, and organizer of the Triple A death squad. Perón's residence in Spain lasted from January 1960 until June 1973, though there was an attempted return to Argentina, which got as far as Rio, in December 1964, and an officially-tolerated return visit in November-December 1972.

[72] For an example of Montonero apologetics, see Ignacio González Janzen, *Argentina: 20 años de luchas peronistas* (Mexico: Ediciones de la Patria Grande, 1975), p. 48.

the Montonero slogans were not intentionally insincere, nor merely self-legitimating, when they read 'Evita — Perón — Revolution!'; 'Evita, Present, in every Combatant!'; and the favourite of all, 'If Evita were alive today, she would be a Montonero'.

URBAN GUERRILLA THEORY AND THE APPEAL OF ARMED STRUGGLE

Those who founded and joined the Montoneros were convinced that armed struggle was the only effective means open to them — a question of 'responding with armed struggle to the armed struggle which [the Argentine military] was waging from the State'.[73] In 1969, both the *Cordobazo* and the crushing of the CGT of the Argentines were interpreted as validating this conviction. Though the former upheaval had critically undermined the Onganía regime, such events were essentially sporadic and transitory: 'continuity is indispensable if we are to advance against the enemy on all terrains of the struggle, including the decisive military terrain',[74] they declared. Later in the year, the success of a government ban, widespread arrests, and the sacking of hundreds of printing workers in paralysing the CGTA only strengthened the attraction of and need for clandestinity. Of course the need for armed struggle was not the only 'lesson' that could possibly have been drawn from these events. Ongaro and other revolutionary Peronists concentrated from 1970 upon building Rank-and-File Peronism (PB), especially in the factories of Córdoba, where, along with the Marxist plant unions SITRAC-SITRAM and combative Peronist trade unionists, they pursued a far more militant course than that taken by the reunified CGT and its leaders in Buenos Aires.[75] For the Montoneros, however, quite apart from the limited nature of their radicalism, this option was precluded by a class membership which rendered a decisive orientation towards *clasismo* and participation in working-class struggles impracticable.

[73] 'La unidad de FAR y Montoneros', *El Descamisado*, no. 22 (16 October 1973), pp. 6–7.

[74] 'Córdoba: a cinco años del 29 de mayo, un montonero cuenta el Cordobazo', *El Peronista*, no. 6 (28 May 1974), pp. 26–9.

[75] On the CGTA, PB, and Córdoban militancy, see my 'The Peronist Left', pp. 455–84.

Nor did rural guerrilla warfare in emulation of the Cuban model hold much attraction for the Montoneros. Efforts to apply *foquismo* after 1959 in mainland countries had ended in calamity. Guevara's own 1967 death in Bolivia had demonstrated how much better prepared US and Latin American counter-insurgency agencies were to rapidly respond to guerrilla activity in the countryside, and persuaded many revolutionaries of the need to take greater cognizance of the peculiar characteristics of their own countries when devising strategies. Inside Argentina, neither the Uturuncos in 1959-60, nor Masetti's People's Guerrilla Army in 1963-4, nor the FAP's 17 October Detachment in 1968 really got off the ground, none of them attracting significant popular assistance even in the provinces of Tucumán and Salta where they attempted to operate.[76] To think in terms of mountains and rugged terrain proved disastrous in a country in which all the decisive popular struggles were taking place in the big cities of Buenos Aires, Córdoba, and Rosario, and in nearby industrial zones.

In looking to urban guerrilla warfare in 1968, the Montoneros acknowledged the geographical isolation of the rural pioneers. Of Argentina's 23 million inhabitants, about 75 per cent were urbanites, living in towns of over 2,000 residents.[77] Virtually half the population was concentrated in the City and Province of Buenos Aires, and two-thirds in this region plus the adjoining provinces of Santa Fe and Córdoba.[78] The remaining one-third populated nineteen out of the twenty-two provinces. Yet, while avoiding geographical isolation, the Montonero strategy militated in favour of social isolation. Experience had suggested to most working-

---

[76] On the Uturuncos, see Emilio Morales, *Uturunco y las guerrillas en la Argentina* (Montevideo: Editorial Sepe, 1964); on the EGP, see Jorge Ricardo Masetti, *Los que luchan y los que lloran* (Buenos Aires: Editorial Jorge Alvarez, 1969), C.7 of Ricardo Rojo, *My Friend Che* (New York: Grove Press, 1968), and Luis Mercier Vega, *Las guerrillas en América Latina* (Buenos Aires: Editorial Paídos, 1969), pp. 117-20 and 153-64; and for the FAP Detachment's statement concerning their defeat at Taco Ralo, see 'Nuestros errores pueden servir de lección y ejemplo, pero no de negación de la única salida del pueblo ante la violencia gorila', *Con Todo*, no. 2 (December 1968), p. 4.

[77] Scobie, p. 304.

[78] Snow, pp. 3-4. By the time of the 1980 Census, the total population had reached 27,862,771, signifying a 39.2 per cent increase over the previous twenty years. See *La Nación*, international edition, no. 1050 (3 November 1980).

class activists that their strength lay in collective industrial muscle rather than in firearms. Economic constraints upon working-class involvement with the guerrillas were, moreover, often prohibitive. Workers might collaborate or sympathize with the guerrillas, but few could afford to go underground as 'professional' combatants, especially when married and with their wage as the sole financial support of themselves and their dependents. Middle-class radicals had considerably greater economic independence here, and students, whose university studies normally lasted five or six years, had much more time available for the demanding life of the *guerrillero*. Not surprisingly then, urban guerrilla warfare in Latin America prospered most in Argentina and Uruguay, both highly-urbanized countries with huge, culturally-sophisticated middle classes, increasingly affected by the curbing of political and cultural liberties as governments in each country introduced authoritarian controls along with unpopular economic measures.[79] Out of an economically-active Argentine population of 9 million in 1970, 70 per cent were wage or salary earners (and within this category the balance had been 70 per cent manual and 30 per cent non-manual back in 1960).[80] About 40 per cent of the total population belonged to the 'middle sectors' by the time the Montoneros were founded.[81]

Most Montonero recruits and sympathizers were to be drawn from these sectors, yet overall attitudes to radical politics here remained typically ambiguous and unstable, marked by the dependence of many middle-class people upon the State. A lot were State employees, vulnerable to 'rationalization' measures and the political pressures of powerholders; others belonged to the more independent professional groups, but government higher education attitudes still conditioned their access-routes to careers. When university autonomy was violated, the bureaucracy pruned, or cultural activity exceptionally censored, or when

---

[79] Although the Uruguayan military did not seize power until 1973 civil liberties were increasingly curbed by civilian governments from 1965 and emergency provisions were exploited to enhance the powers of the President and security forces from 1968. For a comparative approach, see R. Gillespie, 'A Critique of the Urban Guerrilla: Argentina, Uruguay and Brazil', *Conflict Quarterly* (New Brunswick, Canada), no. 2 (Fall 1980), pp. 39–53.

[80] CICSO, pp. 131 and 96.

[81] Snow, p. 5.

inflation appeared uncontainable, these sectors demonstrated a capacity for militancy, but by no means always and unitedly a sympathy for left-wing solutions, especially at times when government-augmented union power or populist demagogy seemed to challenge their status. They generally applauded the overthrow of Perón in 1955, in part favoured radical proposals fifteen years later, and then initially tended to accept or support the installation of another authoritarian military regime in 1976. In terms of income most were situated closer to the better-paid workers of the more modern capital-intensive industries than to the top 5 per cent of income recipients who in 1961 accounted for almost 30 per cent of total family income with average annual incomes per family of 14,800 dollars — six times higher than the national average and seventeen times more than the average income of families at the base of the social pyramid.[82] However, considerations of status, more comfortable working environments, greater social mobility, and other advantages over labour rendered middle-class sponsorship of left-wing and popular causes strictly conditional upon short-term political and economic trends, and hence unreliable. Had the Montoneros' emergence not coincided with the beginnings of a popular upsurge, they might have paid more attention to the analysis of class behaviour; as it was, they regarded the main revolutionary problem as being one of strategy, and trusted that the 'people', including most middle-class Argentines, would continue to repudiate military authoritarianism as they were doing at the end of the 1960s.

From early on, two strategic influences exercised Montonero minds, one of revolutionary and the other of classical military inspiration. Providing the former was Spanish Civil War veteran, Abraham Guillén, who had developed his originally-Bakuninist ideas in association with MNRT militants early in the 1960s. Like Guevara and Debray, Guillén insisted that revolutionary warfare should be waged under a unified politico-military leadership, but for him the rural *foquismo* envisaged by the Cuban school of strategic studies could only fulfil a support function in Uruguay and Argentina: demography and economy dictated urban strategies, for 'the revolution's potential is where the population is' and 'Buenos

[82] Lesseps and Traveler, p. 128.

Aires represents approximately 70 per cent of the wealth, the consumption of energy, the transportation, the industry, the commerce, and in general the greater part of the Argentine economy'.[83] So long as the population was favourable, the terrain suitable, and the enemy vulnerable, Guillén maintained, the revolutionary war could be initiated by ten to twenty-five 'well-tested, physically-apt, morally-resistant, politically-educated men' — after all, its pioneers in China had only numbered a couple of dozen, in Algeria twenty-four, in Cuba twelve.[84]

Apart from advocacy of the urban setting, much of Guillén's writing simply publicized classical formulae for guerrilla struggle. Hence: 'Operations should consist of scattered surprise attacks by quick and mobile units superior in arms and numbers at designated points but avoiding barricades in order not to attract the enemy's attention at one place. The units will then attack with the greatest part of their strength the enemy's least fortified or weakest links in the city.' The struggle would be 'prolonged', consisting of 'many small military victories which together will render the final victory',[85] but it would not be an exclusively military affair. Without a positive orientation towards working-class and popular struggles, without a conscious effort by combatants to coordinate their activities with these and progressively incorporate the masses at large into an eventual liberation army, revolutionary warfare would degenerate into terrorism.[86] Guillén therefore urged a 'total war: economic, social (strikes), demonstrations, protests against the cost of living, isolated violent actions, well-directed propaganda, [and] a coherent international policy, but all combined with the liberation

---

[83] Donald C. Hodges (ed), *Philosophy of the Urban Guerrilla: The Revolutionary Writings of Abraham Guillén* (New York: William Morrow & Co., 1973), pp. 237-9.

[84] Abraham Guillén, *Teoría de la violencia* (Buenos Aires: Editorial Jamcana, 1965), pp. 201 and 210.

[85] *Philosophy*, pp. 238-9.

[86] The terms 'terrorism' and 'terrorist' refer to terror-inspiring methods and agents, and, though often used loosely in political invective, do not properly characterize the Montoneros. Political terror is concerned with 'the use of coercive intimidation by revolutionary movements, regimes, or individuals for political motives'; 'Political terrorists always resort to political murder in order to induce the psychic state of terror' [Paul Wilkinson, *Political Terrorism* (London: Macmillan, 1974), pp. 11-12]. Anti-State terrorists set out to intimidate and to show

army and the guerrilla (located at the enemy's back).'[87] As to exactly how all facets of warfare were to be combined, Guillén had little advice to offer. His 'total war' found parallels in Perón's 'integral strategy', aimed at weakening the enemy through the simultaneous activities of guerrillas, strikers, protestors, rioters, and political campaigners, but whereas Perón saw their effective integration within Argentina as a potential threat to his own management of the Movement, this was for Guillén the key to politico-military success. For Perón was concerned with pressurizing the military into conceding elections which he would win; Guillén's objective, a revolutionary seizure of power, was distinctly more ambitious.

Accompanying Guillén as a rather ungainly strategic mentor of the Montoneros was Carl von Clausewitz — a figure whose teachings were relayed through Guillén's own writings, possibly through Perón's military works (which, as an Argentine would put it, were a 'poor translation' of Clausewitz), and through old nationalists like Hernández Arregui during their late 1960s discussions with proto-Montoneros in the offices of Mario Hernández's legal practice. More than assuring them that military struggles belonged to the realm

---

that the State is incapable of guaranteeing public security and order. The more indiscriminate and unpredictable their violence, the more likely they are to succeed in their objectives. But those who engage in urban guerrilla warfare — 'a form of unconventional war waged in urban and suburban areas for political objectives' [Idem, *Terrorism and the Liberal State* (London: Macmillan, 1977), p. 60] — are after the conquest of State power by means of a politico-military strategy which demands considerable public support and involvement. Their violence therefore tends to be both discriminate and predictable, though it often provokes a far less discriminate backlash. Whereas terrorists may regard innocent civilians as legitimate targets, urban guerrillas generally limit their attacks to State agents (especially military and police personnel) and clearly-defined political enemies (often associated in some way with State or right-wing violence). Since their activities were guided by aims to incorporate rather than terrorize ordinary people, the Montoneros and Tupamaros should properly be regarded as urban guerrillas. However, urban guerrilla warfare and political terrorism are not always mutually-exclusive phenomena. Whether or not individual acts of violence should be classified as instances of terrorism depends greatly upon specific circumstances, for terror is 'a subjective experience' [*Political Terrorism*, p. 11]. And terrorism may be employed by urban guerrillas as an 'auxiliary weapon' [ibid., p. 38] especially when they are weak and socially isolated. Nevertheless, it must be stressed that insurrectional partisan violence in Argentina has been devoid of the random terrorism (bombs in crowded public places) witnessed in recent years by Europeans.

[87] Guillén, *Teoría*, p. 230.

of politics rather than criminology, Clausewitz seemed of particular relevance to the fledgling Montoneros because of his thesis that 'the defensive form of warfare is intrinsically stronger than the offensive'.[88] As the guerrillas saw it, the Armed Forces had launched an offensive against the Argentine people in 1966, but one which could be contained by a defensive campaign of exhausting the enemy, prior to a counter-offensive by the popular forces. Clausewitz had never advocated pure defence, since war by definition has to be waged by both sides. Rather, his was a relative concept of defence, one which included offensive battles, for 'the defensive form of war is not a simple shield, but a shield made up of well-directed blows'.[89] The analogies were of course far-fetched, but just about sustainable: they involved the application of vintage discussion about the advisability of waiting and parrying when an enemy advances (on the basis that 'it is easier to hold ground then take it')[90] to a situation where the enemy had, in a sense, already triumphed, through seizing State power, and where its 'attack' now took the form of military decrees.

The Montoneros envisaged a popular war, Guillén class warfare in its fullest sense, yet in practice this war was neither decreed by the people nor by the working class: only by a handful of combative middle-class youths, so few in number that their attempts to apply Clausewitz to the concrete jungles of Buenos Aires, Córdoba, and Rosario would seem with hindsight patently ridiculous had the outcome not been so tragic. What was valid was the advice only to strike when possessing tactical supremacy, and not to over-commit one's forces through over-ambition, but this was surely only common sense for any insurrectionist. Nevertheless, it was the writings of Guillén and Clausewitz which shaped the discourse of Montonero strategics, with, as will be seen, Clausewitz in time totally overshadowing Guillén. As the Montoneros developed, the more their military pretensions became guided by considerations of regular warfare, and they rapidly forgot the lessons which Guillén drew from the Tupamaro decline in Uruguay: chiefly,

---

[88] Carl von Clausewitz, *On War*, edited and translated by Michael Howard and Peter Paret (New Jersey: Princeton University Press, 1976), p. 358.
[89] Ibid., p. 357.   [90] Ibid.

avoid the establishment of fixed urban bases which jeopardize guerrilla mobility and security; do not build a 'microstate'; discard the use of 'peoples prisons' the existence of which focuses 'unnecessarily on a parallel system of repression'; and — most important of all — remember that 'to be victorious in a people's war, one has to act in conformity with the interests, sentiments, and will of the people. A military victory is worthless if it fails to be politically convincing'. The Tupamaros had become fatally 'overly professionalized, militarized, and isolated from the urban masses',[91] and the Montoneros, invoking the authority of Clausewitz, were to share their fate.

PREPARING FOR WARFARE

Back in 1968, however, the Tupamaros, though formed five years earlier, were only just beginning to mount a sustained guerrilla campaign in Montevideo, and the State response to it was not immediately effective. Those who organized the Montoneros in Argentina did so full of optimism, confident of victory even if it involved the loss of their own lives. 'All or Nothing!' became the tiro guerrillas' internal motto, Peronism's traditional cry of 'Perón or Death!' being regarded as the 'all or nothing' for the Movement as a whole. But immeasurably more important in favouring their rapid growth was the selection, from a shortlist of fifteen proposals, of the name 'Montoneros'. Chosen in preference to some sterile acronym, its adoption was motivated by more than romantic nostalgia for a partly-imaginary idyllic pastoral age when *gauchos* roamed as free men over the pampas. By calling themselves Montoneros, the young militants were affirming the merits of the common people while also resurrecting powerful symbols of nationalism with which xenophobes and anti-imperialists alike could identify. 'Montoneros' and its revisionist associations offered young Argentines a national past and national heroes; they offered a national identity in a country where the process of nation-building is still qualified by the immigrant origins of not so distant generations; and they represented an assertion of 'Argentinity'

---

[91] Hodges (ed), *Philosophy*, pp. 263-71.

against dominant foreign interests and alien ideas. After two decades of US economic penetration and its cultural repercussions, the attraction of 'things Argentine' was substantially enhanced, though middle-class reactions to them were by no means uniform. Many members of the middle classes enjoyed living standards comparable to those of their North American counterparts, and a lot were only too pleased to see imported consumer goods saturating local markets. Yet others, even if living far better than manual workers, were clearly offended by the brashness and artificiality of the *gringo* consumer society. Its values bombarded them through the mass media and advertising, but the accompanying evocation of the 'free society' clashed harshly with the political reality of Argentina. They rebelled against *yanqui* influence, embraced the legends and symbols of a national past, and identified contemporary Argentina internationally with the Third World and its liberation struggles against imperialism.

Two of the original Montoneros — Fernando Abal Medina and Nélida Esther ('Norma') Arrostito — travelled to Cuba in 1967-8 for military instruction. The rest started out with a subsequently-admitted 'absolute ignorance of what armed struggle was', and only gradually attained military proficiency through on-the-job training during operations in which the means of warfare — mainly money and arms — were seized. Owing to their inexperience of clandestine struggle, they behaved in an 'almost suicidal' manner: 'We went about in stolen cars without any kind of papers. We didn't even have false [identity] documents. The only one who had was Fernando ... He also had a police badge and this was the only thing we had to get us out of difficult situations.' During their early operations, such as the 'expropriation' of guns from the Federal Shooting Range of Córdoba in February 1969, the proto-Montoneros, 'in order not to be detected, pretended to be common delinquents',[92] and it would appear that they were successful in protecting their identity. There is no evidence to suggest that the authorities knew of the existence of the group before the start of 1970. For the same reason, though, few details are known about its early activities. It would appear that, although the initial nucleus was established

[92] '7 de setiembre'; and 'La unidad de FAR y Montoneros'.

by Abal Medina, Ramus, and Firmenich in Buenos Aires, most of the early action took place in Córdoba Province, where Emilio Maza organized a second network and became the local *comandante*. The Córdoba group raided the Bank of La Calera and a guard post of the Córdoba Military Hospital; and there were also raids on quarry stores, a few banks, and police posts. Surprised policemen were disarmed. None of the early actions were spectacular, yet they were indispensable for the preparation and equipping of an effective combat force. And each, it is important to stress, seemed to their protagonists a step forward: each had a tangible pay-off which appeared somewhat lacking from leaflet distribution, paper sales, and the other activities which Leninist groups engaged in.

Organizationally the Montoneros subscribed to the principles of 'compartmentalization', already practised across the *Río de la Plata* by the Tupamaros, and before them as *cloisonnement* by anti-Nazi resistance forces in Europe. Accordingly, for reasons of security, the organization had a molecular structure, with each unit possessing the minimal knowledge of the whole construct as was required for its own efficient functioning. The basic fighting units were the military commands, the *comandos*, which by late 1970 had acquired, sometimes just for occasional use, the following names: 'Eva Perón' (a name which all units eagerly competed for), 'Comandante Uturunco' (*nom de guerre* of Argentina's first modern rural guerrilla leader), 'General José de San Martín' (after the Independence hero), 'Felipe Vallese' (the first Peronist Youth martyr), and '29th May' (date of the *Cordobazo*). Later on, Montonero units were christened predominantly with the names of slain combatants, as in the cases of the *Comandos* Abal Medina-Ramus, José Sabino Navarro, and Marcos Osatinsky. Cross-cutting this structure were functional subdivisions of the organization: Córdoba police reports of mid-1970 spoke of there being a 'maintenance department' (responsible for acquiring vehicles and the logistical side of operations), a 'documents department' (providing counterfeit military and police papers, facilitating freedom of travel), a 'war department' (which planned kidnappings, holdups, etc.), and a 'psychological action department' (in charge of the preparation of declarations and communiqués).[93]

Given that the Montoneros numbered only about twenty by the end of 1970, their structure was remarkably grandiose, indicating ambition and also the first hints of a conviction which equated success with the proliferation of military and political apparata, accompanied by correspondingly large numbers of officers. This *aparatismo*, which was to become far more pronounced as the guerrilla core developed into a movement, went hand in hand with bureaucratism and an authoritarian vertical command system. Internal discussion was far easier to arrange prior to the publication of their identities, yet no efforts were made to instigate or formalize democratic decision-making procedures. Their authoritarianism was partially a legacy from the organizations in which several had previously militated, and was quite acceptable in Peronist circles. It was also a matter of recognition that what internal democracy might bring to an urban guerrilla force in terms of political sophistication and theoretical development was countered by the losses it might facilitate through infiltration, intelligence leaks, and the formation of antagonistic factions. But above all, this authoritarianism emanated from the guerrillas' belief that they were not the political strategists anyway. As they saw it, Perón was chief of the Peronist Movement; a revolutionary chief of a revolutionary movement, of which they were becoming part by constituting themselves into one of its armed nuclei. Their original brief, as a Peronist special formation, was fundamentally one of combat, with this forming just one aspect of a grand design elaborated by General Perón. Put another way, the Montoneros did not see themselves as the sole vanguard of the Argentine revolution and then proceed from such an illusion to confront all of the tasks which this might involve.

Almost all the twelve members won to the organization by May 1970 were students or graduates, and two — including Arrostito — were teachers. According to a later account of the 1968–70 period, the personalities of Abal Medina and Ramus were distinguished by a certain hardness, almost by asceticism, by a belief in absolute self-discipline and the total

[93] *Buenos Aires Herald*, 6 July 1970.

subordination of their personal lives to the political cause they embraced.[94] Little is known about the character of Maza, who together with Abal Medina formed the national leadership of the organization. Arrostito stood out as the sole 'original' to emanate from the traditional Left. Born in 1940, she had broken with the Communist Party in 1967 in the company of thousands of the Party's youth and students who verbally had begun to endorse armed struggle. Many remained *guerrilleros de café*; Arrostito went on to become the most important woman to figure in the Argentine urban guerrilla struggle. She also formed part of two personal relationships which helped to bind the original group together: as sister-in-law of TV cameraman Carlos Maguid, and as the companion of the Montonero leader. Indeed, the latter relationship was so intimate that Arrostito, from Abal Medina's 1971 death until her capture in 1976, was known internally as *La Viuda*, the Widow.

Emilio Maza and Ignacio Vélez were scions of wealthy Córdoba families, but most of the original dozen were lower middle class. Through being working class and the product of a family of indisputable Peronist pedigree, José Sabino Navarro was a lone exception to the general pattern.[95] His father had taken him at the age of two to hear Perón address a mass rally and his mother's life had been saved when Evita sent a plane to Corrientes to bring her to Buenos Aires for an operation. By the late 1960s, this future Montonero leader had become an active trade unionist and shop steward, and worked to get the purportedly-militant Dirk Kloosterman and José Rodríguez elected to lead the car workers' union, SMATA. It was mainly disillusionment with the new leaders, who reputedly collaborated with the management of the DECA car works to ensure his dismissal in 1969, that led Sabino Navarro to form a tiny armed group during the same year to wage revolutionary warfare. Intellectual influences, received through reading Fanon, Perón, and Evita, were far weaker radicalizing factors in his case than in those of student

[94] '7 de setiembre'.
[95] On Sabino Navarro and his group, see 'José Sabino Navarro: un trabajador, un montonero, un peronista', *El Descamisado*, no. 12 (7 August 1973), p. 30; and 'Montonero José Sabino Navarro. Volverás en brazos de tu pueblo', *La Causa Peronista*, no. 4 (30 July 1974), pp. 9–11.

members, he not even having lasted the course at secondary school, but he did share the Catholic background of most of them.

Sabino Navarro's group contributed little to the Montoneros in numbers or military expertise when it affiliated early in 1970, having established contact the previous year. As an autonomous organization, it is only known to have carried out a few minor raids and to have attacked two police posts in Córdoba Province. Nevertheless, the fusion of the two groups was of vital importance to the expansion of the Montonero core, for Sabino Navarro was a man with precious contacts among the combative sectors of Peronism. He had taken part with Cooke and other leading Left Peronists (including Rearte, Di Pasquale, and De Luca) in a secret 1968 'Congress of Revolutionary Peronism', which had failed to reach agreement as to whether suitable conditions for armed struggle were present in Argentina. A second, politically-broader, conference was held in Córdoba the following year, but the divisions over this question only deepened. While Sabino Navarro and others urged the immediate launching of an armed campaign, Gustavo Rearte called for the strengthening of militant working-class organizations as an essential prerequisite for successful armed struggle, and trade unionists like Ricardo De Luca emphasized the building of the CGT of the Argentines. In the end, the conference endorsed the line espoused by Sabino Navarro and his colleagues, but for most participants this commitment went no further than rhetorical bravado. The verbal guerrillas were to brand Sabino Navarro's group *foquista* as soon as it began to implement the conference policy, prior to linking up with Abal Medina's outfit.

By early 1970, then, twelve young people, most of them male, had come together and had completed the hazardous preparatory phase of warfare. Influenced by diverse political, social, economic, and cultural factors, by the apparent limitations of mass resistance initiatives and the ineffectualness of the traditional Left, as well as by radical new ideas and strategies, they were now intent upon responding to military violence with violence in the name of the people. Though few in number and insufficiently active to attract police attention, the twelve were ready for the public curtain to go up. It was time for them to announce their existence to the world, and they did so through an action whose repercussions were out of all proportion to their numbers.

3
For the Return of Perón (1970–1973)

> Ayer Fue la Resistencia,
> hoy Montoneros y FAR,
> y mañana el pueblo entero
> en la guerra popular.
> Con el fusil en la mano
> y Evita en el corazón,
> Montoneros 'Patria o Muerte'
> son soldados de Perón.[1]

EARLY OPERATIONS AND POLITICAL DEFINITIONS

At 9.00 a.m. on 29 May 1970 two young men in military uniform went up to the apartment of a retired general on the 8th floor of a building in Montevideo Street, Buenos Aires. They had come, they claimed, to offer the general a bodyguard. Courteous conversation ensued for several minutes while they partook of coffee, before one of the visitors abruptly announced, 'General, you are coming with us.' Had the general not believed that his captors were military personnel, he would surely have resisted, for he was an extremely important political figure: Pedro Eugenio Aramburu, a leader of the coup which deposed Perón in 1955 and head of the 1955-8 military regime. He would not have gone so quietly had he divined that the 'captain' who was putting what he had learned at military college to dramatic effect was Emilio Angel Maza, that the 'first lieutenant' accompanying him was Fernando Luis Abal Medina, and that together

---

[1] Montonero song:
> Yesterday it was the Resistance,
> Today Montoneros and FAR,
> And tomorrow the whole people
> Will join in the popular war.
> With rifles in their hands
> And Evita in their hearts,
> Montoneros 'Fatherland or Death'
> Are soldiers of Perón.

they formed the leadership of a Peronist urban guerrilla organization called the Montoneros.

Three days later the general was dead and the Montonero organization had completed a breathtaking public entry on to the Argentine political stage. Operation Pindapoy, or the *Aramburazo*[2] as it was subsequently referred to, involved careful planning, daring, and sang-froid on the part of its authors, but might well have led, and almost did, to the collapse of the Montoneros as a result of their over-ambition, amateurism, and adventurism. At the time the organization consisted of just twelve people, of whom ten were risked as members of the *Comando Juan José Valle* which carried out the operation. Their infrastructure was meagre: three or four 'safe houses' in the city of Córdoba; in Buenos Aires, a house in Munro shared by Firmenich and Capuano Martínez, and another in Villa Urquiza rented by Abal Medina and Arrostito. No maximum security 'people's prison' was available in which to conduct the 'revolutionary trial' of their victim before his 'execution' on 1 June. Instead, Aramburu was held at the La Celma *estancia* owned by the Ramus family at Timote in the south of Buenos Aires Province, having been transported there in a Gladiator 380 truck registered in the name of the mother of leading participant, Carlos Gustavo Ramus. It was in every sense an 'all or nothing' operation, through which the Montoneros hoped to achieve three objectives.

The first was to give their organization its public baptism by claiming responsibility for a spectacular action which would have nation-wide repercussions. That it took place on the first anniversary of the *Cordobazo*, while the military were celebrating Army Day, enhanced its impact and calendrical status. A series of five communiqués, drawn up by Emilio Maza and Norma Arrostito, provided step-by-step news of the event and introduced the Montoneros to the public. 'Our Organization', they announced in Communiqué No. 5, 'is a union of men and women who are profoundly Argentine and Peronist, ready to fight with gun in hand for the seizure of power for Perón and his People, and the

[2] Details of the Aramburu case come from press reports and the official Montonero account, 'Como murió Aramburu', *La Causa Peronista*, no. 9 (3 September 1974), pp. 25–31.

construction of a Free, Just, and Sovereign Fatherland.' The Montoneros expressed their commitment to 'the Justicialist doctrine, of Christian and national inspiration', and Catholic influence was also, somewhat extraneously, present in the communiqué announcing Aramburu's death: it ended with the words, 'May God have mercy on his soul'.[3]

In the second place Operation Pindapoy had a punitive aim. After simulated trial proceedings designed to establish the legitimacy of the operation Aramburu, as a leading symbol of anti-Peronism, was submitted to 'revolutionary justice' for his ignominious deeds of the past — above all for his spiriting the body of Eva Perón out of Argentina in 1956 and responsibility for the illegal execution of twenty-seven Peronists in June of the same year. To many people the killing of Aramburu appeared brutal and vindictive, especially given the time lapse between the 'crimes' and the 'punishment', yet both of the 1956 events still stuck firmly in Peronist memories, and the more combative sectors did indeed regard it as an act of justice. Evita had won the affection of millions before her premature death, and Perón himself had said of those who 'kidnapped' her corpse, 'not a single one of those vipers must remain alive'.[4] Soon after the body disappeared, Aramburu's reprisals against a small group of military and civilian Peronist rebels illustrated just how bitter the Peronist/anti-Peronist conflict remained. The revolt led by General Juan José Valle amounted to little more than a token rising, only achieved momentary success in La Plata, and was stifled within twenty-four hours by a regime which possessed foreknowledge of the coup plans. What angered Peronists was not so much the loss of seven insurgents during the brief fighting but the shootings on 10–12 June of eighteen military personnel and nine civilians who had surrendered on the understanding that their lives would be spared. In some cases, martial law was applied retrospectively; in others, initial sentences of detention were over-ruled by the regime.[5]

[3] Ibid., p. 31.
[4] Perón, quoted in González Janzen, p. 97.
[5] On the 1956 events, see Rodolfo Walsh, *Operación Masacre* (Buenos Aires: Ediciones de la Flor, 1972); Salvador Ferla, *Mártires y verdugos: sentido histórico del 9 de junio de 1956* (Buenos Aires: Librería Plus Ultra, 1964); and Julio Troxler, 'Los asesinatos de junio del 56 en el testimonio de un militante', *Peronismo y Socialismo*, no. 1, pp. 94–7.

Fourteen years later, it may not have been Aramburu's victims who returned from the dead to hunt him down, as Valle had promised in a final letter to him, but certainly the Montonero *comando* which bore Valle's name considered that it was avenging the death of patriots.

Paradoxical as it may at first seem, the third reason behind the *Aramburazo* was that Aramburu had begun to conspire against the Onganía regime. From 1969, conscious of the alarming social unrest, Aramburu had been working for the removal of Onganía and for a quasi-Liberal electoral solution to the Argentine crisis. Though never fully articulated by him, the plan revolved around the idea of drawing the more conciliatory Peronist leaders, such as Jorge Daniel Paladino, into a new broad political alliance in an endeavour to overcome the longstanding antagonism between Peronists and anti-Peronists. By splitting the Peronist Movement and offering its 'moderates' places within a new civilian order, the revolutionary wing would be denied the protection and assistance of a multi-class national movement; isolated, the revolutionaries could by annihilated militarily. In broad outline, the scheme foreshadowed General Lanusse's Great National Agreement (GAN) of 1971-73, though Lanusse placed additional stress upon the need for Perón to return in order that he might disavow the young turks of his 'special formations'. So far as the Montoneros were concerned, such plans were far more dangerous than Onganía's quasi-corporatist enterprise and proscription of Peronism. Their reasoning went something like this: Peronism is the revolutionary movement of the Argentine people; as such it cannot be accommodated within any quasi-democratic Liberal regime; any attempts at integration, aimed at conciliatory Peronists, would be primarily motivated by a desire to destroy Peronism as a revolutionary force; at the same time, the military would never permit free elections to take place, for the revolutionary Peronist Movement would not only win but proceed to assail the bastions of privilege; Peronism should therefore pursue an unequivocal revolutionary strategy directed towards the violent seizure of power; conciliatory sectors should be attacked, as should their seducers; otherwise, though the rank and file would never succumb to their blandishments, it might for a while be disoriented and divided by their reformist manoeuvres.

Partial success was achieved by the Montoneros in respect of each objective. The *Aramburazo* certainly put the Montoneros on the scoresheet and propagated their name. On the other hand, though its authors later qualified it as 'the first military deed carried out by a revolutionary organization which in itself implied a politicial definition',[6] that definition was lost upon 'Liberal' public opinion. Friends of Aramburu, such as Próspero Fernández Alvariño (alias Captain Gandhi) either suggested that the Montoneros were merely scapegoats for a crime perpetrated by the Onganía regime or insinuated that the guerrillas were in league with the security services.[7] In support of the former thesis, apologists for the deceased 'soldier of freedom' reminded the public that the kidnappers had worn military uniforms, that later, when the police cornered some of the Montonero suspects, no attempt had been made to take them alive, and that Aramburu's widow had claimed not to recognize the corpses of her husband's abductors after they were gunned down. Supporters of the latter thesis meanwhile rested their case on reports which appeared in *La Vanguardia*, where it was claimed that Mario Firmenich had visited the Ministry of the Interior twenty-two times during April and May of 1970.[8] Both interpretations relied upon highly questionable evidence and, above all, dated biographical appreciations of the Montoneros. The detailed account of Operation Pindapoy, including description of Aramburu's personal effects, which the organization later published,[9] proved beyond doubt that the Montoneros were no scapegoats. Moreover, each interpretation was flawed by an erroneous political characterization of the Montoneros,

[6] 'Hablan los Montoneros', *Cristianismo y Revolución*, no. 26 (November-December 1970), pp. 11-14.
[7] Próspero Germán Fernández Alvariño, *Z.-Argentina. El crimen del siglo* (Buenos Aires: published by the author, 1973).
[8] *La Vanguardia*, 5 August 1970. Even if one were to believe that there was some co-operation between the doomed *Onganiato* and the Montoneros, one would have to interpret this as a question of mutual convenience rather than as collaboration by two forces of the Catholic Right. Both had an interest in destroying Liberal alternatives to the regime; and Mario Firmenich has always been characterized as more of a pragmatist than a man of ideological fervour. However, apart from an acceptance of the premise of Montonero opportunism, belief in the conspiracy theory would also involve characterization of Onganía and Interior Minister Imaz as exceedingly shortsighted, precipitating their own fall whether the guerrilla action failed or succeeded.
[9] 'Como murió Aramburu', purportedly written by Firmenich and Arrostito.

soon to acquire the status of a myth: it was assumed that Abal Medina, Ramus, Firmenich, and Maza were still the right-wing Catholics they had been earlier in the 1960s, and were thus spiritual confrères of Onganía. Liberals underestimated the dynamism of the late 1960s Catholic radicalization and could not comprehend how youths with records of regular attendance at Mass could have turned to armed struggle. The *Aramburazo*, then, made 'Montoneros' a household name and was rejoiced in by many Peronists, but did not fully clarify the political identity of the organization.

The second objective, that of submitting Aramburu to 'revolutionary justice', was achieved, but its potential impact was not fully realized due to restrictions on press freedom. Foreseeing this problem, the Montoneros tape-recorded the 'trial', but later burned the tapes as a security measure during the repressive aftermath of the *Aramburazo*. According to their own account, the tapes would have proved that Aramburu pleaded guilty to charges of 'legalizing' the 1956 shootings, repression of the Peronist Movement, and responsibility for the disappearance of Evita's corpse, while professing his innocence of other charges. Under interrogation, Aramburu reputedly stated, without disclosing any details, that Evita's body now lay in a Rome cemetery;[10] the Montoneros then attempted to exchange their victim's remains for those of their 'standard bearer', until the discovery of the general's body on 16 July upset their plans. It was found at the *estancia*, buried beneath a cellar which had earlier been used to store the guns seized from the Córdoba Federal Shooting Range in February 1969.

Finally, a degree of success was attained in pursuing the Montonero's third aim. Onganía, against whom critical military voices had become increasingly strident since the time of the *Cordobazo*, was deposed by the military commanders just ten days after the *Aramburazo* shook Argentina. His replacement, General Roberto Levingston, former head of the Army Information Service, was soon, in turn, to lose the confidence of the more lucid military officers. Levingston's

---

[10] It is not clear whether Aramburu attempted to deceive his captors or whether they themselves made a mistake when writing the official account of the 'trial', four years afterwards. In fact the corpse of Eva Perón lay in lot 86, garden 41 of the Musocco Cemetery in *Milan.*

ambition to extend the 'Argentine Revolution' for another three to four years, plus the fact that he was only prepared to consult 'currents of opinion' rather than re-legalize the parties and come to terms with Perón and UCR leader Balbín, ignored the threatening realities of widespread public hostility towards the military and growing military factionalism. It was only with his replacement by General Alejandro Lanusse in March 1971 that Aramburu's plan for a military retreat and elections in order to isolate the guerrillas reached fruition. Political parties began to operate again legally the following month. The Montoneros had therefore helped to destabilize the military regime but, through their first public act, had only deferred attempts to ensure a reformist civilian alternative to it.

As 22,000 men joined the search for Aramburu's body and hunted for his kidnappers, the Montoneros felt obliged to launch a second spectacular blow in order to demonstrate that they were capable of a sustained challenge to the regime. Thus on 1 July four Montonero units commanded by Emilio Maza occupied the Córdoban town of La Calera, 17km from the provincial capital. The choice of a place near the base of the Air-transported Infantry Regiment of Córdoba, whose personnel were incapable of reacting with sufficient rapidity, was deliberately calculated to undermine enemy morale. About twenty-five combatants of the *Comandos* Eva Perón, Comandante Uturunco, General José de San Martín, and 29 de Mayo, wearing Montonero armbands and maintaining contact via walkie-talkies, took over the local bank, police station, and town hall, after first knocking out communications equipment at the telegraph centre and post office. A policeman named Argüello, who had been wounded while resisting an earlier (anonymous) Montonero assault on the very same bank, again received a bullet wound for being uncooperative. Some 26,000 dollars were seized from the bank. Guns lost in the course of the previous bank raid were recovered from the police station, where policemen were jailed and forced to sing the Peronist March while guerrillas made off with their station radio. Simultaneously, other guerrillas were painting 'Montoneros' and 'Perón or Death' on the municipal building, while a further unit was attempting, unsuccessfully, to awaken the local population with a taped recording of *La Marcha Peronista*.[11]

Modelled on the Uruguayan Tupamaros' occupation of Pando in 1969, this first major military operation of the Argentine urban guerrilla war was well-planned and perfectly synchronized but, as in the prototypal action, the withdrawal went wrong. The raiders left La Calera in a convoy of cars, scattering nails (*miguelitos*) on the road behind them in order to prevent police pursuit. Other motorists gave way as the cavalcade approached, for in front Capuano Martínez was driving an imitation police car, its siren screaming all the way. But then luck deserted the Montoneros. As the convoy dispersed on the outskirts of Córdoba, one of the cars broke down and Luis Losada and José Fierro were captured by the police, the former wounded. Information presumably extracted from them led the police to proceed to a house in the Los Naranjos barrio of Córdoba, where the Montoneros suffered their first losses. After a gunbattle in which Maza was mortally wounded and Ignacio Vélez seriously wounded in the spine, a dozen Montonero suspects, including Dr. Raúl Héctor Guzzo Conte Grande, were arrested. Several were students from the city's Catholic University and some, like Vélez, belonged to prominent Córdoban families.

Public sympathy for the Montoneros became evident at this time. Three thousand people attended Maza's funeral and collections were held in factories, universities, and shanty towns for those Montoneros being tortured in prison. The losses, though, were tremendous: apart from *comandante* Maza, the Montoneros lost weaponry, bases, a contact list containing 167 names which was found at Vélez's house, and organizational security. After this episode, the police knew that the guerrillas were trying to establish a third network in Santa Fe, and had a better idea of the overall molecular structure of the organization. Another blow fell on 9 July when the Montonero Carlos Maguid, a photographer and TV cameraman, was picked up by the police. His sister-in-law, the teacher Norma Arrostito, and the other authors of the *Aramburazo* — Firmenich, Abal Medina, Ramus, and Capuano Martínez — were now identified and hunted by the security forces.

---

[11] On the occupation of La Calera, see 'Montonero Emilio Maza: La Calera', *La Causa Peronista*, no. 2 (16 June 1974), pp. 22-3; and 'A tres años de La Calera', *Militancia*, no. 4 (5 July 1973), pp. 8-9.

The Montoneros were very nearly wiped out in July–August 1970. Those Córdoban members who managed to evade capture after La Calera dispersed throughout Argentina, while four arrests in Santa Fe on 19 July paralysed efforts to organize a group there. After a 73,000 dollar bank raid in Laguna Larga, Córdoba, executed by four suspected guerrillas who claimed to be avenging the death of Maza, the Montoneros went to ground in these two months, with the prospect of death and destruction staring them in the face. They were saved from extinction primarily by assistance and protection supplied by the senior Peronist urban guerrilla organization, the FAP, launched two years earlier. For two months, while the police were scouring the country and following up reports that the fugitives had been spotted in Salta, in the almost-deserted region between San Rafael and the Chilean border, and other remote places, the key Montonero figures hid in a couple of houses lent by the FAP in Buenos Aires.

Operations resumed on 1 September when Abal Medina, Ramus, and others deprived the Ramos Mejica branch of the Banco de Galicia y Buenos Aires of almost 36,000 dollars, but further traumas were suffered by the organization on the 7th. On that subsequently-designated 'Day of the Montonero', five leading members held a meeting, for reasons which defy common sense, in the La Rueda pizza-house in William Morris, Buenos Aires Province. Security was appalling, consisting of no more than having Ramus posted in a car outside, and the guerrillas were rapidly pinned down after the manager of the establishment reported their presence to the police. Abal Medina and Ramus, comrades for almost a decade, died together in the ensuing gunbattle, during which three police corporals were wounded. The unarmed Luis Rodeiro was arrested, but Sabino Navarro and a fifth guerrilla managed to escape after running out of ammunition.[12]

Owing to their failure to take elementary safety precautions, the organization was now bereft of its original commanders and preserved few secrets. After the William Morris shootout, documents found in the Montoneros' cars provided the police, among other things, with the *noms de guerre* of the fighters. Montonero survival, however,

[12] For accounts, see '7 de setiembre'; and 'El mandato político de Fernando Abal Medina', *Militancia*, no. 13 (6 September 1973), pp. 10–13.

was now enhanced by the growth of popular support, emanating in particular from Third World Priests, broader sectors of Peronism, and youth groups. Roman Catholic Primate Cardinal Caggiano was totally unmoved by a Montonero letter to him justifying the *Aramburazo* as 'an act of higher revolutionary justice',[13] but significant numbers of parish priests and lay Catholics were quick to lay the blame for such violence on the regime and social injustices rather than upon the executioners. After a three-year separation, Father Carlos Mugica rallied to the defence of the Catholic *guerrilleros*; he officiated at the funeral of Abal Medina and Ramus, referring to the deceased as 'an example to youth'. The more conservative Peronist, Father Hernán Benítez, also risked being unfrocked by, on the same occasion, describing the two as having been 'murdered by the nation, which did not know how to understand them . . . Thank you Lord for these two young men. They didn't choose an easy road.'[14] Leading nationalists and Peronists including Arturo Jauretche and Miguel Gazzera paid their respects at the funeral, Perón sent a wreath, and hundreds of youths attended, many of them Catholic Action militants who regarded Maza, Abal Medina, and Ramus as martyrs. Benítez was later accused of providing the cassock worn by Maguid during the abduction of Aramburu, while Father Alberto Carbone received a two-year suspended sentence for being the owner of the typewriter with which Montonero communiqués were written.

The Peronist identity of the Montoneros also provided them with much-needed protection and aid. Unlike the Guevarist guerrilla organizations, they were able from early on to count on valuable surface support, especially from Peronist youth groupings. This showed the regime that the solution to 'subversion' demanded something more than rooting out a few 'terrorists'. The deaths of Ramus and Abal Medina gave rise to the first pro-Montonero demonstration by 1,000 youths in the Barrio Casas shanty town on 14 September, and 7 September entered the Peronist Left calendar as a date on or near which there were annual demonstrations to record the memory of these two leading guerrillas. Eighteen-year-old Ramón Cesaris, like Abal Medina, Ramus,

[13] Reported in the *Buenos Aires Herald*, 13 June 1970.
[14] Ibid., 12 and 15 September 1970.

and Firmenich an alumnus of the *Colegio Nacional de Buenos Aires*,[15] was to become a Peronist Youth martyr when a tear gas grenade was fired into his face from a few metres away during the 1972 homage. It was that killing which inspired President Lanusse to comment that, 'from today, young people will know that we don't carry guns for show'.[16]

During the last quarter of 1970 the Montoneros acquired small sums of money through raids on the Córdoba Jockey Club, a Córdoban railway station, and the city's central post office; they took weapons and communications equipment from a National Institute of Industrial Technology (INTI) guard station in Córdoba, and documents from a civilian registry in Bella Vista; they bombed the home of General Osiris Villegas, Ambassador to Brazil, and they launched an assault on a guard post at the presidential residence in Olivos, claiming one victim. These operations, each involving a handful of activists, kept the Montoneros in the public eye, yet overall, for the year as a whole, recruitment did little more than match Montonero losses: membership stood at about twenty by the end of 1970.[17] Nevertheless the Montoneros had certainly established their public presence. The FAP had been by far the most active Peronist urban guerrillas of the year, but the Montoneros, through the *Aramburazo* and occupation of La Calera, had stolen the limelight, before taking advantage of the FAP offer of refuge. They had shown great daring in their operational planning and had to some extent captured the popular imagination through their more spectacular feats. Fortune also intervened on their behalf: though Carlos Maguid received an eighteen-year prison sentence and Ignacio Vélez two years eight months at the end of the Aramburu trial, Norma Arrostito was able to walk out of court a free woman after being acquitted by her judges.

If the latter months of 1970 were militarily rather fallow

[15] Several members of the Revolutionary Armed Forces (FAR), including Carlos Enrique Olmedo and María Angélica Sabelli, also came to know each other while attending this very same school.

[16] Lanusse, quoted in González Janzen, p. 103.

[17] By the end of 1970, Maza, Abal Medina, and Ramus were dead; Vélez, Liprandi de Vélez, Fierro, Soratti Martínez, Conte Grande, Maguid, and Losada were in prison; and Firmenich, Capuano Martínez, Arrostito, Pujadas, Rodeiro, Susana Lesgart, and Sabino Navarro were among those still operating.

ones for the organization, they were not so politically. The Montoneros devoted many hours to the attraction of political support through drawing up documents and conceding interviews in order to propagate their conceptions. In a document published at the end of 1970 in the radical Catholic review *Cristianismo y Revolución*,[18] they presented themselves as 'part of the final synthesis of a historical process which goes back 160 years'. Their historical revisionism portrayed Argentine history in terms of a constant conflict between two major political currents: 'on the one hand, that of the Liberal Oligarchy, clearly anti-national and *vendepatria*; on the other, that of the People, identified with the defence of their interests, which are the interests of the Nation against the imperialist attacks of each historical situation'. In the past, the national-popular current had been present in 'the struggles of San Martín's Army and the *montonero gauchos* of the last century, in the heroic struggles of the immigrants who gave their lives for the formation of our unions, and in Yrigoyenist nationalism'. More recently, the current had been expressed by Peronism, 'the only expression of national unity in 160 years'. Its liberating enterprise had been interrupted in 1955 because 'power was shared with the enemies of the people and with the traitors. But that counter-revolution purified our ranks, leaving the Movement composed almost exclusively of the popular forces.' There was some truth in this. Peronism had indeed become more of a plebeian force since 1955, shedding some of its opportunist bourgeois elements and acquiring structures which were rooted most firmly in the labour movement. But what the Montoneros did not foresee was that many of those who had deserted the crippled band wagon in the 1950s would all too readily climb back onto it as the 1973 Peronist electoral success drew near, and would moreover be welcomed back by Perón as a counter-weight to working-class and left-wing pressures.

The very simplicity of the Montonero schema, especially its dichotomic appeal, enhanced popular assimilation of it, yet its superficiality was soon to prove to be a liability. When evaluating Argentine national movements, the analysis

[18] 'Hablan los Montoneros'.

understated their limitations and overstated their antagonism with the traditional liberal agro-export structure of the country. Neither Yrigoyenism nor Peronism had in fact attacked the power of the landed bourgeoisie but had rather improved the position of the popular classes within the established social order. Neither had been prepared to mobilize or arm the people when threatened by the approaching military coups of 1930 and 1955. The vindication of these movements illustrated how, for the Montoneros, class conflicts were of secondary importance to nationalist struggles against foreign domination and influence. In practical terms, their appreciation of history therefore led them to suppose that Peronism could and would unitedly embark upon 'national liberation' projects when power was recovered; it left them totally unprepared for the outbreak of bitter internecine conflict within the Peronist Movement which was to reach a peak after 1973.

It is interesting to note here that no political, ideological, or class differentiation appeared in the Montoneros' Peronist hagiography: in lauding the diverse examples of Eva Perón, the late 1950s Resistance commandos, General Valle, the Uturunco rural guerrillas of 1959–60, and the Revolutionary Peronist Movement of 1964, the Montoneros failed to discriminate between those sectors which fought merely for the return of Perón to power and those which sought a socialist transformation of society. They identified with 'every Argentine who struggles... because we feel that the *montonero* spirit breathes in all of them'. A cult of action was implicit in their view that Peronism had historically been composed of two tendencies, one bureaucratic, the other revolutionary; and that what distinguished them were the methods which each employed. The revolutionaries were those who had struggled, employing guerrilla methods, military rebellions, mass mobilizations, and the strike weapon, even if they had never heard of *socialismo nacional.* The bureaucrats, on the other hand, 'objectively' formed part of the enemy camp precisely because they discouraged these methods in favour of bargaining and electoralism. Such was the Montonero vision of the alignment of contending forces, a vision only intelligible if one bears two factors in mind: first, that legal and constitutional methods practised by

Peronists had not produced great successes since 1955, while direct action seemed to be the only means of overcoming the Peronist/anti-Peronist stalemate of the 1960s; and second, that the Montoneros considered that the revolutionary process would pass first through a 'national liberation' stage in which all Peronists, except a few 'traitors', had a role to play.

The Montoneros' first document also enlightened its readership as to the organization's conception of armed struggle. After justifying revolutionary violence as a response to institutional violence, the Montoneros stated that their ambition was 'to become, together with the FAP and other fraternal organizations, the Armed Wing of the people. This means to be the politico-military vanguard of the broadest possible popular base'. They looked to the outbreak of a 'popular war', rather than a mere confrontation between military apparata, and insisted that 'our struggle and the mass struggle must go together, mutually feeding and maintaining each other'.[19] However, while the Montoneros aspired to form part of an 'integral' strategy, involving political, trade union, and student activity as well as the armed element, they were clearly content to promote the guerrilla aspect themselves and to leave the remaining complementary activities to other sectors of the Movement. This meant that the chances of the strategy leading to the establishment of 'national' socialism depended upon Perón and the rest of the Movement being as revolutionary or progressive as the Montoneros mistakenly believed them to be.

Nevertheless, the inadequacies of the Montonero analysis of Peronism and their illusions in Perón should not be permitted to obscure the fact that they were, from the start, distinctly more radical than mainstream Peronists. In an interview conceded early in 1971,[20] the guerrillas made it clear that their project envisaged 'the destruction of the capitalist State and its army, as preconditions for the taking of power by the people'. Concomitantly, they rejected Perón's 'Third Position' of equidistance from US and Soviet 'imperialism', interpreting the concept instead to signify 'a form of active solidarity with the Latin American, Asiatic, and African

[19] Ibid.
[20] 'El llanto del enemigo', *Cristianismo y Revolución*, no. 28 (April 1971), pp. 70-3.

peoples, those of the so-called Third World exploited by colonialism and imperialism'. Here again a readiness to subordinate class struggles to popular national struggles was evident in the Montonero outlook. This attracted an increasing number of lower-middle-class youths, unwilling to entrust their interests to a working-class leadership, but held little appeal for the industrial workers. A small minority of the latter, principally located in Córdoba, rejected the Montoneros' views from a more revolutionary standpoint, whereas the economistic majority looked upon armed strategies as alien to their experiences, struggles, and needs. They did not, for the most part, respond to the Montonero example of taking up arms, relying instead upon their labour unions to effect an improvement in their living standards. The Montoneros demanded too much of these workers and promised them too little. While offering them no greater material benefits than did orthodox Peronism for the duration of their 'national liberation' stage, the Montoneros were calling on the workers totally to subordinate their own traditional, tested, means of struggle to a new, unproven, politico-military strategy. Rather than just collaborate with guerrilla units, the masses were urged by the Montoneros to themselves adopt 'the organizational forms and methods of struggle typical of an armed organization', as a first step towards the 'gradual and organized incorporation of the people into the armed organizations' and their transformation into a popular army.[21] José Sabino Navarro, José Enrique Carral, and Jorge Gustavo Rossi were by no means typical workers in responding to the call to arms.

RELATIONS WITH PERON AND OTHER GUERRILLA ORGANIZATIONS

Encouraging the armed activities of the Montoneros from his Madrid exile, Perón rightly discarded the possibility that the workers would rush *en masse* to join the ranks of the guerrillas. He manipulated his 'special formations' most skillfully, and though current mythology would have it that they were speculating upon the approaching death of an

[21] Ibid.

ageing popular leader, hoping to inherit the leadership of his Movement, there is no evidence to suggest that the manipulation was attempted the other way round. Montonero support for Perón and faith in his quasi-revolutionary pronouncements were genuine, based on the conviction that he had become a sincere convert to a national form of socialism. The guerrillas' failure to grasp the real strategic and political differences which they had with the Peronist leader was seen especially after November 1970. In that month Perón sponsored the 'Hour of the People', a joint declaration calling for elections and signed by Balbín's Radical Party, the Popular Conservative Party, Progressive Democratic Party, Argentine Socialist Party,[22] and the *bloquista* Radicals of San Juan, in addition to the Peronists. The group subsequently issued a series of policy statements of a moderate nationalist-reformist nature, which in many ways anticipated the programme of the Peronist-dominated Justicialist Liberation Front (FREJULI), formed in December 1972 to contest the March 1973 elections.[23] But far from realizing that Perón was wheeling and dealing in classical reformist style, the Montoneros managed to find a revolutionary rationale for his behaviour.

For the Montoneros, the 'Hour of the People' was just an example of their wily leader engaging in a 'tactical manoeuvre designed to keep the regime sitting at the negotiating table while the Movement develops its organization and methods of struggle in preparation for the next steps in the war'.[24] They attacked Paladino, Perón's delegate in charge of the initiative, for confusing strategy with tactics, yet developments were to reveal that it was the Montoneros themselves who mistook Perón's strategy for his tactics and vice versa. Minor doubts which the guerrillas had over the inter-party

---

[22] In this case the PSA led by Jorge Selser, not to be confused with the Argentine Socialist Party led by Juan Carlos Coral.

[23] Prior to the launching of FREJULI, the Civic Front of National Liberation (FRECILINA), formed in July 1972, briefly served as the Peronist-orientated alliance. Within FREJULI, the only major party apart from the Justicialist Party (PJ) was Arturo Frondizi's Movement of Integration and Development (MID). The Revolutionary Christian, UDELPA, and Intransigent parties withdrew from FREJULI in December 1972, protesting against the PJ's reservation of 75 per cent of the Front's share of seats for itself, and rejecting the FREJULI economic programme as being too moderate.

[24] Montoneros: 'Las armas de la Independencia hoy están apuntadas hacia el Pueblo', *Cristianismo y Revolución*, no. 30 (September 1971), pp. 13–15.

For the Return of Perón 105

dealing were swiftly dispelled after an exchange of correspondence with Perón. In a letter of February 1971 delivered by radical labour leader Raimundo Ongaro they characterized the pact as being 'tactically correct', but expressed misgivings over the way in which 'the revolutionary armed option, i.e. us, is being used as a means of pressure to reinforce the tactical offensive, i.e. elections', adding that the continuation of such a state of affairs was 'absolutely impossible'. The Montoneros failed to realize that Perón's electoralism was strategic and were fully satisfied with a reply in which he claimed to be 'completely in agreement' with them ... 'As to the electoral option, I don't believe in it either.'[25]

Perón did not criticize a single Montonero operation during these years and indeed seemed, in November 1971, to be reaffirming the revolutionary perspective when he sacked Paladino and appointed Héctor Cámpora to replace him as delegate. In truth he was doing nothing of the sort. Paladino fell from grace because he had lost sight of Perón's 'integral' strategy and was pursuing the electoral line without simultaneously reinforcing this by encouraging armed, mass, and industrial activity; he had demoted people who disagreed with him and had spent too much time scheming with non-Peronists. But though Cámpora was ready to work with the revolutionary wing of the Movement and to consider the guerrillas 'as respectable as those of us who are on the road of ideas and persuasion',[26] his appointment did not signify a 'Left turn' on the part of Perón. All that the latter was seeking to demonstrate to the military regime was that: 'If the elections do not take place, we are prepared for something else. We are prepared for other things as well as voting.'[27]

[25] Both letters published in 'Como murió Aramburu'.
[26] Héctor Cámpora, quoted in Alejandro A. Lanusse, *Mi testimonio* (Buenos Aires: Lasserre Editores, 1977), p. 316. In these memoires, Lanusse described Cámpora as 'the spearhead of *montonerismo* and of the most virulent opposition', yet he was not ideologically a man of the Left. He participated in a prison escape with Cooke and other Peronist leaders in 1957, but, according to Cooke, during his 1955-7 imprisonment Cámpora 'spent his days praying' and 'made a promise to God that he would never return to political activity ... At all times, he demonstrated that he was not a man of struggle and as such he can be of no use (to the Resistance)' [*Correspondencia Perón-Cooke*, vol. 1, p. 72]. His overtures to the Peronist Left were in part a fulfilment of Perón's directives, and in part a result of the weakness of his support base in the Justicialist Party and lack of trade union backing.
[27] Perón: statement in Rome, *Buenos Aires Herald*, 12 February 1973.

Perhaps the Peronist Left should have attached more importance to Perón's appointment in the same month of Lt.-Col. Jorge Osinde, formerly security chief of army intelligence under the pre-1955 Peronist Government, as his military and political advisor: two years later this appointee was to direct the infamous Ezeiza Massacre against the Peronist Left.

Meanwhile the Montoneros had been reorganizing themselves following their post-La Calera set-backs. José Sabino Navarro took over the leadership of the organization after the deaths of Abal Medina and Ramus. He moved to Córdoba and worked seventeen hours a day to rebuild the Montonero network there, while also travelling frequently as the national link-man. At the expense of Sabino Navarro's family life, the Montonero skeleton began to take on flesh and became a national organization. A handful of working-class Peronist militants, such as the railway worker José Enrique Carral and Catholic Working Youth activist Jorge Gustavo Rossi, both of whom had lost jobs as a result of their trade union activities, were recruited in 1971. Far more important though, in terms of the long-term growth of the organization, were the strengthening of ties with other Peronist 'special formations', leading to mergers, and the Montoneros' promotion of a united Peronist Youth movement.

In 1971 it was the originally Trotskyist, by now predominantly Guevarist, People's Revolutionary Army (ERP) which was the most militarily-active urban guerrilla organization;[28] but a crucial process towards unification was being undertaken by four other organizations which was ultimately to make the Montoneros the most powerful. Apart from the Montoneros, those involved were the Peronist Armed Forces (FAP), Revolutionary Armed Forces (FAR) and the smaller *Descamisados* (literally Shirtless-ones). The FAP had originally been founded for rural warfare in April 1968 and included

[28] In May 1971 the ERP kidnapped Stanley Sylvester, honorary British consul and manager of the Swift meat-packing plant in Rosario; Swift distributed 50,000 dollars in food and clothing to the poor in order to obtain his release, while Graham Greene was inspired to write *The Honorary Consul* (Penguin, 1974). The other major ERP action of the 1970-3 period was less productive: in March 1972 the ERP kidnapped Oberdan Sallustro, general manager of Fiat-Concord, in an effort to secure the reinstatement of sacked workers and the release of imprisoned strikers and guerrillas. The government prohibited the payment of a ransom, and Sallustro was killed by fleeing guerrillas on 10 April when a police patrol arrived at the ERP 'people's prison'.

experienced Peronist militants like Envar El Kadri and Carlos Caride (founders in 1958 of the first Peronist Youth), as well as the radical Catholic ex-seminarists Arturo Ferré Gadea and Gerardo Ferrari. Its rural ambitions were thwarted, however, in September 1968 when, just thirteen days after setting up their training camp, thirteen tiro guerrillas were captured at La Cañada, near Taco Ralo, in Tucumán Province. Despite these losses, followed by the arrest and imprisonment of Caride after a shootout in April 1969, the FAP managed to reorganize itself for urban struggle and was conducting a sustained campaign by 1970. In that year, colleagues of these guerrillas helped trade union veterans who had played leading roles in the CGT of the Argentines to create a revolutionary Peronist organization, Rank-and-File Peronism (PB), for work at factory level. The FAP then became the leading Peronist 'special formation' for a while but proved unable to maintain its pre-eminent position due to crippling divisions, several important casualties in 1971, and the fact that its leaders, El Kadri, Caride, and Verdinelli, remained in prison until 1973.

The FAR's history was radically different: its origins went back to 1966 when a small group of people came together in the hope of becoming the Argentine appendix to Guevara's Bolivian *foco*. Che's death and the collapse of the Bolivian project in October 1967 led the FAR, under the command of Gillette employee Carlos Enrique Olmedo and lawyer Roberto Jorge Quieto, to initiate urban warfare in 1969. In attempting to break out of their social and political isolation, the shift to urban struggle was accompanied by the FAR's 'peronization' — a process finally consolidated in 1971. The most noteworthy early FAR actions were their anonymous fire-bombing in June 1969 of 15 Minimax supermarkets in protest against the visit to Buenos Aires by their owner, Nelson Rockefeller, and the July 1970 occupation of the small town of Garín, a half-hour drive away from Buenos Aires. They went on to become a thorn in the flesh of the military regime, but only after experiencing serious reverses. Raquel Liliana Gelín became the first Argentine woman to die in combat, and several other FAR members were captured, after a Córdoba bank raid right at the end of 1970. Then, in July of the following year, Marcelo Aburnio Verd and his wife were picked up by the security forces and forced, under torture, to talk, before being killed. The information extracted from Verd, whom the police spoke of as the *éminence grise* of the Argentine guerrilla movement, led days later to the illegal kidnapping and assassination of Gillette marketing executive Juan Pablo Maestre (a few hours after Federal Security agents had called at Gillette to ask for his address), the permanent 'disappearance' of his wife Mirta Misetich, and the aforementioned police attempt to abduct Quieto, which became an arrest. Maestre had commanded one of the FAR units at Garín. These were telling losses, but again it was the FAP who came to the rescue, saving the FAR from destruction as they had the Montoneros after La Calera.

Finally the Descamisado Command was a small Peronist group founded in 1968 by, among others, the future leading Montoneros, Horacio Mendizábal and Norberto Habegger. Upon his release from prison in 1969 Dardo Cabo, son of the trade union leader Armando Cabo, became its leader. Previously, he had been in charge of Isabel Perón's bodyguard during her October 1965–July 1966 visit to Argentina; and, as leader of the right-wing New Argentina Movement, led an abortive 'invasion' of the Malvinas (Falkland) Islands in September 1966, designed to provoke an international incident during a visit to Argentina by the Duke of Edinburgh. Cabo was never to become one of the more left-wing Montoneros, even after being appointed editor of their weekly *El Descamisado* in 1973. His name and that of the Descamisados have been associated with that of the 'National Revolutionary Army' (ENR) which, though presented in Montonero accounts as a further independent guerrilla organization which joined them in the early 1970s, appears to have lacked a life of its own. The chimerical ENR only carried out a couple of highly militaristic operations: the assassinations in 1969 and 1970 of Argentina's two principal conciliatory Peronist union leaders of the 1960s, Augusto Timoteo Vandor and José Alonso, both regarded as 'traitors' by their 'executioners'. In all probability, the ENR was no more than a Descamisados' 'hit squad', deployed as a front organization for acts certain to give rise to a major State backlash and anger in Peronist labour circles.

Strenuous efforts were made to bring these organizations together in 1971, but the initiative was premature. Joint operations were conceived and executed but the loose coordinating body established to promote unification, the Peronist Armed Organizations (OAP), never acquired formal structures. The guerrillas could not initially agree over whether they should concentrate solely upon armed struggle or pursue an 'integral' strategy of encouraging multiple forms of action, the latter by now being the Montonero position. They also had to overcome the obstacle posed by the Montoneros' hostility towards Marxism: in November 1971 they claimed that they were 'authentic' Peronists who had nothing to do with the 'foreign ideologies' of the other guerrillas.[29] Moreover with the exception of good relations between the Montoneros and Descamisados from 1971, differences increased for a while over how to respond to Lanusse's announcement of elections: were the guerrillas to seek to turn the electoral opening to their advantage or to continue with their armed struggle regardless? Finally, there was an element of competition between the organizations, with each one trying to direct the unification process.[30]

Agreements over the strategy to be followed, the goal being socialism and the enemy US imperialism, were insufficient to generate real unity between the 'special formations'; what was further needed was agreement over political and organizational conceptions and this was only attained, and mergers implemented, between the Montoneros and Descamisados late in 1972, with the FAR in October 1973, and with a wing of the FAP led by Caride in June 1974. The foundations of this Montonero-enhancing unification were laid, though, in 1971-2. In July 1971 the three foremost Peronist organizations cooperated over the assassination of Major Julio Ricardo Sanmartino, the Prisons Director and former Police Chief of Córdoba, but in November of the same year another combined operation ended in costly failure. In an endeavour to bring about a rescission of a government ban on the Marxist Fiat plant unions, SITRAC and SITRAM, of Córdoba, the FAP, FAR, and Montoneros planned to kidnap a top Fiat executive. For some unknown reason, their intended victim was late in arriving at the place of ambush, the guerrillas tarried too long, were spotted and

[29] *Buenos Aires Herald*, 14 November 1971.
[30] On the process of unification, see 'La unidad de FAR y Montoneros'.

reported to the police, and in the ferocious 'Battle of Ferreyra' which ensued, the Peronist Armed Organizations lost Olmedo, Agustín Villagra, Juan Carlos Peressini, and Juan Baffi.

Discussions also helped to cement the unity of the combatant Peronists and these, ironically, were often easier to conduct inside prison than outside. Most of the bases for the convergence between the Montoneros and FAR were laid during 1972 discussions held by militants in the Rawson maximum security prison down in Patagonia. These culminated in the joint drafting of a document known to militants as 'The Bleat of Rawson', since the prisoners were fed mutton day after day! Perhaps the most decisive unifying experience though, as will be seen later, was the opportunity to work together at a political level during the brief late-1972 return visit of Perón and in the campaign leading up to the March 1973 elections.

THE NATURE AND EFFECTS OF MONTONERO ACTIVITY

To understand the growing popularity of the Montoneros in these years, it is essential to examine the nature of their guerrilla activity. Most of their actions were examples of 'armed propaganda' rather than military operations. Even the June 1971 take-over of the small rural town of San Jerónimo Norte, forty miles from Santa Fe, was a case of psychological warfare rather than an attempt to engage in an armed confrontation with enemy units. As at La Calera eleven months earlier, Montonero aims were partly to seize resources (10,000 dollars from a bank; twenty-seven rifles, other weapons, and uniforms from a police station; documents, identity cards, and driving licences from the law courts) and partly to encourage popular combativity by demonstrating the vulnerability of the military regime. By exploiting the classical guerrilla advantages of surprise and mobility a force of twenty-five could occupy a town of 5,000 people for two hours and thus make the government appear weak and incompetent in the eyes of the public, foreign investors, and international bankers. Even in small-scale actions during these years, the accumulation of financial, military, and logistical resources, and the stimulation of popular sympathy and support, were the prime Montonero motives. There were no assaults on military garrisons and no instances of Montonero *comandos* deliberately setting out to do battle with the army or police.

A sympathetic response to Montonero activities was carefully cultivated by means of a minimal use of offensive violence and extreme discrimination in the selection of targets, as opposed to random terrorism. The guerrillas paid special attention to symbolic operations which all Peronists could relate to. Early in 1971 their Evita Fighting Unit occupied the historic *Casa de Tucumán* where Argentine Independence had been declared in 1816, as 'an act of homage and a reminder of the economic independence which Perón declared in 1946' in the same place.[31] Bombs inevitably exploded in all the major cities on important Peronist anniversaries such as those of the 1956 military revolt and of Eva Perón's death on 26 July 1952. Over 100 bombs went off, destroying foreign businesses, on the twentieth anniversary of the demise of 'Evita Montonera'. And whether they applauded or not, the public at least grasped the political significance of these explosions; far fewer spectators realized that the regular Guevarist 9 October blitzes were intended to record the death of Che. Favourite Montonero targets in these early years were symbols of oligarchic privilege and opulence, such as the numerous Jockey Clubs, golf course buildings, and luxurious country clubs which were blasted. And it was all performed with a lot of verve and style, in such a way as to facilitate the growth of a romantic aura around the authors. While the clubs of the wealthy were being detonated, approach roads were invariably closed off with signs reading 'Danger! Dynamited Zone'.

By killing no army conscripts and very few policemen, most of these being of plebeian origin, the Montoneros in their first three years of public life denied their enemy the boon of being able to successfully present them through the media as 'bloodthirsty terrorists'. They displayed their potential and also their self-control when, for instance, the *Comando* Chaco Peñaloza in February 1971 disarmed police guards outside the West German Embassy, without harming

[31] Montonero communiqué, *Buenos Aires Herald*, 15 February 1971.

them or proceeding to spray machine-gun bullets inside the Embassy. It was only very occasionally that violence was employed less discriminately: when Montoneros placed a bust of Evita in the central *plaza* of San Isidro in July 1972, together with a sign reading 'Plaza Evita — Montoneros', they also laid booby-trap bombs which injured three policemen, blinded a fireman, and killed another. And of course Montoneros at times got themselves into 'them or us' situations and left enemy corpses behind them as they shot their way out of trouble. At the end of June 1971 the *Comando* Juan José Valle, composed of eleven Buenos Aires Montoneros, 'expropriated' 88,000 dollars from the Banco de Boulogne in Villa Ballester after disarming two police guards. Though chief of the organization, José Sabino Navarro knew nothing about the plans for this operation and quite by chance drove into that area from Córdoba on the same day. Two police patrol-car men spotted the suspicious character waiting on a dark corner in his car; they tried to search him, opened fire when he pulled a gun on them, and were both shot dead.[32] As in this incident, most of the people killed by Montoneros only died whey they posed a fatal threat to the guerrillas, though the latter patently engaged in activities which dictated that such eventualities were certain to occur from time to time.

Foreign companies and executives were especially singled out for punishment, but here too assassination was not yet on the Montonero agenda. Discouragement of foreign investment in Argentina came in the form of blowing up executives' houses but not executives:[33] property, not people, was the prime target of Montonero violence. On several occasions, executives involved in industrial disputes learnt that their homes had been set on fire by Montoneros, and in February 1971 the Eva Perón Combat Unit occupied and blew up a new police station under construction in Santa Fe. Nine months later, in solidarity with the struggles of militant car workers, another unit invaded a car plant in Caseros, sprayed thirty-eight Fiats with petrol, and then sent merchandise valued at 98,000 dollars up in smoke.

[32] See 'Montonero José Sabino Navarro. Volverás'.
[33] It is difficult to assess the impact of such activities prior to 1973. However, *Time* of 14 January 1974 estimated that 60 per cent of foreign businessmen left Argentina during 1973, prompted by over 170 business kidnappings in that year.

There were few kidnappings, that of Vicenzo Russo, production manager of Standard Electric Argentina (an ITT subsidiary), in December 1972, being a 1m. dollar-worth exception to the general rule. One reason for this may have been that the only two other publicized Montonero kidnap attempts both resulted in unforeseen deaths: in March 1972, Roberto Uzal, a leading member of the extreme right-wing *Nueva Fuerza* was killed after he had himself slain the Montonero Jorge Rossi and wounded two others; and in April 1973, Colonel Héctor Iribarren, head of the 3rd Army Corps' intelligence service, was gunned down when resisting a kidnap bid by the Mariano Pujadas and Susana Lesgart units of the Montoneros. Altogether, even if one includes joint operations, no more than a dozen deaths could be attributed to the Montoneros during these years of military rule. Although they were never quite as successful as the early Tupamaros in presenting a Robin Hood image to the public, lessons about the politically counter-productive nature of terrorism seemed to have been learned from precedents such as the 'kill a cop a day' campaign waged in the early 1960s by the Venezuelan Tactical Combat Units (UTCs) in Caracas.[34]

By helping to create a climate of insecurity and social disorder, Montonero guerrilla activity certainly became a factor in the military decision to return to barracks and attempt a political solution to the Argentine crisis. But it was by no means the only factor. The change in military tactics was motivated just as much, if not more, by the semi-insurrectional challenges that had shaken the regime from 1969. In March 1971, it was the *Cordobacito* (little *Cordobazo*) which was primarily responsible for the military junta's decision to oust the pretentious Levingston and appoint the electorally-minded Lanusse as President in his stead. On that occasion, it had taken the occupation of Córdoba by 3,500 troops to put an end to a provincial general strike, street demonstrations, and barricade fighting, after Governor José Camilo Uriburu had threatened to 'cut off the snake's head' of rebellion there; over fifty vehicles had been burned and several businesses destroyed in the fighting, and the damage bill ran into millions of dollars. April 1972 saw more mass

---

[34] See Richard Gott, *Guerrilla Movements in Latin America* (London: Nelson, 1970), pp. 128-38.

violence, this time in the Andean city of Mendoza, sparked off by the raising of electricity prices. This *Mendozazo* only subsided after the regime agreed to suspend the increase, and after intervening troops had killed three demonstrators and imprisoned 500. During the next three months, further rioting, demonstrations, and strikes in San Miguel de Tucumán and General Roca maintained the momentum of popular revolt. In the course of the *Rocazo*, the local population went so far as to expel their mayor and run the town themselves.

All these mass challenges to military rule, complemented by a series of national and regional CGT strikes in support of economic claims,[35] persuaded General Lanusse that the regime's position was untenable. Though the guerrillas themselves were considered more of a scourge than an immediate military threat, he and his Minister of the Interior, the Catalan, Arturo Mor Roig, clearly feared the prospect of a growing incorporation of plebeian oppositionists into guerrilla ranks. In memoires published in 1977, Lanusse justified his behaviour during his twenty-six-month presidency on the grounds that 'left totalitarianism can flourish naturally where there are reactionary dictatorships'. 'Democracy' had to be restored 'to deprive the subversives of all their arguments', and the ageing Perón had to be brought back to Argentina if his myth were to be exploded. Otherwise, 'Perón in Spain, deprived of an alternative, would have ended his days as the Commander-in-Chief of subversion, without running any risks'. Back home, Perón would seek a more solid power base than his 'special formations' could offer him. Lanusse feared that the general situation would worsen and military divisions deepen unless the 'legitimacy of power' were restored. Almost cynically, he described his electoral plan as an 'escape valve', but did not, it would appear, consider that Peronism would be the prime beneficiary of it.[36]

Perón's Justicialist Party was recognized by the military regime as a legal political grouping in January 1972, but by stipulating that presidential candidates had to be permanently resident in the country from 25 August of that year, Lanusse virtually ensured that Perón himself would not stand. The

---

[35] There were three general strikes in 1970, five regional strikes in Córdoba in 1971, and three regional strikes in Córdoba, one in Mendoza, and one in San Juan during 1972. [36] Lanusse, op. cit., *passim*.

Peronist leader could not afford to be seen fulfilling military conditions by returning in time, especially when no guarantees had been offered with regard to his personal security. Lanusse seems to have calculated that the Peronist-led FREJULI alliance would obtain something less than 50 per cent of the votes on 11 March 1973, thus necessitating a run-off ballot for the presidency which would then be won by non-Peronist forces; the latter would sink their differences and rally round the Radical Party candidature of Ricardo Balbín.[37] It was a gamble which failed to come off. Though Lanusse was accurate in his estimation of the electoral might of Peronism, he underestimated Perón's capacity to put together a broad electoral front which he could dominate: an achievement only consolidated during Perón's November 1972 visit to Argentina. As it turned out, FREJULI presidential candidate Héctor Cámpora, with 49.59 per cent of the poll, was to come so close to attracting the 50 per cent required for election on 11 March that there was no point in the military enforcing their own second-ballot regulations.[38] In this way Lanusse lost control of the process which he had been instrumental in initiating, and the military were left incapable of conditioning the behaviour of the incoming government.

While pursuing his Great National Agreement, Lanusse did not call a halt to his government's repressive treatment of popular opposition forces. Death squads operated, political prisoners were tortured, and the homes of left-wing lawyers were bombed. Yet to some degree repression was tempered by military divisions over the junta's strategy and by Lanusse's desire to reach agreements with the largest of the civilian parties. Lanusse was politically unable to order a 'no holds barred' drive against the Peronist guerrillas, for given the widespread sympathy and support for them within the Peronist Movement, this would have entailed such an offensive against Peronists in general that military deals with even the most conciliatory Peronist leaders would have been rendered

---

[37] Ibid., pp. 273-4; and 'La muerte de Mor Roig', *La Causa Peronista*, no. 3 (23 July 1974), pp. 20-3.
[38] Out of 11,911,832 valid votes, the FREJULI formula for the Presidency and Vice-Presidency attracted 5,907,464 votes; the Radical (UCR) ticket headed by Balbín gained 2,537,605 votes (21.3 per cent), and came second.

impossible. According to Montonero records, about 100 people were killed and 500 imprisoned for political reasons by the agents of the 1966-73 'Argentine Revolution';[39] far more were to lose their lives or liberty during the first *year* of the post-1976 Videla regime.

GUERRILLA LOSSES AND THE CULT OF THE MARTYR

None the less, the Montoneros lost several leading figures during the early 1970s. José Sabino Navarro, following his narrow escape in Villa Ballester, died a young man's death at the end of July 1971. One of four Montoneros pursued by a large police posse after an 'expropriation' of cars in Río Cuarto, Sabino Navarro was eventually surrounded and gunned down in the Córdoba hills. 'El Negro' Díaz also perished in one of several running battles fought prior to his leader's last stand. Sabino Navarro's position was then filled by the former Catholic Student Youth leader, Mario Firmenich, who, whatever his qualities, lacked his predecessor's proletarian pedigree and experience of Peronist trade unionism. Firmenich survived right through the 1970s, but by the end of November 1971 the foremost precursors of modern urban guerrilla warfare in Argentina were gone. Abal Medina and Sabino Navarro of the Montoneros, Olmedo of the FAR, and Luis Pujals[40] of the ERP paid the price which precursors of their genre tend to pay, though each had his name perpetuated when new guerrilla units were christened.

August 1972 was a black month for the Montoneros and indeed for all the major armed organizations. On the 15th Montoneros held in the Patagonian prison of Rawson combined with ERP and FAR inmates to take over their maximum security gaol, killing a guard in the process, before making a desperate bid to get away and return to their armed activities. Non-Montonero outside operational support groups succeeded in commandeering an Austral jet which awaited the escapees at the nearby Trelew Airport, but faults in the signalling

---

[39] 'Compañeros presos: la aurora de la libertad', *El Descamisado*, no. 1 (22 May 1973), back cover.

[40] Luis Pujals, political leader of the ERP in Buenos Aires, was arrested in September 1971 and allegedly assassinated in the Rosario police barracks soon afterwards.

system between the prisoners and guerrillas outside Rawson created transport problems for the journey from Rawson to Trelew. An advance party, composed of six guerrilla commanders, reached Trelew in time to fly to safety. Santucho, Gorriarán, and Menna of the ERP, Osatinsky and Quieto of the FAR, and the Montonero Fernando Vaca Narvaja got to Allende's Chile, then flew on to Cuba days later, and finally returned clandestinely to Argentina. But because of the transport difficulties, a second group of nineteen guerrillas did not arrive at Trelew until a few minutes after their leaders' plane had taken off. They were surrounded, obliged to surrender, and then taken to the Admiral Zar naval base. There, at 3.30 a.m. on 22 August, the infamous 'Trelew Massacre' took place, in which the ERP lost eleven members, including Santucho's wife Ana María Villarreal, and the FAR three. The Montoneros lost the teacher (and wife of Fernando Vaca Narvaja) Susana Lesgart, and the agronomy student Mariano Pujadas. Lesgart had commanded the Montoneros' Tucumán region in 1971, Pujadas had been a builder of the organization in Córdoba, and both had participated in the takeover of La Calera. Only three of the nineteen, though badly wounded, survived the illegal executions allegedly carried out by Captain Luis Emilio Sosa and Lieutenant Roberto Guillermo Bravo, thanks to the arrival on the scene of officers alien to the massacre plan. The three included twenty-eight-year-old chemical engineer Ricardo Haidar of the Montoneros.[41]

Back in Buenos Aires, meanwhile, a further Montonero founder met his death. On 16 August, conscious of the need to do something to prevent the impending massacre, Carlos Capuano Martínez, by now a Buenos Aires regional leader, ventured into the Capital, breaking his own security rules in so doing. He was shot dead when three policemen entered a Barracas bar where he was chatting with a small number of Montonero colleagues. Jorge Escribano and Gerardo Burgos also lost their lives during the final months of military rule, as did the more senior José Enrique Carral. He had been

[41] For accounts of the whole episode, including the survivors' testimonies, see Francisco Urondo, *La patria fusilada* (Buenos Aires: Ediciones de Crisis, 1973); and Tomás Eloy Martínez, *La pasión según Trelew* (Buenos Aires: Granica Editor, 1973).

sacked as a railway worker in 1970, had joined the Montoneros late in 1971, and had risen to the rank of *comandante*, but his life as an urban guerrilla ended bathetically: Carral was cornered and killed in Lanús by policemen who arrived while he was changing the number plates on a stolen car in February 1973.[42]

Persisting Catholic influence did much to shield many Montoneros from fears that they might meet with similar fates. In Montonero literature, guerrillas were presented as heroic 'sons of the people' who 'fell', rather than died, and were then awarded martyr status. A later epitaph for Capuano Martínez exemplified the glorification of the guerrilla fighter:

> He knew that if he died, it would be at the hands of the enemies of the people, of the enemies of Peronism, which is the most beautiful form of dying. It makes the comrades proud; it distresses our hearts, but makes us happy to know that sacrifice is no mere gesture but a form of life. Just as Evita, the owner of our revolutionary tenderness, would have wanted it . . . You incarnated, little Carlos Capuano Martínez, standing upright with gun in hand in the midst of this Peronist Revolution, the purest essence of our people.[43]

Of course these tributes were nothing new to guerrilla literature, but under the authorship of the Montoneros their quasi-religious conceptions were heavily accentuated. The essential ingredients of their homages were an assertion of the Peronist 'authenticity' of the deceased, some reference to his or her valour, and the notion that to sacrifice one's life for the popular cause would guarantee one a kind of metaphysical existence among 'the people' long after physical death. It mattered not whether these elements were congruent with biographical facts. Of Raquel Liliana Gelín, Alberto Camps's girlfriend, the Montoneros posthumously wrote: 'She fell fighting. Machine-gun in hand. And the people cried . . . Today Liliana, the little Montonero virgin, daughter of Evita, has become [part of the] people.'[44] This was hardly an appropriate tribute for a twenty-one-year-old student, unheard of before her death, who belonged to the FAR, and

---

[42] On Carral, see 'Paco: dió la vida por Perón', *El Descamisado*, no. 40 (19 February 1974), p. 23.

[43] 'Carlos Capuano Martínez, por compañero, por peronista, por montonero, ya sos entraña de tu pueblo', *La Causa Peronista*, no. 7 (20 August 1974), pp. 22-3.

[44] 'Fuiste hija de Evita', *El Descamisado*, no. 36 (22 January 1974), p. 15.

was killed not only three years before it merged with the Montoneros but several months before it even declared itself Peronist.

The Montoneros' readiness to spill their own blood in fighting for a popular cause does not, alone, explain why such an impressive amount of popular support and sympathy came snowballing towards them during and after the second half of 1972. What counted above all here was a decisive strategic turn towards mass political activity as the Montoneros disabused themselves of the idea that Peronism would never be allowed to regain power by electoral means. When asked at a Trelew press conference, prior to surrender, why it was that the guerrillas viewed armed struggle as their only option, Mariano Pujadas had replied: 'the regime is always going to lay some trap... because that is needed by the dominant classes if they are to maintain their privileged position. There will always be some trap laid while the present capitalist system exists, in order to prevent the accession to power of governments which represent popular interests'.[45] After August, however, as Perón's return visit from 17 November to 14 December drew near, the Montoneros re-evaluated the electoral possibility and began to grasp the political realities of the situation. While not totally abandoning their armed struggle, maintaining it in order to indicate to the generals what they could expect if the scheduled elections were cancelled, the Montoneros now redirected most of their energies towards mass work in the Perón Return Campaign and then in the election campaign itself.

PROMOTION OF THE PERONIST YOUTH

The key vehicle for their turn towards the mass movements was the Peronist Youth (JP), within which, after years of disunity and anarchy, strenuous efforts were made from mid-1971 to secure unity and create a dynamic mobilizing, agitational, and organizational force. For this purpose, Perón accepted the nominations of Francisco Julián Licastro, a former lieutenant who had left the Army after publicly

---

[45] Pujadas, quoted in Eloy Martínez, p. 72.

applauding the *Cordobazo*, and Rodolfo Galimberti, leader of the Argentine Youth for National Emancipation (JAEN), as youth representatives on the Superior Council of the National Justicialist Movement. Both had been proposed by the youth groups, but only Galimberti enjoyed widespread support, and he was a much-coveted prize for the Montoneros when recruited in 1972. Through discussions and joint mobilizations, Galimberti was able to construct a very loose alliance of the various youth groups. Political and ideological friction remained, to resurface with a vengeance in 1973-4, but in 1972 and early 1973 joint work for the Return and election campaigns proved feasible. Structurally, the product was not a single Peronist Youth, but the process did give rise to the spectacular growth of one tendency which came to dwarf all the others. This was the pro-Montonero *Juventud Peronista (Regionales)*, formed in the middle of 1972, which thrived on account of both the tactical sponsorship of Galimberti by Cámpora and Perón, and the prestige acquired by the Montoneros through their operations and mergers. Conditional support was also forthcoming from the new Justicialist Party General Secretary, Juan Manuel Abal Medina, the non-Montonero brother of Fernando Luis, whom Perón appointed in November 1972 to revitalize the national leadership.

Beginning in February 1972 the increasingly Montonero-orientated Peronist Youth held a series of unity and campaign rallies at which attendances leapt from 5,000 to almost 100,000 in just twelve months. So spectacular was the youth revival and so widespread was Peronist Youth identification with the 'special formations' that when crowds at a 9 June rally in the Argentine Boxing Federation stadium chanted 'FAR and Montoneros are our comrades', Héctor Cámpora felt moved to reply: 'Your comrades are also mine'.[46] By the final months of 1972, the young Peronists had clearly become the protagonists of the Peronist election campaign. After momentarily denouncing the Cámpora-Solano Lima ticket for President and Vice-President as 'treason', feeling that Perón himself should stand, the pro-Montonero JP coined the slogan, 'Cámpora in government, Perón in power',

[46] Cámpora, quoted in 'Soy leal, total, incondicional a Perón', *El Descamisado*, no. 9 (17 July 1973), p. 12.

For the Return of Perón 121

and saw it immediately adopted by the FREJULI alliance as a whole. It was JP stewards who marshalled the 100,000 or so Peronists who took over the area around Perón's Vicente López residence during his November visit, and who decorated nearby walls with such inscriptions as 'St. Perón Neighbourhood', 'Liberated Zone', 'Perón Street', 'Neighbourhood Taken Over', and 'Government House This Way'.

Though greatly scaled down, armed activity also found its way into the electoral campaign. In a 26 December assassination attempt the Montoneros wounded Luis Guerrero, general secretary of the Avellaneda branch of the Metalworkers' Union. Guerrero, who stood on the Peronist Right, had incurred Perón's wrath by disregarding his orders and getting himself nominated as candidate for the Buenos Aires provincial vice-governorship, as running mate to the wealthy right-wing Peronist landowner, Manuel de Anchorena. The attack, coupled with widespread Peronist opposition to the ticket, persuaded Anchorena and Guerrero to step down but hardly endeared the Montoneros to trade union leaders. Nor did Galimberti's speeches at JP rallies, in which he openly threatened the trade union bureaucracy with extinction: 'We're going to stamp on them like cockroaches,' he promised in February 1972.[47]

As the seven years of military rule drew to a close, the Montoneros were able to display a mobilization capacity running into tens of thousands, but real organizational strength at grass-roots level still eluded them, as did trade union support. The absence of the latter had been the Achilles' heel of the Montoneros ever since 1970, when the CGT had condemned Aramburu's abduction as 'foreign-inspired'.[48] Having selected their name and their targets more intelligently than the other guerrilla organizations, and above all because they were more pragmatic and more political than the others, the Montoneros ended this period as the leading Peronist 'special formation'. But the fact that their guerrilla activities had never been more than, at best, tangentially linked to labour struggles had not helped to overcome the guerrilla-trade union divide — a divide dictated by the rebel security

[47] The key source on the JP revival is Juan Carlos Dante Gullo, 'El país se pregunta: ¿qué es la Juventud Peronista?', ibid., no. 8 (10 July 1973), pp. 10-13.
[48] *Buenos Aires Herald*, 3 June 1970.

requirements of anonymity and isolation, and moreover a class divide separating predominantly middle-class fighters from a generally reformist working class. Only by turning to political campaigning towards the end of 1972 did the Montoneros really break out of their social quarantine in a big way, yet their persistent declamation of union leaders still alienated large numbers of workers.

Perón perceived far more clearly than the Montoneros the limitations of urban guerrilla warfare as a revolutionary method. He sponsored his 'special formations' knowing full well that, while they were harassing the military regime and encouraging it to give way, they were incapable of organizing mass support in such a way as to guarantee that the Peronist restoration would indeed lead to the establishment of their espoused *Patria Socialista*.[49] Paying homage to Capuano Martínez, he wrote: 'All those who struggle for the liberation are our allies and friends. What matter are not the ideological differences but the method and form of this struggle against the common enemy.'[50] The Youth and armed organizations, including the powerful Guevarist ERP, served as battering rams to prise open the defences of the military regime. But once the garrison was occupied, it was the blue and white Argentine flag, rather than one with red trimming, which was raised over the bastion. Once they had served his purpose, Perón's 'marvellous Youth' of yesteryear were soon to be vilified by their leader as 'infiltrators' and 'mercenaries'.

---

[49] This was recognized by Ramón Torres Molina, a Villa Devoto inmate since 1969, who in January 1971 wrote a critique of the urban guerrilla, pointing out that: 'A resistance war exhausts the dictatorship politically and demonstrates its unpopularity, but tends to create political solutions which are not those of the guerrillas themselves. Through urban guerrilla struggle one can force the dictatorship to concede elections. But such a tactical guerrilla triumph would be a strategic defeat, since it would push perspectives for the seizure of power into the distance. ... The generals of the dictatorship know that the counter-insurgency measure par excellence is elections' ['La etapa actual de las guerrillas argentinas', *Cristianismo y Revolución*, no. 29 (June 1971), pp. 17-19]. Torres Molina's prescient words were lost on the Montoneros.

[50] Perón, quoted in 'En nuestro movimiento decide el pueblo, aquí deciden ustedes', *La Causa Peronista*, no. 7 (20 August 1974), pp. 16-19.

4
Coming up for Air
(1973–1974)

¿Qué pasa, qué pasa, qué pasa general? está lleno de gorilas el gobierno popular[1]

THE RETURN OF PERONISM AND THE ADVANCE OF THE PERONIST LEFT

A carnival atmosphere pervaded the centre of Buenos Aires on 25 May 1973 as Héctor Cámpora was formally inaugurated as President of the Argentine Republic. After 18 years of proscription, Peronism returned to office and hundreds of thousands effusively rejoiced. Even the formalities, conducted in the Congress building, were imbued with something of the popular mood of that historic day, thanks to the presence at the swearing-in ceremony of the Presidents of Chile and Cuba, Salvador Allende and Osvaldo Dorticós. Outside, over half a million *peronistas* filled *Plaza Congreso*, the central *Plaza de Mayo* in front of Government House, and the intervening 14 blocks of *Avenida de Mayo*. The heart of Buenos Aires pulsated to chants of 'se van, se van, y nunca volverán' (they're going, they're going, never to return), as jubilant crowds celebrated the departure of the outcast military.[2]

Voices were raised against the soldiers, the police, and symbols of US involvement in Argentina. As if drunk on the triumphal euphoria, some of the younger revellers even attempted to storm the Army Command HQ, and later the dominating ITT-owned Sheraton Hotel; both buildings were stoned by their repulsed assailants. The military were denied the sedate, anaemic rites which they had so meticulously planned: demonstrators refused to allow the Navy Engineering

---

[1] Montonero question chanted at Perón during the main 1974 May Day rally: 'What's going on, General? Why is the popular government full of *gorilas*?'.

[2] The account of the 25 May 1973 events is based upon Eduardo Marín, 'El 25 de mayo de 1973: Cámpora al gobierno', *Transformaciones en el Tercer Mundo*, no. 24 (1974); the *Buenos Aires Herald*, 26-7 May 1973; and *El Descamisado*, no. 2 (29 May 1973), *passim*.

School band to perform; a military march was abandoned after the marchers had been surrounded by crowds and their route occupied; marine infantrymen lining *Avenida de Mayo* had to be protected by the police – and eventually by a cordon of Peronist Youth stewards – from the anger of a bellicose throng; and Lanusse was personally abused and spat upon. Secretary of State William Rogers, representative of Richard M. Nixon, was declared *persona non grata* by demonstrators who blocked the path of his car en route from Congress to the *Casa Rosada* (the pink Government House); with anti-imperialist slogans dinning in his ears, a shaken Rogers was obliged to beat a hasty retreat to the United States Embassy. For almost a day the huge Peronist crowds savoured their anticipation of popular power and experienced an exquisite sensation of 'liberation', while the military seethed and sulked, taking mental snapshots of what they perceived as 'mob rule' and anarchy. The illusion of power was not to last, but the snapshots were: they were to reappear and feature remarkably prominently as illustrations in the speeches of the generals of the post-1976 Videla regime.

But the day itself belonged to the *peronistas*, above all to the left-wing and popular sectors of the Movement. Giant Montonero and FAR banners decorated *Plaza de Mayo*, complemented by the black-and-red standards of the JP. A formidable Montonero banner hung down in front of the box of honour. And even at the *Casa Rosada*, the police were 'persuaded' by the massive popular presence to relinquish control over the entrances and exits to JP stewards. 'Give a half turn and go, we are going to decide who comes in here', JP leader Juan Carlos Dante Gullo told Lt.-Col. Perdini . . . and the Lt.-Col. went. To the extent that public order existed, it was maintained by Peronist Youth officials who, in turn, took their cue from commanders of the 'special formations' like Horacio Mendizábal, the most senior Montonero present in the *Plaza*.

Already, though, there was tension in the air. Fistfights broke out between labour groups chanting demands for a *Patria Peronista* and youngsters demanding a *Patria Socialista*. Repression was also present: in response to stone-throwing, insults, and the disarming of isolated policemen by demonstrators, the security forces wounded at least one dozen people; and more repression was to follow later that night.[3]

For the Montoneros and other armed organizations, the happiest memory of that 25 May was the liberation of their guerrilla colleagues, amnestied as promised by the new Government. From Rawson, Villa Devoto, Córdoba, Resistencia, Chaco, Salta, and Ezeiza, the political prisoners were released, to receive tremendous welcomes from their relatives, friends, and comrades. The solidarity which had bound guerrilla inmates of different organizations together, however, disappeared for many along with the adversity that had engendered it. Immediately, divisions between Peronist and Guevarist combatants deepened, the latter full of distrust for the Government and scepticism over the popular glee. While the pro-Montonero JP considered its task to be merely one of 'guaranteeing' the implementation of the amnesty pledge, via a march to Villa Devoto Prison and a vigil there on the night of Friday 25th, the Guevarist ERP regarded arms as the only means of securing their demands: in April they had kidnapped a retired chief of Naval Intelligence, Francisco Alemán, and a border guard colonel, Jacobo Nasif, in an effort to exchange them for thirty of their fellow guerrillas.[4] In the event the new Government respected its electoral mandate and released all the political prisoners, including over 200 who had taken over their Villa Devoto cell-block on the eve of Cámpora's installation. Nevertheless, after most of the 10,000-plus, mainly JP, demonstrators had dispersed from the prison environs, delighted with the release of Montoneros such as Maguid,[5] Haidar, and Roqué, not to mention FAR peronalities Berger, Camps, and the poet Francisco

---

[3] Ibid.

[4] Nasif was released by the ERP on 5 June after they had 'verified that political prisoners released by the Government are in good health'; Alemán, after sixty-eight days in captivity, was set free on 7 June following the publication and broadcast of a 'confession' in which he referred to the 1966–73 regime as a dictatorship. See the *Buenos Aires Herald*, 6 and 9 June 1973.

[5] Maguid broke with the Montoneros after his release from prison, and opted for a more orthodox line. He attended the Perón-Youth meetings of early 1974 which the Montoneros boycotted. This did not however prevent him from being kidnapped, allegedly by Argentine security agents, while an exile in Peru in 1977. See *Noticias de Argentina*, np, no. 17 (8–15 October 1979).

Urondo,[6] the largely Guevarist remnant was determined not to be completely upstaged by the Peronists. Spurred on by rumours that seventy-eight 'prisoners of war' were still inside the jail, they tried to take it by storm, only to encounter the fury of Itaka rifles, gas grenades, and machine-guns, turned against them by guards and policemen. Oscar Lysak of the Peronist Youth and Carlos Sfeir of Communist Vanguard (VC) were killed and twenty others wounded in this unnecessary *Devotazo*.[7]

Despite this tragic epilogue to an important day in Argentine history, the turn of political events was now quite favourable to the Montoneros. While the Guevarists persisted with their militarism (thereby ignoring a guerrilla maxim elaborated by their own mentor),[8] the Montoneros took advantage of the opportunity to extend their political influence by concentrating on legal activity and operating on multiple fronts. They now acquired a capacity to mobilize tens and even hundreds of thousands of people, yet they still lacked grass roots organizational strength, and this, as much as the opposition of the Political, Trade Union, and Women's Branches of the Peronist Movement, rendered the JP-Montoneros unable to entirely fill the 25 per cent share of political posts that Perón had allocated to the Youth. Had they possessed an independent strategy for gaining power, this would have been relatively unimportant, but since their strategy was one of working through the Peronist Movement both within and outside the Government, conquering as much political territory as possible, this set a strict limitation on their prospects. As *movimientistas*, the Montoneros still depended upon Perón and his Movement being truly revolutionary, for their means of political advancement — a purge of 'bureaucrats' and 'traitors' from the Movement and its generational rejuvenation as promised by

[6] Haidar, Berger, and Camps, the Trelew survivors, were interviewed by Urondo during the guerrilla take-over of part of Villa Devoto Prison, the result being *La patria fusilada*. Julio Roqué became a member of the Montonero national leadership before meeting his death in May 1977.

[7] On the *Devotazo*, see 'Informe especial', *El Descamisado*, no. 3 (5 June 1973), pp. 12-13.

[8] 'Where a government has come into power through some form of popular vote, fraudulent or not, and maintains at least an appearance of constitutional legality, the guerrilla outbreak cannot be promoted, since the possibilities of peaceful struggle have not yet been exhausted'. — Che Guevara, p. 14.

Perón — were moves which they could press for but not ensure themselves. Meanwhile, the much smaller *alternativista* groups[9] continued to dismiss bourgeois Peronists as 'class enemies', to shun contact with the official bodies of the Movement, and to invest all their energy in the construction of an 'independent working-class alternative': the would-be nucleus of a future workers' party and revolutionary army, but one unprepared to break the umbilical cord fastening itself to Peronism until the workers in general were ready for a break with the Peronist leadership.

The Montoneros clarified their views on the new political process in a document of July 1973, produced with the FAR and entitled 'Build Popular Power'.[10] Here, Argentina was depicted as facing the option of 'Liberation or Dependency', with this issue forcing Argentines to side either with 'the Peronist people and their allies' or 'imperialism and its allies'. The huge, foreign-owned monopolies and the 'industrial, financial, commercial, and agricultural oligarchy' were challenged by 'the working class, including 1½ million unemployed and the marginal sectors, the small urban and rural producers, the great majority of students and intellectuals, and their allies, the medium urban and rural producers and all those who identify with the objectives of liberation'. FREJULI was presented as the political expression of this 'class alliance to confront imperialism', and the most radical aspects of its electoral programme — 'To fight against the monopolies and all forms of dependency', 'To redistribute wealth', 'To nationalize and socialize the economy' — were taken at face value. The authors of the document insisted that working-class leadership of the alliance was the only

[9] The main *alternativista* organs were *Militancia (Peronista para la Liberación)*, a weekly review co-edited by Rodolfo Ortega Peña and Eduardo L. Duhalde until banned in March 1974, and its replacement, *De Frente (con las bases peronistas)*, which was suppressed four months later. The circulation figures of Peronist Left publications provide a rough guide to the level of active support for each tendency: while the Montonero daily *Noticias* (edited by Miguel Bonasso) regularly achieved 150,000 sales and the weekly *El Descamisado* over 100,000 [González Janzen, pp. 219-20], *Militancia* only reached the 40,000 mark and was constantly struggling to survive in a battle against rising publication costs ['Militancia entre el ahogo y la clausura', *Militancia*, no. 38 (28 March 1974), p. 3].

[10] 'Construir el poder popular', *El Descamisado*, no. 4 (12 June 1973), pp. 2-4: a document presented by Firmenich and Quieto during a press conference on 8 June 1973.

guarantee that the programme would be implemented, yet in practice they failed to organize with this objective in mind. Largely because of their unquestioning faith in Perón, they reconciled themselves to the dominance of bourgeois and bureaucratic Peronist sectors for the first year of this Government's life, confident that Perón would sooner or later opt for an unequivocal path, so long as the Peronist Left remained a massive alternative power base. While the stage of National Reconstruction and Liberation was deemed transitional towards 'the national construction of socialism', the presence of Perón and the working class in the Movement militated, so far as the Montoneros and FAR were concerned, in favour of a smooth and rapid passage from one stage to the next. As Montonero leader Mario Firmenich saw it when presenting this document to the public, there was 'no difference between the Peronist Fatherland and the Socialist Fatherland, since the Peronist Movement led by General Perón serves the workers' interests and, for that very reason, the construction of *socialismo nacional* is posed'.[11]

All this rested upon two unfounded premises and one exceedingly shaky one: namely, Perón's alleged conversion to *socialismo nacional*; the suicidal preparedness of the bourgeois and bureaucratic sectors of Peronism to accept radical, working-class leadership; and the possibility of maintaining a broad class alliance in office during the so-called 'national liberation' revolutionary stage. Of these the latter was the most persuasive, but nevertheless antiquated. Argentina's late 1940s economic vitality, which had enabled the first Peronist Government to dispense benefits to both sides of industry, no longer existed. Economic crisis rather than prosperity greeted Peronism upon its return to office in 1973: it inherited a sizable budget deficit and an inflation rate of 6.5 per cent per month (over the 5 months down to March 1973).[12] Moreover, the country soon suffered from the July 1974 EEC decision to close its doors to Argentine meat, which affected 70 per cent of the national meat export trade and thus the trade balance;[13] and from the leap

[11] Ibid.
[12] '30 Meses de camino descendente', *Confirmado*, no. 400 (3-9 December 1975), pp. 52-4.
[13] Pablo Kandel and Mario Monteverde, *Entorno y caída* (Buenos Aires: Editorial Planeta Argentina, 1976), p. 26.

in world oil prices which hit her both directly, as an oil importer (though not a major one), and indirectly, through the effect of the rise on her industrial imports. Under these conditions, the Peronist economic development project and the governing alliance itself soon began to disintegrate. In thirty-four months of office, Peronism resorted to six different Economy Ministers yet could not halt the economic decline nor satisfy initially-sympathetic employers and workers simultaneously. Those months witnessed not only the first ever general strike against a Peronist government but also the first real employers' strike in Argentine history; and each clearly undermined Peronism's historic claim as harmonizer of the interests of labour and capital.

The inability of Peronism unitedly to undertake a series of national development tasks and radically to redistribute national income was something which the *alternativistas* understood far better than the *movimientistas*. They, like the Guevarist ERP, quickly recognized that in this case 'national reconstruction' signified nothing more than a national reconstruction of capitalism, which, after early concessions to the workers, would entail attempted wage freezes and the use of repression in the interests of capital accumulation and social order. But prescient analyses brought neither Rank-and-File Peronism nor the ERP much in the way of recruitment success. The ERP's conviction that 'as the people alone cannot face the army in the streets, guerrilla action must continue'[14] only reinforced their own social isolation through inflexibility. At the same time, neither they nor Rank-and-File Peronism could themselves do a lot to undermine popular illusions in Perón and Peronism, given their tremendous strength and the superficially-apparent success of Peronist economics during the first twelve months. Rather than being attributable to the intrinsic merits of their own programmatic documents, the spectacular Montonero advance in these years owed far more to the fact that their political formulae were infused with the prevalent popular myths, misconceptions, and illusions of the time, while possessing for students the attraction of a certain internal logical consistency. Later, in an internal document of

[14] ERP C-in-C Mario Roberto Santucho, at guerrilla press conference reported in the *Buenos Aires Herald*, 9 June 1973.

September 1977, the Montoneros were to admit the political failure of *movimientismo* while, pointing to its popularity, designating it, in an original manner, as the 'correct deviation' for the 1973-4 political situation![15]

Indeed the Montoneros' *movimientismo* did, for a while, earn them fame and fortune, helping them to become indisputably Argentina's largest radical force. During Cámpora's brief forty-nine-day Presidency, before he resigned so as to enable Perón to take the helm in person, the political complexion of the Government reflected the diversity of the Peronist Movement relatively accurately. Looking at the more important positions, a leading representative of the monopolistic sector of the national bourgeoisie, José Ber Gelbard, took control of the Economy Ministry; the Labour Ministry was awarded to Ricardo Otero of the Metalworkers Union; and the ultra-Right, in the sinister guise of Perón's private secretary, José López Rega, established a base at the head of the Social Welfare Ministry. For their part, the Peronist Left acquired a degree of influence for a little more than a month in the Foreign Office, where the Foreign Minister, Juan Carlos Puig, and his deputy, Jorge Alberto Vázquez, facilitated the establishment of diplomatic relations with Cuba, North Vietnam, and North Korea; in the Education Ministry, with Jorge Taiana in charge for considerably longer; and above all in the Ministry of the Interior.

Revolutionary nationalist aspirations for a new alignment of Argentina with Chile, Panama, Peru, and Cuba did not get much further than a speech on 21 June by Vázquez at an Organization of American States meeting in Lima, during which he called for the admission of Cuba. Though Argentina's diplomatic and trading links were diversified, the agreements reached with Communist Party States owed more to EEC trade restrictions than to ideological preferences.[16] This

---

[15] 'Informe del Consejo Nacional del Partido Montonero, septiembre de 1977', p. 5.

[16] On account of European trade restrictions, the EEC's share of Argentine exports fell from 60 per cent to just 37 per cent between 1960-80, and these figures were cited by Videla's Economy Minister, José Alfredo Martínez de Hoz, when explaining to US businessmen the growing volume of Argentine trade with the USSR and China. See *La Nación, Edición Internacional*, 5 May 1980. On the decreasing importance of nationalism in Argentine foreign policy after 1974, see Milenky, *passim*.

being so, they were welcomed or accepted by all sectors of Peronism and even by foreign capital: the establishment of commercial relations with Cuba, for instance, enabled US automobile subsidiaries operating in Argentina to by-pass the official US economic boycott of the Caribbean island. Meanwhile, at the Education Ministry, Taiana's frequent condemnations of student faculty occupations did much to qualify Peronist Left support for him.

The minister closest to the Montoneros was undoubtedly Esteban Righi in the Ministry of the Interior. True, he also went along with a call for an end to the occupations of study- and work-places which characterized the early heady days under Cámpora, but he was also instrumental in shepherding the amnesty bill through Congress, in securing the rapid release of the political prisoners, and in abolishing repressive State organs. On being appointed, he is reputed to have marched into the Federal Police headquarters, accompanied by leather-jacketed Montonero activists, and to have ordered policemen there to 'stand up for the Montonero combatants' whom they had been persecuting for the last three years.[17] It was Righi who was responsible for the dissolution of the Department for Anti-Democratic Information (DIPA), which had witch-hunted the Left, and for the destruction of its files. Later, he delivered an eloquent speech to a gathering of police officers, in which he reprimanded them for their more nefarious activities and ordered them to desist from torture and death-squad pastimes. Not surprisingly, he was the main target of Rightist attacks on the Cámpora administration: newspaper headlines such as 'The Minister of the Interior has still not resigned'[18] appeared throughout his spell in office, which ended with the resignation of Cámpora. Soon afterwards, he was forced to flee the country, to become an exile in Mexico.

Outside the Federal Government, Montonero influence was felt in the National Congress, in provincial administrations, and in the universities. There were only eight Montonero deputies in the 145-strong FREJULI bloc in the Chamber of Deputies: Armando Croatto, Santiago Díaz Ortiz, Jorge Glellel, Aníbal Iturrieta, Carlos Kunkel, Diego Muñiz Barreto,

[17] Personal interview with a Montonero, Buenos Aires, 16 November 1975.
[18] 'Righi: el nuevo orden revolucionario', *Militancia*, no. 5 (12 July 1973), p. 7.

Roberto Vidaña, and Rodolfo Vittar.[19] They all made radical speeches and urged investigation of cases of torture and para-police activity, but could not ensure the implementation of FREJULI's electoral pledges on agrarian reform, socialization, and workers' participation,[20] the eight's effectiveness being greatly reduced by their acceptance of bloc discipline.

Montonero nominees also gained some fifty posts in provincial governments, as well as seats in local legislatures and governments, but were in all places outnumbered by successful candidates nominated by the trade union and other less radical sections of the Movement. Several provincial governors lent their vacillating support to the *movimientista* Peronist Left, or at least tolerated its presence in their administrations, the most sympathetic being Oscar Bidegain (Buenos Aires), Alberto Martínez Baca (Mendoza), Jorge Cepernic (Santa Cruz), Miguel Ragone (Salta), and Ricardo Obregón Cano (Córdoba). The Governors of Santa Cruz and Córdoba had already, by 1973, done much to merit tactical Peronist Left sponsorship, but others made their overtures to the Montonero tendency for largely pragmatic reasons: like Cámpora, they lacked solid bases of support in the Movement. All were under attack from the empire-building trade union barons and the Peronist Right, received little or

[19] Croatto went on to take charge of Montonero trade union work in the late 1970s before being killed in an ambush in September 1979. Kunkel was arrested in September 1975. Muñiz Barreto, of wealthy, anti-Peronist origin, had previously been a legal advisor to the Onganía regime [See Roberto Roth, *Los años de Onganía* (Buenos Aires: Ediciones La Campana, 1980), pp. 82-4]. According to Rodolfo Walsh's Open Letter of March 1977, he was abducted and then killed in a detention camp after the 1976 military coup. Vittar's political evolution went in the opposite direction: following his resignation from Congress, he left the Montoneros to join a new but unsuccessful Peronist Youth group created by Juan Manuel Abal Medina (sacked as General Secretary of the Justicialist Party in May 1974); later, after the 1976 coup, he became identified with the political ambitions of Navy C-in-C, Admiral Emilio Massera.

[20] As summarized in the *Buenos Aires Herald* of 13 March 1973, the March 1973 FREJULI programme promised the establishment of diplomatic relations with Cuba, N. Vietnam, and N. Korea; a general wage rise; an amnesty for political prisoners; nationalization of banking deposits and foreign trade; measures to support local industry; agrarian reform — 'the land must be for those who work it and who produce, not (for those who use it) as an investment or for speculation'; and extensive socialization of the economy through State take-overs of industries whose activities 'imply monopolistic power and/or strategic decisions'. For the full programme, see Héctor Cámpora, *La revolución peronista* (Buenos Aires: Editorial Universitaria de Buenos Aires, 1973), pp. 7-67.

no support from either Juan or Isabel Perón, and were eventually ousted by a mixture of Federal *intervenciones* (Mendoza, Formosa, Santa Cruz), forced resignations (Buenos Aires, Catamarca), a mysterious plane crash (Misiones), and a fascist-inspired police coup (Córdoba). Obregón Cano's popular working-class Vice-Governor, Atilio López, and Miguel Ragone were later assassinated by para-State death squads. Several of the surviving ex-governors, though, went on to throw in their lot completely with the Montoneros, as did Ricardo Omar Sapag, much to the embarrassment of his father, Felipe Sapag, Governor of Neuquén.[21]

The pattern of initial Peronist Left gains, gradually undermined as right-wing and trade union representatives became more and more dominant in the Government, also asserted itself in higher education. Without doubt the most treasured trophy awarded to the *movimientista* Left under Cámpora was the University of Buenos Aires, where former leading Communist Party member and prolific nationalist historian Rodolfo Puiggrós was named *interventor* to prepare the way for reforms. Assisted by sympathetic new faculty deans, Puiggrós as Rector set out to transform the traditionally Liberal institution into a 'National and Popular University of Buenos Aires': lecturers who had backed the previous military regime or who were 'agents of companies that deform the national historical process'[22] were dismissed; the police were ordered off the campus, and freedom of expression was granted to student political groups; lecturers, students, and non-academic staff began to participate in the running of their university; courses such as 'History of the Struggles of the Argentine People for their Emancipation' were introduced; medical facilities and legal aid centres were established by the relevant faculties in poor districts, in an effort to make the university serve ordinary people; and entrance restrictions were lifted.[23] The University of Buenos Aires, and to a lesser

[21] Ricardo Sapag's political loyalties came to light in December 1975 when he participated in a guerrilla bid to kidnap or assassinate Brig. Major Aly Luis Ipres Corbat, 4th in the Air Force hierarchy. Sapag was his aide-de-camp at the time, and escaped with other attackers, leaving Corbat gravely wounded by machine-gun fire. Sapag Sr. resigned a day later.

[22] 'Puiggrós y el avance del pueblo', interview with Puiggrós, *Militancia*, no. 5 (12 July 1973), pp. 16-20.

[23] For a full list of the Puiggrós reforms, see his book, *La universidad del pueblo* (Buenos Aires: Editorial Crisis, 1974), pp. 97-114.

extent those of the Interior, thus underwent some fundamental changes. It became less of an 'island', more democratic, and more involved in plans for national development. However, even left-wing academics baulked at the effects of unrestricted entry: the student population of this single university grew from 80,000 early in 1973 to 237,000 by 1975, with student-lecturer ratios reaching 300:1![24]

For their political work in this period, the Montoneros built front organizations adapted to the needs of each of the major social movements. The JP (*Regionales*), which now concentrated on activity at *barrio* or neighbourhood level, was joined by the Peronist University Youth (JUP), Peronist Working Youth (JTP), Secondary Students Union (UES), Peronist Shanty-Town Dwellers Movement (MVP), the Evita Group of the Feminine Branch (AE), and the Peronist Tenants Movement (MIP),[25] and collectively these organizations became known as the *Tendencia Revolucionaria*, or Revolutionary Tendency of the Peronist Movement.

It was through these organizations that the Montoneros mobilized impressive numbers of people for the rallies and demonstrations of 1973-4, as well as for activity during the September 1973 presidential election campaign. On more than half a dozen occasions, they achieved attendances of

[24] Figures from J. Monahan, 'I agreed to teach'; Jonathan Kendell, 'I cannot imagine what would happen if the police left', *Times Higher Education Supplement*, 7 January 1977; and 'Universidad: o del pueblo o de nadie', *El Descamisado*, no. 45 (26 March 1974), pp. 22-4.
[25] Of the latter four organizations, not analysed in the text, the MVP and UES were the largest. Four thousand people attended an MVP rally in August 1973, and it later claimed the support of 450 *villas miserias* nationally ['Las villas triunfarán', *El Descamisado*, no. 43 (12 March 1974), pp. 12-14]. However, 'lumpenproletarians' were just as likely to support the Right as the Left, and the shanty towns were certainly a source of recruits for the ultra-Right Organizational Command of Alberto Brito Lima. The MIP, which organized slum dwellers, never managed to tempt more than 500 people to a meeting, and its potential social base was weak anyway. The UES was large enough to acquire, as did the JP, JUP, and JTP, a regional structure, but its stronghold remained Buenos Aires and especially that hot-bed of school-student militancy, the *Colegio Nacional*, which was to be occupied by dozens of policemen following the 1976 coup. Finally, the Evita Group failed in its attempts to capture the small Feminine Branch of the Peronist Movement and to mobilize large numbers of women. In part, this can be attributed to over-concentration upon a single issue, described by Firmenich as 'the greatest demand of the Argentine woman, which is the greatest demand of the Argentine working class: the repatriation of our standard-bearer Evita'. ['Palabras de Firmenich', *Militancia*, no. 37 (14 March 1974), pp. 37-42.]

50-150,000 people, and even surpassed such figures on the historic occasion of Perón's definitive homecoming of 20 June 1973: though estimates of the numbers who flocked to Ezeiza Airport ranged wildly between 1½-4m people, the Tendency certainly mobilized at least half of them. Outside Buenos Aires, the crowds were of course smaller, yet still commensurate with Federal Capital attendances if city population differences are taken into account.[26] And whenever rival youth groups sponsored by the Peronist Right or by the labour bureaucracy attempted to compete, their convocational achievements were always exceeded by the Tendency by factors of at least six.[27]

On one occasion, on 31 August 1973, when there was a huge Peronist march past the CGT headquarters to endorse the presidential candidature of Perón, the union leaders and the Montoneros gained the opportunity to openly and directly compete in the numbers game, in full view of Perón. The result in no way discredited the Tendency's contingents: whereas they took 162 minutes to pass the review stand, the CGT-mobilized columns took 165 minutes (according to the JP, walking more slowly!) and two non-Tendency youth groups just eleven minutes together. The CGT had been preparing for a month, had allegedly spent 300,000 dollars on the event, and had hundreds of buses laid on at factory gates; the Tendency had only decided to participate on 28 August and had managed to mobilize their 150,000 marchers in just two days.[28]

---

[26] The largest rally in the Interior was held on 29 May 1973, when 40,000 celebrated the fourth anniversary of the *Cordobazo* in Córdoba, but turn-outs in the provincial cities generally were of 15,000 or fewer people. All estimated attendances are based upon reports contained in the *Buenos Aires Herald*, *La Nación*, *La Razón*, and *El Descamisado*.

[27] Only 1,200 people attended the largest rally organized by the Peronist Youth of the Argentine Republic (JPRA) in February 1974 in Avellaneda; and while 15,000 were attending a pro-Montonero JP 3rd Region rally on 17 October 1973 in Córdoba, the combined forces of the Peronist Right were only able to muster one-tenth of that number for a rival event in the same city. On the trade-union front, when the JTP competed with the pro-bureaucracy Peronist Trade Union Youth (JSP), it triumphed just as impressively: the JSP mobilized 3,000 supporters on 31 October 1973, the JTP 20,000 three days later.

[28] See the special supplement to *El Descamisado*, no. 16 (4 September 1973) and the report in *La Razón*, 1 September 1973. The time-keepers from each publication produced almost identical time-sheets.

LIMITATIONS OF THE REVOLUTIONARY TENDENCY

The tragedy for the Tendency was that Perón was in no way impressed by its massiveness. He had used the Youth and the guerrilla formations as spearheads in the battles against the 1966-73 stratocracy, then used them to do most of the March and September 1973 election work, and was finally in a position to dispense with their services. Once back in power, Perón, while ideally seeking to keep his Movement united, was not bent upon retaining the adhesion of the radicalized wing *at all costs*, so long as he could retain the support of, or at least control, the labour movement. When it became clear that, in spite of their frequent preparedness to compromise, the Tendency could not be 'domesticated', Perón's interest lay not in making concessions aimed at the preservation of an increasingly unrealistic unity, but rather in driving the Left out of his Movement in an attempt to isolate the 'virus' of socialism. In February 1974, he displayed his contempt for the Left when he told right-wing youth groups linked to the labour bureaucracy that he preferred 'an honest leader with ten people behind him to a dishonest one with 10,000';[29] and in June, he proceeded simply to close down the whole Youth Branch, after explaining that he did not want 'to take the apple of discord into the Movement'.[30] If shows of popular support were needed again, Perón's personal pull could, with the assistance of the labour apparatus, still be relied upon to fill *Plaza de Mayo*. Despite a Tendency boycott, Perón's last public appearance in the *Plaza* on 12 June 1974 was witnessed by a crowd of 60-100,000, even if they did have to be prodded: Perón had threatened to resign, and the CGT had decreed a ten-hour strike beginning mid-morning so as to be able to transport workers straight from their work-places to the rally.

Numbers, though, were of lessening significance in the internal Peronist power struggles once Perón had returned to the Presidency; street mobilizations, without organizational and economic muscle to back them up, risked becoming sheer exhibitionism, yet the Tendency continued to lack

---

[29] Perón, quoted in 'Semana política: entre la definición y la violencia', *Militancia*, no. 35 (21 February 1974), pp. 4-9.

[30] 'Definiciones del general Perón', *El Peronista*, no. 6 (28 May 1974), p. 8.

these crucial reinforcements. Its organizational weakness was a direct result of the inheritance by the front organizations of the elitist practices and bureaucratic-authoritarian structures[31] which had characterized all the special formations, not least the Montoneros. Each front organization had a national leadership, and the larger ones (the JUP, JTP, and UES, as well as the JP itself) regional executives too, but all were chosen by the Montonero leadership instead of by their own rank and file. Rather than develop these fronts as cadre organizations, the Montoneros were highly selective over who was to be 'brought on' and who was merely of use for mobilizations and electioneering. Only the most noticeably capable Peronist youths were picked out for specialized military and political training, to prepare them for their incorporation into the Montoneros. This meant that the huge numbers regularly mobilized by the latter through their agencies could not be legitimately equated with numerical support for a revolutionary political project. Mobilization was not based upon a coherent analysis of Argentine problems, a clearly-defined socialist alternative, or a theory to guide the mobilized along the road from the existing to the new society. They were mobilized, for the most part, around slogans and specific policy stances which were generally unrelated to a global project for societal transformation; and through the emotive appeal of Montonero rallies and marches, with all their colour, chanting, and drum-beating, with their exuberance, their sense of power and solidarity, and their sheer arrogance.

Adhesion to the front organizations often expressed a genuine desire for change, but one which was inarticulate and confused, and remained so: a smallish minority became cadres, capable of leadership, organization, and political initiative, while the vast majority did little more than contribute bodies and voices at the mass events plus stamina and enthusiasm during National Reconstruction social work projects.[32] This state of affairs, not recognized as a problem

[31] After much criticism of these features from other left-wing groups, the JP in January 1974 admitted: 'We are conscious of the fact that our organization is still a long way from being totally democratic.' ['Habla Juventud Peronista', *El Descamisado*, no. 36 (22 January 1974), pp. 4–5].

[32] Typical Peronist Youth projects included street repairs, the building of schools and health units, and the removal of election propaganda from walls. The

by the Montoneros until early 1974, not only meant that a lot of potential political talent was wasted, but also encouraged schisms. In the absence of mechanisms for rank-and-file participation in the elaboration of policy, denied democratic internal means of challenging the leadership, dissident groupings tended to form themselves into rebel factions and then break away or be expelled. Splinters to the Left and to the Right of Montonero orthodoxy emerged in this highly-charged period of political activity.

On the Left, based in the city of Córdoba, 1973 saw the emergence of the short-lived José Sabino Navarro Column, whose leaders included Luis Losada, the Montonero wounded and captured after the occupation of La Calera, and Luis Rodeiro, a survivor of the gunbattle in which Abal Medina and Ramus were slain. Rodeiro became editor of the Column's mouthpiece, *Puro Pueblo*.[33] The tendency failed to grow, for it lacked positive proposals of its own, but its critique of the Montoneros, developed through a series of 'Notes for Militants',[34] was written with the authority of experience. Rejecting the Montoneros' *movimientismo* and their conception of revolutionary stages, the critics attributed the principal weaknesses of their parent organization to the fact that it had been launched 'from above' as a 'response of the radicalized petty bourgeoisie to the general problems of the country', rather than having emerged in response to the direct needs of Argentine labour; armed struggle, lacking labour involvement, had then militarized 'all aspects of life' in the Montoneros, with the result that when they did eventually turn to political activity, this had been hampered by the stifling of dissent and criticism by the bureaucratic military structure.[35]

In turn, all that the Rightist splinter had to offer was an obsequious loyalty to Perón: the *Leal* or Loyalist Tendency,

---

MVP, despite the ministerial opposition of López Rega, attempted to establish self-help schemes in the shanty towns, while the UES early in 1974 mobilized 500 youngsters for *Operativo Güemes*, aimed at helping and organizing people living in the south of Salta Province.

[33] *Puro Pueblo* (later *Puro Pueblo Venceremos*) was launched as a weekly publication in July 1974, but only five issues appeared.

[34] At least five 'Notes for Militants' were issued, of which four were published in *Militancia*, nos. 20, 26, 30 and 35 (October 1973–February 1974).

[35] Montoneros José Sabino Navarro, 'Cartilla para militantes no. 4', *Militancia*, no. 30 (3 January 1974), pp. 20-2.

which broke ranks early in 1974, merely stood for an end to Montonero criticism of Perón. It attracted to its leadership Jorge Obeid, the former head of the JP 2nd Region (covering Santa Fe and Entre Ríos), but only significantly affected the JUP, and even on the university front its ticket only attracted 350 votes to the JUP's 21,000 in the 1974 University of Buenos Aires student elections.[36] Both of the breakaway groups faded into oblivion towards the end of 1974, but their fleeting existence at least illustrated a fundamental organizational, and basically political, weakness of the Montoneros: namely, their militaristic lack of any forms of internal democracy whereby differences could be resolved. Dissent was equated with treason, criticism with hostility; minority groups were regarded as threats to be exorcized by means of ostracism and expulsion, never through the strength of political argumentation.

Even more serious a problem for the Montoneros was the economic weakness of the Revolutionary Tendency, something which derived from its social composition. The Peronist Government was susceptible to the pressures of those wielding economic power, as the mid-1975 general strike, which cost over 800m dollars in lost production,[37] was to demonstrate; but the Tendency's labour group, the JTP, only experienced spectacular growth among non-industrial workers. Though it could muster 20,000 people for a November 1973 rally in Luna Park,[38] though it won control of the State Workers Association (ATE) regional councils in Córdoba, Rosario, and Misiones, and though it won strong positions among the bus drivers (UTA), State Gas workers, and bank employees of Buenos Aires, the JTP never acquired industrial muscle. Providing a rough measure of the JTP's weakness within the labour movement, press stopwatches at the 31 August 1973 CGT demonstration, mentioned above, revealed that whereas the JTP's State Workers and State Gas columns took ten and six minutes respectively to pass the review stand, the blue-collar columns controlled by the labour bureaucracy took far longer: the Metalworkers (UOM) forty minutes, the Car Workers

---

[36] Carta Política, no. 20 (1st week of April 1974), pp. 14–16.
[37] La Opinión, 6 July 1975.
[38] Crowd estimate from El Descamisado, no. 25 (6 November 1973).

(SMATA) thirty-three minutes, and the Power Workers (*Luz y Fuerza*) and Railway Workers (UF) twenty minutes each. Moreover, the sixteen-minute JTP total fell far short of the 146 minutes which it took the rest of the Revolutionary Tendency to march past the CGT headquarters on the same occasion.[39] Even if one takes into account the fact that small JTP groups marched with the official union columns, no reasonable estimate of the social make-up of the Tendency could put the working-class element at more than 20–30 per cent, with students constituting a further 50 per cent, and the remaining 20–30 per cent being other middle-class participants, including school students and professional people. The largest front organization to come under the Montonero umbrella was undoubtedly the Peronist University Youth (JUP), which, making its debut in University of Buenos Aires student elections in 1973, attracted 23,176 votes (44 per cent of the poll) and took control of nine out of thirteen student centres.[40]

Organizational defects and a lack of strategic economic power thus imposed limits on the Montonero Tendency's ability to exert influence within the Peronist Movement and upon the Government, but then so did the Montoneros' own vacillating political behaviour of this period. The latter first came to light in April 1973 when Rodolfo Galimberti was dismissed by Perón from his position as youth delegate, after calling for the creation of a 'people's militia' of workers and students to safeguard Justicialist principles. Though the Peronist Youth leader had initially stated that the question of whether or not it should be armed depended upon developments, when summoned peremptorily to Madrid he began to claim to have been 'misunderstood' and declared that there was absolutely no question of the proposed militia being armed! Successive retreats from the original JP plan eventually

[39] Special supplement to ibid., no. 16; and *La Razón*, 1 September 1973.
[40] In 1972, the Communist Party's 'Reformist' student organization (MOR) had won an easy victory here, with 55.5 per cent of the poll, *Franja Morada* (Leftish Radicals who supported Raúl Alfonsín's *Movimiento de Renovación y Cambio* UCR tendency) coming second; but the Left Peronists had boycotted the election and four-fifths of the students had abstained. Now, *Franja Morada* attracted 21 per cent of the votes and the MOR just 18 per cent. Moreover, the JUP victory was more representative: about 50 per cent of the metropolitan student population voted in 1973, quadrupling the 1972 turn-out. See the *Buenos Aires Herald*, 6 November 1972; and *La Nación*, 4 and 6 December 1973.

led the scheme to signify no more than a youth labour corps, but that did not save Galimberti. He was forced to resign, was withdrawn from public circulation for a year by the Montoneros as if he were in disgrace, and had to suffer the humiliation of the JP leadership, quite hypocritically, publicly endorsing Perón's decision. It condemned Galimberti for attempting to introduce 'extreme left-wing policies' into the Movement, and accused him of 'infantilism and a certain elitism'.[41]

This set the keynote for the Revolutionary Tendency's reactions to successive decisions by Perón which favoured the less radical sectors of his Movement. Their criticisms of Perón-sponsored legislation did not, they maintained, imply political differences with him, but rather were motivated by fears over how the laws would be implemented by right-wing 'agents' infiltrated in the State apparatus. In the case of each anti-popular piece of legislation, the Montonero Tendency was to claim that the 'spirit' and intentions of the bill were fine but that Perón's intent in promoting it might be subverted by the 'infiltrators'.

Quite uncritically at first, the Montoneros supported the Social Pact, an agreement between the CGT and the national entrepreneurs' General Economic Confederation (CGE) patronized by the new Peronist Government, under which labour was promised an increased share in national income from 35 per cent (the May 1973 level) to 48 per cent (the 1955 level), plus price controls, in return for a two-year suspension of free collective bargaining rights. In Montonero eyes, the Pact was the economic keystone of their illusory 'national liberation front', yet common economic sense dictated that the agreement would soon founder: it was quite unrealistic, given Argentina's economic problems of 1973-4, to expect entrepreneurs to invest in a development enterprise while having their prices frozen and facing steeper wage bills; and it was doubly unrealistic to expect this, as the Montoneros did, from the weakest sectors of the business community, just because they were 'national' and had interests deemed 'objectively' opposed to those of foreign capital. Under the

[41] Juan Carlos Dante Gullo, 'El país se pregunta'; and the *Buenos Aires Herald*, 27 April and 1 May 1973. Gullo took over the JP leadership after Galimberti's dismissal and also, under Cámpora, served as presidential advisor on youth affairs.

circumstances, the only means found by the Peronists to provide cheap credit for the national bourgeoisie and to encourage expansion was to permit the amount of money in circulation to grow astronomically: in their first sixteen months in office, they authorized the printing of 2½ times as much money as had been printed in the previous hundred years![42] Hyper-inflation lay just around the corner.

Economically, the Social Pact was quite utopian; politically, it was potentially repressive, at least in its implications. Under it and associated legislation, strikes could be declared illegal by the Government, obligatory 'conciliation' could be imposed by the Labour Ministry, and unions which organized strikes became liable to suspension or loss of their legal status. Nevertheless, bound by a highly-schematic conception of revolutionary stages, the Montoneros waited several weeks before joining militant labour sectors in criticizing the Pact, and then only to call for 'modifications'. They did not issue a call for the Pact to be 'smashed' until one year after Cámpora's election, when Montonero commander Mario Firmenich told a mass rally in the Atlanta Stadium that a new pact had to be negotiated, so as to give the workers '51 per cent of the power'. In response to insistent crowd chants of 'ALL the power', he went on to declare that 'in the process which we are going through, all the power cannot belong to the working class. It is a problem of the balance of forces, it is a problem of the passage through national liberation towards *socialismo nacional*.'[43]

Statements such as these highlighted the political dilemma facing the Montoneros: as critical Peronist loyalists, they could not possibly win over the class-conscious labour minority which was beginning to challenge the Government's economic strategy, though revolutionary canon suggested that this minority should have been the priority recruitment target; on the other hand, to have come out more sharply with a radical critique of the drift of government policy would have been to risk isolation from the rest of the Peronist Movement, including the economistic majority of workers, thus leaving the unions in the hands of the reformist labour bureaucracy.

[42] Alvaro Alsogaray, article in *La Prensa*, 8 September 1974.
[43] 'Palabras de Firmenich'.

In the end, the Montoneros got the worst of both worlds by falling between the two stools. Their attitude to government measures was too critical to be tolerated by the Peronist leadership quick to demand the 'orthodoxy' and 'loyalty' traditionally required of the Movement's adherents but insufficiently censorious to prelude the formulation of a genuine political alternative to orthodox Peronism. Nevertheless, the balance of Montonero behaviour in the 1973-4 biennium was inclined towards the pursuit of an accommodation with the Government. Thus, the JTP abandoned the work-place occupations which took place during the early weeks of the Cámpora administration as soon as Perón wagged his finger reprovingly; only parts of the new Law of Professional Associations, which strengthened the union bureaucracy by empowering the national CGT to 'intervene' its regional sections and federations to 'intervene' participant unions, were selected for criticism, even though Tendency influence in Congress was far too weak for the procurement of amendments; and the Tendency supported a new Redundancy Law, trusting that it would be used against 'reactionaries' and not, as it was, against left-wing militants. Finally, on the Penal Code reform approved in January 1974, whereby stiffer penalties for guerrilla activities than existed under the previous military regime were introduced, the Montoneros made every effort to reach a compromise by, in the end, just trying to get two clauses altered. Under this piece of legislation, arms possession could lead to a harsher sentence than could murder.

All the legislative compromises were made in the vain hope that, with Perón at the helm, the legislation would be interpreted according to its 'true' (i.e. 'progressive') spirit, especially if the Left mobilized its numerous followers to counter the possibility of Perón succumbing to Rightist pressures. Montonero faith in Perón was so great that 'deviations' from the expected national liberation path were either ignored or only criticized in muted tones for several months. After the departure of Cámpora from the Presidency on 13 July 1973, the nomination by Perón of his third wife, Isabel, as his running mate for the 23 September elections was something which the stunned Montoneros 'neither understood nor understand'. They commented that 'she was not the most representative of those 18 years of [Peronist oppositional] struggle', but decided to remain 'silent in a disciplined manner', confident that Perón would soon put things right: 'we are going to do what he orders'.[44] No criticism was made of Cámpora's resignation, only of the way in which the Peronist Right attempted to portray the 13 July events as a 'palace revolution' engineered by themselves rather than as the fulfillment of an arrangement made earlier by Perón and Cámpora.[45]

PERON ATTACKS THE MONTONEROS

When Perón formally took over the Presidency on 12 October, the Montoneros celebrated by announcing their merger with the FAR. Full of optimism, they joyfully declared: 'Today, Perón is Argentina. He is Sovereignty. He is Fatherland.'[46] At the same time, through an incredulous editiorial in their weekly *El Descamisado* entitled 'What on Earth's this?',[47] they claimed that Perón had nothing to do with a Peronist leadership 'Reserved Document', issued after the assassination of CGT General Secretary José Rucci, which was a declaration of war against the 'terrorist and subversive Marxist groups' that had supposedly 'infiltrated' the Movement.[48] Yet it was Perón who publicly announced the document and whose signature appeared at the bottom of it! Disbelief at Perón's defence of the Peronist Right and labour leaders paralysed Montonero initiative for weeks, while they stoically soaked up the verbal punishment he was meting out to them. After Perón's speech on 8 November at the CGT HQ, in which he likened the so-called 'infiltrators' to 'germs' which were 'contaminating' the Movement, the Montoneros went so far as to obey his order not to criticize government ministers, in this way accepting the Peronist principle of *verticalismo*, or vertical discipline and authority. As Dardo Cabo (who had

[44] Dardo Cabo, 'Carta del director: Compañeros', *El Descamisado*, no. 13 (14 August 1973), pp. 2-3.
[45] For Cámpora's own version of the controversial event, see his *El mandato de Perón* (Argentina: Ediciones Quehacer Nacional, 1975).
[46] 'El final de una batalla: Perón Presidente; El comienzo de otra: Liberación', *El Descamisado*, no. 19 (26 September 1973), pp. 2-3.
[47] 'Y esto, ¿qué es?', ibid., no. 21 (9 October 1973), pp. 2-3.
[48] For the text, see *La Opinión*, 2 October 1973.

taken over the editorship of *El Descamisado* from the more left-wing Mario Hernández after the first issue) wrote: 'He who leads is Perón. Either one accepts his leadership or one is outside the Movement ... because this is a revolutionary process, it is a war, and although one may differ, when the General gives an order for all [the Movement] it must be obeyed'[49] — a rather long-winded way of saying, 'Perón Rules — OK?'.

During these weeks the Montoneros fantasized about Perón's 'strange' behaviour: rather than immediately question their own political characterization of Perón, they depicted him as an innocent prisoner of a clique of imperialist agents, traitors, and bureaucrats who had constituted themselves into a cordon surrounding him, isolating the leader from his mass following. Social Welfare Minister José López Rega entered this fanciful drama in the role of villain-in-chief, distorting Perón's orders and preventing mass opinion from reaching him. For weeks, the Montoneros thought that all they needed to do in order to rectify the political process was to use their mobilizing muscle to break through the cordon, to renew the direct contact between Perón and the masses which they believed had traditionally supplied the Peronist Movement with its revolutionary dynamism. Hence the Montonero claim, 'when Perón and his people come together, only Perón and the people triumph'.[50]

Only in January 1974, when Perón told a group of dissident FREJULI deputies either to vote for his regressive Penal Code reform bill in Congress or to resign, did things begin to come to a head. The Montoneros, who had been muttering veiled threats about withdrawing their parliamentary representatives, now had to implement their sanction or risk losing face. With Perón indicating no preparedness to make concessions in order to maintain the unity of the Peronist Movement, the eight Peronist Youth deputies resigned on 24 January. They attempted to evoke memories of Evita and her so-called 'rejection' of the Vice-Presidency in 1951, stating that they were 'resigning the honours, but not from the struggle',[51] yet their stand was hardly a principled one: of the eight people

---

[49] Cabo, 'Compañeros', *El Descamisado*, no. 26 (13 November 1973), pp. 2–3.
[50] 'Con el Pueblo hacia Perón', ibid., no. 16 (4 September 1973), pp. 2–3.
[51] *Buenos Aires Herald*, 25 January 1974.

who, by virtue of their being next on the FREJULI lists, filled the empty seats, two were the Montoneros Leonardo Bettanín and Miguel Domingo Zavala Rodríguez. Both differentiated themselves from the other newcomers at the swearing-in ceremony by swearing 'for God and country, for the memory of Evita, and for those who fell in the battle for national liberation', and, not unexpectedly, were refused admittance to the FREJULI bloc.[52]

In the same month the Montoneros went in for some mild self-criticism and began to discover that they had political differences with Perón. Addressing a Peronist Youth Week-End School, Mario Firmenich now admitted that, prior to Perón's return, 'we created our own Perón, someone greater than the person he really is. Now that Perón is here, Perón is Perón and not the man we wish him to be'. He recognised that Perón was remaining loyal to his traditional Third Position and that for him, '*socialismo nacional* is not socialism. What Perón defines as *socialismo nacional* is *Justicialismo*', emphasizing class alliance rather than class struggle.[53] The discovery of an ideological gulf between Perón and the Montonero leaders did not, however, lead to a withdrawal of support, for the Montoneros still felt strategically at one with Perón: they still agreed with Perón's postulation of a national multiclass alliance, though, whereas Perón regarded class conciliation as an end, they believed that such an alliance, implementing anti-imperialist measures, would inevitably initiate a process towards socialism. It is important to record that this distinction between Perón's ideology and his strategy was not an idea which the Montoneros released for public consumption, even among their own sympathizers. Ever hopeful for some concessionary gesture from Perón in their favour, the Montonero leadership minimized their differences with him in public, the result being that their old illusions about him being a socialist lived on in the minds of many of their supporters, soon to give way to a 'Perón betrayed us' attitude.[54] The official line continued to be that, despite

[52] Ibid., 15 March 1974.
[53] Firmenich, 'Etapa y conjuntura', typescript of talk given at JP School, January 1974, p. 7.
[54] Such an attitude was expressed by many former JP members interviewed by the author between June 1975 and October 1976.

'errors' attributable to 'a poor analysis of the national situation', Perón was still a revolutionary and an anti-imperialist, even if he was envisaging a 'very long-term liberation process' of a type that would 'deceive' imperialism![55]

The second 'stand' made by the Montoneros and their Tendency, again designed to extract concessions from Perón through threatening, implicitly, to leave the Movement, came on 31 January when they boycotted a meeting between Perón and the youth organizations at the Olivos presidential residence. They objected to the invitation of ultra-Right groups such as the National University Concentration (CNU) and Organizational Command (C de O), on the grounds that they were not only unrepresentative of Peronist youth but had also been responsible for assassinations and other attacks on Peronist Left militants. Among those who sat down with Perón at this and other weekly meetings was CNU leader Alejandro Giovenco who, having joined Dardo Cabo and 15 others in the ill-fated 1966 Malvinas Islands 'invasion' and having been jailed for it, became a bodyguard of CGT General Secretary José Rucci. Persuasive evidence of links between the Peronist Right and the increasing incidence of terrorism[56] was provided on 18 February when Giovenco, heading for an unknown destination in the centre of Buenos Aires at midnight, was blown to pieces by a bomb which he was carrying in his brief-case. Again though, the Revolutionary Tendency's boycott of Perón's meetings with the youth organizations was more of a tactical manoeuvre than a principled act of defiance: Alberto Molina of the Montoneros, as well as leaders of the front organizations, attended a 25 April meeting to discuss arrangements for the celebration of

[55] 'Qué votamos el 11 de marzo', *El Descamisado*, no. 43 (12 March 1974), pp. 2–3.

[56] In differentiating between political terrorism and urban guerrilla warfare when characterizing the violent methods of the Peronist Right and Left, several distinctions must be made: the evidence shows that the Right's use of mortal violence was far less discriminate than that of the Left and was indeed aimed for the most part against non-combatants; that this was so because the Right consciously worked to sow a climate of terror throughout society, so as to discourage opposition to the Government once Perón had recovered the Presidency; that in this respect the Rightist violence was in defence of the status quo rather than being an instrument of a politico-military strategy directed towards the seizure of power; and, finally, that whereas the Left generally respected the conventions of war, victims of right-wing violence were not infrequently raped or tortured before their mutilated corpses were discovered.

May Day, even though Perón had refused to debar the young fascists.

One year after the Peronist electoral triumph, on 11 March 1974 at the JP-Montoneros last mass rally, 50,000 people packed the Atlanta Stadium, eager to hear what Tendency leaders had to say in response to the recent reverses. It was the occasion of Galimberti's public reappearance, but Firmenich was the man to chart the course of future Montonero policy. In his speech the Montonero number one spoke of how the purported Liberation process had been 'distorted' and 'betrayed' by the 'traitors' to the Movement, especially the trade union nominees who had filed provincial vice-governorships only to conspire against popular governors, and the people who had taken command of the official structures of the Movement, who had purged Peronist Left militants. To 'redirect' the process along national liberation lines, Firmenich emphasized three proposals: that the existing Social Pact had to be scrapped rather than reformed; that it was necessary to 'recover the government for the people and Perón' rather than, as their earlier slogan demanded, 'Support, Control, and Defend the Popular Government'; and that the Peronist Youth and other collaterals had to pay more attention to organizational tasks.[57] What he did not say was that the biggest 'traitor' to the Montoneros' conception of what Peronism should be and do was Juan Domingo Perón himself.

Nevertheless, a major confrontation was by now inevitable. It occurred in *Plaza de Mayo*, arena of popular jubilation just a year earlier, when the Montoneros attempted to transform what Peronist leaders intended as a May Day jamboree into a popular assembly at which 'the people' could engage in 'dialogue' with their leader.[58] For the last time, the Revolutionary Tendency flaunted its enormousness, mobilizing 60,000 people, perhaps more, out of a total attendance of about 100,000, of whom the remainder were largely mobilized by the unions. Had Peronist officials had their way, it would

---

[57] For the full text of Firmenich's speech, see 'Palabras de Firmenich'. The speech formed the basis of a programme called 'Un documento para la Liberación', which appeared with *El Peronista*, no. 1 (19 April 1974), and was in fact the only programme produced by the Montonero Tendency as a whole.

[58] The account of the 1974 May Day rally is based upon reports published in the *Buenos Aires Herald*, 2 May 1974; *De Frente*, no. 1 (2 May 1974); and *El Peronista*, no. 3 (4 May 1974).

have been a well-orchestrated rally which would have applauded a bland Perón speech urging national unity; as it was, it revealed Peronism to be on the verge of fratricidal warfare.

The Montoneros and their devotees were irrepressible that day. Only union banners and national flags were permitted by the organizers to be carried into the *Plaza*, but those in Montonero hands, once there, changed radically. The view which greeted Perón as he stepped out onto the balcony of the *Casa Rosada* was one of UTA bus drivers' union banners with their lettering adjusted to read 'JTP' and of Argentine banners sprayed by means of aerosol cans with the name 'MONTONEROS'. And their bearers were not content to intone 'Argentina, Argentina' and 'Perón, Perón', as officialdom had stipulated. They whistled with merciless derision as Isabel Martínez, wife of Perón, crowned the 'Queen of Labour'. 'We don't want a carnival, we want a popular assembly', came the chants, before claims that 'If Evita lived, she would be a Montonero' succeeded them. Then, as a minute's silence in memory of Eva Perón and all departed Peronists commenced, a JP drum sounded and the names of slain Montoneros were read out loud, to Tendency responses of 'Present' after each one: 'Fernando Abal Medina' ... '¡*PRESENTE!*' 'Carlos Gustavo Ramus' ... '¡*PRESENTE!*' 'José Sabino Navarro' ... '¡*PRESENTE!*' ... [59]

Perón was furious. More so when, approaching the microphone, he was welcomed with the persistently-chanted Montonero question, 'What's going on, General? Why is the popular government full of *gorilas*?'. He lost his self-control, abandoned his national unity speech, and unleashed an attack on the Peronist Left which amounted to a declaration of war. After just fifty seconds of praise for the quality of Argentine trade unionism, hearing slogans against the union leaders from the Left, Perón made his first reference to 'those stupid idiots who are shouting'; but the Tendency at first did not react. Perón continued, 'I was saying that through these [last] 21 years, the trade unions have remained intransigent, yet

---

[59] The idea of the martyr who has gained eternal life is not a recent one, nor is it the exclusive property of the Left: the fascist Legionnaires of the Rumanian Iron Guard also practised the rite of calling the names of their dead at parades and answering 'Present!', during the 1930s. See Walter Laqueur, *Terrorism* (London: Sphere Books Ltd., 1978), p. 157.

today some beardless wonders try to claim more credit than those who fought for 20 years'. Soon after, having heard Montonero celebratory slogans about two of the assassinated labour leaders ('Rucci, traitor, say hello to Vandor'), Perón referred ominously to 'comrades who have seen their leaders assassinated, without punishment having been implemented yet'. He lambasted the Revolutionary Tendency as 'infiltrators who work within and who in terms of treachery are more dangerous than those who work outside, in addition to most of them being mercenaries in the service of foreign money'; and he called for an internal war 'if the pernicious elements don't give way'. But the 'pernicious elements' were no longer there: they had long since had enough of his tirade and had withdrawn from the *Plaza* in a reasonably orderly manner, chanting 'the people are leaving' and 'if these are not the people, where are the people?' — with Perón still in full cry. Two-thirds of the *Plaza* was left unpopulated.

Predictably, the Montonero autopsy after the events of 1 May revealed that 'something broke after 30 years',[60] that 'something' being the magical revolutionary relationship which they had believed to exist between Perón and the masses, and which they had hoped to experience in the *Plaza*. Far from engaging in dialogue, Perón had attempted to deliver a monologue, and one which laid bare his contempt and distaste for the Left. Clearly, nothing could now be expected of Perón who a fortnight later, protected by 1,000 troops, personally welcomed the visiting General Pinochet of Chile at the Morón air force base and declared that 'Our relations with Chile are excellent'[61] — just eight months after the bloody September 1973 coup. At a Montonero press conference on 15 May, spokesmen Alberto Molina and Fernando Vaca Narvaja raised the possibility of a 'return to the resistance' in the event of an 'attack by imperialism' on a weakened government and demobilized Peronist

---

[60] Miguel Lizaso, 'General, el peronismo no está de acuerdo', *El Peronista*, no. 3 (4 May 1974), pp. 2–4.

[61] Perón, quoted in the *Buenos Aires Herald*, 17 May 1974. It is ironic that whereas Allende's Chile awarded General Lanusse the highest Chilean decoration, the Bernardo O'Higgins Order of Merit, in 1971, Peronist Argentina awarded the Order of May to General Pinochet in 1974. Back in September 1973, Perón had referred to the Chilean coup as a tragedy for Latin America, and had said that he suspected US participation [ibid., 13 September 1973].

Movement.⁶² After months of soaking up body-blows from the Right like punch-drunk boxers, the Montoneros were becoming more critical of the Government and losing their naivety concerning Perón. However, their basic underlying political conceptions remained intact: just a fortnight after the May Day clash, Miguel Lizaso, in an editorial in the Montonero weekly *El Peronista*, asserted that 'The Peronist Movement continues to be the only way of advancing along the road of National Liberation towards the construction of *socialismo nacional*.⁶³ Had Perón lived, the Montoneros might well have been driven by the reactionary drift of the Peronist Government to further radicalize their political formulations. But Perón died on 1 July 1974, victim of a heart attack brought on by pneumonia, at the age of seventy-eight.

Perón's death prevented political experiences from forcing the Montoneros to move on from respectful criticism of his 'errors', and then bewildered silence, to a full understanding and critique of his political project. His last major speech of 12 June, in which he had denounced an 'imperialist plot', was now presented by the Montoneros as evidence that the deceased leader was 'to a great extent taking up the orientations and many of the criticisms which we were formulating'.⁶⁴ Deputies Bettanín and Zavala Rodríguez were the first to call for popular unity in defence of the political process initiated on 11 March 1973, with Perón's 12 June speech as the guide for the Justicialist Party to follow. Leading Montoneros Mario Firmenich, Roberto Quieto, and Carlos Caride, JP leaders Juan Añon and Juan Carlos Dante Gullo, and JTP leader Enrique Juárez were among the mourners who went to pay their last respects to Perón as he lay in state in the Congress building. The Tendency's leaders closed their eyes to the experience of recent months, with Galimberti rendering homage to Perón for 'never defending any cause other than that of the people'.⁶⁵ Since Perón by the time of his death had not exhausted his political credit in

⁶² Ibid., 16 May 1974.
⁶³ Lizaso, '1 de mayo: ¿quién ganó? ¿qué cambió?', *El Peronista*, no. 4 (14 May 1974), pp. 2–3.
⁶⁴ 'Hablan los Montoneros', text of speech by Roberto Quieto in La Plata, *La Causa Peronista*, no. 4 (30 July 1974), pp. 6–8.
⁶⁵ Rodolfo Galimberti, 'Unidad nacional o "Gran Acuerdo Nacional"', ibid., no. 3 (23 July 1974), pp. 2–3.

the minds of many workers, and perhaps having really convinced themselves that Perón had indeed learnt from his May Day 'mistake', the Montoneros continued to use his name as their principal banner of struggle, asserting their own Peronist orthodoxy while whitewashing all the anti-popular actions and declarations from recollections of Argentina's departed *caudillo*.

Yet Perón had promoted or at least condoned the legislation which the Montoneros had criticized; he had been President when in 1974 Quieto, Caride, and Firmenich were each, in turn, temporarily arrested; he had been in power when the Montonero weeklies *El Descamisado* and *El Peronista*[66] were closed by governmental decree; and he had done absolutely nothing to curb Rightist violence against the Peronist Left. If one excludes the minor shootout which occurred during a homage on 10 June 1973 to the Peronists executed in 1956, the attacks on left-wing activists can be said to have been launched on 20 June 1973, date of the Ezeiza Massacre and of Perón's definitive return to Argentina. The Tendency mobilized hundreds of thousands to go to welcome Perón home, but were kept off the organizing committee by the Right. When columns marching behind Montonero, FAR, and JP banners arrived at Ezeiza, the airport at which Perón was due to land, they were fired upon from the improvised speakers' platform as they tried to occupy the already-crowded area right in front of it. A few Tendency members were armed but only with irrelevant hand guns which were no match for machine-guns and rifles. At least twenty-five people were killed, including the Montonero Horacio Beto Simone; the Peruvian-born journalist Antonio Quispe, a leader of the FAR's southern region, was mortally wounded;

---

[66] *El Descamisado* was banned for 'causing ideological chaos and a crisis of concept by deforming reality' [*Buenos Aires Herald*, 11 April 1974], after its 46th edition had blamed López Rega for the killing of MVP militant Alberto Chejolán during a protest outside the Social Welfare Ministry, and had published a photograph of a policeman apparently shooting him. *El Peronista* was edited by Miguel Lizaso, whose brother Carlos Alberto was shot after the 1956 Peronist rebellion. He himself, along with Julio Troxler, was a survivor of the 1956 shootings, but died in a Navy detention camp after the 1976 coup. The decree which closed *El Peronista* in June 1974 referred specifically to an article about a Peronist Youth group in the Armed Forces and asserted that it sought to provoke indiscipline and disunity there.

and over 400 people were injured.[67] Perón's main comment after being informed of the tragedy (his plane having been diverted to Morón) was that 'there must be a return to legal and constitutional order'.[68] The Left unanimously accused retired army colonel Jorge Osinde, Sports Under-Secretary at the Social Welfare Ministry, C de O leader Alberto Brito Lima, right-wing Peronist Norma Kennedy, and Captain Ciro Ahumada of responsibility; and they even published photographs showing Ahumada and others firing guns into the multitude, but Perón did nothing.[69]

THE TRIPLE A AND THE RIGHTIST OFFENSIVE

The Montoneros should have taken more account of the fact that Osinde was a subordinate of Social Welfare Minister, José López Rega. Only later did they claim that Ezeiza, the biggest popular mobilization in Argentine history, had witnessed the 'birth' of the Triple A death squad, the Argentine Anti-Communist Alliance which was to claim so many Peronist Left lives. Whether launched at Ezeiza or not, it is now clear that López Rega was assembling a death squad, based in his Ministry, in 1973, though it did not christen itself the Triple A until 1974. As his lieutenants, López Rega chose Commissioner Juan Ramón Morales, whom he made Security Chief at the Social Welfare Ministry, and Inspector Rodolfo Eduardo Almirón, a member of the presidential security team who became Isabel Perón's chief bodyguard when Perón died. True to the Triple A recruitment pattern, both men had earlier been thrown out of the Federal Police for gangsterism but were re-incorporated on the eve of Perón's final assumption of the Presidency. Within months, Morales rose two ranks and Almirón four, but this was

[67] Among those wounded was the Montonero José Luis Nell, who back in 1963 had led the MNRT into Argentina's first urban guerrilla action (though legend has it that Joe Baxter led the group). The wounds received by Nell at Ezeiza caused paralysis, which rapidly demoralized him, and finally led him to shoot himself in September 1974.
[68] Perón, quoted in the *Buenos Aires Herald*, 22 June 1973.
[69] Newspaper coverage of the event was appalling, mainly because the journalists present lay low as soon as the firing started, but for Peronist Left reports, see *Militancia*, no. 3 (28 June 1973); and *El Descamisado*, nos. 6 (26 June 1973), 7 (3 July 1973), and 8 (10 July 1973). Issue no. 7 suggested that former OAS agents, like Francois Chiappe, had been involved in the massacre.

nothing compared to the meteoric rise of their boss: on 10 May 1974, retired policeman José López Rega was promoted by decree from Corporal to Commissioner General, and thus leapt through 15 ranks!⁷⁰ As if to celebrate the triumph, the following day the Triple A assassinated Father Carlos Mugica as he left his church in the Materdos district of Buenos Aires, their intention being to implicate and thus discredit the Montoneros.

The Triple A could not possibly have achieved the deadly efficiency that it did were it not for the toleration or active involvement of the Federal Police command, achieved through the promotion of Alberto Villar. Already a police chief under Lanusse (in charge of the Urban Order Department), Villar was appointed as Assistant Chief of the Federal Police at the end of January 1974, and then occupied the top position after the resignation of Iñíguez in April. Having resisted the rise of Villar and having referred to Mario Firmenich as 'a good nationalist, Peronist, and Catholic',⁷¹ Iñíguez (who led an abortive Peronist military rising against the Frondizi Government in November 1960) was persuaded that retirement was the only means of safeguarding his health.

Attacks on individuals by the Triple A appear to have begun on 21 November 1973 when a bomb almost claimed the life of Radical Party senator Hipólito Solari Yrigoyen, an outspoken critic of the Peronists' labour legislation. Among the more prominent early victims were the revolutionary Peronist deputy, Rodolfo Ortega Peña, co-editor of *Militancia*; Peronist Resistance heroes Horacio Chávez and Julio Troxler, both of whom had participated in the June 1956 Valle rising; the former Vice-Governor of Córdoba, Atilio López, who had played a leading part in the *Cordobazo*; the Marxist, Silvio Frondizi, brother of the ex-President, killed for publicly denouncing the alleged massacre of sixteen captured ERP guerrillas, and charging that Villar had personally presided over the torture of twelve more in Catamarca in August 1974; and Alfredo Curutchet, formerly

---

⁷⁰ For the Montoneros' own exposé of the Triple A, see 'La historia de la Triple A', *El Auténtico*, nos. 6 (26 November 1975), 7 (10 December 1975), and 8 (24 December 1975). For corroboration from somebody at one time linked to the Triple A, see 'Las revelaciones de Paino', *La Opinión, segunda sección*, 12 February 1976.

⁷¹ Iñíguez, quoted in the *Buenos Aires Herald*, 14 April 1974.

a defender of political prisoners until he joined them in Rawson, more recently legal advisor to the left-wing Córdoba section of the car workers' union, SMATA. Most were Peronists but a substantial minority belonged to the non-Peronist Left or were — like General Carlos Prats (Chilean C-in-C under Allende) and his wife, and several former Tupamaros — political refugees from neighbouring Latin American countries. The Montoneros Eduardo Beckerman and Pablo Van Lierde were assassinated, all of the Tendency organizations suffered losses, and dozens of JP, JUP, and JTP local headquarters were blown up. Altogether, some 200 people had been killed by the Triple A and civilian fascist commandos by September 1974, and the Montoneros, if one includes members of their collateral organizations, had lost more militants, killed, than they had in the 1970-3 period.[72] Of course, political violence did not merely afflict the Left: fierce guerrilla campaigns were maintained throughout the 1973-4 years by both the ERP and the *Comando Nacional* wing of the FAP, organizations which merged in October 1974.[73] Triple A and fascist violence cannot, however, be regarded as a response to left-wing militarism, for the vast majority of right-wing attacks were directed against those who were attempting to develop the Left politically through exploiting legal means of struggle, or against those who merely defended existing democratic rights.

[72] Ibid., 7 September 1974; and 'Respuesta socialista al llamamiento montonero', *Avanzada Socialista*, no. 120 (9 September 1974), pp. 8-9.
[73] The ERP concentrated mainly on kidnapping business executives in 1973 and raised over 30 million dollars in ransom money. Military targets were also attacked: on 6 September 1973, ERP guerrillas took over the Army's Medical HQ and engaged in a five-hour gun-battle just thirty blocks from Government House before some surrendered and others escaped; on 20 January 1974, sixty to seventy ERP members attacked the 10th Armoured Cavalry garrison at Azul, 170 miles south of Buenos Aires, and not only failed in their mission but also supplied Perón with a pretext for ousting the popular Governor of Buenos Aires, Oscar Bidegain, and for introducing the Penal Code reforms; and on 11 August 1974, synchronized attacks on a Córdoba arms factory and the Catamarca paratroop garrison provided the ERP with hundreds of automatic weapons, but at the cost of heavy losses. During 1974 the ERP began to turn its attention to a rural guerrilla enterprise in the northern province of Tucumán, hoping that it would become 'the Cuba of Argentina'. Meanwhile, FAP *Comando Nacional* activity was less spectacular in military terms, but equally insensitive to public opinion. Beginning on 22 May 1973 with the assassination of Car Workers Union (SMATA) General Secretary Dirk Henry Kloosterman, it devoted itself to the punishment of 'traitors', other vengeance attacks, and the intimidation of foreign businessmen.

On several occasions, police guards were withdrawn from the homes of Triple A victims shortly before the death squad struck,[74] and both the CNU and C de O clearly had some police members. After Peronist Youth activist Elsa Calia Algañaraz de Román was raped and assassinated by the C de O in Don Torcuato in July 1974, her husband was immediately beaten up when he went to a police station to recover her body.[75] Perón's failure to do anything about such outrages verged on condonation of them, and he brooked no criticism of the police. In February 1974, when Ana Guzzetti, a Peronist journalist working for the ERP-orientated daily *El Mundo*, asked him at a press conference whether his Government was investigating the right-wing para-police organizations, which had killed twelve militants and destroyed twenty-five Peronist local headquarters during the previous fortnight, Perón ordered legal proceedings for slander to be taken against her.[76] She was arrested the same month. Then, fourteen months later, Ana Guzzetti was herself abducted by the men she had denounced; the ones who drove around in Ford Falcons, identical to those used by the Federal Police. Six days later, she was found beaten but still alive on the Pan American highway, following a protest strike by members of the Buenos Aires Press Association.

Ideologically, the Rightist offensive came through the pages of Felipe Romeo's anti-Semitic magazine, *El Caudillo*. Allegedly financed by the Social Welfare Ministry through paid advertisements, it called for the elimination of the 'rearguard guerrillas' (i.e. all the Left) and took as its watchword, 'the best enemy is a dead enemy'.[77] After August 1974, when the octogenarian fascist Oscar Ivanissevich replaced Taiana at the head of the Education Ministry, the offensive was reinforced in the Montoneros' university heartland. Ivanissevich made Alberto Ottalango Rector of

[74] For example, in the case of the Triple A bomb attack on 7 September 1974 on the home of the Peronist Left Rector of the University of Buenos Aires, Raúl Laguzzi. He survived it, but his four-month-old baby son Pablo was killed. The Montoneros sent Laguzzi a message of condolence: 'your son is the youngest martyr in the Peronist resistance' [*Buenos Aires Herald*, 8-9 September 1974].

[75] Ibid., 8 July 1974.

[76] For the full text of this revealing exchange, see *La Nación*, 9 February 1974.

[77] See Kandel and Monteverde, pp. 30 and 77; and 'Volvemos para triunfar o morir junto a Isabel', *El Caudillo*, no. 68 (15 October 1975), p. 3.

the University of Buenos Aires a month later[78] and together they undertook a 'mission' to 'purify' the campuses. Fifteen of the sixteen universities were 'intervened' and their rectors in some cases replaced by fascists. By July 1975, after 4,000 lecturers had been sacked, 1,600 students had been imprisoned, and dozens had fled after receiving death threats, the Argentine University Teachers Confederation had to admit that Ivanissevich had succeeded in establishing 'a peace of the graveyards' on the campuses.[79]

In this way the Montoneros lost an invaluable base, or at least their legal title to it; but the defeat there, as in other spheres, was greatly enhanced by their own vacillation when attacked by the Right. When, for example, the new University Law was passed early in March 1974, JUP leader Juan Pablo Ventura declared that his organization was 'convinced' that it was not 'thought up to throw us out',[80] yet, as amended in the Senate, it provided for a ban on campus politics, ideologically discriminated against left-wing lecturers, and restricted the free operation of student unions. Under it, university trustees were to be replaced by 'normalizing rectors', which in practice meant that Tendency supporters with university positions would have to submit their resignations. Here, not untypically, the Montoneros marched their soldiers up to the top of the hill only to march them down again: mobilization after mobilization aimed at securing a progressive University Law was followed by the usual climb-down, by the 'tactical retreat' which soon became a strategic rout. The JUP dismissed calls for 'no resignations' as 'ultra Left' and made its customary semantic distinction between the 'spirit' and 'content' of the Law, relying upon sympathetic decisions from above to ensure that the 'spirit' of the Law triumphed.[81] The result was the successive displacement of

---

[78] Ottalango claimed that the only choice open to Argentines was to be 'Justicialists or Marxists . . . Political parties will be a thing of the past . . . All the Liberal parties will have to choose between Justicialism and Marxism. Here and now, one has to be either with Christ or against Christ . . . An attempt has been made to construct a pluralist society and one can see the consequences. We possess the truth and reason: the others do not and we will treat them accordingly' — quoted in Kandel and Monteverde, p. 31.

[79] Monahan, 'I agreed to teach', p. 10.

[80] 'La Universidad al borde de la opción: liberación o continuismo gorila', *El Descamisado*, no. 43 (12 March 1974), pp. 7-8.

[81] Ibid.; and 'Universidad: o del pueblo o de nadie'.

popular rectors Rodolfo Puiggrós, Ernesto Villanueva, and Raúl Laguzzi,[82] and a fascist takeover of the University of Buenos Aires; for, once the legislation was on the statute books, the Right was able to operate with the full force of the law behind it.

Similar vacillations, in addition to its youth image, hindered the growth of the other main collateral, the JTP. Quite apart from its temporization when faced with the Social Pact, Law of Professional Associations, and the Redundancy Law, its illusions in the Government led it, during the mid-1974 struggle of the Córdoban car workers, to initially oppose the use of strike action in furtherance of a wage claim exceeding the Social Pact ceiling; to condemn René Salamanca and other local workers' leaders for their 'incendiary speeches'; and finally, when the strike went ahead anyway and the local branch of the SMATA car workers' union was threatened with national 'intervention', the JTP proposed that the wage claim be 'disguised' with demands for other improvements in order 'to avoid a level of confrontation which [the union] was not in a condition to face up to due to the great isolation of the struggle'. While a tactical retreat here may or may not have been advisable, such a position was not likely to win the support of militants among the highly class-conscious workers of Córdoba. In fact, the Montoneros had nothing but militarism to offer to these workers: 'If our enemies advance with arms, we are going to stop them with arms', Firmenich declared, when, during the Córdoba dispute, he gained his only opportunity to address a workers' assembly.[83]

Many such criticisms can be made of the Montoneros' behaviour during these months, but these should not be allowed to obscure the fact that they were up against powerful enemies. To effectively challenge the power of the union

---

[82] In fact, the Conservative Solano Lima, formerly Cámpora's Vice-President, occupied the position for a while between the rectorships of Villanueva and Laguzzi. Triple A death threats obliged both Puiggrós and Laguzzi to flee to Mexico in September 1974. Villanueva was imprisoned in 1975, charged with the possession of arms and false documents, but was not released following his completion of a five-year sentence in March 1980.

[83] 'Córdoba: el porqué del conflicto de SMATA', *La Causa Peronista*, no. 4 (30 June 1974), pp. 30–1; and 'Córdoba: si es necesario aquí pondremos sangre montonera', ibid., no. 6 (13 August 1974), pp. 26–31.

bureaucracy, the JTP badly needed success in the Metalworkers Union, which, besides being the most influential union in the CGT, controlled the Labour Ministry via Minister Ricardo Otero. Participation in the March 1974 union elections, though, was all too easy for the bureaucracy to deny. At the end of November 1973, a National Congress of Delegates, all nominated by the bureaucracy, met and changed the union statutes so as to effectively prevent opposition lists from being presented in the election. Otero condoned the manoeuvre, accusing the JTP metalworkers' group activists of being 'Bolshies and Trots',[84] before the police executed the *coup de grâce* by raiding the JTP headquarters and seizing group lists which theoretically entitled the JTP to compete. Since most workers were still adopting 'wait-and-see' or supportive attitudes towards the Government, there was little that the Montoneros' labour front could do in the face of these frauds; and JTP spirits must have reached an all-time low in August 1974 when the two most militant, though non-Montonero, union strongholds fell: SMATA Córdoba was 'intervened' by its national executive, while Raimundo Ongaro's Printers Union, the FGB, was simply outlawed by the Government, just three months after Ongaro's 'Green List' had defeated the Peronist labour bureaucracy in union elections by 4,800 to 682 votes.[85]

THE FAILURE OF THE *MOVIMIENTISTA* STRATEGY

By now the Montoneros' *movimientista* strategy had demonstrably failed: the Left had been pushed out of the positions it had controlled in the Movement and had, moreover, seen its influence disappear or decline in the national Congress, provincial governments, and in university administrations. With Isabel Perón as President no favourable change of governmental course was to be expected, especially given López Rega's dominance within the new Government. The Montoneros now saw their daily newspaper, *Noticias*, and their last weekly, *La Causa Peronista*, banned by

---

[84] Communiqué issued by the JTP Agrupación Metalúrgica 17 de Octubre, *El Descamisado*, no. 43 (12 March 1974), p. 15.
[85] Results from 'La federación gráfica es de los gráficos', *De Frente*, no. 1 (2 May 1974), p. 50.

decree;[86] they were denied permission to hold further rallies and demonstrations, even to mark the 22 August Trelew anniversary; illegal attempts at demonstrations were fiercely repressed by the police; and, as one national newspaper put it, political murder had become almost a 'natural' form of death.[87] It was imperative for the Montoneros to opt for a new strategy if they were to avoid annihilation.

Politically they might in theory have now formed a common front with the combative labour and left-wing organizations in order to build the embryo of a socialist alternative to the Government. That they did not, however, was entirely in line with their earlier behaviour. The Montoneros had shunned all unitarian overtures made to them by both the armed and non-armed Left, whether emanating from the ERP and seeking a guerrilla alliance or from the Socialist Workers Party (PST) with the more modest proposal for joint activity against the Bank Employees Association (AB) bureaucracy. Instead, seeking 'tactical allies' in the strangest of places, they had courted the youth of the pro-capitalist political parties while searching for a reformist 'Peruvian' sector with which to ally in the Armed Forces. Both initiatives had come to naught.

A Multi-Party Assembly of Youth for Reconstruction and National Liberation held, portentously, in the luxurious Savoy Hotel under JP auspices in August 1973, attracted sixteen youth sections, including the Radical Youth and Popular Conservative Youth. It resulted in the launching of a popular youth front, the Argentine Political Youth (JPA), on 17 August, but its unity, based upon the lowest common denominator of a shared desire for 'national' and 'popular' unity against imperialism and the oligarchy, was far too fragile for it to achieve anything. The JPA mobilized 120,000 youths to demonstrate against the Chilean coup that September but was incapable of further initiatives. For to seriously struggle against imperialism and the oligarchy, the youth organizations would have had to have discarded their

---

[86] *Noticias* was banned in August 1974 for 'not contributing to national pacification' [*Buenos Aires Herald*, 29 August 1974]. *La Causa Peronista*, edited by Rodolfo Galimberti, was closed on 6 September 1974 after publishing an account of the *Aramburazo* signed by Arrostito and Firmenich.

[87] La Opinión, 2 August 1974.

implicit assumption that imperialism was something lurking in the United States and the oligarchy in the countryside; they would have needed to have examined more closely the links between foreign and national capital and between the landed oligarchy and other sectors of the bourgeoisie. Yet to have done so would have been totally incompatible with the allegiances of most of these youth groups to conservative and reformist adult parties.

Meanwhile, once Galimberti had received his dressing down from Perón over the radical militia proposal, the Montoneros had attempted to win friends and influence people in the Armed Forces. Apart from early calls for the remnants of the 'military clique' to be purged, no further reforms of the Armed Forces were proposed. Instead, they organized small Peronist Youth branches in each of the three Forces (for junior officers rather than conscripts), which made no impact whatsoever; they tried to woo the new Army Commander, General Carcagno, who, for all his populist rhetoric of 1973,[88] had participated in the putting down of the 1956 Peronist revolt and 1969 *Cordobazo*; and they arranged for 8,000 JP militants to join forces with 5,000 troops of the 1st Army Corps in the Colonel Manuel Dorrego National Reconstruction Operation in October 1973. The latter, apart from giving practical aid to the population of flood-affected areas of Buenos Aires, was sponsored by the JP who, 'without holding out much hope for the conversion of those military sectors most linked to the imperialist project', thought that the scheme might contribute to 'a broadening of the National Liberation Front and the isolation of the main enemy: Yankee imperialism'.[89] Only when the operation, just one of dozens of community work projects undertaken by the Tendency, was over did the truth about the Army's motives hit the JP: that whereas the JP had gone into the Operation with idealistic notions of contributing to 'national reconstruction', the Army 'seems to have gone

---

[88] Carcagno, addressing the 10th Conference of American Commanders-in-Chief, had said that 'the Army cannot be the praetorian guard of an unjust social and political order' — *Buenos Aires Herald*, 6 September 1973.

[89] 'La JP y la Reconstrucción Nacional', *El Descamisado*, no. 20 (2 October 1973), p. 25.

to gain political space'.[90] After the treatment it had received during the Peronist electoral celebrations of 25 May 1973, what the Army most dearly wanted and needed was an event such as this to provide it with a national-popular image, and this is what the JP to some extent supplied it with.[91]

Both of these initiatives revealed the Montoneros, mindful of the limited support for socialism in the labour movement, to be to an extent trimming their sails to the prevailing wind, as well as remaining loyal to the stages conception of revolutionary development. Their behaviour, which thus appeared more populist than socialist, with its emphasis upon 'the people' rather than the working class, was denounced by the ultra-Left as an example of petty-bourgeois reformism. And indeed, in a sense, it was: one can certainly question whether some of the lower-middle-class members of the Tendency had a one hundred per cent commitment to the establishment of socialism; and suggest that some may have perceived their personal and class interests more in terms of the achievement of a left-wing technocracy,[92] thus refuting socialist claims that the petty bourgeoisie had become 'proletarianized'. The inadequacy of reducing explanations of Montonero behaviour merely to class composition is, however, clearly evident in the fact that the social make-up of both the ERP and PST was broadly similar to that of the Montoneros.[93] What is more relevant here is the way in which the Montoneros, through their early 1970s guerrilla mergers, had become accustomed to being the senior partners in acts of unification and had, in the immediate past, revealed themselves at rallies

[90] 'Balance de Operativo Dorrego: la Juventud Peronista fue a trabajar', ibid., no. 25 (6 November 1973), p. 27.

[91] During the Operation the JP worked alongside the future Minister of the Interior under Videla, Colonel Albano Harguindeguy, whom they referred to as an 'intelligent Liberal' who had realized that 'co-existence' with Peronism was possible ['Operativo Dorrego', ibid., no. 22 (16 October 1973), pp. 28-30)].
By the time the exercise was over, they had decided that he was in fact an 'intelligent *gorila*' ['Balance de Operativo Dorrego'].

[92] As Poulantzas put it, the radical petty bourgeoisie may not 'want to break the ladders by which it imagines it can climb'. — Nicos Poulantzas, *Classes in Contemporary Capitalism* (London: Verso, 1978), p. 292.

[93] In August 1974, ERP leader Santucho admitted that the PRT-ERP suffered from 'weaknesses in social composition (only 30% factory workers)' [Mario Roberto Santucho, *Argentina: Bourgeois Power, Revolutionary Power* (Oakland, California: Resistance Publications, nd), p.29]. PST data pertain to the 1973 elections but are as yet unpublished.

and marches to have far greater political support than those urging a 'unity between equals'. Now, they were only interested, organizationally, in mergers involving subordination to their leadership and acceptance of their political outlook and strategy. Their own history was also relevant in explaining why the Montoneros, contemporaneously, discarded the strategic option of continuing to perform mass work but on a clandestine basis. As the dissident José Sabino Navarro Column had pointed out, the practice of urban guerrilla warfare, originally regarded solely as a method, had brought about a thoroughgoing militarization of the organization, which the Montoneros had in 1973-4 carried with them into the political arena. They had retained their option on the guerrilla card during the sixteen months since 25 May 1973 and still had a tendency to equate revolutionary struggle with armed struggle, or at least to view the latter as the quintessence of the former.[94]

Excluded from the official Argentine political system, the Montoneros now turned violently against it. By 6 September 1974, they were underground again, having declared war on a government deemed 'neither popular nor Peronist'. They felt that they were back where they had been prior to the March 1973 election, and asked: 'What is the difference between that military dictatorship and this government? . . . In the name of Peronism and constitutional legality it does the same as the military before.'[95] But time had not stood still. The Montoneros now possessed a tremendous reserve of support, thanks to their mass political initiatives and their responsiveness to radical public opinion. They had suspended their guerrilla campaign as the leading Peronist special formation; they now resumed it as the most powerful politico-military organization in Argentina; and within the next twelve months they were to establish themselves as the mightiest urban guerrilla force ever seen in the whole of Latin America.

[94] 'The guerrilla is only one of the forms of developing the armed struggle; it is without doubt the highest level of political struggle. This method is developed when political objectives cannot be obtained through non-armed forms of political struggle.' — Mario Firmenich interview, *El Descamisado*, no. 17 (11 September 1973), pp. 2-4.

[95] '¿Quién votó a Isabel, López Rega?', *La Causa Peronista*, no. 8 (27 August 1974), pp. 2-3.

5
The Return to Arms (1974–1976)
Isabel no es Perón[1]

Flanked by Adriana Lesgart, Juan Carlos Dante Gullo, Juan Pablo Ventura, and Enrique Juárez, leaders respectively of the Evita Group, JP, JUP, and JTP, Mario Firmenich announced the Montonero decision to 'return to the resistance' at a secret press conference in Buenos Aires on 6 September 1974. Armed struggle, the twenty-seven-year-old guerrilla leader pledged, would continue so long as repression, trade union *intervenciones*, undemocratic labour legislation, the Social Pact, and political prisoners remained features of Argentine political life; only when collective wage bargaining was permitted and all political forces allowed to express themselves freely would there be a cease-fire. Since 'all legal forms of carrying on the struggle have been used up', Firmenich declared, the only option left open was to wage an 'integral popular war', involving the establishment of 'Peronist militias', against national and foreign monopolies and against a government increasingly dominated by José López Rega.[2]

In fact, the resumption of sustained warfare had taken place a week beforehand. Half a dozen operations 'in the popular cause', including revenge killings, were claimed at the press conference: the destruction of four sugar-harvesting machines, as a protest against rural unemployment in Tucumán Province; the bombing of IKA-Renault car salesrooms in Buenos Aires and Córdoba in support of the SMATA car workers strike; the kidnapping of a Propulsora Siderúrgica executive, Enrique Mascardi, held for a week to reinforce

[1] 'Isabel is not Perón', a common Montonero daubing of 1974–6, frequently preceded by, 'The prices provide the reason'. Another anti-Isabel favourite was 'Evita hay una sola' — 'There's only one Evita'.
[2] For reports of the press conference, see the *Buenos Aires Herald*, 7 September 1974; *The Sunday Times* (England), 8 September 1974; and *The Guardian* (England), 9 September 1974.

workers' demands for wage rises and the rehiring of dismissed workmates; the 'execution' of Quilmes policeman Orlando Fernández, accused of slaying Beckerman and Van Lierde; the assassination of Rosario policeman Rubén San Juan, charged by the Montoneros with the killing of revolutionary Peronist Carlos Brandazza in 1972; and a raid on a La Plata courthouse to 'recover guns seized from the people'.[3] All these acts had taken place within days of each other, yet were mundane in comparison with the occasional, anonymous 1973-4 Montonero operations which still remained unacknowledged — perhaps in an attempt to preserve the legality of the Revolutionary Tendency's front organizations; more certainly, because some of those operations had met with a cool reception in the labour movement.

Even with Perón alive, the Montoneros had not refrained from building up their capital reserves and occasionally implementing their own version of 'popular justice', while successfully concealing their responsibility. During their sixteen months 'above ground', they had probably assassinated CGT General Secretary José Ignacio Rucci;[4] they had certainly killed former Builders Union (UOCRA) leader Rogelio Coria, UOCRA bodyguard Félix Navazo, Lanusse's Interior Minister Arturo Mor Roig, newspaper owner David Kraiselburd, and ultra-Right CNU leader Martín Salas; and they had seriously wounded Leando Salato, Director of the Social Emergencies Department in the Social Welfare

---

[3] *Buenos Aires Herald*, 7 September 1974.

[4] Most fingers were pointed at the ERP or at Rucci's trade-union rivals at the time of his death. The Montoneros seemed publicly to lament the killing, though their authorship was clearly suspected by somebody: Enrique Grynberg, a leading member of the JP's *Ateneo Evita*, was gunned down in the doorway of his home in a reprisal attack the next day. Rucci had certainly been 'condemned to death' at pro-Montonero rallies: 90,000 people at a 26 July 1973 Eva Perón commemoration event in Saavedra had repeatedly chanted, 'Rucci traidor, a vos te vas a pasar lo que le pasó a Vandor', intimating that he would receive the same 'punishment' as Vandor for being a 'traitor to Peronism' [*El Descamisado*, no. 11 (31 July 1973), pp. 2-6]. But it was more than a year after the assassination that the Montoneros 'assumed' (rather than claimed) responsibility for it. The probability is that they did actually kill Rucci, though some rumours suggested that they were opportunistically trying to take the 'credit' for an act which was really the work of the breakaway Montonero Sabino Navarro Column. Either way the most important thing so far as Montonero-labour relations were concerned was that the Montoneros were generally believed to be Rucci's assassins.

Ministry.⁵ Both Rucci and Coria had been accused of treason to Peronism and the working class; Mor Roig had been in office at the time of the Trelew Massacre; Navazo had been photographed incriminatingly during the Ezeiza Massacre; both he and Salas had allegedly engaged in para-police activity in La Plata;⁶ and Salato was one of López Rega's men in the self-styled 'Ministry of the People'.⁷ Kraiselburd had attracted Montonero attention because he had been handed the *El Día* newspaper, previously union-owned, after the 1955 military coup, and ran a press monopoly in La Plata — along with Buenos Aires, Córdoba and Rosario, one of the Montoneros' main strongholds. He was seized by guerrillas towards the end of June 1974 and held at a house rented to Carlos Iriart, apparently with the aim of securing a ransom. But a police raid on the house, during which the Montonero Carlos Starita was wounded and captured (to die or be killed six days later), led Kraiselburd's captors to kill him.⁸

Bearing in mind the number of Peronist Left losses in the early 1970s, one can understand the appeal of vengeance killings and the guerrilla conviction that 'popular justice' was being done; but in no way did political benefits accrue to the Montoneros through such activity. Crowds at the FREJULI election rallies prior to March 1973 had certainly chanted 'Soon they're going to see / Soon they're going to see / When we avenge the Trelew killings';⁹ and both the ERP and the FAR had acted in fulfillment of that promise.¹⁰

⁵ Dates of operations: Rucci, 25 September 1973; Coria, 22 March 1974; Navazo, 1 July 1974; Mor Roig, 15 July 1974; Kraiselburd, 17 July 1974; Salas, 24 August 1974; Salato, 12 July 1974.

⁶ González Janzen, p. 184.

⁷ For Montonero coverage of the most controversial assassinations, see 'Ante la muerte de José Rucci' and 'La vida y muerte de José Rucci', *El Descamisado*, no. 20 (2 October 1973), pp. 2-3 and 4-5; 'Por qué murió Coria', ibid., no. 45 (26 March 1974), pp. 2-3 and 8; and 'La muerte de Mor Roig', *La Causa Peronista*, no. 3 (23 July 1974), pp. 20-3.

⁸ One can assume that the Montoneros abducted other businessmen, with a view to endowment of their war chest, as the 6 September 1974 announcement of a return to sustained warfare approached. A number of executives, reluctant to finance guerrilla enterprises, began to direct their business operations from hotels and apartments in the Uruguayan capital of Montevideo [*The Guardian*, 3 September 1974].

⁹ 'Ya van a ver / ya van a ver / cuando venguemos los muertos de Trelew.'

¹⁰ The FAR had killed Rear Admiral Emilio Berisso, a top Navy intelligence officer, on 28 December 1972; the ERP had assassinated Rear Admiral Hermes Quijada, retired chairman of the Joint Chiefs of Staff, on 30 April 1973.

Arturo Mor Roig had now been *ajusticiado* in the eyes of and by the Montoneros, yet one must seriously doubt whether the popularity of the killing extended beyond the combatant Left: the victim was, after all, a civilian, a former member of a political party which still enjoyed considerable middle-class patronage (the UCR), a man regarded by Liberals as having, with Lanusse, brought about the 1973 elections (if by Peronists as the architect of a deceitful GAN), and he had not been politically active since the March poll.

GUERRILLA ATTACKS ON THE LABOUR BUREAUCRACY

The reprisals against Rucci and Coria were no more productive, though clearly merit more attention, given that they directly affected the Montonero bid to attract massive working-class support. Coria had won the UOCRA general secretaryship from the Communist Party in 1963 and had subsequently risen to positions of leadership in the Peronist 62 Organizations and Justicialist Party, before, on being accused of corruption and collaboration with the military regime, he was obliged to resign all three posts by the end of January 1973. He had opposed the FREJULI formula of Cámpora-Solano Lima and had claimed that its lists of candidates had been infiltrated by Marxists. During his decade at the top, while claiming to represent ordinary building workers, he had himself become a construction magnate and landowner, had acquired a fabulous apartment in fashionable *Barrio Norte*, and had also invested his wealth in a bullet-proof car, bodyguards, and other security facilities.[11] In 1973, he had taken refuge on his *estancia* in Stroessner's Paraguay, but made occasional trips to Buenos Aires — his last on 22 March 1974.

Rucci, too, was a wealthy union boss; he was a playboy, the owner of several apartments and cars, a man with foreign investments and a regular security retinue of fifteen *pistoleros*, at least two of whom were implicated in the killing of

---

[11] The lifestyles of Coria and Rucci, and other labour leaders, are described in Jorge Correa, *Los jerarcas sindicales* (Buenos Aires: Editorial Obrador, 1974), a greatly extended and updated version of the original [Buenos Aires: Editorial Polémica, 1972] and the best source on Argentine trade union corruption.

Peronist Youth activists.[12] It was a serious mistake, however, for the Montoneros to assume that the labour movement as a whole shared their characterization of Rucci as a 'traitor', just as it was self-deluding for Firmenich to dismiss him and the other labour signatories to the Social Pact as 'four bureaucrats who don't even represent their own grandmothers'.[13] For though important anti-bureaucratic labour tendencies, associated with the names of Raimundo Ongaro, Jorge Di Pasquale, Agustín Tosco, Armando Jaime, René Salamanca, and Alberto Piccinini, had developed in the late 1960s and early 1970s, their power bases were either regional or lay in militant but small unions.[14] Large numbers of workers were still prepared to tolerate corrupt, wealthy union leaders so long as they won economic benefits for their members from time to time. Here the Montoneros, partly due to the nature of their own social composition, underestimated the economism of Argentine labour, envisaging their 'Vandorist' foe as merely a *superstructural* union phenomenon. They erroneously equated high levels of labour militancy over economic issues with political radicalism at rank-and-file level, and portrayed the *burocracia sindical* as a totally alien growth on the labour movement, something imposed from the outside rather than being an expression of the non-preparedness of Argentine labour for revolutionary politics.

[12] Correa [1974, pp. 89-90] mentions the case of Juan Carlos Gómez, one of the CNU assassins of Mar del Plata student Silvia Filler in December 1971, and that of Tomás Roberto Cardozo, who killed the San Nicolás JP Press Secretary Benito Miguel Span in July 1973. Gómez was released from prison under the May 1973 amnesty.

[13] 'Atlanta', text of 22 August 1973 speech by Mario Firmenich, *Militancia*, no. 12 (30 August 1973), pp. 26-9.

[14] Ongaro's Buenos Aires Printers Federation (FGB) and Di Pasquale's Association of Pharmacy Workers were, along with the publicity workers union, the main strongholds of the *alternativista* Rank-and-File Peronism (PB). PB's other major centre was the city of Córdoba. Tosco and Salamanca were both Córdoban regional leaders, the former of the power workers (*Luz y Fuerza*) and the latter of the car workers (SMATA). Jaime's base lay primarily in Salta Province: militant workers established a *CGT Peronista-Clasista-Antiimperialista de Salta* there in July 1973, but it was violently suppressed by official CGT forces five weeks later. Finally, Piccinini was the leader of the sixty-one-day Villa Constitución strike of March-May 1975, begun when the national UOM bureaucracy attempted to take over the local union branch after having lost the November 1974 leadership elections there to a joint list of JTP, PST, and PRT candidates [See 'Entre el tiempo y la sangre', *Carta Política*, no. 21 (3rd week of April 1975), pp. 4-6 and 8]. Reasons for the pronounced radicalism of Córdoban workers are presented in Beba Balvé *et al.*, pp. 155-67; and Delich, *passim*.

Historically the labour bureaucracy had its roots in the early Peronist and pre-Peronist years after the 1943 nationalist coup, when State patronage of labour and genuine working-class advancement had been achieved at the cost of a loss of trade union independence. Its consolidation as a power factor was interrupted by the 1955 anti-Peronist coup and subsequent military *intervención* of the CGT, but it gradually became a feature of Argentine trade unionism again after the March 1961 'normalization' of the labour confederation, with cautious, conciliatory leaders like Vandor and Coria being quite prepared to negotiate and reach an understanding with the post-1966 military rulers.[15] The point that the Montoneros normally missed, though, when describing the bureaucracy as an instrument of imperialism and a 'daughter' of the 1955 'Liberating Revolution',[16] was that the bureaucracy had possessed a genuine basis of, at first, support and, later, at least sufferance in the labour movement: quite apart from the bureaucracy's historical claims to a Peronist birthright, the labour barons of the late 1960s and early 1970s were, in many cases, the militants of the late 1950s who had led the struggle to regain the CGT;[17] they were certainly subject to 'external' pressures and influences, but could not and did not persistently ignore their members' economic needs;[18] and, indeed, the leaders of the Vandorist unions, most strongly organized in monopolies with a *capacity* for relatively high remuneration, were often successful, if

---

[15] On the power base and rise of Vandorism, see especially Daniel James, 'Power and Politics in Peronist Trade Unions'. The same author provides an introduction to the combative unions in his 'The Peronist Left, 1955-1975', *Journal of Latin American Studies*, vol. 8, no. 2 (1976), pp. 273-96.

[16] 'La burocracia traidora es hija de la Libertadora' was a common Montonero slogan in 1975.

[17] In fact on one occasion the Montoneros did recognize the early combative records of conciliatory union leaders but without appreciating the credit which these had earned them in the labour movement during the 1960s. That occasion was just a few days after Rucci's assassination when, in a bizarre editorial, the Montoneros commented: 'Rucci was a good lad . . . he was not a bad type. He had his history of resistance, of prison.' The same editorial referred also to the late 1950s militancy of Vandor and Coria: 'They were loyal, they had arrived in the unions through elections and they represented the rank and file' ['Ante la muerte de José Rucci'.]

[18] As when, in 1964, the CGT launched a Plan of Struggle (*Plan de Lucha*) which involved the occupation of some 11,000 work-places by almost four million workers [Peralta Ramos, p. 166].

judged solely in terms of economic achievements.[19]

Once ensconced in powerful positions, many of these union leaders did resort to the proscription of opposition lists, electoral frauds, and even US-style labour gangsterism. Several amassed huge personal fortunes and all were decidedly anti-communist. But the Montoneros were surely mistaken in assuming that the workers *en masse* shared their own radical Catholic moral revulsion over the labour leaders' ostentatious displays of wealth and corruption,[20] especially in a country where a spoils system is both traditional and pervasive; where complaints about corruption are often tempered by a sneaking admiration for the successful social climber, an admiration born from the knowledge that the complainant would also grasp any enrichment opportunities that might arise. An even more grave error was for many Montoneros to assume that the methods which the bureaucracy used to maintain its power were those it had employed to achieve it: in September 1973, the JTP had stated that one of its priority goals was 'to get the bureaucracy out of the unions they have *taken by assault*'[21] (my italic).

The logic behind the Rucci and Coria killings, present again in the February 1975 Montonero assassinations of Hipólito Acuña and Teodoro Ponce,[22] was identical to that which had cost Vandor and Alonso their lives at the hands of the ENR a few years earlier. One aspect was purely punitive: it was a question of 'executing traitors', Vandor's elimination

---

[19] Peralta Ramos [pp. 58-63] points to the growing heterogeneity of the working class after 1955 as the wages of workers in dynamic industrial sectors increased and differentials separating them from workers in declining areas of production grew. By 1966 unskilled metalworkers were better paid than skilled workers in other sectors of production and, whether one regards metalworkers as a 'labour aristocracy' or not, their union, the UOM, was naturally the leading bastion of Vandorism.

[20] One leading militant who was, exceptionally, drawn towards socialist politics as a result of radical Catholic influence was Raimundo Ongaro, as comes across strongly in *Sólo el pueblo salvará al pueblo*. During his many terms in prison, he is reputed to have endured the agonies of torture by reciting chunks from the Bible to his police tormentors.

[21] 'Hacia la toma de la batuta', *El Descamisado*, no. 17 (11 September 1973), p. 11.

[22] Hipólito Acuña was the national FREJULI deputy for Santa Fe and Assistant Secretary of the Peronist 62 Organizations; Teodoro Ponce was the interim leader of the Rosario UOM.

being code-named 'Operation Judas'.[23] A second was a belief that 'treachery' could be cleaned out of the Peronist Movement by the force of fire-power, and this came across most clearly in an apologia for Alonso's August 1970 assassination, written four years after the event by 'executioners' who were by now Montoneros. In it, Argentina was depicted as split into two warring camps: 'On the one hand, imperialism; on the other, the Nation. The principal force of the Nation was the Peronist Movement and within that the working class. Any traitor, therefore, from the imperialist camp within the heart of the Nation, i.e. within the Movement and the Peronist working class, was a priority target for being eliminated'. Elitist, supercilious, deaf to workers' real opinions, the ENR's descendants went on to explain that the Alonso operation had been undertaken 'to show the whole Peronist working class that it had a superior weapon to all those employed during those eighteen years [of resistance]' and to demonstrate that the 'main mission of revolutionaries' was 'crushing traitors'.[24] In other words, propaganda of the deed by the deed.

Publication of the latter communiqué by the Montoneros just ten days before their official resumption of hostilities was their way of announcing that punitive operations, including, for a while, those against labour leaders, were now to become a major item in the guerrilla repertoire; and that military means were regarded as legitimate and efficient means, combined with less spectacular agitational activity in the factories, of securing a more militant labour leadership. In January 1974, when questioned privately about what the Montoneros might offer union leaders in order to interest them in negotiations, Firmenich had suggested that one way would be to offer *not to kill* Lorenzo Miguel, leader of the UOM and 62 Organizations.[25]

Through their militarism (though not through this alone), the Montoneros needlessly isolated themselves from some of the more radical labour sectors. Ricardo De Luca, on

[23] 'Declaración del ENR con motivo del ajusticiamiento de Augusto T. Vandor', *Cristianismo y Revolución*, no. 28 (April 1971), pp. 52–3.
[24] 'Quiénes cómo y por qué lo ejecutaron. La muerte de José Alonso', *La Causa Peronista*, no. 8 (27 August 1974), pp. 25–9.
[25] Firmenich, 'Etapa y conjuntura', p. 17.

behalf of the combative CGT of the Argentines, had, back in 1969 in the case of Vandor, condemned the assassination, pointing out that it was 'not Argentine labour's way of solving disputes'.[26] And the Peronist Armed Forces had made an equally apposite criticism of Alonso's 'execution' when they commented: 'If the workers movement is not strong enough to get rid of its own parasites, it won't be strong enough to make a revolution.'[27] In self-defence, the Montoneros claimed Perón's authorization for the elimination of 'traitors', yet the Peronist leader's apparent condonation of the Alonso killing in a February 1971 letter to them was the most recent evidence of approval that the Montoneros could cite.[28] Since then, Rucci as CGT leader had demonstrably attempted to bridle strike movements, but had done so on the orders of Perón,[29] a Perón eager to provide the military regime with practical displays of his professed ability to control the labour movement. Rucci had also embraced the Social Pact, which was now restraining wage rises as prices once more increased, but then so had the Montoneros momentarily and Perón unequivocally. His death led to a thirty-hour general strike, was used as a pretext for a purge of 'Marxists' from the official Peronist Movement, and Perón indicated his disapproval by attending the funeral. Only the Peronist Left and the Guevarists rejoiced, as though the revolutionary cause had been advanced, yet none of the assassinations of labour leaders — Vandor, Alonso, Kloosterman, Mansilla, Rucci, Coria, Santillán[30] — produced shifts to the Left when their replacements were chosen.

[26] De Luca, quoted in the *Buenos Aires Herald*, 1 July 1969.
[27] 'Con las armas en la mano', interview with FAP representatives, *Cristianismo y Revolución*, no. 28 (April 1971), pp. 77–80. An English version of the interview appears in Kohl and Litt, pp. 365–73.
[28] 'Perón a los Montoneros', 20 February 1971, *La Causa Peronista*, no. 9 (3 September 1974), pp. 28–9.
[29] *Buenos Aires Herald*, 19 March 1972.
[30] Marcelino Mansilla, General Secretary of the Mar del Plata CGT Region, right-wing Peronist and wealthy leader of UOCRA in La Plata for a decade, was assassinated by the Belloni-Frondizi Detachment of the *Comando Nacional* wing of the FAP on 27 August 1973, the third anniversary of Alonso's death; Atilio Santillán, General Secretary of the Federation of Sugar Industry Workers (FOTIA), was gunned down by an ERP unit on 22 March 1976 in the centre of Buenos Aires. Santillán had been a combative Peronist union leader for many years but then supported the Army when it moved into Tucumán Province early in 1975 to counter ERP activity there.

Nevertheless, down to the time of the mid-1975 general strike, the Montoneros persisted with their militaristic 'labour policy' rather than reserving their fury for the Right. As they saw it their Peronist enemies were now the *brujo-vandoristas*: a Montonero neologism implying an alliance between the Peronist Right, headed by 'the Sorcerer' (*el brujo*)[31] López Rega, and the *vandoristas*, grouped around the UOM bureaucracy and allegedly seeking to transform Argentina into a *Patria Metalúrgica*, a metalworkers' fatherland. But here notions of 'loyalty', 'authenticity' and 'treason' proved totally inadequate guides to the real divisions within Peronism: these two sectors *had* combined in a pincer movement to force the resignation of Economy Minister Gelbard in October 1974, but had soon fallen out over economic policy. While López Rega sponsored liberal Economy Ministers like Celestino Rodrigo and Emilio Mondelli, who attempted to offload the burden of a worsening economic crisis onto the backs of the workers, the labour bureaucracy harked back to the economic nationalism and income distribution of the late 1940s.[32] Contradictions between the López Rega–Isabel Perón faction and the labour leadership came most clearly into focus in June and July 1975 during the *Rodrigazo*, when Rodrigo's economic 'shock' tactics provoked a *de facto* general strike (the first ever against a Peronist government) which the CGT leaders were obliged to recognize, 'declare', and belatedly lead; and it was used by them to help oust López Rega and some of his allies from the Government, momentarily increasing their own power in so doing.[33]

[31] The nickname was derived from López Rega's obsession with astrology and the occult. Among his often self-financed books on these subjects was one which he claimed had been co-authored by the Archangel Gabriel! Parallels were drawn between López Rega and Rasputin. See Tomás Eloy Martínez, 'El asenso, triunfo, decadencia y derrota de José López Rega', *La Opinión*, 22 July 1975; and Jane Monahan, 'Fallen star who guided Señora Perón', *The Times*, 23 July 1975.

[32] See for example, 'El movimiento obrero argentino ante la situación nacional', a CGT-62 Organizations' paid press advertisement, *La Razón*, 22 July 1975. In September 1975, the Montoneros claimed that Antonio Cafiero, the most pro-CGT Economy Minister of this administration, stood for a continuation of Rodrigo's policies ['Otra vez el poder militar', *Evita Montonera*, no. 7 (September 1975), pp. 2–4].

[33] Relations between the López Rega faction and the union leaders are analysed in Santiago Senén González, *El poder sindical* (Buenos Aires: Editorial Plus Ultra, 1978), *passim*.

It has been shown elsewhere that the power of the CGT leadership was, in any case, more apparent than real,[34] that it was mainly confined to trade union issues and, following the death of Perón, consisted more of successfully vetoing governmental initiatives than imposing its own policy proposals. By tending to lump the rest of the Peronist Movement together in the camp of treason, the Montoneros isolated themselves politically before reinforcing their isolation militarily. They were slow to recognize the emergence of fractures within the labour bureaucracy and broader Peronist Movement when these became visible in 1974-5. There was conflict between the UOM and SMATA, competitors for unionization rights; between Lorenzo Miguel and Victorio Calabró, Bidegain's replacement as Governor of Buenos Aires Province; and between 'verticalist' supporters of Isabel Perón and her disenchanted centrist critics inside the Peronist Movement. A more penetrating political and sociological analysis of Peronism, as opposed to moral denunciations of treason, might have enabled the Montoneros to have reached tactical agreements with other anti-Isabel sectors[35] had it not been for the guerrillas' increasing commitment to a highly militaristic strategy.

THE ATTEMPT TO BUILD A MONTONERO ARMY

The return to clandestinity was intended as a defensive measure, a 'strategic withdrawal' in response to an 'enemy offensive' involving the Triple A and regular police forces, but predicted to shortly include the Armed Forces.[36] This

[34] Ibid., especially pp. 24-5.
[35] There was never, however, any chance of an alliance between the Montoneros and the trade union leadership. The CGT executive firmly supported the security forces' drive against 'subversion' in the 1973-6 period. It organized a fifteen-minute general strike 'in repudiation of terrorism' in October 1974, paid homage to officers killed in the anti-guerrilla struggle the following month, and expressed its 'permanent identification with the soldiers of our glorious Army . . . in the struggle against the terrorists' in August 1975. At times, the Army also assisted the labour bureaucracy: in October 1974, Brig.-Maj. Raúl Lacabanne, appointed as Federal *Interventor* to run Córdoba Province after the police coup against the elected Government of Obregón Cano, supported the SMATA national executive's decision to expel Salamanca and his supporters, referring to them as 'mercenaries' [ibid., pp. 28, 50-8 and 71].
[36] 'Informe del Consejo Nacional del Partido Montonero, septiembre de 1977', p. 10.

'retreat' was unrecognizable to those observers who regarded every guerrilla move as an act of aggression; for it was in no way a passive retreat, but rather, in Clausewitzian terms, the 'retreat of a wounded lion'.[37] While the enemy advanced, the Montoneros' self-appointed tasks were to protect their own forces, to manoeuvre in order to minimize damage at enemy hands, to take military initiatives in order to harass, demoralize, and disorientate the opposing forces, and throughout to prepare at every level for their own eventual counter-offensive. Once the 'retreat' itself was over and the guerrillas safely underground, something achieved by the end of 1974, 'tactical military offensives' of increasing might were to be launched, but always within the strategically-defensive context of a *guerra de desgaste* in which the Montoneros' prime aim was the 'exhaustion' rather than the annihilation of their enemy.[38] Only after the enemy offensive had, with Montonero assistance, come grinding to a halt, could the guerrillas pass to a phase of strategic counter-offensive, in which popular triumphs would provoke splits and the winning over of sectors of the Armed Forces; but that phase was considered, even in the minds of the Montoneros' most optimistic strategists, some years away.

No political radicalization was implied by the return to clandestine warfare. Though now faced with a government deemed 'pro-imperialist' (and certainly prepared to abandon the more nationalistic development strategy of 1973-4), the Montoneros still aspired to the leadership of a National Liberation Movement, based upon Peronism, which would spearhead a broader National Liberation Front, including 'the medium national enterprise and its political expressions, with an interest in the ending of dependency', under working-class leadership.[39] The only novelty was that, with Perón dead, the Montoneros now saw themselves rather than the official Peronist leaders as the principal architects and builders of such structures.

This political bridge-building was, however, less easy than

---

[37] Clausewitz, p. 271.
[38] 'Parar a los milicos cipayos, preparar el avance popular', *Evita Montonera*, no. 12 (February-March 1976), pp. 7-8.
[39] 'La clase obrera y el movimiento peronista', ibid., no. 7 (September 1975), pp. 14-15.

it looked on paper and highly dependent upon the Montoneros retaining a legal foothold in the established political system. An attempt was therefore made to leave the 1973-4 front organizations 'above ground', guerrilla activity being scaled right down for three weeks in November 1974 as the Peronist Youth struggled to reassert itself as at least a semi-legal force. But front activists, like Florencio Fernández and Roberto Silvesti, continued to be picked off by right-wing gunmen, and pressures to either denounce the guerrillas or become an outlaw oneself were particularly strong upon the JUP: its student activists were threatened by Education Minister Ivanissevich in October with the loss of a term or exams as a penalty for continued activism, and leaders José Pablo Ventura and Miguel Talento were arrested, along with Marcela Cuesta, a month later. The Montonero resumption of warfare greatly increased the risks involved in participating in the fronts — the most visible and vulnerable face of the organization. And whether for this reason, or on account of political dissent, or even the way in which the resumption was decided by guerrilla chieftains who left many of their supporters to read about it in the newspapers the following morning,[40] by no means all of the guerrilla periphery went along with the combatants on 6 September. Mario Kestelboim was only the most prominent figure to dissociate himself from the Revolutionary Tendency at this time, resigning as University of Buenos Aires Law School Dean rather than rely upon the JUP, and therefore the Montoneros, for support against the Rightist university offensive.

Within weeks it became obvious that the front organizations were far too closely identified with the Montoneros to serve as legal expressions of their politics. The larger ones (the territorial Peronist Youth and the functional JUP, JTP, and UES) continued to exist into 1975, but as clandestine organizations composed of a series of *agrupaciones* (groups). Indeed, for several months, the Montoneros had their access to the constitutional political system totally blocked: their last remaining deputies, Zavala Rodríguez and Bettanín, resigned from Congress in mid-September, protesting that it had 'proved useless for the defence of the people's causes',

[40] Personal interview with a Montonero supporter who held a minor government post during Cámpora's Presidency, Buenos Aires, 27 September 1975.

having only passed government bills;[41] and by the end of November, their last two sympathetic provincial governors, Jorge Cepernic and Miguel Ragone, had been ousted by Federal *intervenciones*. Now, with the temporary loss of all shreds of legality, new organizational forms became imperative.[42]

During the early 1970s the basic guerrilla unit had been the *comando*, with several of these combining for major operations and with the Peronist Youth *Regionales* and a few Montonero-created combative Peronist branches (*unidades básicas de combate*) as their 'mass front' expressions. For 1973-4, when mass work was clearly the priority, an equally straightforward system of 'integrated platoons', or cells of activists for both mass work and military tasks, had been devised. But now the Montoneros had thousands of activists ready to be organized at one level or another and so 'specialization' became the order of the day: political and military structures became, to an extent, segregated. A specifically military network with combat platoons (*pelotones de combate*) as the basic cell units was built towards the end of 1974. The platoons were roughly the equivalents of the old *comandos*, and like them mainly bore the names of slain guerrillas, but the new fighting units were only part of a far more elaborate structure composed militarily of Columns[43] (like the *Columna Abal Medina* in Buenos Aires) and geographically of Regions and Zones. Along with these

[41] *Buenos Aires Herald*, 13 September 1974. Zavala Rodríguez went on to become a national leader of the Montoneros' Authentic Peronist Party (PPA) and editor of *El Auténtico* in 1975, before being killed in a December 1976 gun-battle with the police. Leonardo Bettanín, who had earlier worked for *Primera Plana*, was killed, resisting detention, in January 1977, months after the abduction and probable assassination of his brother Guillermo Juan. Leonardo's wife Cristina, with him at the end, committed suicide to avoid being taken alive.

[42] An attempt is made in Appendix B to illustrate the organizational development of the Montoneros.

[43] The idea of the guerrilla 'column', influenced by Tupamaro organizational thinking, was that of self-sufficient guerrilla units, each possessing its own recruitment, intelligence, military, and technical apparata, as well as organizing its own mass work. Theoretically, even if several columns were totally wiped out, the others would be unimpaired and therefore able to fight on and multiply. Within a year of beginning to construct columns, the Montoneros abandoned them as being too large and unwieldy. On Tupamaro structures, see Kohl and Litt, pp. 188-91; MLN Tupamaros, *Actas tupamaras* (Buenos Aires: Schapire Editor, 1971); and Alberto Islas and Clara Ferreira, 'Apuntes para una historia crítica del MLN (tupamaros)', *Combate* (Sweden), nos. 31-7 (March-September 1978).

innovations came a vast infrastructural expansion involving the acquisition of bases, 'safe houses', meeting places, printing equipment, 'peoples prisons', training facilities, and munitions workshops. Military ranks were also introduced, *comandantes* now being joined by aspirants, officials, and three different grades of officer. From early in 1975, the illusion was entertained that one could build a regular Montonero Army,[44] not too dissimilar to what the Montoneros termed 'the self-styled Argentine Army', in the concrete jungle of the cities.

The 'politico-military' nature of the Montonero organization (often referred to internally as the 'OPM' — *organización político-militar* — when not as 'La M' of Peronist Left argot) was to be preserved through the simultaneous formation of Peronist militias, composed of activists who, as in 1973-4, continued to perform both political and military tasks: political tasks through the *agrupaciones*, operating especially in the universities and factories; and military tasks in the guise of combat militias (*milicias de combate*). While the platoons, composed of *combatientes*, specialized in military combat and technically-sophisticated operations, their members trained to use a variety of weapons, the militias, composed of *milicianos*, employed hand guns and molotov bombs, and performed a para-military function — at times in support of the platoons of the embryonic Montonero Army, on other occasions independently. Whereas many *combatientes* lived totally clandestine existences (especially when they were *quemados*, known to the authorities), the *miliciano* would typically combine his politico-military activities with the maintenance of a regular job or studies, with 'public' accommodation, and the appearance of 'normality'.[45]

These structures enabled the Montoneros, during their peak year of 1975, to organize as *combatientes* or *milicianos* at least five thousand people, with the latter obviously being more numerous than the former.[46] To mark the 16 September

---

[44] Much of the information concerning the 1974-5 organizational developments derives from a personal interview with two members of the Montonero Peronist Movement (MPM), August 1980.

[45] 'Hacia la construcción del Ejército Montonero', *Evita Montonera*, no. 8 (October 1975), pp. 25-6.

[46] Other estimates of the peak strength of the Montoneros tend to put their numbers under arms higher: Christopher Roper [*The Guardian*, 26 March 1979]

1955 anti-Peronist coup in 1974, 1,500 people were mobilized nationally to carry out about 100 *operaciones* — molotov attacks on targets with imperialist, oligarchic, and repressive associations, plus leafleting, occupations, and lightning demonstrations.[47] However, though the new structure enabled the Montoneros to integrate militants at two levels, it also facilitated the advance of militarism. Theoretically, the emergence of a military caste was to have been thwarted by the participation of professional combatants in the mass front *agrupaciones*, but in practice security considerations rendered this an uncommon phenomenon. On the other hand, the military significance of the militias decreased as the operations became more and more ambitious and required mainly the services of professionals. Structurally then, right from the start of this new phase of warfare, there were indications that military factors might outweigh political criteria in Montonero decision-making.

One of the more impressive, ever-improving, aspects of the burgeoning guerrilla apparatus was undeniably its intelligence service, the *Servicio de Informaciones Montonero*. Its proficiency, unlike that of a State agency, rested upon the unpaid collaboration of individuals in nearly all spheres of Argentine public life. Primarily through the *agrupaciones*, data were channelled to it concerning the security forces, 'traitors', employers, the lay-out of barracks and police stations, and the operation of public services. But an appeal also went out early in 1975 to the Buenos Aires Provincial Police (regarded by the Montoneros as less repressive than their Federal counterparts), and it and similar solicitations may well have reaped information about the Triple A death squad — information from ordinary policemen who despised the latter's activities, who saw how the lust for vengeance engendered by Triple A 'hits' was gradually transforming all uniformed personnel into guerrilla targets, or who resented the promotion of Triple A thugs in preference to career policemen. The Provincial Police were also requested to

---

put their 1975 size at 7,000, as did *The Economist* [26 January 1980] in a survey on Argentina; Robert Cox, absentee editor of the *Buenos Aires Herald*, put it at over 10,000 [*The Observer*, 3 February 1980].

[47] 'Las milicias peronistas son posibles', *Evita Montonera*, no. 3 (March 1975), pp. 22-3.

offer no resistance to guerrilla actions, to covertly assist captured Montoneros, and to minimize the effect of orders to repress:[48] requests far less likely to have been granted, especially after the guerrillas' February 1975 ambush of a police patrol in Buenos Aires, which resulted in three policemen being killed and one seriously wounded.

Apart from an intelligence service, the building of a genuine guerrilla army demanded an abundant supply of finance and weaponry. The Montoneros turned their efforts to the resolution of the liquidity problem before the month of September 1974 was out, moving against *Bunge y Born*, a leading monopoly possessing grain and flour mills throughout the world, as well as diverse agricultural and industrial interests. Juan and Jorge Born, the director and general manager of this business empire, were followed as they drove away from their home in the Buenos Aires suburb of Beccar on 19 September, were diverted from a main road by 'policemen' with a battery-operated traffic light, and were then ambushed by between twenty and thirty 'telephone repair men': four combat platoons of the Eva Perón Column of the Montoneros. Alberto Bosch, manager of *Molinos Río de la Plata SA*, and a Molinos chauffeur, Juan Carlos Pérez, died resisting the abduction.

Within hours, a Montonero 'war communiqué' announced that the Born brothers would be put 'on trial' for 'acts against the workers, the people, and national interests', and claimed that the Government had recently returned confiscated goods, which had been allegedly hoarded in order to force up prices, to the company.[49] Confined in a 'peoples prison', the kidnapped businessmen were questioned about their activities and then 'sentenced' to one year's imprisonment (commuted to nine months when the company yielded to the guerrillas). The Montoneros' self-confidence was as great as their demands: a *sixty million* US dollar world record ransom, described as 'bail for the freeing of Jorge and Juan Born, and a fine for the crime of exchange irregularities, this sum being handed over to the Montoneros as the representatives of the national interest'; the distribution of a further 1.2m dollars in merchandise as a punishment for

---

[48] 'Carta a la policía', ibid., p. 47.
[49] *Buenos Aires Herald*, 20 September 1974.

hoarding and the creation of shortages; concession of their workers' demands; and finally, for alleged involvement in the 1955 coup, *Bunge y Born* were ordered to place busts of Juan and Eva Perón in all their factories.[50]

Negotiations were long and drawn out. To expedite matters, the guerrillas applied pressure through bombing and machine-gunning the homes of Molinos managers during a February 1975 labour dispute there, the kidnapping of another *Bunge y Born* executive (ransomed for half a million dollars), and numerous death threats, until the company finally gave in. *Bunge y Born* representatives in Britain, Germany, France, and Italy met to make the arrangements; giant Montonero publicity advertisements appeared in five Western papers; dozens of truckloads of food and clothing were distributed in the *villas miserias* and working-class *barrios* of Argentina by Montoneros who announced that it was *'Bunge y Born* money being returned to the people';[51] modifications were made in industrial relations and working conditions at some of the group's member companies, including Molinos; Firmenich and Jorge Born appeared at a secret press conference in Accassuso to give details of the package; and the executive regained his freedom the same day, 20 June 1975.

Though sectors of the Left referred to the industrial achievements of the operation as 'paternalistic', it was undoubtedly a success in other senses. While financially corpulent enough to meet the guerrilla demands, the company, even in distress, was unable to evoke any noticeable sympathy among Argentines, allegations of hoarding (denied by *Bunge y Born*) being highly plausible in 1975. On the other hand, the Montoneros had demonstrated the strength of their organization, described by Jorge Born as being 'as good as *Bunge y Born*'; the violence employed had been counterbalanced by displays of compassion — visits by the Borns' family doctor were permitted and Juan was released after just six months for medical reasons; and the Robin Hood stunt with which the episode ended helped to refurbish the Montoneros' romantic image. Above all, the huge pay-off was a guarantor of the Montonero policy of

[50] *The Guardian*, 19 June 1975.
[51] *Buenos Aires Herald*, 18–19 June 1975.

financial independence, amounting, as Jorge Born pointed out, to one-third of the national defence budget.[52] A further five million dollars were to flow into the Montonero coffers the following December, this time as a 'fine' paid by Mercedes Benz to obtain the release, after two months in a Montonero cell, of Enrique Metz. Again, the operation was linked to an industrial dispute, the company was coerced into meeting workers' demands for wage rises and the reinstatement of sacked employees, and the guerrillas gained forcible access to the world's leading newspapers, here to publicize a call for early elections.[53]

With their income for 1975, largely derived from just these kidnappings, exceeding seventy million dollars, the Montoneros were in a position to purchase large quantities of automatic weapons, but very few were ever bought. A guerrilla raid on the Halcón arms factory in Banfield at the end of July 1975 saved them that expense. According to press reports reliant upon the official news agency, the raiders made off with parts to assemble 100 nine millimetre submachineguns and 150 cal. 765 rifles, the former being put together for the Coast Guard and the latter being modified for the Navy;[54] according to the Montoneros, however, they stripped the place bare, leaving it devoid of weapons, parts, machinery, and even fittings. The Halcón production manager was a Montonero.[55]

This operation enabled the guerrillas to venture into the arms business themselves. They acquired the potential to manufacture Halcón machine-guns, though never did[56] — presumably because their technical expertise was insufficient

[52] Ibid., 22 June 1975.
[53] For details of the Metz kidnapping, see *La Opinión* and ibid., 26 December 1975, plus the guerrilla communiqué in *Evita Montonera*, no. 11 (January 1976), pp. 22. For examples of the publicity achieved, see *Le Monde* and *The Guardian*, 24 December 1975.
[54] *Buenos Aires Herald*, 29 July 1975.
[55] Personal interview in August 1980 with MPM members, London.
[56] The Revolutionary Coordinating Council (JCR), composed of the Argentine PRT-ERP, the Uruguayan MLN Tupamaros, the Chilean Movement of the Revolutionary Left (MIR), and the Bolivian National Liberation Army (ELN), whose existence was publicly announced by the ERP in February 1974, did however start to manufacture the JCR-1 machine-pistol. In April 1975, Argentine police discovered a JCR arms factory in Caseros where 500 of the guns were being produced, mainly by Uruguayan members [*Buenos Aires Herald*, 15 February 1974 and 12 April 1975].

(and the importation of gunsmiths too risky) and because, anyway, contrary to television stereotypes, the rifle rather than the machine-gun is (along with hand guns and grenades) the standard weapon of the urban guerrilla. In built-up, populous cities, the accent had to be upon accuracy, so not surprisingly the FAL rifle, as used by the Argentine Army, remained the Montonero favourite, accompanied by Browning and Halcón pistols, the former usually snatched from policemen.[57] But Montonero products — especially grenades and grenade launchers for attachment to FAL rifles — began to appear, indicating the creation of a *Servicio de Fabricaciones Montoneras*, consisting of one large workshop (the Sabino Navarro arms factory in Greater Buenos Aires) and a number of smaller units dispersed throughout various zones of the country. Predictably, the smaller workshops remained undetected far longer.[58]

A NEW PHASE OF ARMED STRUGGLE

Financially secure, better armed, and more numerous, the Montoneros became more ambitious in their new phase of warfare, though they almost discredited themselves early on through a macabre reunion with the remains of General Aramburu. The coffin of the Montoneros' first victim was spirited out of the Recoleta Cemetery in mid-October 1974, only to be relinquished a month later, a few hours after López Rega had returned from Spain bringing with him the cadaver of Eva Perón. Many people viewed the repatriation of the Peronist heroine as a cheap bid for popularity by Isabel Perón and *el brujo*, but the Montonero effort to upstage the Government fell flat: observers tended to see the abduction of Aramburu's corpse — presented by the Montoneros as a means of 'ensuring' the return of Evita Montonera — as either trivial or repulsive.[59]

---

[57] Personal interview in August 1980 with MPM members, London.
[58] The main products were the LG22 rifle grenade launcher, the SFM-4 hand grenade, and the G-40 rifle grenade for use against armoured vehicles. A report on the production of grenades and explosives appeared in the Montonero Army's *Estrella Federal*, no. 5 (September 1978), p. 13.
[59] *Buenos Aires Herald*, 20 October and 18 November 1974.

'Montonero justice'

Vengeance killings (*ajusticiamientos* in the guerrilla lexicon) now became an integral part of the Montonero repertoire as violence, though still discriminate, became more freely used against people as well as property. Top of the list was Federal Police Chief Alberto Villar, blown to pieces in November 1974 as he steered his motor launch away from a Tigre boat dock. Villar was so unpopular that many commentators tended to ignore the fact that his spouse also perished in the blast. An expert in anti-guerrilla warfare, he stood condemned by the Montoneros for his role in creating the blue-helmet Anti-Subversive Brigade in 1970; for directing the storming of the Justicialist Party headquarters in August 1972 to seize the corpses of three Trelew victims (allegedly to prevent it being medically proven that Ana María Villarreal de Santucho, wife of the ERP leader, was pregnant when shot); for police attacks on the funeral processions of Rodolfo Ortega Peña and Silvio Frondizi in 1974; for leading assaults on JP and JTP headquarters; and, above all, for his participation in, or at least collaboration with, the Triple A. His death had been demanded at the Montoneros' March 1974 Atlanta rally when Firmenich, to chants of 'Montonero, the people have a request, we want the heads of Villar and Margaride', replied, 'we inherit all the slogans of our Movement'.[60]

The killing of Villar delighted the Peronist Left, was publicly lamented by few, and showed the Montonero technical advance, but its only political outcome was the governmental imposition of a state of siege on 6 November 1974 — a 'temporary' suspension of constitutional rights which remained firmly in force six years later. For the Montoneros, the state of siege represented a mere institutionalization of the status quo, their legal rights to march, assemble, and publish already having been denied; but it certainly made life harder for other left-wing forces. Despite Government promises that decree 1386, imposing the state of siege, would not be used against legal parties, it was, in the space of just a fortnight, invoked to justify a raid on the Socialist Workers Party (PST) headquarters and bans on a Popular Left Front (FIP) congress and a Communist

---
[60] 'Palabras de Firmenich'.

Party (PCA) rally to recall the Bolshevik Revolution.[61] Villar's successor, Commissioner General Luis Margaride, proved no more humane than his predecessor and distinctly more durable: in December, the ERP launched a truck packed with explosives towards his car, but it was the Police Chief's motorcycle outriders[62] who took the blast. Nevertheless, the Montoneros developed a penchant for assassinating police chiefs, killing General Jorge Esteban Cáceres Monié (Federal Police Chief 1970-2, then appointed as Security Secretary by Perón in June 1974) and Brig. Gen. Cesario Angel Cardozo (Videla's first Federal Police Chief) during the next biennium, thus reviving a practice initiated way back in November 1909 when the anarchist Simón Radowitzky slew the notorious Ramón Falcón.[63] Feelings of Montonero elation at having snatched press headlines must have rapidly dissipated, however, as each backlash came: literally hundreds of 'suspects' were arrested in intensified anti-guerrilla operations during the week following Cáceres Monié's death and, in reprisal for it, a 'General Cáceres Monié Platoon' of the Liberators of America Command[64] invaded a student meeting, dragged out five Bolivians, three Argentines, and a Peruvian, and took them to an isolated spot outside Córdoba, where, bound hand and foot and blindfolded, they were all shot.[65]

Villar was only one of several victims in a sustained Montonero campaign against the Triple A, affecting policemen and Social Welfare Ministry personnel. José Mario Russo, a right-wing Ministry employee was gunned down in Santa Fe in October 1974; retired police commissioner Juan Ramón Morales, *Jefe operativo* of the Triple A according to the Montoneros, was wounded but survived a Montonero ambush in April 1975, thanks to Army intervention;[66] in

[61] *Buenos Aires Herald*, 17 November 1974.
[62] Around this time VIPs were driven amid flotillas of police cars and motorcycles, often with side roads temporarily closed off. Many private security vehicles carried flame-throwers.
[63] Viñas, pp. 231-41.
[64] The *Comando Libertadores de América* was a death squad which operated in 1974-6, reputedly linked to the Army in Córdoba.
[65] *La Opinión*, 5 December 1975; and *El Cronista*, 8 December 1975.
[66] Morales's car was ambushed in the Palermo district of Buenos Aires by the Gustavo Natalio Stenfer Combat Unit (two platoons); but Army troops arrived on the scene and a gun-fight started, Lt. Col. Colombo and a bodyguard being killed during it. See the Montonero communiqué in González Janzen, pp. 243-54.

August television worker Adolfo Dibatista, allegedly the Triple A killer of two Montoneros,[67] was assassinated; and finally, in February 1976, another Social Welfare Ministry official, José Miguel Tarquini, ex-editorial chief of the fascist *El Caudillo*, was ambushed and killed in Quilmes.[68] While totally ineffective as a response to right-wing violence — and indeed stoking it — these assassinations were not devoid of legitimacy in quite a number of minds. The Triple A was widely regarded as sinister and fought a far dirtier war than the most unprincipled guerrillas. On several occasions wounded Montoneros were picked up off the streets by doctors, carried to waiting Social Welfare Ministry ambulances, and never reached a hospital: they were either killed in the vehicles, taken to torture centres before being finished off at rubbish tips, or hung from trees.[69] Moreover, the Triple A enjoyed official protection and seemed immune from lawful challenges: no Triple A henchmen or 'Ministry of Death' employees were arrested.[70] Government officials publicly appeared to justify Rightist violence. Internal Security under-secretary García Rey was reported as saying in Tucumán that 'to get rid of the guerrilla, the same non-conventional methods used by the delinquents will be used';[71] López Rega came out with the statement that his opponents had such hard heads that hammers should be used on them;[72] and *la Presidenta* herself, at a poorly-attended 1975 May Day rally, expressed a desire to 'take a whip' to the guerrillas.[73] There was also evidence of public

[67] Jorge Ernesto Araya and Adriana Estevez, whose bodies were found in the River Carcaraña on 19 July 1975.

[68] The names of Morales and Tarquini featured prominently in the testimony of Triple A deserter Héctor Paino in February 1976 ['Las revelaciones de Paino', *La Opinión, segunda sección*, 12 February 1976]. Paino's organigram of the Triple A showed López Rega at the top, with Carlos Villone (briefly Social Welfare Minister after López Rega's fall) and Jorge Conti (Social Welfare Ministry press advisor) as 'link men'. Among the Triple A groups allegedly organized by Conti was one led by Julio Yessi (leader of the right-wing Peronist Youth of the Argentine Republic — JPRA) and another by Felipe Romeo, which included Tarquini. Paino left the Triple A and was jailed, he claimed, for refusing to kill somebody [*Buenos Aires Herald*, 5 February 1976; and *La Nación*, 14 February 1976].

[69] *The Times*, 29 July 1975.
[70] *La Opinión*, 28 September 1975.
[71] Ibid., 11 July 1975. He later denied having made the statement.
[72] *Buenos Aires Herald*, 30 June 1975.
[73] Ibid., 2 May 1975. Only 20–30,000 people attended the rally.

funds being channelled to fascist groups.[74]

On the other hand there were just as many Montonero vengeance killings whose significance was lost on the general public. One wonders, for instance, how many people knew and remembered, when Monte Grande councillor Rubén Domínico was assassinated in December 1974, that eight months earlier he had been accused by the Peronist Youth of responsibility for the rape and murder of JP activist Liliana Ivanoff?[75] Here, the danger for the guerrillas was that, even for civilians undisturbed by the killing of Police Chiefs, the less 'obvious' vengeance attacks would be seen as part of a private war between armed gangs. They did not contribute to the guerrilla aim of transforming their combat units into a people's army; all that they contributed to was a growing exchange of assassins' bullets between Left and Right, with those of the Right being the more diffusely targeted. Rightist violence became less and less discriminate following the death of Villar, its list of victims including dozens of political refugees from neighbouring military regimes and people whose only crime was to be related to guerrillas.[76] Looked at purely in instrumental terms, the Right's usage of terror was logical: it already wielded control over key power centres and could thus rest its might upon State resources rather than popular support. The anti-State

[74] The Organizational Command (C de O), led by Peronist deputy Alberto Brito Lima, received over 1,000 dollars from the Social Welfare Ministry in February 1975, ostensibly for a sports camp belonging to a primary school, the *Escuela Hogar No. 11* of Ezeira. The C de O was in the process of taking control of the school at the time. Under its management, which lasted for most of 1975, school children were frequently harangued by C de O propagandists and during PE lessons were forced to march in columns and make the Nazi salute [*La Opinión*, 12 and 14 October 1975].

[75] *Buenos Aires Herald*, 26, 27 and 30 April 1974 and 9 December 1974.

[76] Firmenich's cousin, Mario Norberto, was reported to have 'disappeared' after being arrested and then allegedly released [*Buenos Aires Herald*, 16 December 1974]; then, to mark the 3rd anniversary of the Rawson guerrilla jailbreak, the Liberators of America Command killed the parents, a brother, and a sister of Trelew victim Mariano Pujadas in Córdoba, provoking a considerable public outcry, including protest strikes by Transax, IKA-Renault, Thompson Ramco, and Fiat workers [*La Opinión*, 14 and 16 August 1975; *El Cronista*, 20 February 1976]; Dr. Hugo Vaca Narvaja, once Frondizi's Interior Minister, father of another Rawson escapee and leading Montonero Fernando Vaca Narvaja, was abducted in Buenos Aires by men claiming to be policemen two weeks before the military coup, and never seen again [*La Nación*, 11 March 1976]; and the father of Montonero 'original', Carlos Capuano Martínez, was killed in Córdoba on the eve of the Army takeover [*La Tarde*, 23 March 1976].

violence of the Left, conversely, had to be selective, for the winning and retaining of popular support were essential to its strategy for the seizure of power.

Vengeance killings were not always selective enough, in terms of the public appreciating their significance, but two other means of countering Rightist violence were also pursued. The first demonstrated the quality of the Montoneros' intelligence service and consisted of compiling a dossier on the Triple A for use in encouraging constitutionalist politicians and the Army to move against it. It is almost certain that this was sent to Radical Party leader Ricardo Balbín, though in July 1975 he failed to attend an investigation into the Triple A and denied having received it. A brother ascribed his absence to *force majeure*.[77] The Montonero ploy failed, yet they were correct in assuming that the Army was in many ways hostile to the Triple A: 'internal security' was not a task for 'private enterprise' and the generals wanted full control over it themselves. It was largely they and the trade unions who forced the resignation (and subsequent departure from Argentina) of López Rega in July 1975, and they alone who became dominant in fighting the guerrillas that same year: in February they took charge of operations against the ERP in Tucumán Province; in October they gained national control over all security matters . . . though this in no way produced a curbing of death-squad activity.

The other Montonero effort at dealing with the same problem was even less effective and highlighted an ever-increasing difficulty for the guerrillas: that concerning communications. On 26 February 1975 the Hugo Baretta and Hugo Figueroa Platoons[78] of the Emilio Maza Column occupied the offices of the US honorary consul in Córdoba, John Patrick Egan, autographed the walls using aerosol cans, deposited leaflets, and then carried off their sixty-two-year-old victim. A Montonero 'War Report' issued that day stated that Egan 'as the direct representative of Yankee interests in our province has been condemned to death by

[77] *Buenos Aires Herald*, 25 July 1975.
[78] The operation was planned for 24 February to coincide with the anniversary of Perón's 1946 electoral victory, but had to be postponed when two would-be participants, Baretta and Figueroa, were killed in the Córdoba suburbs on 21 February, shot by the police when attempting to retrieve guns from an abandoned car.

shooting', but that he would have the sentence 'commuted' and be released if the Government and Armed Forces showed that five 'missing' guerrillas were alive and well before 19.00 hours on 28 February. A letter from Egan to the US Ambassador in Buenos Aires referred to the five Montoneros: 'I know that you have enough power to get the Argentine Government and the Army to meet the Montonero demands. If these people are not dead, please use all your influence to ensure that they show up.'[79] It had no effect. Egan was shot at the stipulated time, and his body was discovered wrapped in a Montonero flag and newspapers reporting the deaths of Baretta and Figueroa.

In this case, the Montoneros' demands appeared quite reasonable, but they were not realistic. Either the five had already been killed or the Government and Army were guilty of abduction. To have responded in any manner would therefore have politically discredited the Government and might easily have made it appear a tool of the USA. The dilemma, of their own making, which faced Egan's captors was thus similar to that which confronted the Tupamaros in the case of Dan Mitrione,[80] though the Montoneros' prisoner was neither a CIA nor an FBI agent. To release Egan would have been a humane act, but one likely to be interpreted as a sign of weakness and hence cause demoralization among Montonero supporters; to kill the consul was to show that they could and would fulfil promises and threats, yet in indicating firmness the guerrillas ran a great risk of being seen by the public as the authors of a terrorist act of kidnapping and murder, devoid of a political rationale. Without exception the latter was indeed how the assassination was presented in the far from 'free' Spanish-language press, its coverage here typifying the communications problem facing the guerrillas.

---

[79] For the texts of the 'War Report' and Egan's letter, see *Evita Montonera*, no. 3 (March 1975), pp. 46-8. The leading name on the list was that of Gustavo Stenfer, the son of a small businessman, who joined the guerrillas during the early 1970s. Jailed for an attack on a policeman in August 1972, he took part in the Villa Devoto Prison takeover in May 1973, but 'disappeared' on 21 October 1974.

[80] On the Mitrione case, see Alain Labrousse, *The Tupamaros* (Harmondsworth, Middlesex: Penguin, 1973), pp. 99-112. Costa-Gavras's film, *State of Siege*, brilliantly portrays the Tupamaro dilemma.

Communications problems and the growth of militarism

Pressures for self-censorship by editors had increased at the end of September 1974 when a new Anti-Subversion Law established prison sentences of up to five years for journalists and editors reproducing information considered to be aimed at 'altering or eliminating institutional order'.[81] Before long a specific ban on even mentioning guerrilla organizations by name was in force and practically no information about guerrilla activity from unauthorized sources appeared in print. With the noble exception of the English-language *Buenos Aires Herald*, and occasionally *La Opinión*, the political objectives of guerrilla operations were largely ignored by the press, which only indicated the specific authorship of actions in about 10 per cent of reported incidents.[82] Then, instead of the usual references to 'subversive delinquents', the ERP (illegal since September 1973) gained mention as the 'ODI' or *organización declarada ilegal*, while the Montoneros, considered to have 'proscribed themselves' by going underground, appeared as the *organización autoproscripta* or as the *guerrilla peronista*. Talk of 'journalistic terrorism' found its way into right-wing rhetoric, and it was a sad reflection on the state of the Argentine press when in August 1975 Interior Minister Antonio Benítez, denying any restrictions on its freedom, pointed out that 'only' *Crónica, Militancia, El Mundo, El Descamisado, Noticias, La Calle*, and *Satiricón* had been banned.[83]

Tremendous obstacles therefore stood in the way of the Montoneros explaining their actions to the public. They seized radio stations for brief bandit broadcasts on a couple of occasions, but this was poor compensation for the lack of a legal mouthpiece: no freely-accessible Montonero publication existed from the September 1974 *La Causa Peronista* ban until the launching one year later of *El Auténtico*, and the latter was only a fortnightly, had to pose as merely sympathetic to the Montoneros, only ran to eight editions, and was, even so, a paper which one brought at news-stands

---

[81] *Buenos Aires Herald*, 27 September 1974.
[82] Author's examination of the Argentine press, June 1975–March 1976.
[83] *Buenos Aires Herald*, 7 August 1975. On the same occasion, this minister with responsibility for the police claimed that he did not know whether the Triple A existed: 'They could be left-wingers in disguise.'

only while looking nervously over one's shoulder.[84] *Evita Montonera*, a clandestine magazine containing political commentary on events and details of guerrilla and labour activity, appeared at the start of 1975 but, distributed by post and hand, never acquired a readership beyond members and active supporters. The eight numbers published that year had a total circulation of 96,000 copies and generally arrived three to four months late.[85]

This all meant that, for operations to have a chance of succeeding in their political ambitions, guerrilla actions had to be self-explanatory; otherwise, as guerrilla strategist Abraham Guillén had warned, they would be 'politically useless'.[86] For them to have been self-explanatory, however, would have involved far greater discrimination in the Montonero choice of targets and operational methods, something which would have run counter to the growing momentum of the guerrilla struggle and to the increasing tendency of the Montoneros to equate revolutionary struggle with regular military warfare. Guillén had always insisted that 'to win the support of the population, arms must be used directly on its behalf',[87] but the maxims of this veteran of the Spanish anarcho-syndicalist movement (FAI-CNT) were by now largely ignored by the Montoneros. In his stead, to the extent that one may speak of strategic influences upon the Montoneros, stood the imposing figure of Carl von Clausewitz, the dialectician of war, commonly known for having noted that 'War is not an independent phenomenon, but the continuation of politics by other means'.[88] This at first had

[84] Similarly, Peronist Left books remained on sale, yet if one spent more than a few minutes examining them in major bookstores in the centre of Buenos Aires, plainclothes policemen would demand to know why (personal experiences).

[85] Partido Montonero, untitled internal document, October 1977: a synthesis made by the *Conducción Nacional* of the September 1977 meeting of the *Consejo Nacional* of the party, p. 16. *Evita Montonera* was briefly joined by *El Montonero* early in 1976. On the eve of the military coup, one edition of the Montonero-backed *Información* came out, to voice the demand of Centre-Left groups for elections. Its editor, Holver Martínez Borelli, was a former university rector and Popular Christian Party leader in Salta. In 1977 he became a leader of the Professionals, Intellectuals, and Artists Branch of the MPM. The best source on the problems affecting journalism is Andrew Graham-Yooll, *The Press in Argentina 1973–8* (London: Writers & Scholars Educational Trust, 1979).

[86] Hodges (ed), *Philosophy of the Urban Guerrilla*, p. 266.

[87] Ibid., p. 267.

[88] Clausewitz, p. 7.

been cited by the Montoneros to emphasize that their guerrilla activity formed part of a political struggle, but now the dictum served as a substitute for revolutionary theory: it was used to present the guerrilla escalation of 1975 as not only a military advance but also *ipso facto* as a political advance. Militarism became the dominant guerrilla trait as strategic declarations not only outlined the guerrilla methodology but also doubled for revolutionary theory. Armed struggle had developed a dynamic of its own, with Montonero moves dictated, in addition to national political events, by two things: a theory of armed struggle which demanded periodic *saltos* to higher levels of warfare; and, as the death toll rose, by the desire for vengeance. It was the latter above all which drew the guerrillas into what they termed the 'dialectic of confrontation' — a reactive spiral of violence which tempted Montoneros to increasingly *respond* to enemy moves rather than seize and retain the initiative.

Two years later militarism was to appear with *movimientismo* as the subject of a guerrilla *autocrítica*, though as a sin which could be excused as one of several 'correct deviations of the period'.[89] Nevertheless, the Montoneros in 1975 at least demonstrated to sceptics the *possibility* of urban guerrilla warfare. Bolstered by a healthy guerrilla exchequer, the operations of that year included but went far beyond kidnapping, assassination, and bombings: by exploiting the classical guerrilla advantages of surprise and mobility, the Montoneros were able on two occasions totally to undermine State control over a major city, and on several occasions over neighbourhoods; they were to strike telling blows against the Navy and Air Force; and they were to mount a 'monster operation' against the Army which drove deep into the frontier terrain separating regular from irregular warfare. The phase was not to last. The Montoneros remained strategically on the defensive. But their exploits of that year took them to the centre of the Argentine political stage, elevated them to Latin American urban guerrilla pre-eminence, and illustrated both the potential and the limitations of a strategy which showed itself to be clearly of a different qualitative order to political terrorism.[90]

[89] 'Informe del Consejo Nacional . . . septiembre de 1977', p. 6.
[90] Urban guerrilla warfare has been referred to by Walter Laqueur [*The Guerrilla*

Raising the level of warfare

Within the 'defensive' context defined by Montonero strategists, which was to last until 1979, three 'tactical military offensives' were launched in the 1974-6 period. Of these, the first military campaign (January–March 1975), while producing 150 *operativos*, consisted mainly of armed propaganda and the settling of accounts with Peronist 'traitors' and members of security apparata.[91] July saw the initiation of a second campaign and the onset of genuine military and para-military activity. At first this involved blocking roads, establishing temporary control over urban areas, and attacks on police stations, with both platoons and militias intervening in efforts specifically designed to boost popular confidence in Montonero military ability; but a new *salto* was achieved, as part of the same campaign, from late August to October with, for the first time, major attacks on the Armed Forces taking place. Finally, a new phase of 'withdrawal and preparation' (for a Montonero counter-offensive) was announced at the end of the year, in response to the military's 'annihilation campaign', though this was not to prevent a 'third military campaign', directed principally against policemen, from being set in motion on the eve of the March 1976 coup. In all some 500 operations, of vastly differing dimensions, went onto the Montonero score-sheet in 1975.[92]

Of these the most noteworthy were the occasions upon which Montoneros rampaged at will through Argentina's major cities, and the blows struck against the three military services. Twice in July 1975 the guerrillas displayed their developing military muscle through superbly-synchronized attacks in Córdoba, then the focal point of urban political

---

Reader (Philadelphia: Temple University Press, 1977), p. 7] as 'only terrorism in a new guise', yet both Marighela and Guillén feature in the cited work. John Ellis [*A Short History of Guerrilla Warfare* (London: Ian Allan Ltd., 1975), pp. 6-8] also sees 'urban guerrilla warfare' as a misnomer, and moreover accuses its practitioners of 'half-baked gangsterism', yet the Argentine armed struggle of 1975 did at least satisfy his definition of warfare as implying 'a certain level of organized violence which is above and beyond isolated acts of sniping, kidnapping, and robbery'.

[91] 'Hacia la construcción del Ejército Montonero'.
[92] Partido Montonero, untitled internal document, October 1977, pp. 15-16.

repression.[93] In the first operation, a couple of days after the victorious general strike, they bombed two police stations, twenty stores, and two press offices, yet this blitz, accompanied by a call for a popular rising against the Government, was no real substitute for attaining a leadership capacity in the strike movement. After a similar escapade in Buenos Aires Province on 25 July, during which seven police stations, three town halls, and the Ciudadela Artillery HQ were attacked, the Montoneros again hit Córdoba on the 30th, barricading off approach roads to the city with chains and overturned cars before launching a machine-gun attack on the provincial Government House. Though the police lost control of Córdoba for one hour on this latter occasion, what all these actions so blatantly lacked was mass participation.[94] If genuinely intended to ignite the fuse of popular rebellion, and not to serve merely as guerrilla training exercises, these operations were *blanquist* in the extreme: their impact on workers was an external, military one, to which actual Montonero participation in mass struggles was subordinated. What they achieved, at the cost of several Montonero losses, was to show that the police alone could not maintain order. Despite the introduction of sand-bagged machine-gun nests outside police stations and strict control over motorist usage of passing roads, police casualties were now rising at least as rapidly as those of the Montoneros,[95] prompting Army demands for a counter-insurgency monopoly for itself.

Up to August 1975 the Montoneros concentrated their fire upon the police, monopolies, and Peronist Right, having

---

[93] Unofficial data, probably from the Ministry of the Interior, cited in *La Nación* of 21 June 1975, suggests a shift in armed struggle away from Córdoba after 1973, possibly owing to the harshness of counter-insurgency methods used there after the police coup and Federal *intervención* of February–March 1974. According to this source, there were 689 'acts of terrorism' in Argentina in 1973 and 3,178 in 1974; Córdoba was the principal venue in 1973, followed by Buenos Aires Province, but in 1974 Buenos Aires Province became the main area, followed by the Federal Capital.

[94] For details, see the *Buenos Aires Herald*, 11, 26 and 31 July 1975; *La Opinión*, 11 July 1975; and *La Nación*, 11–12 July 1975.

[95] The *Buenos Aires Herald* of 13 August 1975 calculated that sixty-five policemen had died in clashes with guerrillas or guerrilla attacks since July 1974. One heard rumours in 1975 about police stations in the Buenos Aires suburbs having been abandoned due to their vulnerability to guerrilla attack. Though never confirmed (or denied), their credibility conveys something of the political atmosphere of the time.

reached a tactical agreement with the ERP which left attacks on the military a preserve of the Guevarists.[96] Intelligence exchanges took place between the two organizations, typically of plans of enemy installations, but no major joint operations were hazarded and no progress made towards unity. All guerrillas could now agree on armed opposition to an increasingly unpopular government, yet the basic Peronist/Guevarist divide remained, with the Montoneros seeking to establish a broader front than the ERP and insisting upon their own hegemony. Roberto Quieto pointed out in an interview in October 1974 that, whereas the ERP regarded the Armed Forces as a reactionary monolith, the Montoneros still stood for 'a programme of national liberation that will be supported by a broad front in which the petty bourgeoisie and progressive sectors of the Armed Forces will participate'.[97] Moreover, the Montoneros viewed the ERP's rural *foquismo* as old-fashioned and inappropriate: Tucumán Province, where the ERP began rural operations in 1974, was not the 'Cuba of Argentina' and soon became, in Army appraisals, the 'Stalingrad of the ERP'.[98]

As the ERP became more and more tied down in Tucumán,

[96] After the alleged massacre of sixteen captured guerrillas in Catamarca in August 1974, the ERP announced that it would shoot sixteen Army officers in retaliation, and began to do so on 25 September. By 10 December ten officers had been assassinated, but the campaign was then called off due to the accidental death of a three-year-old girl, caught in the crossfire during the killing of her father, Captain Viola. After that, the ERP concentrated on rural guerrilla warfare in Tucumán for a year, achieving initial success when faced with only police opposition, but then gradually succumbing to the Army in 1975. ERP support there, won by its PRT parent party during the 1960s through its participation in struggles against sugar mill closures, was undermined by the Army creating 'protected' areas and destroying isolated dwellings in order to cut the guerrillas off from the rural population. By January 1976 official sources suggested that the ERP had lost 150 fighters in Tucumán, against Army losses of 50; the ERP claimed 100 enemy losses against 50 of their own, but they were clearly in decline by this time. See the *Buenos Aires Herald*, 7 January 1976; and *La Opinión*, 8 January 1976.
[97] 'Under the Shadow of a Gunman', Roberto Quieto interviewed by Richard Gott, *The Guardian*, 18 October 1974.
[98] Brig.-Gen. Luciano Benjamín Menéndez, Commander of the 3rd Army Corps, quoted in *La Opinión*, 18 December 1975. The ERP likened Tucumán to Cuba because of the province's sugar economy and extensive mountainous terrain; but besides romantic Guevarist notions, the selection of Tucumán as a war zone almost certainly had something to do with the fact that PRT-ERP leaders Mario Roberto Santucho, Manuel Carrizo, and Luis Sbédico had all been students of the Faculty of Economic Sciences at Tucumán University, and all qualified as public accountants on the same day.

generally on the losing end of skirmishes with regular troops, the onus was upon the Montoneros to 'lift' the guerrilla struggle to new heights. The latter months of 1975 were thus characterized by generalized, well-coordinated operations of high technical proficiency. Over 100 Montonero bombs, directed against property, exploded throughout Argentina on the Trelew anniversary of 22 August, followed by an encore performance of equal magnitude to commemorate the 1955 coup on 15–16 September. Then, each of the Armed Forces suffered a psychological blow, if not a military defeat. Still holding the Navy primarily responsible for the Trelew Massacre, the Montoneros' Arturo Lewinger[99] Combat Platoon recorded the date by blowing up the force's prize possession: its first modern missile-carrying frigate, the 3,500-ton *Santísima Trinidad*. This *niña bonita* of the Argentine Navy was particularly tempting for the Montoneros, it being built with British assistance as part of a 350m dollar deal which outraged their nationalist sentiments: warships such as this, the guerrillas maintained, should be used to recover the Malvinas Islands for Argentina, not to strengthen ties with 'British Imperialism'.

Conceived in November 1974 the operation was meticulously planned by a unit which studied and then adapted lessons drawn from Second World War underwater attacks. A celluloid version might have conveyed the scene better than the guerrillas' printed accounts of it:[100] the vessel lying in Ensenada's Río Santiago Naval Shipyards, where it was being outfitted, protected by unsuspecting Naval Guards; the stealthy nocturnal approach of the saboteurs in a collapsible, camouflaged boat; the three-and-a-half-hour labours of Montonero frogmen, close enough to hear the guards chatting as they attached 170kg of underwater demolition charges to the hull; and the climactic explosion which, without sinking the boat, knocked out all the electronic computation apparata

---

[99] Lewinger was a former staff-writer for *Primera Plana* and a senior officer in the Montoneros. He led the unit which eventually launched the attack on the Navy, though he himself was killed when directing an attempt on 24 May 1975 to take over a Mar del Plata police station and free the Montonero, Eduardo Soares. The father of Soares was killed the following day, allegedly by the police [*Evita Montonera*, no. 7 (September 1975), p. 12].

[100] Ibid., pp. 28–9; and no. 8 (October 1975), pp. 16–18. See also *La Opinión*, 23 August 1975.

designed to steer it, setting back construction schedules by at least a year.[101]

Next it was the turn of the Air Force, which also suffered an attack in the name of revenge, this time for the killing of leading Montonero Marcos Osatinsky.[102] At the end of August, a platoon bearing his name blew up the runway of the Benjamín Matienzo Airport of San Miguel de Tucumán by remote control, destroying a Hercules C-130 transport plane carrying anti-guerrilla personnel as it took off. Five people were killed and forty injured in this, the most direct Montonero response to the military anti-guerrilla Tucumán mission. It happened in a guarded military zone, but security had become slack and the existence of a tunnel beneath the airstrip, from which explosives could be packed into a drainage pipe, appears to have been forgotten. Again, months of work had been invested in the operation, coldly referred to in Montonero boasts as 'a genuine work of military engineering'.[103]

The Army, however, had the honour of being the subject of the most elaborate operation of the Argentine guerrilla struggle. The date: 5 October 1975; the place: Formosa, 930km north of Buenos Aires, close to the Paraguayan border; the principal target: the garrison of the 29th Regiment of the Mounted Infantry (R29), one of Argentina's strongest. This northern provincial capital was not a Montonero stronghold, a place where 'locals' might alone stage a surprise attack and then disappear 'like fish in water':

[101] A mini-replay of this operation occurred on 14 December 1975 when the Montoneros mined and seriously damaged the Itatí yacht, owned by the Navy High Command but generally used by C-in-C Emilio Massera.
[102] Osatinsky had earlier been a leader of the FAR. Arrested in February 1971, he was one of the guerrilla leaders to escape in the big Rawson break-out of August 1972. After the Montonero-FAR merger, he joined the National Leadership and took command of the Montoneros' Western Zone until 7 August 1975, when he was arrested by police in Córdoba following 'betrayal' by Fernando Haymal. He was killed two weeks later, either by the police (according to the Montoneros) or by would-be Montonero rescuers (according to the police). His wife was imprisoned, one son killed, and another — aged fifteen — kidnapped after the March 1976 coup. See *La Opinión*, 10, 22 and 26 August 1975.
[103] 'Tucumán: golpe a las fuerzas de ocupación', *Evita Montonera*, no. 7 (September 1975), pp. 16–18; *Buenos Aires Herald*, 29 August 1975; and *La Opinión*, 30–1 August 1975. The only other Montonero attack of this period was the December attack on Corbat (mentioned in the previous chapter): a response to the November announcement that Skyhawk combat planes were being used in Tucumán for the saturation bombing of high mountain areas frequented by ERP contingents.

combatants and equipment had to be transported 800km from Rosario to Formosa and then evacuated 700km. Emphasis therefore had to be placed upon economy, both of personnel and matériel, and the only secure means of evacuation was by air. Just thirty-nine fighters, organized in nine platoons, formed the assault force, though the existence of support groups in Buenos Aires, Santa Fe, and Formosa apparently brought the number of those actively involved to sixty. With the assault force were 11 FAL rifles, 5 FN rifles, 18 Halcón machine-pistols, 1 Madsen machine-gun, 2 shotguns, 5 mines, and 51 grenades, plus hand guns for each member.[104]

Success depended upon precise synchronization of three operations: the hijacking of the *Aerolíneas Argentinas 'Ciudad de Trelew'* Boeing 739 on flight 706 from Buenos Aires to Corrientes — a task entrusted to a platoon of four guerrillas, including doctors, who were to force the pilot to land at the Formosan provincial airport of El Pucú; the takeover of the airport by a further two platoons (nine guerrillas) as the plane was circling overhead; and all this while a caravan of six vehicles containing seven platoons (twenty-six people) wound its way undetected towards the R29 garrison. Moves one and two were successfully accomplished; the third was a tougher proposition. It was too much to demand that the garrison surrender, yet the fact that the Montoneros made such a demand speaks of their self-confidence, as does the fact that the attackers wore uniform: the three members of platoon five in Army apparel, the rest in the Montoneros' own berets, sky-blue shirts, and blue denim trousers.

Resistance proved more robust than the assailants had foreseen: the garrison's heavy machine-gun soon sprang to life and guards who had been allowed to flee opened fire from a distance, occasioning several guerrilla losses. Nevertheless, the assault force penetrated as far as the garrison armoury. There it was obliged by Army gunfire to be satisfied with only fifty of the two hundred FAL rifles it had hoped for. An FAP machine-gun was also seized and immediately put

---

[104] 'Formosa: el ejército gorila oculta su derrota', *Evita Montonera*, no. 8 (October 1975), pp. 2–8. See also *La Opinión*, and the *Buenos Aires Herald*, 6–10 October 1975, which include accounts given by the security forces.

to use. The battle was brief but furious. Before long, platoons two, three, and four were reduced to just two survivors, five out of the six Montonero vehicles had been immobilized, and Army reinforcements from nearby residential quarters began to arrive. Fortunately for the guerrillas, the remaining vehicle was an F 350 truck, just large enough for eleven attackers plus weaponry to get away in. A further four guerrillas who failed to hear the order to pull out none the less managed to reach the airport independently. Eleven guerrillas, at least, lay dead inside the garrison.

Army losses were put at twelve dead, eighteen wounded; and the police also suffered casualties, one of them fatal, in minor skirmishes. 'Mopping-up' operations by the security forces during the following days carried the overall body count to forty-seven, a figure which may or may not have included further Montonero losses. What is certain is that those guerrillas who managed to withdraw from the garrison made a clean escape: they reached El Pucú, took off with their spoils in the Boeing and a four-seater Cessna 182 (later found near Corrientes), and provided their wounded with blood transfusions aboard the plane. Eventually the Boeing landed in the field of a Santa Fe *estancia* where a welcoming party with ten vehicles greeted them.[105] The guerrillas and their weaponry then vanished, preventing police pursuit simply by scattering nails on the roads behind them.

Commentators' military evaluations of the Formosa operation depended upon whether or not they believed the official accounts, and especially the claim that the people gunned down after the operation was over were really Montoneros;[106] if so, they were almost certainly 'locals'. Yet

---

[105] The question of why there was no aerial pursuit or attempt to shoot the Boeing out of the sky has never been satisfactorily answered. In addition to the crew, the Montoneros apparently took a coast guard officer with them as hostage on the flight to Santa Fe, yet it would be surprising if it were to transpire that this alone caused ruthless security personnel to desist from pursuit if not interception. Possibly the need for the authorization of the military commanders and Defence Minister in order to take action against the plane was a factor in retarding possible counter-measures. More likely, though, poor coordination between the Army and Air Force, stemming from inter-service rivalry, explains the mystery.

[106] So far as one can determine, Montonero accounts of their own activities were factually accurate so far as they went. What distortion there was emanated from the omission of relevant facts: in this case, the fact that the R29 attackers had inside assistance provided by the conscript, Roberto Mayol, killed by soldiers during the battle. On the other hand, security force accounts, at least on this

whether Montonero losses were set at eleven or at thirty, many, while condemning the guerrilla initiative, were impressed by its magnitude and audacity. One newspaper speculated that at least 500 guerrillas must have been mobilized for the operation, either as combatants or as auxiliaries.[107] But even those with a sneaking admiration for the purely technical aspects of the feat asked, 'Why?' — 'What was the point of it all?'. Really, it lacked any political logic. The Montoneros' own detailed account, in which they claimed that 'the self-styled Argentine Army, armed wing of the oligarchy and imperialism, suffered one of its biggest defeats at the hands of the revolutionary forces ...', did not mention, as was customary, any specific *political* aims of the attack.[108] Formosa was primarily a military spectacular, designed to secure a large number of arms, to humiliate the Army, and to do both as showily as possible. It brought the Montoneros no great political kudos: nearly all the political parties publicly condemned the action, the Socialist Workers Party not being alone in noting that most of the Army fatalities were 'workers who by force of circumstance found themselves in the Armed Forces as conscripts'.[109] Ironically, the only Army officer to die, sub-lieutenant Ricardo Eduardo Massaferro, was the son of a participant in General Valle's 1956 Peronist rising.

Other Montonero attacks on the Army were similarly, and indeed inevitably, militaristic: the so-called 'recovery' of six FAL rifles by ambushing an Army lorry in La Plata in September 1975, and a similar act in Bahía Blanca in December. In both cases, the vehicles were painted with guerrilla slogans, and in Bahía Blanca leaflets were scattered announcing that

---

occasion, were characterized by positive distortion as well as omissions: the loss of arms from the R29 arsenal was denied, yet eye-witnesses saw them being loaded aboard the escape plane [*La Opinión*, 11 October 1975]; and official claims that there were also Montonero attacks on other Formosa buildings, including a hospital and prison, were never substantiated. Whereas the Montoneros reported eleven losses in the garrison as their total, official reports spoke of sixteen guerrilla deaths there, five more in a hospital attack denied by the Montoneros, and nine more in skirmishes during which four civilians allegedly died in cross-fire.

[107] *La Opinión*, 7 October 1975.
[108] 'Formosa: el ejército gorila', op. cit.
[109] PST statement, quoted in *La Opinión*, 8 October 1975.

'the weapons of the army which represses Sierra Grande pass into the hands of the Montonero Army';[110] yet, apart from passers-by and sympathizers, few Argentines knew that the action was a response to the repressive intervention of the Army and Police to crush an illegal strike by the Sierra Grande miners. All that most people learned was that a sergeant had died resisting the La Plata ambush and an NCO and conscript had been killed in Bahía Blanca.

The Montoneros never resorted to strategic terrorism, in the proper sense of the term, but did, within a year of resuming warfare, begin to treat all soldiers and policemen as legitimate targets. After slaying Cáceres Monié and, unintentionally, his wife, they threatened that 'all those who have persecuted, assassinated or exploited the people will, sooner or later, wherever they may be, have to face the Montonero rifles';[111] and by March 1976, 'attacks on all representatives of repressive institutions' were considered justified: 'from the moment the Armed Forces took control of all the security organs, every uniformed and armed man — irrespective of his class extraction and ideas — contributes to the anti-popular repression and shares responsibility for the atrocities and assassinations committed by the repressive forces'.[112] However, the more the Montoneros concentrated upon reprisals, the more they began to resemble the State-sponsored death squads. Two weeks before the Videla coup, a Montonero aspirant transporting a bag containing revolvers was stopped by plainclothes policemen at a bus stop in William Morris: he resisted arrest, injured two policemen with a grenade, and escaped. The following day, 13 March, the Montonero response was to mount their own 'police patrol' in the area. The Calá López platoon stopped pedestrians, checked their papers, and explained, 'We are Montoneros and we're looking for policemen.' After half an hour, they found one unfortunate Ramón Echeverría, 'executed' him, and disappeared with his Browning.[113]

On paper, the Montoneros still stood by two principles:

[110] 'Contra el ejército represor de Sierra Grande', *Evita Montonera*, no. 11 (January 1976), pp. 9-11.
[111] *Evita Montonera*, no. 11, p. 20.
[112] 'Tercera Campaña Militar Nacional Montonero', ibid., no. 12 (February-March 1976), pp. 32-5.
[113] Ibid.

the maintenance of a 'permanent link with the masses' and 'recognition of military tasks as the principal aspect of our action, based on the conception that although war is the continuation of politics by other means, one cannot achieve major political objectives if one does not possess sufficient military power'[114] — the rider also stemming from the pen of Clausewitz. In practice the two were manifestly incompatible: political and military criteria clashed when it came to real operational decision-making. Political reasoning demanded that the Montoneros deepen their insertion in mass movements, military logic dictated a high level of isolation purely for security reasons. And one can appreciate why it was the military pole of the contradiction which increasingly asserted its dominance. Quite apart from the insistence upon military escalation contained in guerrilla theories, and the tendency of vengeance to motivate spiralling reactive violence, other factors encouraged militarism. First, there was what might loosely be termed 'technological determinism': the tendency for available technical resources to become a determining factor in deciding what kind of operations to mount, and thus for guerrilla actions to get larger and larger as a result of military successes, regardless of the political wisdom of the operations and their relevance to mass movements and developments. Secondly, there existed a guerrilla worry that, unless increasingly audacious and spectacular operations were brought off, their public would soon tire of repetitious acts of violence. And, thirdly, the limited extent of political backing for the Peronist Left also encouraged the attempted substitution of military might for social support, at least as a stop-gap measure.

As the size of guerrilla operations grew the Montoneros appeared more and more obviously to non-combatants as performers rather than participants in the unfolding social dramas. To some they were heroes, to others villains, but either way their stage became more and more distant from ordinary Argentines. In terms of public response the most successful guerrilla activities by far were those of the Robin Hood variety, yet these became less and less frequent as political conflict intensified. Operations of this type, such as

[114] *Evita Montonera*, no. 11, p. 17.

the June 1975 *Bunge y Born* distribution of food and clothing, faded from the guerrilla scene at the end of that year, though the last was particularly amusing: on Christmas Eve, uniformed Montoneros visited a community within a military-controlled zone in Tucumán, dispensed *pan dulce* (the Argentine version of Christmas cake) to the locals, and then marched off in military formation![115] But both here and in their 'monster' operations of 1975, the problem for the Montoneros as political militants was that their military activities demanded nothing of the masses except applause. As in Uruguay, the more successful urban guerrilla warfare was in military terms, the more it degenerated into a 'technological battle between specialists in clandestine violence, with the masses in the role of spectators around the ring where the professionals were fighting it out'.[116]

A huge gulf separated the Montoneros' armed struggle from the struggles waged by industrial militants, including those of Montonero persuasion. Even where support for the guerrillas was relatively high, there was never any possibility of them organizing the local population with any certainty of permanence. Since they operated 'behind enemy lines', where State forces were concentrated, the Montoneros could not, like rural guerrillas, establish 'liberated zones' within which the local population could be politically organized and militarily protected. Their chosen strategy inevitably involved the physical isolation of combatants from the people in whose name they fought. Nevertheless, the State response to insurgent violence was to strike hard against militant workers as well as against guerrillas. The September 1974 Anti-Subversion Law, for example, while principally introduced to counter guerrilla propaganda, also stipulated prison sentences of one to three years for the leaders of strikes declared illegal.[117] Government references to 'industrial subversion' and *la guerrilla industrial* frequently accompanied the illegalization of strikes in 1975, though one magazine noted that the alleged appearance of this new 'threat' was remarkably convenient for the union bureaucracy to invoke

---

[115] Ibid., p. 21.
[116] Régis Debray, *The Revolution on Trial*, vol. 2 of *A Critique of Arms* (Harmondsworth: Penguin, 1978), p. 164.
[117] *Buenos Aires Herald*, 27 September 1974.

when attempting to clamp down on dissident union branches.[118]

Urban guerrilla warfare served as a pretext for the Right to undermine many of the democratic gains of 1973 well before the March 1976 military seizure of power.[119] It catalysed reaction far more than revolution; but the Montoneros were not unaware of its effects. 'The accumulation of political power,' they remarked, 'objectively, at certain times, provides the *golpistas* with justifications, hardens enemy positions, and encourages the advance of the most reactionary forces.' This was deemed 'unavoidable', for 'popular power cannot be developed without confronting the enemy and without aggravating our contradictions with the camp of the imperialists and their allies.'[120] The logic of the argument was that workers would flock into the ranks of the Montonero Army as repressive conditions became unbearable. Instead, many either came to regard the guerrillas as solely responsible for the repression or became victims of it themselves. It is significant that the first major 'anti-subversive' drive once the Army had control over counter-insurgency was directed against the miners of Sierra Grande.[121] But how could they rally to the Montonero cause when the mines, the source of

---

[118] 'Guerrilla: ¿ahora está en el Paraná?', *Cuestionario* (Buenos Aires), April 1975, p. 7.

[119] The major steps in the military advance were as follows: prior to February 1975, the Army was only officially involved in counter-insurgency in a support capacity; that month it was sent to fight the ERP in Tucumán; in August the right-wing Peronist General Laplane was deposed as C-in-C in a move led by Videla, who then replaced him; within twenty-four hours of the Formosa spectacular, the Armed Forces acquired participation in a new Internal Security Council headed by the President; nine days later the provincial police were placed under military control. Big counter-insurgency operations involving the Army, Navy, police, and border guards began in Bahía Blanca in November and by the middle of that month had been extended, under Army authority, to the whole of Argentina. As in the Uruguay of 1972-3, guerrilla activity was used to justify considerable militarization prior to the actual *golpe de estado*. For example, when Catamarca Governor Hugo Mott decided to release seven detainees in November 1975, the Army disapproved and so simply recaptured them [*La Opinión*, 23 November 1975].

[120] 'Los militares cipayos: una nueva etapa de la guerra', *Evita Montonera*, no. 11 (January 1976), pp. 12-15.

[121] The Sierra Grande mines had been occupied by miners for forty-two days when the security forces intervened in November 1975. Workers' demands there included wage rises but were above all, as in the earlier Villa Constitución strike, for the right of the miners to choose their own local trade union representatives. See *El Cronista*, 24 November 1975; and *La Opinión*, 20-3 November 1975.

their livelihood, were occupied by the Army, when 300 miners had been jailed and 400 had lost their jobs? Only by abandoning the mines to make a military contribution to the guerrilla struggle, when what the Montoneros really needed was to cultivate their mass following and remedy their traditional weakness in the strategic industries. It was pointless, in this sense, to recruit working-class militants if they were only going to become professional combatants or live in clandestinity, cut off from their area of influence. Yet that is precisely what considerations of security demanded. The repressive backlash against Montonero activity hit the real, potential, and imagined guerrilla periphery at first far harder than the combatants themselves, encouraging the passage of 'legal' activists into clandestinity but thereby stunting the growth of the periphery even more than as a direct result of repressive violence. The periphery was the life-line between the combatants and sectors of the mass movements, and its paralysis posed a mortal threat to the future of the Montoneros as a whole. Indeed, for all their military extravaganzas of 1975, by the time of the March 1976 coup the guerrillas appeared to be more isolated than at the end of 1974.

POLITICAL INITIATIVES THROUGH THE *AUTENTICOS*

The year 1975 also saw attempts by the Montoneros to reassert themselves as a mass political force, and to prepare for the eventuality of an electoral solution to the crisis in which the Isabel Perón Government was by now floundering. Since the old front organizations were being treated by the authorities as if they were illegal, a new public face was needed. Misiones provincial elections, called as a result of the deaths of the Governor and Lieutenant-Governor in a November 1974 plane crash, were due in April and provided the Montoneros with an opportunity for an attempted exposure of the official Justicialist Party as unrepresentative of the Peronist Movement. It was with this electoral contest in mind that the idea of a Descamisado Party was mooted early in the year, but by 11 March, when the party was formally launched in Nino's Restaurant, its name had become the Authentic Peronist Party (PPA), the courts having ruled sympathetically on a Justicialist Party claim to exclusive property rights over the word *descamisado*. Before long further Justicialist litigation had deprived the infant party of even the *peronista* label, leaving it the Authentic Party (PA), although continuity with the past was preserved in the slogan, 'Peronism Returns with the Authentic Party'.[122]

Essentially, the PA was an alliance formed by the Montonero *Tendencia Revolucionaria* of 1973-4, most of the ousted provincial governors (Bidegain, Martínez Baca, Cepernic, and Obregón Cano), and a few trade union veterans of the post-1955 Peronist oppositional struggles. The alignment was not entirely new: a year earlier, the veterans had created the 'Permanent Commission of Homage to the 11th of March' to defend the electoral programme on which Cámpora had been elected and to campaign for internal democracy in the Peronist Movement. Big names from the late 1950s *Resistencia* years and the 1960s labour battles, such as Sebastián Borro, Armando Cabo, Avelino Fernández, Andrés Framini, Arnaldo Lizaso, and Dante Viel,[123] had appeared at the Tendency's 11 March 1974 Atlanta rally and had shortly afterwards formed the Authentic Peronist Group (APA). Both the ex-governors and the veterans had shared the Montoneros' identification with the Peronist electoral mandate and also their vacillating political behaviour of 1973-4. Martínez Baca had, when ordered by Peronist superiors to purge 'Marxists' from his administration, sacrificed two provincial ministers belonging to the left-wing Peronist Youth before losing power himself in Mendoza; and Framini had, like the JP, momentarily called upon Peronists to rally around Isabel following the death of Perón.[124]

[122] Special supplement to *El Auténtico*, no. 6 (26 November 1975).

[123] Borro was an outstanding leader of the defeated 'Revolutionary' General Strike of 1959; Cabo, the father of Dardo, was a metalworker and former member of the CGT executive; Fernández was a former interim General Secretary of the UOM, who had fought and lost a battle against Lorenzo Miguel for the Buenos Aires leadership of the union in the late 1960s and early 1970s; Framini was a textile workers' leader and a prominent figure in the post-1955 union struggles, before being elected as Governor of Buenos Aires Province in the annulled elections of 1962; Lizaso was a Radical and FORJA member in his youth, but opted for Peronism in 1945 and later participated in the post-1955 *Resistencia*; and Viel was a former General Secretary of the Coordinating and Supervisory Council of Peronism and an ex-leader of the State Workers Union (ATE).

[124] Andrés Framini, 'Hacia la unidad que nos marcaba Perón', *La Causa Peronista*, no. 1 (9 July 1974), p. 46.

Since the Montoneros had abandoned all hope of 'recovering' the Justicialist Party from within, the PA was itself presented as the legitimate heir to the party of Perón and as part of an equally-legitimate Authentic Peronist Movement (MPA).[125] But it failed to excel in its first and last electoral competition, held in the northern province of Misiones. Allied with the ominously-named local Peronist Left party, Third Position (TP), the *Auténticos* attracted only 5 per cent and the Peronist Left alliance 9 per cent of the votes, leaving the PA-TP a distant third to the FREJULI alliance with 46 per cent and the Radicals (UCR) with 38 per cent in the elections for Governor and Lieutenant-Governor. Whereas Third Position, standing alone, had gained 29,000 votes (compared with FREJULI's 51,000) in March 1973, now, allied with the *Auténticos*, the vote for Peronist Left gubernatorial candidates fell to 15,000. The PA's only consolation prizes were places in the thirty-two-seat provincial legislature for Pablo Fernández Long[126] and Juan Figueredo, and the satisfaction of knowing that the official Justicialist vote had lost ground to the Radicals and that the non-Peronist Left had fared even worse than they had themselves.[127]

It must be emphasized that Misiones is no microcosm of the Argentine Republic and that the *Auténticos* would have been expected to have done better in a national contest. Perón himself had estimated the strength of his left wing as 'at the most' 10 per cent of his seven million electors of September 1973.[128] As for the province, it is underdeveloped and hence possesses little in the way of industry or of a working class. Only 40 per cent of the provincial population live in urban areas, the rest inhabiting small closed communities.

---

[125] For the basic structure of the MPA, see the organigram in Appendix B.

[126] Fernández Long, who later became an international youth representative of the Montoneros, had spent the previous four years as a legal advisor of the Misiones Agrarian Leagues, founded in 1970.

[127] The 'non-Peronist Left' here signifies the PCA, PI, PST, and FIP (though the FIP had campaigned for Perón votes in September 1973). The Montoneros had rejected an alliance with the PCA, PI, and PST, saying that the battle was in the Peronist Movement. In the elections for Governor and Lieutenant-Governor, the non-Peronist Left together received 4,593 votes to the PA-TP's 15,244. In the election of provincial deputies, the non-Peronist Left obtained a total of 5,239 votes to the PA's 9,178 and TP's 6,362. All Misiones electoral data from *La Nación*, 13–14 April 1975.

[128] Perón, quoted in *The Sunday Times*, 8 September 1974.

There is a higher proportion of foreigners, especially Paraguayans, than in most provinces, and experience has shown that support for the party of Federal government is often stronger for employment reasons. Moreover, it is no secret that López Rega's Social Welfare Ministry spent a small fortune on *Operación Misiones* to ensure the FREJULI victory: as the election approached, the creation of thirty cooperatives was announced, pensions and the prices paid to tea producers were raised, tax rebates were introduced, and food, clothing, refrigerators, ambulances, school equipment, and sewing machines were distributed as the most persuasive political arguments that the Government had to offer.[129]

In the circumstances, while not impressive, the *Auténtico* showing was respectable. The party had yet to demonstrate its viability as an electoral alternative to Justicialism and Radicalism, but was clearly the leading left-wing force. To enhance their credibility, the *Auténticos* now sent envoys to Mexico in an attempt to persuade Cámpora[130] to become their national figurehead, but to no avail: when the former President returned to his homeland at the end of 1975, his message was essentially the same as in 1973 – 'I want to govern for everybody, without exceptions'[131] – which meant attempting to reconcile warring Peronist factions rather than opting for Left or Right. This was in spite of the Justicialist Party's having expelled him for 'treason and disloyalty',[132] presuming him to be a PA supporter merely because he refused to actively support the Government.

After the mid-1975 general strike, with pressures on Isabel Perón to resign and call early general elections mounting, the Authentic Party built a national organization covering an area

---

[129] *Buenos Aires Herald*, 27 February 1975; and 11 and 13 March 1975.

[130] Cámpora remained in Mexico after an October 1973–June 1974 spell as Argentine Ambassador there. With Obregón Cano and two Mexicans, he opened a dental clinic in May 1975, before returning home later in the year. He was still in Argentina when the coup came, but managed to escape arrest when troops raided his San Andrés de Giles house, and took refuge in the Mexican Embassy. Despite medical problems, the military regime did not permit him to leave the country until November 1979, when he rejoined the Mexican colony of Puiggrós, Righi, Laguzzi, Obregón Cano *et al.* Cámpora died in Cuernavaca, Mexico, on 19 December 1980, aged seventy-one.

[131] Cámpora, quoted in the *Buenos Aires Herald*, 9 April 1973.

[132] *La Opinión*, 23 April 1975.

inhabited by 95 per cent of the electorate.[133] By the end of October, it had 40,000 registered members,[134] mainly people previously mobilized by the Tendency fronts created around 1973. Announcing in the first edition of their fortnightly *El Auténtico* that 'the workers have initiated a new resistance, organizing themselves to recover the government',[135] the *Auténticos* introduced themselves as an expression of proletarian militancy. Yet, when the Authentic Peronist Movement was officially launched, in the distinctly unproletarian Savoy Hotel on 21 September 1975, only one-third of the people chosen to form its Superior Council had trade union credentials.[136] And although the basic document approved at the founding conference maintained that 'we cannot repeat old errors', the political line embodied therein was hardly novel. Liberation versus Dependency remained the fundamental Montonero dichotomy, with this serving as the bed-rock of a project envisaging the creation of a 'National Liberation Front of all sectors objectively opposed to imperialism'.[137] Criticism of Perón was minimal, limited to his 1974 decision to close down the never-institutionalized Youth Branch of the Movement, and a sharp demarcation line was drawn between the Governments of Perón and Isabel Martínez: headlines such as 'Under Perón, things were different'[138] and 'This Government betrayed the people and

---

[133] Ibid., 28 December 1975.
[134] 'Congreso Nacional del PPA', *El Auténtico*, no. 4 (29 October 1975), p. 6.
[135] Ibid., no. 1 (17 September 1975), p. 1.
[136] 'La conducción del MPA: hombres y mujeres con trayectoria de lucha en defensa de los intereses populares', ibid., no. 2 (1 October 1975), p. 4. One reason for this was that the MPA, being modelled on the traditional Peronist Movement, had an executive composed of an equal number of representatives from each of the four branches. The sixteen-person Council was thus composed of four political councillors (Framini, Cepernic, Zavala Rodríguez, Bidegain); four trade union councillors (Gonzalo Chávez, Roberto Tapia, Heriberto Torres, Mario Aguirre), four female councillors (Diana Alac, Delia Castelazzi, René Chávez, Susana Sanz de Llorente); and four youth councillors (Rodolfo Galimberti, Ramón Puch, Claudio Slemenson, Ismael Salame). Of the workers, apart from Andrés Framini, Chávez had been dismissed by the State telephone company in 1969 for rank-and-file activity, Tapia had led the bus drivers' union UTA in Córdoba during the early 1970s, Torres had been an active trade unionist since the early 1940s and held a CGT post in 1957, and Aguirre had twice been General Secretary of the Rosario State Workers Association between 1961 and 1974.
[137] MPA, Consejo Superior, 'Emprendemos la histórica transformación del Movimiento', ibid., p. 5.
[138] 'Con Perón era otra cosa', ibid., no. 1, p. 6.

Perón'[139] frequently appeared in *El Auténtico*.

The *Auténticos*' organizational frenzy reached a climax with the staging of the first 'Perón-Evita' National Congress of the Party on 16 November 1975, using a hall supplied by the Czech Cultural Association after the intended Córdoban venue had been dynamited on the morning of the event by the para-military Liberators of America Command. Already, however, many Montoneros were privately expressing doubts over the desirability of the new party: some felt that a party of cadres, rather than a mass movement (MPA) with an electoral party (PA), should be the objective; many simply regarded any electoral strategems as mistaken, arguing that the military would never permit Peronism the opportunity to be returned at the polls, even if by a reduced majority; and fears concerning the security risks involved in displaying a public face were widespread.[140] Those fears were well-founded. *Auténtico* canvassers were arrested during the Misiones campaign, and later, as the Authentic Party prepared itself for a future general election, the names of 40,000 Montonero supporters were presented, on a plate, to the authorities in order to fulfil party registration requirements.[141]

Had the Armed Forces and Peronist Right possessed greater political acumen, they might have permitted the *Auténticos* to retain their legal status, thereby encouraging a Montonero division into militarists and *políticos* before destroying both. Certainly, guerrilla actions embarrassed *Auténtico* leaders on occasions: in November 1975, former Córdoban Social Welfare Minister, Dr Antonio Lombardich, as *Auténtico* National Council member for his province, declared, 'we have nothing to do with what happened in Formosa' (yet was nevertheless arrested in December); and Framini denounced the Montoneros' assassination of Cáceres Monié and mortal wounding of the victim's wife.[142] Pressures on Authentic Party politicians to disavow the guerrillas grew after 8 September 1975, when the Montoneros were finally outlawed by a military-pressured Government in response to the

---

[139] 'Este gobierno traicionó al pueblo y a Perón', ibid., no. 5 (12 November 1975), p. 6.

[140] Several personal interviews with Montoneros in Buenos Aires, late 1975.

[141] According to a photographic supplement to *El Auténtico*, no. 8 (24 December 1975), the party reached a membership of 98,000 in just eight months.

[142] *La Opinión*, 16 November 1975; and 26 December 1975.

commencement of Montonero attacks on the Armed Forces.[143]

The political parentage of the *Auténticos*, though publicly disclaimed, was an open secret. When the Buenos Aires section of the party was founded on 21 September, the Montoneros sent a message of support and received enthusiastic *vivas* from the assembled delegates. It was the Montoneros who provided the party with its political line and finance, besides most of its leaders, and this was clear to all — not least the Armed Forces. To them the Montoneros and *Auténticos* were attempting an Argentine dramatization of Jekyll and Hyde whose plot was only too obvious — and only too easy to bring the curtain down on after just an eight-month run. The PA was proscribed on Christmas Eve 1975, the ban being premised on the fiction that the Montoneros had participated in the ERP's disastrous attack on the Monte Chingolo 601st army arsenal unit the previous night.[144]

Perhaps the real motivation behind the ban arose out of fears that initiatives aimed at the establishment of a Centre-Left electoral front might prosper. On 21 October, Bidegain for the *Auténticos* had shared a public platform with Oscar Alende of the Intransigent Party (PI) and Héctor Sandler of the Argentine Revolutionary Current (CAR) during an Avenida Theatre meeting ostensibly to discuss the university situation. Negotiations also went ahead with Horacio Sueldo's

---

[143] The ban itself was of little practical significance: it just meant that if guerrillas were brought to trial, which was seldom, a further charge of illicit association could be levelled against them. What it represented, however, was the fact that the Peronist credits earned by the Montoneros in the pre-1973 struggles were by now greatly devalued in the official Movement. Until now, these credits had made the Government hold back from unleashing the full power of the security forces against the Peronist guerrillas, while taking a harder line against the ERP.

[144] In a report published in *La Opinión* of 31 January 1976, the Army was later to admit that its original claim regarding Montonero participation had been false. The report also revealed that of the 29 ERP losses identified, only one was a worker and the rest university and secondary school students. The total number of deaths may have reached 160: several hundred guerrillas took part in the assaullt and unofficial military sources cited by *The Times* of 29 December 1975 put guerrilla losses at 137, and Army and civilian losses at about 20. The ERP admitted 61 losses (28 dead, 10 arrested, 23 disappeared) and denounced the way in which aeroplanes and helicopter gunships had allegedly fired at anything that moved in the *barrio* where the garrison was located ['Monte Chingolo: equivocarse conduce a la derrota', *Evita Montonera*, no. 11, pp. 18-19]. Certainly the Army had foreknowledge of this operation, probably provided by the ERP traitor Jesús Ranier: the guerrillas shot him weeks later but never recovered from this defeat.

Revolutionary Christian Party (PRC) and other small parties in an effort to construct something similar to Chile's Popular Unity alliance, to be headed by Alende if Cámpora could not be cajoled into filling its candidature. But in fact both hopes and fears concerning the crystallization of a popular front were, as Alende put it in November, 'premature'.[145] Such an alliance would have been futile without the Intransigents, yet they formed a bloc with the Communists (PCA) in Congress,[146] and the PCA had always looked upon armed struggle as anathema. Moreover, a tremendous gulf separated the pro-Moscow party's call for a 'broad democratic civilian-military coalition cabinet'[147] from that of the *Auténticos*, for the former was intended to shore up the existing Government, through the co-optation of civilian and military critics, whereas the latter posed a radical alternative, though one fraught with all the dangers encountered by the Chilean prototype of 1970-3. Alende's reluctance to transform unitary declarations into deeds may well have had something to do with PCE distrust of the Montoneros, as well as the threat of *Auténtico* proscription.

That proscription was accompanied by a ban on the Montoneros' last legal paper, *El Auténtico*. Edition No. 6 had contained a list of almost 300 Triple A victims; the eighth and final edition named 4,000 political prisoners, including the Montonero Dardo Cabo and Peronist Youth leaders Juan Carlos Dante Gullo and Miguel Angel Mosse.[148]

[145] Alende, quoted in *La Opinión*, 4 November 1975.

[146] As a result of the March 1973 elections, the Revolutionary Popular Alliance (APR) had one senator and thirteen deputies in Congress, out of totals of sixty-nine and 243. The bloc was composed of: PI five deputies; PRC one senator, three deputies; PCA two deputies; UDELPA (*Unión del Pueblo Adelante*) three deputies. APR's ticket of Alende-Sueldo for the Presidency and Vice-Presidency attracted 885,201 votes (7.43 per cent) in March out of almost 12 million. There were no APR candidates in the September 1973 poll. See *Carta Política*, no. 9 (third week of October 1974), p. 13; and Graham-Yooll, *Tiempo de violencia*, op. cit., p. 59.

[147] PCA communiqué: 'El Partido Comunista apoya la decisión de la CGT y reclama la formación de un gabinete cívico-militar de amplia coalición democrática', published in *La Opinión*, 6 July 1975.

[148] *El Auténtico*, no. 6 (26 November 1975), p. 5; and no. 8, photographic supplement. Cabo, Gullo, and six others were arrested in two Morón restaurants in April 1975. Press speculation had it that they were either planning an operation to coincide with a visit to Argentina by Gen. Pinochet or awaiting an installment of the *Bunge y Born* ransom. Gullo's mother was later reported kidnapped [*La Tarde*, 9 August 1976], and Cabo, along with Rufino Uriz, was almost certainly subjected to a summary execution, though officialdom spoke of an escape bid,

Armed struggle and the State response to it were also detrimental to the non-electoral mass activity of the Montoneros. Of necessity, but also impressed by the grass-roots militancy on view during the general strike, they now operated solely at rank-and-file level. The second half of 1975 witnessed redoubled Montonero efforts to organize labour *agrupaciones*. A Coordinating Council of Unions, Shop Stewards Committees, and Bodies of Delegates in Struggle of the Capital and Greater Buenos Aires was established with Montonero participation, and former leading JTP figure Gonzalo Chávez, whose father and sister had been killed by the Triple A, became its leader. By December 1975 this *coordinadora* was claiming the support of 130 *agrupaciones* in the Federal Capital and Greater Buenos Aires,[149] but by no means all were pro-Montonero. Though it is impossible to gauge the precise strength of the *Auténtico* Trade Union Bloc (which replaced the JTP), it is clear that it was weak outside Buenos Aires and La Plata. Significance may also be attached to the fact that the trade unionists present at the first *Auténtico* National Congress were there in an individual capacity rather than as representatives of workers' organizations.

The impression given by the available evidence is that the Montoneros with their *agrupaciones* were not quantitatively an advance upon the 1973-4 *Tendencia*: recruitment was steady, but then so were losses through death, imprisonment, and 'disappearances'. Disillusionment rather than radicalization and the resort to arms was the effect of governmental behaviour on many, perhaps most, Peronists. The costs and risks of involvement rose as the threshold of political violence fell. Growing numbers agreed with the sign surrounding the obelisk in *Avenida 9 de Julio* which read 'Silence is Health'; few suspected that it had anything to do with an attempt to reduce metropolitan noise levels. By the end of 1975, the

---

on 6 January 1977. One of his arms had already been paralysed as a result of torture. Mosse was arrested in July 1975 in Córdoba and, with five others, was killed in June 1976. Amnesty International [*Report of an Amnesty International Mission to Argentina*, 6-15 November 1976 (Great Britain, 1977), p. 24] described their killings as summary executions.

[149] Coordinadora de Gremios en Lucha, 'La guerrilla industrial, un nuevo cuento para perseguir a los trabajadores', *El Auténtico*, no. 8 (24 December 1975, p. 6.

presence of 200 'protection agencies' bore witness to the depth of insecurity in the Capital.[150]

What gains were made at rank-and-file level by the *Auténtico* Trade Union Bloc were achieved in the Buenos Aires area; Córdoba and Villa Constitución remained pockets of non-Peronist Left intransigence; and the Government and labour bureaucracy still had their own power bases — among workers who, at least, saw them as ultimately responsive to grass roots' pressures and as a lesser evil than the only real power alternative in the short term: the Armed Forces. Montonero claims that they were themselves the prime driving force behind the general strike[151] only revealed an immodest tendency towards self-aggrandizement. After all, the average circulation figure for *Evita Montonera* was only twelve thousand around the time of the strike. Early in 1976 the guerrillas were to admit that 'the political space lost by the treacherous Justicialists has only been partially occupied by us'; and concurrently spoke of the 'backwardness of the vanguard in relation to the mass movement ... in organizational development we are falling behind the high level of spontaneous response of the masses'. But the fact that the Montoneros had 'not acquired the necessary representativity for uniting and leading the whole people'[152] was inevitable, owing, among other reasons, to their own militarism. It was only in their 1977 *autocrítica* that the Montoneros, having clarified the fact that 'only a very low percentage' of their 500 *operaciones* of 1975 'were in support of mass conflicts', admitted that 'each military campaign paralysed political activity'.[153] 'Logistical production' had been wholly based on the guerrilla apparatus rather than in the mass movements, and 'comrades who had the possibility of operating legally instead invited those who were in their union to go underground.'[154]

---

[150] 'Guardaespaldas: imagen de la Argentina', *Cuestionario*, no. 32 (December 1975), p. 17.

[151] Montoneros, 'Argentina: la guerra continúa', *Marka* (Peru), c. June 1976.

[152] 'Los trabajadores hundiremos al régimen, porque queremos el poder para el pueblo', *Evita Montonera*, no. 12, pp. 2-5.

[153] Partido Montonero, untitled October 1977 document, op. cit., p. 16.

[154] 'Argentina: un país en guerra', a *Cuadernos Políticos* interview with leading Montonero Julio Roqué, published in *Revolución* (Np: December 1977), a defunct joint bulletin brought out by several Chilean revolutionary tendencies.

Presumably a similar transfer of militants from mass activity to clandestine combat duties occurred in the other major area of interest to the Montoneros: the universities. There, in the clandestine student elections of late 1975, the pro-Montonero JUP showed signs of minor decline, though the repressive circumstances in which they took place militated against their constituting an accurate barometer of student political loyalties. Nationally, in elections in which 50,620 students participated, the JUP's Blue and White List won 16,129 votes, 32 per cent of the poll, and twenty student centres, the percentage achievement being lower than the 35 per cent obtained nationally by the JUP in 1973. Centres were lost to reformist student tendencies (the progressive Radicals' FM, the Communists' MOR, and the Popular Socialists' MNR) which condemned right- and left-wing 'terrorism' and together represented 45 per cent of the total vote.[155] JUP endeavours to attract Radical and Popular Socialist students away from the rival Argentine University Federation (FUA) into the JUP-led National Council of Federations and Centres (CNFC) also foundered, mainly on the question of armed struggle, leaving the Argentine student movement by the end of 1975 almost as fragmented as at any time during the previous decade.

THE COST OF INVOLVEMENT

One of the strongest disincentives to responding positively to Montonero recruitment appeals was the fact that casualty figures showed the combatant Left to be now more often than not on the receiving end of bullets. The specific number of Montonero losses for this period was never announced but a breakdown of the 705 *reported* political deaths during the fourteen months from July 1974 to September 1975 pointed to more than half of them being at least left-wingers.[156]

[155] Election results from *El Auténtico*, no. 7 (10 December 1975); and *La Opinión*, 19 December 1975. Percentage performances from year to year are the best indices of student political trends. In 1975, the pro-Isabel student groups gained a pathetic total of only 2,584 votes, just 5 per cent of the poll.
[156] The *Buenos Aires Herald* of 12 September 1975 estimated that the 705 political deaths between 1 July 1974 and 12 September 1975 were composed of: left-wing losses 248; killed in gunfights (mainly left-wing) 131; right-wing losses 41; police 75; Army 34; businessmen 19; people of unidentified political orientation

Overall, whereas 200 political deaths had been reported in 1974, there were at least 860 in 1975; and by the time of the 24 March 1976 military intervention, a further 149 victims' names had been added to the lists.[157] In a number of cases, the escalating violence did in fact draw people towards the Montoneros — relatives and lovers of death squad victims and, when right-wing violence began to strike at the families of guerrillas, the spouses of living combatants too — but many more drew back as the stakes of involvement rose and as the Montonero resort to less discriminate attacks eroded the guerrillas' romantic image: a vital antidote to the essential ugliness of violence.

Another disincentive to becoming a Montonero was the absence of any prospect of short-term success, given the tenuousness of the guerrillas' foothold in the labour movement and signs that important sectors of the middle classes, influenced by spiralling inflation and insecurity, were now resigning themselves to, or welcoming the prospect of, a military takeover.[158] But even Montonero admirers must have occasionally baulked at the superhuman standards demanded of combatants. To become a professional guerrilla involved not only breaking, often, with one's family and friends, and one's means of subsisting independently of the organization, but also behaving in accordance with the heroic imagery which guerrilla publications and communiqués sought at all times to project. The stern disciplinary response to those whose conduct failed to measure up to the Montonero code, while vital in the long term in so far as security was concerned, did their political image no good at all — especially in a country where, despite the widespread occurrence of illegal executions by State forces, capital punishment has not

---

35; unidentified bodies 122. For the entire May 1973 to March 1976 Peronist period, the security forces estimated a total of 1,358 deaths from 'terrorism': military 66; provincial police 136; Federal police 34; civilians 677; subversives 445 [*La Prensa*, 22 March 1976]. *La Nación Internacional* of 3 July 1978 cited an Amnesty estimate that the right-wing violence organized by López Rega was responsible for the assassination of over 1,500 people in 18 months.

[157] *Buenos Aires Herald*, 12 January 1975; *La Opinión*, 2 January 1976; and *La Tarde*, 22 March 1976.

[158] See Ronaldo Munck, 'The Crisis of Late Peronism and the Working Class 1973-1976', *SLAS*, Bulletin of the Society for Latin American Studies (UK), no. 30 (April 1979), pp. 25-8.

been officially implemented in recent years.

Two examples of Montonero internal discipline attracted differing degrees of publicity, the first being the case of Fernando Haymal, a twenty-six-year-old student shot for informing in 1975. Upon being arrested and tortured by State security forces, Haymal had given away the locations of a Montonero's house and a base, and had allegedly caused ten colleagues to be tortured; he was reputedly responsible for the death of Osatinsky, had brought about a loss of money and arms, had obliged several guerrillas to become 'illegal', and had thus provided his captors with a politico-military triumph. When subsequently tried by his former comrades, Haymal's first line of defence was that he had been tortured, but this was dismissed: all prisoners were tortured as a matter of routine, it was claimed, and by August 1975, of the 800–1,000 Montoneros tortured so far, 95 per cent had surrendered no information of any importance, 4 per cent had given some information, and just 1 per cent had told all that they knew. 'Torture is perfectly endurable,' the *Tribunal Revolucionario* affirmed, pointing to cold statistics, 'it is not a problem of physical weakness but of ideological firmness, since comrades with weak physiques have managed to hold out completely.' Nor was the plea that he had held out for four days prior to 'talking' accepted in mitigation of his misdeeds: to talk under any circumstances was damaging to the organization and betrayed ideological weakness. Haymal thus received a death sentence on 26 August.[159] Police found his body in the city of Córdoba a week later.

Here the Montoneros were reacting to a threat to their existence in the manner of an army and not of a revolutionary organization. Haymal was not an enemy infiltrator:[160] his crime was simply human weakness. The media was therefore

---

[159] All information about Haymal's case comes from 'Juicio revolucionario a un delator', *Evita Montonera*, no. 8, p. 21. The commercial press simply reported that he had been shot for treason.

[160] Haymal's 'offences' were of lesser gravity than those of Carlos Roth, a Montonero who really did turn traitor and went with the security forces through the streets of Córdoba, pointing out any militants whom he recognized; yet both received the same sentence. And the main charge against Haymal — that of betraying the location of the base he was in charge of, thus enabling the capture of leaders Osatinsky and Mendizábal — was highly questionable: sources close to the Montoneros revealed that the latter pair had not taken the elementary security precaution of telephoning the base before going there for a meeting.

presented with a golden opportunity to portray the Montoneros as inhumane by omitting to link his death with the deaths and arrests of other Montoneros. Haymal's death provoked some guerrilla introspection but had a far slighter impact than did the ignominious treatment received by Roberto Quieto in one of the most puzzling episodes in Montonero history. Many questions surrounding it remain unanswered; nevertheless, it enabled observers to catch a glimpse of internal Montonero life, and what they saw was not particularly impressive.

As Christmas approached in 1975 Roberto Quieto, as a Montonero *official superior*, had sat down at a desk and typed out orders in which it was stressed that under no circumstances were combatants to risk contacting their families during the festive season. Two weeks later, at 7.30 pm on 28 December, Quieto was himself picked up, unarmed and without bodyguards, while playing with his family on a beach in San Isidro, Buenos Aires. As in so many cases, the Federal Police and Army personnel who, here led by an Inspector Rosas, carried him off wore civilian dress, claimed it was a legal proceeding, and stated that Quieto was being taken to the Federal Police headquarters.[161]

Within hours the Montoneros had launched a vociferous campaign, demanding that his detention be legalized by the authorities and that he be treated according to the law. *QUE APAREZCA QUIETO SECUESTRADO POR LAS FUERZAS ARMADAS GORILAS* and *QUIETO PRESO POR EL EJERCITO GORILA* were the slogans which appeared overnight on hundreds of walls throughout Buenos Aires. On 3 January 1976, a hundred *milicianos* ran riot in the centre of the Capital, setting cars ablaze, throwing incendiary bombs at business establishments, and scattering leaflets demanding respect for Quieto's 'physical integrity'. The victim's wife, Alicia Beatriz Testai, and his mother were meanwhile busy mobilizing international support for the captive's human rights, and were meeting with considerable success: telegrams were dispatched by, among others, François Mitterand, Jean-Paul Sartre, Simone de Beauvoir, Paco Ibañez, Pierre Vilar, Alain Touraine, and the Italian Socialist Party.

[161] See the paid advertisement, '¿Dónde está Roberto Quieto?', in *La Opinión*, 31 December 1975; and *El Cronista*, 29 December 1975.

But the Government refused to acknowledge Quieto's detention. And no sooner had the Montonero campaign got into full swing than it was suspended, the reason rapidly becoming apparent: during the night following the leading Montonero's disappearance, troops raided two important guerrilla bases and seized valuable equipment; then came a rash of kidnappings, arrests, disappearances, and infrastructural losses which, together, could only mean one thing: Roberto Quieto was talking. In the space of just a fortnight, twenty-five people 'disappeared' in Córdoba alone in identical incidents: their abductors were strongly armed, identified themselves as policemen, and were never impeded by the security forces.[162] Because they were the security forces.

So the *Tribunal Revolucionario* sat in judgement of Quieto in February, its verdict unlikely to evoke surprise. In his absence the accused was condemned for allowing himself to be captured (since this, even had he remained silent, automatically necessitated the abandonment of infrastructure known to the prisoner and, at least in theory, the provision of protection for militants likely to be affected) and for 'informing'. Quieto had transgressed the Montonero canon, 'Don't surrender alive; resist until you escape or die in the attempt': he had on several occasions been to the same beach in the company of his family, even though the latter had not adopted false identities and did not practise *anti-seguimiento* (procedures to prevent oneself being followed); he had not been armed; and had offered no more than passive resistance. The offence of passing information to the enemy was, in turn, considered aggravated by the rank of the accused, the importance of the betrayed information, and the speed with which it was delivered.[163]

The most interesting aspects of the episode were the Montonero explanation of Quieto's behaviour and the external impact of the case in general. As the guerrilla judges saw it, the accused's offences could only be ascribed to his 'liberal and individualist behaviour', previously seen in the 'poor resolution of family problems, his first detention, and

---

[162] *La Opinión*, 10 and 17 January 1976; *El Cronista*, 12 January 1976; *Buenos Aires Herald*, 14 January 1976.
[163] For the Montonero account of the trial, see 'Juicio revolucionario a Roberto Quieto', *Evita Montonera* no. 12, pp. 13-14.

his non-assumption of the fullest implications of clandestinity'. These were references to Quieto's failure to reconcile himself to the solitude of life in a 'safe house', to his recent habit of sharing a 'public' house with another comrade, and to the fact that his marriage was at risk — his wife had never been a militant, had never come round to the idea of sharing an underground existence with him. The pressures to which their marriage was subjected almost certainly defined the context of their discourse that Christmas, their last together. But to the *Tribunal*, such problems constituted no defence whatsoever; they were merely confirmation of Quieto's 'extreme liberalism', of his unpreparedness to accept the personal sacrifices of revolutionary warfare. Found guilty of 'desertion and informing', he was sentenced to 'humiliation and death', a judgement ratified days later by the Montonero National Council.[164]

Quieto's death sentence stunned many Montoneros and appalled sympathizers[165] . . . though within weeks it was generally assumed that the Armed Forces had 'implemented' it. To Peronist Left militants, Quieto was a revolutionary giant, a *Jefe Montonero*. His political record stretched back as far as the early 1960s, to his years as a Communist Party rebel;[166] it included his role in building and eventually commanding the Revolutionary Armed Forces; he had been a prisoner of *la dictadura* but had participated in the legendary Rawson Prison breakout and flight to Chile and Cuba in 1972; he had addressed several of the multitudinous Montonero rallies of 1973-4; and since then had been in charge of the organization's military apparatus, being popularly thought of as Firmenich's deputy though actually number three in the

[164] Ibid. In all probability, Quieto had earlier endorsed Haymal's death sentence.
[165] The author was present at discussions held by Montonero supporters in Buenos Aires, January 1976.
[166] Quieto participated in the breakaway from the PCA led by Juan Carlos Portantiero around 1963. He subsequently became a leading light in the small, transient Revolutionary Vanguard (VR). VR's passing successes before 1966 were in the student arena and in Press Workers Union elections: VR militant Eduardo Jozami became the union's general secretary and Quieto its legal advisor. After the demise of VR, while Quieto and some of his comrades entered the FAR, Jozami joined the Armed Liberation Forces (FAL), formed principally by PCA dissidents who had in 1967 created the breakaway Revolutionary Communist Party (PCR). In 1974, however, Quieto and Jozami were reunited when Jozami's splinter from a deeply-divided FAL, the small Popular Liberation Commands (CPL), was incorporated into the Montoneros.

guerrilla hierarchy. Quieto commanded tremendous respect due to his military expertise, acquired in Cuba, but through his public appearances he had also earned much affection. To many, he was known fondly as 'el negro Roberto', and his reputation as an outstanding revolutionary extended beyond the frontiers of Argentina. His personal weapon was a machine-pistol presented to him by Fidel Castro.[167]

The sentencing of Roberto Quieto greatly, if not permanently, disturbed Peronist Left militants: neither his alleged betrayal nor the Montonero response conformed to their romantic notions of what revolutionary warfare *should be* about. *Evita Montonera*, in an attempt to reassure the faithful, was suddenly full of reported instances of heroism and intransigence,[168] combined with condemnations of individualism: 'The individualist ... is not a hero but a potential traitor', it insisted.[169] But here the cant reached the height of hypocrisy. How could anybody take denunciations of 'individualism' seriously in a renowned nation of individualists such as Argentina? Neither urban guerrilla warfare nor any form of struggle could have flourished so much were it not precisely for this individualism, now attributed by the Montoneros to Liberalism, to the ideology of the dominant classes. What the Montoneros were in fact demanding was that their members should be like Che Guevara's 'New Man', that their present conduct be that of an ideal socialist society, unaffected by the competitiveness, egoism, and individualism associated with the material conditions of a capitalist society.[170] But here they were sounding like Stalinists, disregarding the intricacy of the human character in the name of an awkward hybrid of fanciful idealism and crude determinism, failing to recognize Argentine flamboyancy and egoism, failing to acknowledge the traits of their own class. Nor did the Montoneros really come to terms with the

[167] Information concerning Quieto's early militancy and private life comes from interviews which took place during 1980 with one of the former guerrilla chief's personal friends.

[168] The most notable was the account of the January 1976 escape-rescue of Montonero superior officer Horacio Mendizábal from a court-house, involving the assistance of his defence lawyer. See 'La conducta revolucionaria', *Evita Montonera*, no. 12, p. 36. Mendizábal went on to become Commander of the Montonero Army.

[169] 'El heroismo y el individualismo en las guerras populares', ibid., additional unnumbered pages. [170] Ibid.

strength of the family institution in their country: it was one thing to attract dynamic, assertive youths, eager to demonstrate their political *machismo*, into guerrilla ranks, and another thing to persuade middle-aged radicals, courted by the temptations of security, and often with children of their own, to become *guerrilleros*. It was not mere chance that most guerrillas happened to be in their twenties, especially in the twenty-three to twenty-six age group. Quieto was thirty-seven. His black hair was already beginning to show signs of grey.[171]

Perhaps, in the circumstances,[172] it was understandable that the men and women who set themselves up as Quieto's judges were intolerant of human weakness and indiscipline, but one can doubt whether they themselves really attained the standards of Che's 'New Man'. During 1975, several people claimed that, while enjoying a day at the Palermo races, they had spotted no less a celebrity than Mario Firmenich among the spectators. And one can certainly question the realism upon which the judgement was based: would pain alone, in just twenty-four hours, have broken Roberto Quieto, a man who, for all his 'individualism', had experienced prison life on two previous occasions? Were not the Montoneros not only misjudging Quieto but also their enemy in not even considering the possibility that the disorienting effects of hallucinogenic drugs had been utilized to facilitate the extraction of information from the prisoner?

The whole episode reflected discreditably on all those involved, but at least the shock waves which it sent through Montonero ranks and into their periphery contributed to the dawning of self-criticism. After Quieto had been well and truly 'condemned', it had to be admitted that the most serious aspect of the whole affair was not his 'betrayal' but 'that we failed to notice it beforehand; that we considered him a *Jefe* right up to the moment of his treason'. Quieto's 'individualism' had only gone unnoticed, it was now argued,

---

[171] It is interesting to recall Richard Gott's 1974 interview impressions of Quieto ['Under the Shadow of a Gunman']: 'In conversation he seems diffident and hesitating, almost dangerously undogmatic for a revolutionary. He smiles with the air of a man seeking confirmation and assurance.'

[172] Montonero losses as a result of 'treason' were, however, far less serious than in the Uruguayan Tupamaro cases of Héctor Amodio Pérez and Mario Piriz. See my 'A Critique of the Urban Guerrilla: Argentina, Uruguay and Brazil', p. 48.

due to the presence of individualism, liberalism, and bureaucratization in the organization itself; and such traits were symptomatic of a general lack of criticism and self-criticism, the non-socialization of organizational practices, and the non-participation of militants in decision-making. Democratic centralism had been adopted, recently, in principle, but bureaucratic centralism remained the practice.[173] What might also have been beneficially noted by the more critical Montoneros was how considerations of organizational security had ridden roughshod over all thought of how Quieto's condemnation would be received by those whose support was vital if the Montoneros were to develop further as a political force. Militarily, they had come a long way in just one year, yet their very success had helped nurture militarism, cramping the political style and health of the organization, and thus jeopardizing future military prospects too.

A COUP APPROACHES

As the period of Peronist government came to an end, inflation was galloping towards world records and Argentina was approaching a cessation of debt payments. One political killing was occurring every five hours and a bomb explosion every three.[174] In the face of a power vacuum caused by the disunity of Peronism and the ineptitude of the Government, and with opposition to it from both labour and entrepreneurial groups mounting, a military *golpe de estado* was generally regarded as inevitable by the start of 1976. Considerable numbers, especially among the middle classes, even encouraged such a development, some apologetically, others enthusiastically. It was not something sought by the Montoneros, though in effect their attacks on the Armed Forces did everything to hasten it. Rather than considering it desirable, the guerrillas viewed military intervention as an inevitable enemy move which would come as the revolutionary war reached a certain level of intensity. Nevertheless, within this fatalistic panorama, right up to March 1976 the Montoneros entertained the hope that they might, through direct attacks on the military, provoke its disunity. By frontal assault, inter-service rivalry

[173] 'El heroismo y el individualismo'.
[174] *La Opinión*, 19 March 1976.

might be exploited so as to engineer a split over how the subversive challenge was to be dealt with. Momentarily, in December 1975, such a situation seemed to have arisen when Brigadier Jesús Orlando Capellini led a Rightist Air Force *putsch*, but Army supremacy was rapidly reasserted.

In anticipation of the coup, the Montoneros began to act with reckless abandon, while stopping short of random terrorism. The threshold of guerrilla violence reached its lowest to date as insurgent aims were reduced to the mere demoralization and exhaustion of the enemy. At the end of January 1976, three guerrilla platoons invaded the Bendix factory in the industrial area of Munro, Buenos Aires, near to where sixteen metalworkers had recently been abducted; they shot dead two leading executives, painted 'The boss who collaborates with repression is the boss who will go to the execution wall' in the factory, and then left, killing a police corporal on their way out.[175] Nobody bothered to find out what the workers' reaction was, but three months earlier, when the Montoneros killed Fiat executive Samuel Salas in Córdoba, during an industrial dispute, the workforce had struck in protest.[176]

A force established to operate in the mountains of Tucumán, the *Fuerza de Monte del Ejército Montonero*,[177] began operations around this time, possibly as a gesture to the fast-declining ERP, but more probably just for training purposes and to disperse enemy forces as much as they could.[178] Some Montonero influence became discernible in the Agrarian Leagues, which had led struggles by agricultural workers in Chaco, Formosa, Misiones, and northern Santa Fe Province during the first half of the 1970s. The Leagues' General Secretary, Osvaldo Lovey, became a Montonero. But the cities remained the decisive foci of conflict; and, calculating

[175] 'Bendix: patrón que colabore con la represión irá al paredón', *Evita Montonera*, no. 12, pp. 18-20.
[176] *El Cronista*, 30 October 1975.
[177] The mountain unit's first fatal casualty was Juan Carlos Alsogaray, son of General Julio Rodolfo Alsogaray, Army C-in-C under Onganía. He was killed by an Army patrol near El Cadillal, Tucumán, on 13 February 1976 [*Evita Montonera*, no. 12, p. 24].
[178] After the coup, the mountain units were either destroyed or isolated. Some guerrillas in Chaco took to the mountains for two years and did not learn about the 1977 Montonero reorganization until they tuned in to the BBC World Service [*Boletín Interno del Partido Montonero*, no. 13 (February 1980)].

that the police would play the principal physical role in the urban component of the enemy offensive (they having a better knowledge of the terrain of urban guerrilla warfare than troops), the Montoneros chose the police as their priority target for 1976. On 12 January, between fifteen and twenty combatants tried to break into the Juan Vucetich Police College in La Plata to hijack the College helicopters, but were beaten off. Twenty days later they returned, this time numbering fifty guerrillas, but were again repulsed. A 'Third Montonero National Military Campaign' was then initiated on 11 March and within a week its 'annihilation and arms recovery' operations had claimed the lives of sixteen people, including thirteen policemen, and had left a further ten policemen injured.[179]

The Montoneros were roving deeper and deeper into the penumbra between urban guerrilla warfare and terrorism and stood on the brink of what the press termed 'collective terrorism' with their last big bang of the period. On 15 March, a device containing 20kg of trotyl, located in a car parked outside the Army General Command HQ (the *Libertador* building) was exploded by remote control as high-ranking military officers entered the building. Four colonels on the General Staff were slightly injured, as were twelve other military figures. But so were a dozen civilians, and a lorry driver perished in the blast, just 150 metres from the *Casa Rosada*. The Montoneros were able to classify this attack as one on 'the centre of gravity of the enemy', and it may have imperilled the life of Army Chief *teniente general* Jorge Rafael Videla, but it also endangered civilian lives.[180] So did the events of the following day: not only were bombs similar to that at the Army HQ found close to where a funeral cortège for two assassinated policemen was due to pass, led by Federal Police Chief, General Harguindeguy, but there were also at least half a dozen bombings of luxury apartments — including, the Montoneros affirmed, one owned by CGT General Secretary Casildo Herreras — in

---

[179] 'Tercera campaña militar nacional montonera'.
[180] The Montoneros ['Crónica de la resistencia', *Evita Montonera*, no. 12, p. 29] claimed that Videla missed death by a hair's breadth and that 15 soldiers were injured. But *La Opinión*, 16 March 1976, and other newspapers made no mention of General Videla's alleged presence at the scene. *Teniente general* (Lt.Gen.) is the highest rank in the Argentine Army, equivalent to the British Brigadier-General.

Barrio Norte. 'We have mined *Barrio Norte*', Montonero telephone callers announced to the press.[181]

By now the Montoneros' striking power was indisputably high and was being used with growing aggression against the security forces and their elite patrons. The *Auténtico* ban had removed all restraints upon the guerrillas stepping up their harassment of State forces. Their 'tactical military offensive' was not, however, the only rebel action to spur on the Armed Forces in their charge for power: labour unrest was again becoming generalized, this time in response to the Mondelli Plan — a caricature of the Rodrigo Plan (which had provoked the 1975 general strike), offering price rises of 100 per cent and wage increases of 20 per cent as the formula to cure the nation's economic ills. Despite the outlawing of strikes, major sectors of the labour movement resorted to them, hunger marches, work-to-rules, and demonstrations in efforts to bring about a volte-face in Government economic strategy. Metalworkers, carworkers, and many other groups paralysed their industries in Buenos Aires, La Plata, and Córdoba, even though Mondelli's proposals enjoyed CGT support. Yet the guerrillas played no organic role in the March 1976 workers' mobilizations. Predicting the advent of raids and systematic mass arrests, they withdrew their remaining militants from the factories weeks before the 24 March coup. This was orthodox guerrilla behaviour: retreat when up against superior military might. It was absolutely essential as a security measure, but it was not a move calculated to advance the political cause of a would-be vanguard of the working people. As the enemy advanced, the 'vanguard' withdrew from the industrial battlefield.

---

[181] *La Tarde*, 17 March 1976; and *La Opinión*, 18 March 1976.

6
The Retreat from Argentina (1976–1981)

> Our organization is a means, merely a means, and therefore we have been prepared to sacrifice the organization in combat in return for political prestige. We have lost five thousand cadres, but how much more mass support have we won? That is the real point.
> — Mario E. Firmenich[1]

> Sacrifice is not a political argument and martyrdom does not constitute proof. When the list of martyrs grows long, when every act of courage is converted into martyrdom, it is because something is wrong.
> — Régis Debray[2]

THE VIDELA REGIME

Many Argentines believed the new military junta when on 24 March 1976 it claimed to have ousted the Peronists from office in order to 'put an end to the lack of government, the corruption, and the subversive scourge'. With inflation rising faster than in Germany in 1921-2,[3] with Argentina having come within days of a cessation of international debt payments, Argentina's latest military rulers were able to point persuasively to the constitutional government's 'irresponsibility in dealing with the economy'. With Peronism in crisis and multiply-fractured, with evidence of graft on the part of Isabel Perón now public and her administration thoroughly discredited, the military commanders further justified their intervention on the grounds of the deposed government's lack of ethical and moral standards, and presented the 'tremendous power vacuum' as having threatened Argentina

---

[1] Firmenich interview, 'La base del triunfo está siempre en la masa', *Bohemia* (Havana), 9 January 1981; reproduced in *Resumen* (Madrid), 17 February 1981.

[2] Debray, *Revolution in the Revolution?*, p. 86.

[3] *La Tarde*, 23 March 1976. The inflation rate for the March 1975 to March 1976 period was 566.3 per cent; and had the rate of inflation during the first quarter of 1976 been maintained throughout that year, the annual figure would have reached 788.8 per cent. See *La Opinión*, 3 April 1976.

with 'dissolution and anarchy'. There was also the time-honoured *golpista* claim that the responsibility of government had been 'assumed' solely in the interests of the *Patria*; that the latest *golpe de estado* was not directed against any 'social sector', merely against 'those who have committed crimes or abused their power'. Such were the pledges and self-justifications presented to the public by Lt. Gen. Jorge Rafael Videla for the Army, Admiral Emilio Eduardo Massera for the Navy, and Brig. Gen. Orlando Ramón Agosti for the Air Force.[4]

As in 1966 Congress and the provincial legislatures were dissolved, the President, legislators, governors, and judges ousted, and political party and student activity banned. This, though, was a far 'harder' *golpe* than its forerunner, especially in its assault on the power of organized labour: the CGT and the major unions were 'intervened', trade union funds frozen, and activities relating to strikes and collective bargaining declared illegal. Leading Peronist politicians and trade unionists were imprisoned, the 62 Organizations dissolved, and five parties of the revolutionary Left completely outlawed. Military 'Councils of War', empowered to hand out death sentences for a variety of offences, were set up to summarily try those considered subversive. Yet the official, emphatically-stated message of the military commanders was that 'only the corrupt, the criminal and the subversive need fear the new authority'.[5]

Liberals, in particular, drew reassurance from the fact that before long a 'moderate' Videla-Viola military axis appeared to gain the upper hand, resisting the more extreme exhortations of Generals Menéndez, Díaz Bessone, and Suárez Masón. They interpreted the military mission as being one primarily destined to annihilate the guerrillas, and secondarily to put the economy 'in order'. But a year later, the regime's erstwhile apologists were already confused and alarmed: not only was the economy in a worse mess than when José Alfredo Martínez de Hoz took charge of the Economy Ministry; the drive against subversion seemed also to have escaped control, and was striking against democratic liberties

---

[4] Proclamation of the Military Junta, 24 March 1976, in Kandel and Monteverde, pp. 223-6.
[5] Graham-Yooll, *The Press*, p. 115.

in all areas of life and committing massive violations of elementary human rights.

Those commentators disappointed by the new regime erred in their appreciation of it in two fundamental ways: in vastly underestimating the dimensions of the Argentine military's conception of 'subversion', and in failing to see that its profoundly unpopular economic strategy demanded widespread repression and not merely firm government as a political concomitant. Although the military's outstanding ambition in March 1976 was indeed to finish with 'subversion', the manhunt which ensued was far from confined to guerrilla targets. Large numbers of trade unionists, student activists, journalists, and political refugees from neighbouring countries were also treated as delinquents. General Videla himself claimed that 'a terrorist is not just someone with a gun or a bomb but also someone who spreads ideas that are contrary to Western and Christian civilization'.[6] To his way of thinking, ex-President Cámpora was a 'political delinquent'.[7] General Vilas, while conducting a university purge in Bahía Blanca, also voiced a broad view of subversion: 'Until the present time, only the tip of the iceberg has been touched in our war against subversion ... It is necessary to destroy the sources which feed, form, and indoctrinate the subversive delinquent, and this source is in the universities and the secondary schools themselves.'[8] For his part, Foreign Affairs Minister, Admiral César Guzzetti, claimed that there was no such thing as right-wing subversion in Argentina, only 'antibodies' which were the 'natural reaction of a sick body' to the guerrilla 'germ'.[9] And when the regime produced a fat dossier on 'terrorist delinquency', the Socialist Workers Party, which had operated constitutionally and had consistently criticized all of the armed revolutionary organizations, was described therein as a 'terrorist gang'.[10]

Many who misjudged the Armed Forces' anti-subversive intentions were also slow to question the economic project

[6] Videla, quoted in *The Times*, 4 January 1978.
[7] Videla, quoted in *La Nación*, international edition, no. 997 (29 October 1979).
[8] Vilas, quoted in Amnesty Report (1977), p. 65.
[9] Guzzetti, quoted in the *Buenos Aires Herald*, 4 October 1976.
[10] República Argentina, Poder Ejecutivo Nacional, *Terrorism in Argentina*, 7 January 1980, p. 419.

of Martínez de Hoz and fully recognize its implications for civil liberties. It was to be expected that this product of a 'traditional' family, President of the Argentine Entrepreneurs' Council, of the large Acindar steel enterprise, of the Argentine Sugar Centre, and so on, would look after the interests of his economic peers and their international partners. What was not immediately perceived was his readiness, while pursuing policies of benefit to foreign capital, landed interests, and some big financiers, to permit major deindustrialization to take place. Local industry was greatly damaged as a result of a gross over-valuation of the peso (which stymied exports while attracting imports), the gradual dismantlement of tariffs, and a huge drop in the purchasing power of workers' incomes. By the end of September 1976, real wages were down to 50 per cent of their 1974 level,[11] and only experienced a minor recovery after 1978. Labour opposition to the wage cuts, to the 'rationalization' and privatization of State enterprises, to the dismissal of militants, and to the loss of the unions' social service agencies was not slow in expressing itself, though disunity hampered its effectiveness. But just as inevitable was the regime's response to it. The September 1976 car workers' protests against wage reductions, lay-offs, and three-day working weeks were met with a military occupation of Ford's General Pacheco plant and an 'Industrial Security' decree (21400) which provided for up to ten years' imprisonment for incitement to strike. Hundreds of workers were arrested (or like union leader Oscar Smith abducted) during the power workers' struggles of October 1976 and early 1977 against plans to increase their working week from thirty-six to forty-two hours and make 300,000 public sector workers redundant — beginning with 200 leaders and shop floor delegates of the Power Workers Union.

From the outset, then, the plans of the new military rulers and their civilian advisors implied not only ruthless repression of the guerrillas and their periphery, but also the stifling and intimidation of all organized opposition to unpopular political, economic, and labour measures. Media personnel who were over-enthusiastic about providing a news service for their public also suffered, as did academics who found the right-

[11] *La Opinión*, 26 September 1976.

wing nationalism of some officers and the non-democratic 'Liberalism'[12] of others unpalatable. The guerrillas helped in no small way to generate this state of affairs, yet should not be held exclusively responsible for it. The chronic economic crisis, the highly recessive IMF-endorsed prescription of Dr. Martínez de Hoz for its treatment, and the combative response of a powerful labour movement to it, together militated strongly in favour of a draconian authoritarianism, quite irrespective of the putative guerrilla threat — a threat qualified by the decline of the Guevarist ERP during the four months preceding the coup, and by its virtual disarticulation four months after it.

Regardless of how one may wish to apportion the 'blame' for the human tragedy of these years, it is clear that Martínez de Hoz ended his quinquennium with fewer admirers inside Argentina than when he began it. In his March 1981 swansong speech prior to retirement, he seemed to regret only the high interest rates which had recently provoked a number of financial crashes. Inflation, his declared economic enemy number one, had been reduced to about 100 per cent, yet remained an intractable and major problem.[13] Moreover, the national debt had increased more than threefold to 30,000m dollars, GNP per capita was lower in 1980 than in 1974,[14] and political forces which had attracted almost four-fifths of the votes in the March 1973 elections were unequivocally condemning his performance as a failure.[15] Perhaps even more disconcerting for him personally, as he left office and General Roberto Viola replaced Videla as President, was the revelation that at least two members of the replacement

[12] Many statements by General Videla suggest that he regards himself as a democrat merely because of self-identification with the Western World. As far as Argentina's internal political future is concerned, he has said that Peronism, unless it changes fundamentally, had no place in a democratic society. See *La Nación*, international ed., no. 1004 (17 December 1979).

[13] The inflation figure for 1980 was officially put at 87.6 per cent, but this was generally regarded as some 20 points below the real figure. See the *Financial Times* survey, 1 December 1980.

[14] *Clarín*, 1 February 1981.

[15] For the views of Arturo Frondizi and the MID, see ibid.; for those of Ricardo Balbín's UCR, see *La Nación*, international ed., no. 1069 (16 March 1981); and by the Peronists, see Partido Justicialista, 'Primeras jornadas de economía social: declaración final', Buenos Aires, 16 December 1980. The latter document, drafted by Antonio Cafiero, is especially important for its rejection of dependency theory and acceptance of the concept of interdependent development.

economy team were in private agreement with those who deemed the economic situation to be worse than when the military seized power.[16]

THE MONTONERO RESPONSE: 'ACTIVE DEFENCE'

The Montoneros characterized the military take-over of 24 March 1976 as a 'generalized offensive against the popular camp', a *golpe* sponsored by 'the oligarchy, the imperialist monopolies, and the upper strata of the national bourgeoisie', enjoying considerable but not durable middle-class approval. It was regarded as a response to 'the definitive crisis of dependent capitalism in Argentina', aggravated by the deepening Western recession, the path of the military having been cleared by the 'definitive crisis of the Peronist Movement and the treason practiced at governmental level by Isabel and López Rega'. And its aim: 'to immobilize the working class and annihilate the revolutionary forces.'[17]

Faced with the new regime, the guerrillas decided upon a strategy of 'active defence', designed to prevent its consolidation and to prepare the ground for an eventual popular counter-offensive. In theory, the role of the Montonero Army was now to hold back the enemy advance, enabling the masses to reorganize and resist. Translated into practice, this involved the launching of economical but telling attacks on the 'centre of gravity' of the enemy: on key personnel and installations, the destruction of whom and which would, it was hoped, demonstrate the vulnerability of the regime and thereby encourage diverse forms of mass resistance. The guerrilla force was sufficiently numerous for survival not to be a prime consideration. Despite the hundreds of arrests and abductions of activists which accompanied the military power-seizure, the Montoneros were self-confident enough to embark in April upon a 4th Tactical Offensive Campaign conceived prior to 24 March. In doing so, however, they badly misjudged the power and strategy of their enemy, allowing themselves to be guided for much of 1976 by the October 1975 Armed Forces' announcement that, while

[16] *La Nación*, no. 1069, which also contains the text of Martínez de Hoz's last ministerial speech.
[17] 'Un balance de 1976', *Evita Montonera*, no. 15 (February 1977), pp. 2-11.

the military would continue to repress the rural guerrilla in Tucumán, it would only intervene against the urban guerrillas on occasions when the police could not cope.[18] In fact, though the police contribution to the counter-insurgency campaign remained important, though the death-squad activities undertaken in the past by the Triple A became officially-condoned police practice, the Armed Forces clearly took over the task of Montonero destruction early in 1976. The Army had not fought a war in a century and was not going to miss out on one now. Nevertheless, the bombing campaign waged by the Montoneros throughout that year was based for months on the erroneous assumption that their enemy's 'centre of gravity' was located, at least for tactical purposes, in its police forces.

Four huge blasts struck the police: the first on 18 June, when Federal Police Chief, General Cesáreo Cardozo fell victim to 700 grams of trotyl planted in bellows beneath the mattress of his bed; the second on 2 July, when 9kg of trotyl brought down the roof of the dining room in the Federal Police Security Branch (*Coordinación Federal*) headquarters, killing twenty-five to thirty people and injuring over sixty; the third on 12 September, when a Citroën packed with explosives was detonated by remote control as a police bus was passing by, claiming eleven police and two civilian lives; and the fourth on 9 November, when a Montonero bomb wrecked the Buenos Aires Provincial Police headquarters in La Plata, killing one and injuring eleven police officers who were meeting in the office of assistant provincial police chief, Colonel Trotz.

The Montoneros sought to justify this blitz on the grounds that nearly all of their victims had tortured or oppressed with impunity; and to legitimize it with the claim that a 'collective decision' had been taken on the 'executions'.[19] Without information passed on by the public, their argument went, the Montonero Army could not possibly have mounted such operations. In three of the above cases, however, no external assistance was visible; Cardozo perished because eighteen-year-old *asesina*, Ana María González, had deliberately befriended his daughter in order to gain access to the Cardozo household;

[18] *La Opinión*, 14 October 1975.
[19] 'Crónica de la resistencia', *Evita Montonera*, no. 15, p. 27.

the *Coordinación Federal* carnage was the deed of an infiltrator who was able to carry the explosives into the building unchallenged; and the Montonero responsible for the La Plata bombing had been, until that day, Col. Trotz's private secretary. It would be misleading to suggest that the victims were universally loved, respected, or mourned by Argentines: antipathy to the police, especially the security branch, was not uncommon, and distrust and fear of them widespread. Yet now more than ever the guerrillas had the problem of a regime-manipulated press to contend with, a press from 22 April 1976 only permitted to relay 'official' news about the 'delinquents'. The initial impression which it gave was that the *Coordinación Federal* explosion had claimed as casualties many civilian employees: an impression not manifestly rectified when the published casualty lists mentioned only one victim without a police rank.[20] With few exceptions, newspaper editors complied with the regime's policy of giving guerrilla activity as little publicity as possible. This policy actually encouraged the Montoneros to go in for massacres and audacious assassinations. As Ana María González explained when interviewed by a Spanish journalist about the Cardozo killing, a number of earlier Montonero operations had failed to 'break the press embargo set up by the enemy. With this type of action [Cardozo], we weren't going to have any publicity problems as the act would immediately draw the public eye.'[21]

Certainly each one of the above blows demonstrated a degree of State vulnerability, and no doubt boosted guerrilla morale at a time when heavy losses were tending to undermine it. But each provoked furious responses from the security forces which hit Montoneros and non-combatants alike. The Cardozo assassination led to the official introduction on the death penalty for killers of members of the security forces and government or judicial officials; and to a series of unofficial massacres, often presented through the press as unsuccessful guerrilla attacks on police stations and military convoys, resulting in high fatalities but only on the

[20] *Buenos Aires Herald*, 3 July; *La Opinión*, 3–4 July 1976.
[21] *Buenos Aires Herald*, 13 September 1976. For full details of this clandestine Buenos Aires press conference, at which Mendizábal also spoke, see *Cambio 16* (Madrid), no. 245 (16 August 1976).

side of the attackers. Reprisals were particularly unrestrained following the *Coordinación Federal* blast. Reporters outside the building were beaten up by the police. A young man, gagged and bound, was thrust up against the obelisk in the middle of *9 de Julio* street and 'executed' by a 'firing squad'. The bodies of eight detainees were found in a San Telmo car park. And-three priests and two trainees of the Pallotine order were shot full of bullets, while praying in a Belgrano church, by assassins who scrawled 'For our dynamited police comrades' on a door as they left.[22] The incident also sparked a successful police revolt against Federal Police Chief, General Arturo Corbetta, who was replaced less than two weeks after urging organized and centralized but 'legitimate' repression, rather than the use of death squads.

Other massacres which bore all the hallmarks of reprisals included those which left thirty bullet-riddled and dynamited corpses on wasteland near Pilar and seventeen bodies in Lomas de Zamora in August. The Pilar victims were believed to have been held at *Coordinación Federal*, and eye-witnesses observed that they, like many of the people officially termed 'guerrillas killed in combat', were not wearing ties, belts, or shoelaces — items always confiscated from detainees.[23] Possibly the worst reprisals were taken in La Plata, where fifty-five 'suspects' were slaughtered in the vicinity of the bombed police headquarters in November.[24] Commentators who, with classical terrorist tactics in mind, asserted that the Montonero bombers were deliberately seeking such reprisals, in order to enhance the attraction of counter-State armed responses, took insufficient note of the damage which the backlash inflicted, 'innocents' apart, on the guerrilla organization itself. Quite prominent Montoneros, like Miguel Mosse, Hugo Vaca Narvaja Jr., Dardo Cabo, and Rufino Uriz, were among the prisoners killed, officially while trying to escape, but probably by summary execution.[25] By the last quarter of 1976, an average of fifteen abductions were being carried out every day by para-police and para-military units.

[22] *Buenos Aires Herald*, 5 July 1976.
[23] Ibid., 21 August 1976; *La Razón*, 20 August 1976; Amnesty Report (1977), p. 35. [24] *The Times*, 17 November 1976.
[25] Amnesty Report (1977), pp. 24–5; Organization of American States (OAS), *Report on the Situation of Human Rights in Argentina* (Washington, 1980), pp. 41–4; *The Times*, 4 February 1977.

At the end of the year, official sources put the annual political death toll at 1,354, the victims including 391 guerrilla and 167 police and military losses. Amnesty International estimated that there were 5–6,000 political prisoners by January 1977, and reckoned that the security forces and para-police groups had probably claimed 1,000 victims, to the armed Left's 4–500, in 1976.[26]

In the new circumstances the Montoneros lacked a capacity for direct engagement of the Armed Forces. Their 'jungle guerrilla', after a brief and largely uneventful appearance in Tucumán, was disbanded towards the end of 1976; a small rural unit was established in the North-East (Formosa, Chaco), but only as a token presence, dodging shadows. Urban activity remained the rule, with the Montoneros late in 1976 and during the first half of 1977 aiming selective blows, similar in character to their attacks on the police, against strategic military targets. At the start of October, an explosive device placed under a review stand at *Campo de Mayo* blew a metre-wide hole at the exact spot where President Videla, by then 55m away, had been standing. Two weeks later, on the eve of the Peronist anniversary of 17 October, a bomb destroyed a cinema in the *Círculo Militar* Army officers' club, injuring sixty retired officers and relatives. There were also individual assassinations, such as the 1 December slaying of Col. Leonardo D'Amico, Director of Courses at the Superior War School, the 17th senior military official to be killed by guerrillas since the coup. But security targets and destructive blasts provided the only guarantee of capturing press headlines, and the Montonero Norma Arrostito Combat Platoon was well aware of this when it placed a 6kg fragmentation bomb in a Defence Ministry hall during an anti-subversion conference in mid-December: fourteen senior military and intelligence officers were killed and a further thirty injured.

In all, there were some 400 Montonero guerrilla operations in 1976, and responsibility was 'claimed' for the death or injury of about 300 entrepreneurs and members of the military and police forces.[27] Several munitions workshops

[26] Amnesty Report (1977), pp. 10, 18, 33 and 49.
[27] Ejército Montonero, *600 Operaciones en 1977* (Np, 1978), p. 5; *Evita Montonera*, no. 15, p. 7.

were uncovered, but what the guerrillas called 'logistical production' was not halted until late in 1978. On at least one occasion, in November 1976, the Montoneros were forewarned of a raid and managed to evacuate all their equipment in time, leaving only mines to greet the raiding party. Between 1976-8, their central logistics unit produced 780kg of high-power plastic explosives (C-2) and their zonal logistics units a further 1,500kg of medium-power explosives, used for grenade attacks and major bombing operations.[28] There were fewer of the latter in 1977. Although 600 actions were recorded, only four were presented as 'centre of gravity operations': the incapacitation of Foreign Minister Guzzetti in a bid to kill him; an explosion in the Condor Building, headquarters of the Air Force Command; an attack with a multiple grenade launcher on General Videla's platform, two hours before a ceremony in Rosario; and another explosion in the office of Labour Minister, General Liendo.[29] For some unknown reason, the explosion of a bomb at the Metropolitan Airport, which left a crater 9m wide as the President's plane passed just 50m overhead in February 1977, was not so classified.

Towards the end of 1976 and during 1977, hundreds of minor labour-orientated *operaciones* were also carried out as the Montoneros were obliged by circumstances to become less militarily ambitious and to pay increased attention to renewing their decimated social base. Of the social groups to which they had previously looked for support, only labour proved capable of serious resistance to the new authorities, and this remained so into the early 1980s. In efforts to assist and encourage that resistance, the Montoneros contributed acts of sabotage to the October 1976 power workers' strike; they killed or wounded several dozen managers involved in industrial conflicts; and they blew up railway wagons, tracks, and stations during the protracted rail dispute which ended with a workers' victory in November 1977. Without doubt, there were occasions when employers yielded

---

[28] 'Las armas montoneras en nuestro accionar militar' *Estrella Federal* (organ of the *Ejército Montonero*), no. 5 (September 1978), p. 13.
[29] For details, see *600 Operaciones*. Of the other guerrilla operations, 253 were classified as 'in support of the workers' struggles', 114 as 'anti-repressive operations', and 238 as 'propaganda operations'.

to intimidation and the threat of damage to property, but there was no resultant flood of thankful workers into Montonero ranks.

Guerrilla activities, even if closely coordinated with labour struggles, could not seriously rival trade unionism as a means of consistently fighting for workers' demands; and the Army response to any signs of guerrilla involvement greatly hampered efforts to rebuild the shop stewards committees and rank-and-file bodies. When the Montoneros attempted to become more directly involved in labour struggles, by launching a CGT in the Resistance on 14 August 1976, they soon came up against a wall of suspicion: perhaps unfairly, this CGT-R was widely suspected of 'parallel trade unionism', of seeking to replace the CGT rather than recover it from military control. Even surviving militants of the non-Peronist Left declined to participate, accusing its Montonero promoters of 'sectarianism'.[30]

Involvement with the Montoneros was seen, anyway, by most realistic trade unionists as a virtually suicidal option. While the guerrillas offensive capacity declined in 1977, claiming fewer than thirty-five military, police, and entrepreneurial victims,[31] Montonero losses continued to rise. Indeed, the unrelenting repressive drive against the battered Montoneros and all forces considered subversive by the regime seemed to grow even fiercer during the second half of 1977, as General Videla and his colleagues attempted to fulfil their promise of a 'peaceful Christmas' and to remove the Montoneros from the scene well in advance of the approaching World Cup football championship. One year after the March 1976 military coup, Montonero casualties stood at 2,000, one-third more than had been envisaged in the guerrillas' own estimates.[32] By August 1978, they were putting their post-coup fatalities at 4,500,[33] and the Armed Forces were showing no interest in Montonero cease-fire proposals.

[30] Personal interview with a PRT-ERP member, England, 15 September 1978.
[31] *600 Operaciones, passim.*
[32] 'Informe del Consejo Nacional del Partido Montonero, septiembre de 1977', p. 17; and personal interview with MPM members, London, 15 December 1979.
[33] Personal interview with leading Montonero, Manuel Pedreira, Havana, August 1978, Pedreira was killed a few weeks later, back in Argentina.

REORGANIZATION, RETHINKING, AND THE GROWTH OF INTERNAL DISSENT

The relative ease with which the Montoneros were militarily shattered in 1976-7 needs to be seen in the light of a more general political failure, of which the CGT-R disappointment was only one aspect. Superficially the guerrillas were now radicalized by the crises affecting Peronism and the economy, with Marxist influences becoming more discernible in their political and organizational proposals. Following all the introspection and self-criticism provoked by the so-called 'treason' of Quieto, the National Council,[34] meeting in April 1976, decreed the transformation of the Montoneros from a politico-military organization into a revolutionary party, the *Partido Montonero*. The OPM thus became the PM, theoretically a party of cadres, organizationally based upon the Leninist principles of democratic centralism, and committed to an ideology termed 'Dialectical and Historical Materialism':[35] the nationalists' euphemism for Marxism.

Still in the realm of ideals, the PM was to be a vanguard party, linked by means of a Montonero Movement to the working masses which it sought to lead. For now, like so many pundits on past occasions, the Montoneros declared Peronism to be dead ... only to discover, a little later, that the corpse was stubbornly and almost vivaciously resisting burial. The pronouncement of death was publicized in what was certainly the most left-wing document ever issued by the Montoneros.[36] In it, criticism of the 1973-4 'Errors of Perón' went further than ever before: he had failed to challenge the power of the military; had used the trade union

---

[34] The National Council was roughly equivalent to a Central Committee, and indeed took that name when enlarged in 1979. The National Leadership was the Montonero equivalent of an Executive Committee or Politburo, and at the time of the 1976 coup was composed of Firmenich, Roberto C. Perdía, Carlos Hobert, and Raúl Yäger. When Hobert was killed later that year, Julio Roqué replaced him. Horacio Mendizábal joined the leadership when Roqué was killed in May 1977, as did Fernando Vaca Narvaja and Horacio Campiglia when it was enlarged at the end of 1978. The National Leadership of the PM was the High Command of the EM.
[35] Footnote 1, *Vencer* (Mexico), no. 2/3 (1979), p. XXVIII.
[36] Partido Montonero, 'Hacia una nueva política para la conquista del poder por los trabajadores y el pueblo peronista' (Buenos Aires, August 1976) — a modified version of a more extensive original draft published in *El Montonero*, no. 11 (24 April 1976).

bureaucracy as his power base while purging the Left and facilitating the rise of López Rega; he had retained the 'fingering' principle of personal nomination rather than the democratic election of officials; and he had opted for a vacillating programme based upon European, Arab, and even Yankee capital, instead of expropriating the oligarchy and monopolies, insisting upon internal saving, and seeking the commercial and financial support of the 'Socialist Countries'. The failure of his last Presidency, followed by 'the treason of Isabel and López Rega' and the militant mass opposition to them, prompted the Montoneros to conclude: 'Peronism is finished and the people are orphans'. Justicialist doctrine, with its advocacy of a harmonious capital-labour relationship nurtured by a neutral State, was no longer adequate to the needs of the people: 'Now in 1976 the workers know that when power is shared with the bosses, the latter end up winning, allying themselves with imperialism as happened in 1955 and 1974. Therefore, today the People do not want to share power with capitalism, the People want *all the power* . . . of the State, which is neither independent nor neutral but rather a workers' or a bosses' State.' Ambiguity was present, almost in the form of self-parody, *'all the power'* in fact being followed by 'or at least more than 50%', but the general tone of the document was, in terms of the Montonero political spectrum, decidedly ultra-Left.

The 1976 line implicitly abandoned the discredited theory of revolutionary stages, and suggested an immediate 'transition to socialism' upon the seizure of power. Industrial, agricultural, and financial capital would be expropriated from the oligarchy and monopolies; the 'large national companies' would be encouraged to participate in the Montonero venture, and would be nationalized if they demurred. Finally, the document argued the need to replace the traditional unipersonal leadership of Peronism with that of a more durable revolutionary party — the PM — and ended on a pretentious note: since the popular revolutionary movement in Argentina had historically taken the name of its strategic leadership ('before Perón, now Montoneros'), it was only right that that Movement should now be rechristened the Montonero Movement.[37]

[37] Ibid. On the naming of the Montonero Movement, see also the interview

Other instances of fleeting Leftism involved extending fraternal hands to the non-Peronist revolutionary Left, especially to the ERP and the Workers Power Communist Organization (OCPO). The latter had become newsworthy through its activities during the 1975 Villa Constitución strike, and more recently, with ERP logistical assistance, had kidnapped the military *interventor* of the CGT, Colonel Pita, in May. However, joint activity got no further than exploratory discussions: the Argentine Liberation Organization (OLA), proposed in June 1976, never materialized, while the CGT-R, in the face of ERP and OCPO reservations, was launched solely by the Montoneros. Even the aspiration for unity deserted some Montoneros after the annihilation of the ERP leadership, Mario Roberto Santucho, José Benito Urteaga, and Domingo Menna on 19 July. Rumour had it that the ERP had asked the Montoneros for 'protection'.

What was the reality behind all these developments? The reality was that the new party was composed exclusively of the guerrrillas, of members of the Montonero Army (EM); and that the Montonero Movement remained a figment of the imagination of the National Leadership. Political positions now joined military ranks, 'Pepe' Firmenich becoming First Secretary of the PM as well as First Commander of the EM, but the organizational changes fell far short of Leninist prescriptions. To attempt to build a revolutionary party against the repressive backcloth of 1976 was like trying to launch a pleasure boat during a hurricane. The consultation of activists over major decisions was significantly expanded, but as Julio Roqué admitted late in 1976, democratic centralism remained defective, the training of party cadres having been greatly hampered by the security forces.[38] Later the National Leadership acknowledged that the Party had been created 'without the participation of the masses', as part of an ambitious 'triumphalist' plan which really had no clear perspectives for achieving political power. Militarism had continued to characterize Montonero activity, at least until October 1976 when a new emphasis on operating in support

---

with Firmenich reported in *The Guardian*, 2 March 1977; and 'Firmenich: A Political Analysis', *NACLA Report*, vol. 11, no. 1 (January 1977), pp. 17-22.

[38] 'Argentina: un país en guerra'.

of mass struggles appeared: 'politico-social weapons should prevail, and military weapons be subordinated to them', had then become the guiding principle,[39] though many workers regarded the assassination of their employers as just as 'militaristic' as the big blast methodology.

During the course of 1976, internal discussions gave rise to a number of dissident viewpoints, with opposition to the National Leadership being strongest among militants of the Greater Buenos Aires North Column and in La Plata. In its late 1977 report on the disputes, the Leadership described the dissidents as 'classist, ideologist, and militarist' for, among other things, persisting with calls for mergers with the armed Left; and as *aparatistas* for urging further expansion of the Montonero infrastructure. While the La Plata Secretariat apparently claimed that it needed almost forty cars for a city of just 300,000 people, the Buenos Aires North Zone Secretariat called for ten million dollars to be allocated to the annual housing plan, in order to provide clandestine accommodation for industrial militants who were being hunted by the security forces. Other than contend that the protection of persecuted factory activists was the responsibility of the mass movement rather than the party, the Leadership in turn presented the issues as being largely just disagreements over the 1976 organizational budget. It made a caricature of the *Columna Norte* dissidence, claiming that its logic would be to transform the PM into a 'National Mortgage Bank' which might solve the national housing problem but not those of the Argentine revolution.[40] In fact, despite the doubtful practicality of the housing proposal, the North Column's motives were anything but *militarista* and *aparatista*: behind its tentative proposals was a desire to transform Montoneros into an organization which would serve the labour movement, rather than act upon it mainly from the outside.

For this, the dissidents were pilloried and belittled by the National Leadership: by October 1976, it claimed, the deviations were only being insisted upon inside *Columna Norte*. No mention was made of the fact that this Column

---

[39] 'Informe del Consejo Nacional ... septiembre de 1977', *passim*. The same document was published in English, as 'Criticism and Self-Criticism', in *Vencer* (international MPM magazine), no. 2/3.
[40] Ibid.

represented 900 Montoneros,[41] and that it, along with the La Plata Column, had been the most successful in developing Montonero work in the labour movement.[42] The dissidents' demands for the holding of a national party congress, as promised by the executive in April, were now rejected by the National Leadership as 'suicidal', which it probably would have been. Instead the four guerrilla *comandantes* laid down the law on how 'democratic centralism' was to function: a poll was ordered, with all the superior, major, first, and second officers participating, but with the voting option restricted to just two motions which in effect made the affair a vote of confidence in the National Leadership, authorizing it to 'impose the hegemony of the majority lines'. It was impossible, through the poll, to express disagreement with the leadership on the political issues at stake without accusing it of being generally unrepresentative of the organization. As a result, even *Columna Norte* joined in the unanimous vote ratifying the existing leadership.[43] A measure of unity was restored, but only by restricting the parameters of political debate; and though that restriction may have been justifiable for security reasons, it only postponed the damaging loss of the dissidents for a few more years.

Nevertheless, the National Leadership and the organization as a whole could not ignore the fact that neither the Montonero Movement nor the OLA and CGT-R initiatives had met with an encouraging external response. If the expected transmutation of *peronismo* into *montonerismo* were taking place, it was doing so exceedingly slowly, leaving the Montonero 'vanguard' dangerously isolated. Without abandoning their efforts to construct a party, the Montoneros therefore backtracked in search of popular support. On 20 April 1977, they launched a Montonero Peronist Movement (MPM), modelled on the Peronist Movement but incorporating, in addition to the traditional *Ramas*, an Agrarian Branch and a Professionals, Intellectuals, and Artists Branch.[44] Again though, the

[41] Number provided by a former leader of *Columna Norte*, now living in exile.

[42] For the dissidents' case, see Peronismo en la Resistencia, *Reflexiones para la construcción de una alternative peronista montonera auténtica* (Np, June 1979), p. 12.

[43] 'Informe del Consejo Nacional . . . septiembre de 1977'.

[44] See Appendix B.

Montoneros proved more imaginative in the design-work than competent in the construction. On paper they now had a revolutionary party of cadres (the PM), a revolutionary army (the EM), and a mass organization rooted in the major popular social sectors (the MPM); in theory, they had now brought together the Authentic Peronists — Bidegain, Obregón Cano, Puiggrós — in an open merger with the Montoneros, adding extra Peronist legitimacy to themselves. Yet in practice, the leadership and membership of the PM and EM were both identical; PM-EM leaders were a majority in the MPM Branch leaderships; and Mario Eduardo Firmenich was now First Secretary of the PM, Commander-in-Chief of the EM, and General Secretary of the MPM — the latter 'in order to guarantee the dominance of the ideology of the Party in the Movement', so it was said.[45]

In effect, the growing addiction to hierarchy and elaborate structures meant that the real physical division became one between 'officers' and 'troops'. That between the MPM and PM denoted somewhat less important differences in levels of commitment and responsibility, though not trivial ones: a dissident MPM activist might be summoned before a Disciplinary Tribunal and expelled; an errant PM-EM cadre could be hauled before a Revolutionary Tribunal whose maximum penalty, implemented on at least half-a-dozen occasions, was death by shooting. Those who held the real power were the few with top military ranks and control over the war chest. It was they who took the initiative to launch the MPM in April 1977, and it was to the great consternation of many of those who were expected to build it in Argentina that their leaders, having unilaterally decided to get out themselves, announced the establishment of the new Movement from the safety of distant Rome.

THE USE OF 'STATE TERRORISM' TO ERADICATE 'SUBVERSION'

The methods used by the Argentine Armed Forces to eradicate 'subversion' took the Montoneros by surprise. They expected fierce armed confrontations in the streets, vehicle

[45] Personal interview with two MPM members, London, 26 August 1980.

checks, raids, house-by-house searches, and mass detention, but assumed that the latter would be as before: about ten days to endure torture before the detention was legalized, followed by the re-establishment of contact with one's family and organization. Only slowly did they detect the new repressive infrastructure and methods: officially-sanctioned but clandestine concentration camps and torture centres, plus special units based on the military services and police whose function was to abduct, interrogate, torture, and kill.[46] Under the new regime, not only was torture more savage: the detainee was now at the disposal of captors who had all the time in the world, were unmolested by judicial interference, could totally isolate the prisoner from society, and had no need to produce a living person at the end. The new regime was not fascist. It lacked the organized civilian mass base, the mobilized petty-bourgeois support, of a fascist regime, but many of its agents boasted of their Nazi sympathies, and the methods they used, and were permitted to use, were not exactly alien to those of the Gestapo.

As envisaged by the Montoneros, hundreds of guerrillas were indeed gunned down in the streets, putting up desperate resistance to the would-be abductors of the Task Forces. Carlos Caride, Carlos Hobert, Sergio Puiggrós, Miguel Zavala Rodríguez, and Rodolfo Walsh[47] were only the most prominent. Some encircled guerrillas, like Montonero Captain Francisco Urondo, one of Argentina's most outstanding poets, swallowed the *pastilla*, the dreadful cyanide capsule, as their final act of defiance.[48] Others were trapped in houses and meeting places, and fought to the last. At the

---

[46] See especially Amnesty International, *Testimony on Secret Detention Camps in Argentina* (London, 1980).

[47] Sergio Puiggrós was the son of Rodolfo Puiggrós and his private secretary when the latter was Rector of the University of Buenos Aires in 1973. Puiggrós Jr. is said to have directed the Formosa spectacular in 1975. The writer and journalist Rodolfo Walsh, a founder of the *Prensa Latina* news agency and later of the Montonero daily *Noticias*, had become a Montonero second officer, and was reputedly in charge of the police section of the guerrilla intelligence service. He was killed resisting abduction on 25 March 1977, a day after denouncing the military regime in a famous Open Letter. His San Vicente house was later demolished by Army tanks.

[48] On the death of Urondo, see *Los papeles de Walsh* (Np: Cuadernos del Peronismo Montonero Auténtico, 1979), p. 25. The obligation of cornered Montoneros to commit suicide was rescinded by the National Leadership in May 1978.

end of September 1976, the National Political Secretariat[49] of the organization was surrounded while meeting in a house in Corro Street, Floresta, by troops who used a tank, bazookas, and a helicopter in the furious one-and-a-half-hour battle that ensued. After the Montoneros, Coronel, Salame, and Beltrán, ceased firing downstairs, the final rites were performed on an upstairs balcony by national political secretary, Alberto 'Tito' Molina, and Maria Victoria Walsh, daughter of Rodolfo. Stunned, disbelieving soldiers watched as the young woman put down her Halcón machine-gun, stood up straight, opened her arms wide, and called to them, 'You cannot kill us ... we choose death!' Accompanied by Molina, she then ended her life with a bullet through the temple.[50] These five deaths represented a considerable loss to the Montoneros, though they were not as strategically-crippling as the ERP's July losses, and it was said that the sacrifice of the five permitted the escape of Firmenich and Galimberti. Another blow fell in May 1977 when Julio Roqué, the only member of the National Leadership designated to stay in Argentina, was trapped with another Montonero in a house. Unable to escape, they set fire to the house and then blew it up.[51]

The real key to the Montonero collapse, however, were the kidnappings and their sequel. Towards the end of 1977, the guerrillas claimed that during the first five months after the coup, 90 per cent of those abducted had refused to talk, and were later killed; and that though 10 per cent talked, only about 1 per cent of the total casualties really turned traitor and patrolled with mobile units, pointing out their former comrades. Without doubt, the real number of those who talked without collaborating was far higher, but the Montoneros did realize, belatedly, the seriousness of even their own figures: one traitor alone might denounce 20-30 members, of whom 3-4 might talk without collaborating, denouncing

---

[49] In April 1976 a National Secretariat was established as the tactical leadership organ. Initially, it encompassed three secretariats – political; military; and press, propaganda, and indoctrination – but secretariats for organization and foreign relations were added later.

[50] On the Corro Street battle and the death of his daughter, see Rodolfo Walsh, 'A Letter to my Friends', *Vencer*, no. 4 (1980), p. 37. For press coverage, see *La Opinión*, 2 October 1976.

[51] *The Times*, 6 June 1977.

another 8-10, of whom one might become a *dedo* — someone prepared to go out on the streets (*pasear*) and point out (*marcar*) Montoneros known to him or her.[52] In the face of these enemy tactics, the guerrillas fell victim to their own *aparatismo*. Failing to appreciate the true nature of the counter-insurgency operation until it was too late, they maintained their vast infrastructure into 1977, though it was constantly diminishing as a result of detainees 'talking'; and with each piece of the apparatus, fell further comrades.

Those few Montoneros who survived the nightmare of detention were quite clear, in their subsequent testimonies, that the vast majority of Montoneros who fell into enemy hands did so 'with their morale practically destroyed';[53] most of them talked and without great delay. That is not to say that barbarities were not committed as a matter of routine. In addition to the *picana* (electric prod), the *submarino* (immersion), and rape, the methods included 'putting prisoners in pens with vicious dogs trained by their captors, until they are almost dismembered'.[54] The physical pressures were tremendous, yet the testimony of survivors of the Navy Engineering School (ESMA), whose G.T.3.3. unit was held responsible for 3,000 deaths alone,[55] records that most Montoneros arrived there with no confidence in the political future of their organization. Taken chained and hooded to the torture chamber most of them cooperated, soon concerned solely, but hopelessly, about their own individual survival. 'Without the Montoneros, the Armed Forces would not have been able to destroy the Montoneros', the testimony records.[56] Prompted by pain, Montoneros talked because of the political bankruptcy of their organization and its military decline; they talked because they knew their friends were talking; because their leaders had taken off and abandoned them. Far too much was expected of these prisoners by guerrilla chiefs who demanded heroism and solidarity as

[52] 'Informe del Consejo Nacional... septiembre de 1977', p. 17.
[53] 'Memorandum 1: Explicitación política de la experiencia mantenida por militantes montoneros con la Marina de Guerra, en calidad de detenidos y bajo condiciones de secuestro', July 1979, p. 11. This unpublished document, emanating from Geneva, relates the experience of prominent Montoneros held in the *Escuela de Mecánica de la Armada* (ESMA).
[54] OAS (1980), pp. 199-200.   [55] 'Memorandum I', p. 6.
[56] Ibid., p. 15.

the norms of conduct and who refused to tolerate the less glorious aspects of human nature. In Algeria, detainees had been set a realistic objective: to hold out for forty-eight hours, so that bases known to the captive might be evacuated and colleagues protected. Montoneros, however, were ordered to resist until death.

Some Montoneros were betrayed by their own militarism — appealed to successfully on the basis of a realistic assessment of the balance of forces between the two opposing 'armies'. Whether their lives were spared once their collaboration had outlived its utility is not known. Those still at large had no effective response to offer to the repressive machine which was devouring their comrades. All they could do was denounce the horrors of ESMA and other centres, and launch token militaristic reprisals (often using teams coming in from abroad for specific missions) against those most visibly responsible for them. In August 1978 they demolished the house of Rear-Admiral Lambruschini, shortly to become Navy C-in-C, using 30kg of explosives. But Lambruschini was not there; a guard, an old woman, and his young daughter were; and their deaths brought the Montoneros no credit whatsoever.

Inside ESMA, however, some of the prisoners managed to devise a stategy which, over the 1977-9 period, saved their lives. By simulating collaboration with their Navy captors, they avoided the fate of the vast majority. These were people like Martín Gras, a senior member of the Montonero international service, and Sara Solarz, the widow of Marcos Osatinsky, whom the Navy regarded as important guerrillas who should be kept alive, perhaps in case the international human rights pressures became too strong and it became necessary to produce some of the 'disappeared' people. Before long, it also became apparent that C-in-C Massera, as his term on the military junta drew to a close, had begun to develop presidential ambitions, and, with the war against the guerrillas largely won by the end of 1977, was beginning to cast around for political support. This enabled the group inside ESMA to gradually improve its material and psychological position by becoming, indirectly and incredibly, 'political advisors' to the Navy Chief — a kind of left-wing 'think tank' which between 1977-9, while not the major influence upon Massera, seems to have been listened to in respect of two areas of policy: one concerning the need to legalize the situation of the detainees and replace mass extermination with selective killing in order to improve the international image of the regime; the other with regard to contemporary international disputes with Chile, Brazil, and Britain. Knowing that Massera wanted to evade his personal responsibility for repressive measures and that his best strategy would be to pose a populist alternative to the Army chiefs, the advisers, often using Captain Acosta as an intermediary, urged him to ease up on repression, to offload the responsibility for it on the Army, and to seek a nationalist triumph in the Beagle dispute, over the Falkland Islands, or against Brazil, ostensibly in order to improve his presidential chances. Their real motives of course were to save lives and to shift military attention away from internal 'subversion' to external issues.[57]

The precise degree of this group's influence will never be known, but by appearing to collaborate the detainees certainly improved their lot. Their living conditions improved, their chains were taken away, they were permitted limited contact with their families, and, through the political dialogue, they managed to sow growing doubts in their captors' minds as to whether they were really 'monsters' who had eventually to be killed. By 1979, some sixty to seventy prisoners had in this way worked their way into a position where they were allowed to leave for Europe. It was a strange experience: a two-year psychological battle with several bizarre features. One of the inmates, known to the Montoneros as 'Ana' and to the Navy as 'Lucy', developed such a close relationship with a Navy officer that she ended up as his wife. It is also said that when Arrostito died, the officer who had been in charge of her was greatly upset and wept upon hearing the news.[58]

The above case, though, was exceptional; the others far

[57] Ibid., *passim*.

[58] Arrostito was reported as having been killed in an ambush in December 1976, but according to ESMA escapee Horacio Maggio's testimony [MPM, Secretaría de Prensa, 1978], she lived until 15 January 1978, when she was given an injection and died in the Naval Hospital. Former Peronist deputy Jaime Dri also escaped from ESMA, but was criticized for so doing by the other Montoneros referred to in 'Memorandum 1' for jeopardizing their strategy.

more grim. In general, prisoners were most 'useful' during the first forty-eight hours, when information extracted would immediately produce further guerrilla losses. After that there would be demands for more detailed information, for the prisoner to go out on patrols with the Task Forces, to appear at press conferences. Finally, once most had outlived their usefulness to their captors, they were 'transferred'. Early on, 'transferees' tended to be found riddled with bullets, strangled, or dynamited; later, they simply 'disappeared'. The accumulated evidence suggests that their 'final destination' was the sea. They were injected with a powerful sedative, taken to aircraft, and never seen again. Guards who were asked by detainees about the fate of those 'transferred' made 'jokes' about 'fishfood' and 'the Naval Solution'.[59]

There are also reasons to believe that two major massacres took place: a right-wing Air Force chaplain claimed that, soon after the coup, he was called to give extreme unction to the Catholics among hundreds of people in a Córdoba field, and then saw them shot and buried;[60] and what the regime described as the killing of sixty inmates during a riot at Villa Devoto Prison in March 1978 was denounced by some journalists as the 'Devoto Massacre' of over 200 political prisoners and criminals.[61]

The norm was extreme ruthlessness, and not only in eliminating guerrilla suspects. While the junta's defence was that it had been forced to fight a 'dirty war' in which certain 'excesses' and 'errors' had been unavoidable,[62] the pattern of repression followed far more closely the statement of intent made by Buenos Aires Governor, General Ibérico Saint-Jean, at the time of the military takeover: 'First we will kill all the subversives; then we will kill their collaborators; then ... their sympathizers; then ... those who remain indifferent; and finally we will kill the timid.'[63] By the end of 1977 Argentina, with an estimated 18,000 political prisoners, was top of the list for jailing innocents compiled in Washington by the Council on Hemispheric Affairs.[64] The junta

[59] OAS (1980), p. 80; Amnesty (1980), pp. 22–7.
[60] *The Guardian*, 24 May 1978.   [61] *Triunfo* (Madrid), April 1978.
[62] Statement by Minister of the Interior, General Harguindeguy, *La Nación*, international ed., no. 1071 (30 March 1981).
[63] *The Guardian*, 6 May 1977.   [64] *The Times*, 24 December 1977.

never admitted holding more than 5,108 detainees at any one time (May 1977) and by January 1981 claimed to have only 900 held at the disposition of the Executive power.[65] No reliable estimate of the numbers killed by State forces since March 1976 is available, though provisional estimates generally put the figure at between ten and twenty thousand,[66] and the number of political exiles at multiples of these figures. The Organization of American States investigating team, which visited Argentina in 1979, implicitly accused the junta of 'state terrorism' and explicitly found the 'governmental authorities and their agents' responsible for 'numerous serious violations of fundamental human rights'.[67] In reply the regime produced a list of 1,025 guerrilla attacks since 1969 and published details of a total of 688 murders by 'terrorist delinquency' since 1970.[68] That few observers considered the repression thereby justified was symbolized by the award in October 1980 of the Nobel Peace Prize to Adolfo Pérez Esquivel, a former Argentine political prisoner, for his activity in defence of human rights.

The broad sweep of the repressive drive, and especially its impact on the student movement, helped to prevent Montonero recruitment from matching losses. By the end of 1977, the guerrillas were putting their membership at 40 per cent of the 1975 level, having recovered, they claimed, from a low of 20 per cent.[69] Apart from casualties, they had suffered numerous 'desertions', including the departure of one of their leading trade unionists, Guillermo Grecco, a man who

[65] *La Nación*, international ed., no. 1059 (5 January 1981).

[66] By 1980, the Permanent Assembly for Human Rights had data on 6,000 missing people, and Amnesty on 4,000, while the OAS spoke of 5,000 'disappeared' people, 'presumed executed' [*The Guardian*, 25 November 1980]. Many of the abductions have not been publicized. The OAS team in Argentina in 1979 received 5,580 depositions about human rights violations, of which 4,153 were new [OAS (1980), p. 6]. No data has been published concerning the number killed by the security forces in armed confrontations or during raids since the military coup, though it is probably around 5,000. The most frequently-quoted Montonero claims were 10,000 killed, 30,000 disappeared (many of them dead), and 15,000 imprisoned.

[67] OAS (1980), pp. 27 and 263.

[68] *La Nación*, international ed., no. 1025 (12 May 1980); and *Terrorism in Argentina*, p. 314. Of the 688 victims of political killings, 515 were members of the Armed Forces, Gendarmerie, and police (over 70 per cent of the total). With entrepreneurs, these victims accounted for 82 per cent of the total. Trade unionists killed by guerrillas numbered 24.

[69] PM, untitled internal document, October 1977, p. 15.

had reputedly begun to have second thoughts after the assassination of Rucci. At the end of the year, most of the remaining Montoneros at liberty abandoned the country, hoping in exile to be safe from the manhunters for a while and then to make a triumphant return to Argentina when conditions improved. They were to be disappointed on both counts.

THE MONTONERO EMIGRATION

The Montoneros survived their 1976-7 nightmare on account of the great numerical strength they had achieved by the end of 1975, the evacuation of their leaders, and their financial corpulence. Abroad — in Madrid, Mexico City, Rome, Paris, Caracas, and other capitals — more than 1,000 Montoneros were able to regroup, and possibly for a while attract other exiles towards them. Preservation of the lives of the leaders was essential to what remained of guerrilla morale, providing as the *comandantes* did some continuity with memories of a more glorious past. And the war chest was still quite adequate to Montonero needs. It had suffered a haemorrhage of funds in August 1976 when the private plane of David Graiver crashed into a mountainside while *en route* from New York to Acapulco. With him, presumably, went the 17 million dollars which he had been 'laundering' for the guerrillas, investing it in banks, industrial plant, and real estate, with interest payments of 130,000 dollars a month accruing to the Montoneros as a result.[70] But caution had persuaded the kidnappers of the Born brothers to channel 50 million dollars to Cuba in 1975 and there, though it yielded no interest, it was absolutely safe.[71] Some 30 million dollars remained by the beginning of 1979.[72]

In 1977, not surprisingly, the leaders who controlled the funds and weaponry made Havana their strategic base. Firmenich and the other *comandantes* began to globe-trot in search of international allies, yet their principal *pied-à-terre*

---

[70] On the Graiver case, see *The Sunday Times*, 5 June 1977; and Christopher Dobson and Ronald Payne, *The Weapons of Terror* (London: Macmillan, 1979), pp. 87-90.

[71] Personal interview with a former Montonero, England, January 1981.

[72] Peronismo en la Resistencia, *Reflexiones*, p. 12.

remained in Cuba where, although they maintained a low profile, Commander Firmenich would appear at major anniversary celebrations as the guest of the Government and Cuban Communist Party. Money being no problem, a major propaganda offensive against the Argentine regime was now mounted. Montonero publications multiplied: *Evita Montonera*, technically the party organ, was joined by regular trade union news bulletins, a Montonero Army organ, a general news synthesis, an international MPM magazine, and a whole host of occasional items.[73] A radio station was legally installed in Costa Rica, beaming short-wave denunciations of the regime into Argentina and throughout the region.[74] Of Montonero invention, *Radio Liberación* was also born — a small portable box which could be taken into Argentina, plugged into any electricity supply, and broadcast short taped messages through television sets over a radius of eight to ten blocks. The Montonero voice was further to be heard at major international conferences, but that voice was primarily that of the leaders. It was the leaders who joined the revolutionary jet set, who had the financial freedom to travel, while the ordinary exiles, many of them now jobless graduates, suffered economic hardship. Away from Argentina, the rank-and-file became far more dependent on their leaders, both for news and for monetary allocations, but they also became more critical of them. After all, if Mario Firmenich, Roberto Perdía, Horacio Mendizábal, and Fernando Vaca Narvaja agreed upon the need to invest millions of dollars in travel, often lavish publications, and new infrastructure, why was it that a fraction of this expenditure could not now, in the relative security of exile, be devoted to financing that long-promised Montonero Party Congress?

Abroad the Montoneros, at least as an organization, refrained from military activities. Argentine diplomatic

---

[73] Respectively, *Crónica de la resistencia sindical argentina, Estrella Federal, Noticias (de Argentina)*, and *Vencer*. Of less regular appearance were *Movimiento*, organ of the MPM Superior Council, and *El 17*, produced by the Trade Union Bloc of Montonero Peronism. Booklets were also issued by the latter and in the name of the Montonero Peronist Youth (JPM), and a *Boletín Informativo* was circulated by the CGT-R.

[74] *Radio Noticias del Continente* was silenced by the Costa Rican Government in February 1981 as a result of Argentine governmental pressures and Montonero indiscretion.

buildings were bombed in Colombia, Geneva, and El Salvador, but by local opponents of the military regime; in 1980, the Montonero leader declared that 'it would have been an honour for us to have killed Somoza', but it was the ERP that in fact claimed the life of the deposed Nicaraguan dictator.[75] Instead the Montoneros concentrated their efforts on building international support and isolating the junta, directing their approaches to human rights organizations, the Catholic Church, the world labour movement, the Socialist International, 'Socialist Countries', and national liberation movements, wearing a variety of hats in the process.

They never dominated, nor sought to dominate, the movement of protest against human rights violations. Many of the courageous 'Mothers of Plaza de Mayo', who regularly assembled outside Government House to demand news of their abducted sons and daughters, had Montonero ties — but ties of blood more often than of politics. As for the Argentine Church, there was no response from the episcopate to a Montonero letter in late 1976 proposing dialogue with a view to achieving 'pacification'.[76] Nor was there any reply from the Vatican to *comandante* Mendizábal's letter of 1978 to his Eminence Cardinal Jean Villot informing him that, in order to encourage Catholics to join the Montonero Army, the latter (without becoming a confessional entity) had established a chaplaincy and had appointed Father Jorge Adur as its chaplain.[77] The MPM Superior Council also sported a Reverend Father, Rafael Iaccuzzi, but the Montonero arguments no longer held much credibility in Church circles. A more sympathetic response came from labour, Montonero delegations being permitted to attend International Labour Organization meetings and trade union conferences in Algeria and elsewhere, yet in most cases this was merely an expression of solidarity with the hundreds of trade unionists imprisoned or 'missing' in Argentina — not specifically with the Montoneros, though they did have their own labour casualties, such

---

[75] Firmenich interview, 'Nos honraría haber matado a Somoza', republished in *Noticias*, 1-15 September 1980; and 'Así se mató a Somoza', *El Socialista* (Madrid), no. 172 (24-30 September 1980), p. 50.

[76] Montoneros, *Lettre al 'Episcopat d'Argentine du Commandement National du Parti Montonero* (France, December 1976).

[77] 'Comunicación oficial del Ejército Montonero al Vaticano', special supplement to *Estrella Federal*, no. 5 (August 1978), pp. 2-4.

as Mario Aguirre, former General Secretary of the State Workers' Association in Rosario, who was arrested in September 1976.

Montonero relations with the Social Democrats, 'Socialist Countries', and national liberation movements were more complex. Within the Socialist International, Montonero representatives were received by the leaders of the Swedish, West German, and Spanish member parties. The Austrian Socialists even proposed the Montoneros for membership, unsuccessfully.[78] Such progress as was made though, especially with the Spanish and Austrian parties, was to some extent a product of the earlier support-building activities for the *Auténticos* by Juan Gelman while based in Rome, and again more an expression of general sympathy for Argentine workers than specifically for the Montoneros. It waned as Montonero claims to be leading the Argentine resistance were exposed as arrogant self-delusion, and in Spain as the PSOE increasingly came to regard ETA as a threat to the post-Franco political process.

As for the so-called Socialist Countries, Montonero hopes for solidarity were dashed by the attraction of commerce. Contrary to some expectations, the military government found it so convenient to further exploit the trading avenues opened up by its Peronist predecessor with the Soviet camp that Argentina even broke the attempted US grain embargo imposed by President Carter following the Soviet intervention in Afghanistan.[79] This marriage of convenience explains why the slavishly pro-Moscow Argentine Communist Party (PCA) retained its legality in 1976, why it lent its 'critical support' to General Videla's Government as a putative 'Liberal' bulwark against *pinochetista* challengers, why it sent thirty representatives to Europe in an effort to neutralize the effects of Montonero propaganda,[80] and why the Soviet Union blocked attempts to condemn Argentina's human rights record in a number of international forums. China also found it advantageous to increase its trade with the regime, to play host to Videla and Martínez de Hoz, and in 1978 to

[78] *La Nación*, international ed., nos. 941 and 943 (2 and 16 October 1978).
[79] In 1980 the Soviet Union purchased 52 per cent of the Argentine grain harvest (volume). Ibid., no. 1060 (12 January 1981).
[80] Ibid., no. 913 (20 March 1978).

praise 'the dizzy progress made by Argentina in the last two years'.[81] Cuba's position was more ambiguous, as was seen at the time of the 1978 World Youth Festival in Havana. On the one hand, Cuba accepted a PCA veto on Montonero participation in the Argentine delegation to the Festival,[82] and organized solidarity rallies for every major Latin American country under military rule except Argentina; on the other hand, fifteen Montoneros were present as individual guests of the Cuban Government, and in two speeches Fidel Castro included Argentina in his lists of denounced regimes. While it should not be exaggerated, there is something in the Montonero view that the Cuban regime contains both a solidly pro-Moscow line and a *fidelista* line more sympathetic to themselves. Addressing a rally on 26 July 1980, the Cuban leader reaffirmed: 'That there is only one path: revolution! That there is only one way: revolutionary armed struggle!'.[83]

The most unequivocal support for the Montoneros came, however, from the liberation movements, mainly those of Africa and the Middle East. MPM representatives issued a joint communiqué with the Tanzanian ruling party and established a permanent office in Dar-es-Salaam in 1977. Later a similar declaration was signed in Iraq, there were official visits to Mozambique and Ethiopia, and Montoneros were guests of ZANU during the independence celebrations in Zimbabwe.[84] In organizational terms the firmest bonds were secured with revolutionary nationalist movements favouring armed struggle: chiefly the PLO and the Nicaraguan Sandinistas (FSLN).[85] Firmenich and military commander Mendizábal went to Beirut to discuss political and military matters in September 1978.[86] Montonero backing for the Sandinista struggle against Somoza the following year included a financial contribution, the presence of Fernando Vaca

[81] Ibid., no. 1029 (9 June 1980); *The Guardian*, 2 June 1978.
[82] The Montoneros published the eight letters through which they sought to at least be accepted as part of the Argentine delegation. None received a reply.
[83] *Granma Weekly Review* (Havana), 3 August 1980.
[84] Further details about Montonero international activity are to be found in PM, untitled internal document, October 1977; MPM, *With the People of the World* (Np, 1978); and *Vencer*, nos. 1-4, *passim*.
[85] MPM Superior Council, 'Interview with Commandant Mario Eduardo Firmenich', 16 March 1979 (London, 1979), p. 10.
[86] *Latin America Weekly Report* (London), 15 February 1980.

Narvaja in Nicaragua during the final month of the fighting, and the sending of the 'Adriana Haidar' Medical Brigade to treat wounded Sandinistas in the region of Masaya.[87] The pay-off was provided, theoretically, by the lessons to be drawn from the FSLN triumph and the experience of post-insurrectional reconstruction; and, practically, by the defeat of an ally of the Argentine regime and the acquisition of a further venue for holding undisturbed meetings.[88] The latter was no mean conquest: more than a dozen Montoneros and presumed Montoneros were picked up or off outside Argentina, as Latin American intelligence and security agents demonstrated what 'internationalism' meant to them.[89]

Meanwhile inside Argentina football became the focus of popular attention, with millions enthusing over the chances of their team winning the mid-1978 *Mundial*. The Montoneros declared that it would be a 'people's festival' which they would transform into a 'giant press conference to inform the world of the tragedy which our people are suffering'.[90] In pursuit of this objective they issued a pamphlet as decorative as the prospectus of any multinational corporation;[91] they held press conferences in Buenos Aires addressed by Juan Gelman, Norberto Habegger, and Armando

[87] *Evita Montonera*, no. 25 (August 1979), a special edition dedicated to the Sandinista triumph.
[88] Personal interview with two MPM members, London, 26 August 1980.
[89] In 1976 the former parliamentarians Zelmar Michelini and Héctor Gutiérrez Ruiz were only the most prominent of the Uruguayan exiles to be assassinated in Buenos Aires; former Bolivian President, Juan Torres, was also killed, and at one stage some twenty Chileans were 'disappearing' each week, perhaps because there were forty Chilean police agents based in the central police headquarters in Buenos Aires [*L'Europeo* (Italy), 10 September 1976]. The cases which the Montoneros publicized in seeking to demonstrate the existence of 'international State terrorism' against their activists were as follows: 1977 — former member Carlos Maguid kidnapped in Lima; in Uruguay, Jaime Dri and Oscar de Gregorio arrested and transported to ESMA, Alejandro Barry (PM Political Secretary) and Carlos Valladares killed. 1978 — Norberto Habegger kidnapped in Rio de Janeiro; unsuccessful attempts to abduct or kill Montonero leaders in Madrid and Mexico; internationally-famous pianist Miguel Estrella jailed in Uruguay, accused of being a 'Montonero terrorist'. 1980 — National leader Horacio Campiglia and Susana Binstock kidnapped in Brazil; María Inés Raverta, Julio César Ramírez, and Noemí Esther Giannotti de Molfino kidnapped in Peru, the latter to be found dead, assassinated, in a Madrid apartment weeks later; and Montonero chaplain, Father Jorge Adur, kidnapped in Brazil, where he had gone for the papal visit.
[90] Statements by Juan Gelman, *Le Monde* (Paris), 15–16 January 1978.
[91] *Argentina '78* (Np, 1978).

Croatto;[92] and they urged supporters to attend the matches and chant, 'Argentina Champion — Videla to the Wall!'. Simultaneously, the Montonero Army went into action, well away from football crowds, aiming to show that it still possessed a military capacity and to pin-point the centres of repression. Using RPG-7 portable rocket-launchers for the first time, eighteen attacks were launched against the homes of Army officers, the Superior War School, ESMA, the Army Intelligence Service HQ, Government House, the Army High Command, and police stations, and a *Gendarmería* commander was assassinated.[93] Sadly for the Montoneros, this activity was far too successful: the guerrillas hit their targets, managed to avoid killing civilians, and then withdrew without losses. The press therefore ignored it, thereby nullifying its political value and in effect encouraging a recurrence of the politically-counterproductive big explosions and major assassinations that nobody could hush up.

Propaganda-wise, despite Montonero claims that 'We won the World Cup',[94] the championship stimulated the kind of nationalism from which the regime would benefit. The only real consolation for its opponents was the spectacle of General Videla twitching nervously as delays provoked loud whistling from the spectators during the final presentation ceremony. International audiences saw little of the secret detention centres, just a well-organized Argentine side taking the honours, defeating Holland 3-1 in the final with two goals from Kempes and a third from Bertoni.

On this and other issues, the Montonero leadership, full of an unconvincing triumphalism, proved thoroughly incapable of recognizing failures, set-backs, and defeat. Only the distance of exile enabled them to convince their members, if indeed they did, that 'all the workers sympathize with our policies which time has shown to be correct', that 'Today Montonero Peronism is the majority force within Peronism', and that 'Montonero Peronism is the soul of this

---

[92] At these press conferences, the Montoneros condemned the kidnapping and killing of Aldo Moro in Italy, arguing that constitutional expressions of political dissent were possible there. See *The Guardian*, 8 June 1978.

[93] For details see *Estrella Federal*, no. 5 (September 1978), pp. 16-17.

[94] Ibid., pp. 3-5. See also the Firmenich interview, 'Por qué Videla perdió el Mundial', *Resistencia Socialista* (bulletin of the P. Socialista CNR, Gran Bretaña), 1978, pp. 3-5.

Resistance'.⁹⁵ Perhaps even the leaders managed to convince themselves that their illusions were reality. Certainly at first their pretentiousness was based on confidence in their future: though the *Casa Montonera* (the Montonero House) which they opened in Mexico had to suspend its public activities as a result of Argentine Government pressures on the Mexican Government, its twin in Puerta de Hierro, Madrid, was initially envisaged as the place to which the 'generals of the dictatorship' would eventually come to negotiate the terms of their surrender, just as Lanusse's envoys had come to the same city to 'surrender' to Perón in the early 1970s.⁹⁶ Efforts to evoke memories of that triumph ruined the 1977 Montonero film, *To Resist is to Win*, half of which was marred by a camera fixation with Mario Firmenich who, attempting to don the mantle of Perón and emulate the Peronist leader's appearance in a film sent into Argentina years earlier, delivered an exceedingly tedious monologue.

The determination to persist with claims of victories despite the patent failure of the MPM to take root inside Argentina was fundamentally an expression of political opportunism. For now the 'pragmatists' and militarists were in full control. The outstanding revolutionaries — Osatinsky, Quieto, Urondo, Roqué — were all dead. Suspicions even surfaced in some minds as to whether the National Leadership had not in fact been infiltrated. Was it pure chance that the leading former cadres of the FAR, the Montonero component most strongly influenced by Marxism, had all been eliminated? Whatever the truth, the 1976 programme was hastily buried. It was replaced, first, with the April 1977 'Eight Points of Rome', a minimum programme calling for the removal of Martínez de Hoz, the holding of elections, the release of the prisoners, and a restoration of all constitutional, political, and trade union rights.⁹⁷ Then, in June 1978, came a document which, while still mentioning socialism, urged the reunification and transformation of Peronism, with the Right, Left, and Centre participating in a joint leadership.⁹⁸

[95] PM, untitled internal document, October 1977, p. 16; Firmenich interview, 'Nos honraría'; and 'Organizarse para vencer', *Evita Montonera*, no. 23 (January 1979), pp. 3-10.
[96] Personal interview with two MPM members, London, 26 August 1980.
[97] MPM, *Victory is Born with People's Unity* (Np, 1978).
[98] Mario Firmenich, 'Acerca de la unidad del peronismo' (Np), June 1978.

And finally, in April 1980, the evolution arrived at a programme which appealed for anti-oligarchic and anti-dictatorial unity without any mention of socialism. In four years, Leninist-influenced schemas had given way to talk of 'national pacification', the desire for 'democratic stability', and 'social justice'. Even the military were now assured of an institutional role in the Montonero 'Revolutionary National Project'.[99]

None of the Montonero proposals prospered. The minimum demands, though they were those of millions of Argentines, failed to politically differentiate the organization from the mainstream opposition forces which, in turn, all regarded association with the Montoneros as a liability as they strove for a return of party political freedoms. Among Peronists, even Héctor Cámpora, for whose liberty the MPM had been campaigning since 1977, condemned 'subversion' when permitted to leave Argentina, and refused to meet Obregón Cano and Rodolfo Puiggrós when he reached Mexico.[100] Negotiations with national entrepreneurs, conducted by Ernesto Jauretche in 1979, also proved fruitless: condemnation of the policies of Martínez de Hoz was expressed, yet so were plausible claims that significantly higher wages would bankrupt the ailing companies concerned.[101]

As if to make up for the political failures, militarism became even more pronounced. Uniforms were worn by Montoneros during the Cuban Youth Festival, much to the amusement of Red Army delegates wearing civilian dress. Days later, it was announced that the leader of the Martyrs of the Resistance and the members of the Miguel Zavala Rodríguez Combat Platoons, both belonging to the Captain Alberto Camps Special Troops Section of the Montonero Army, had been decorated with the Order of Hero in Combat, Commander Carlos Olmedo grade, for their RPG-7 exploits during the World Cup Tactical Offensive Campaign.[102] After the latter, the Montoneros claimed that the resistance movement had detained the enemy offensive, had provoked internal contradictions in the regime, and had

---

[99] MPM, 'Al pueblo argentino: la justicia social y la soberanía popular son el camino hacia la democracia y la paz' (Np), April 1980. An English translation of this document was published in *Vencer*, no. 4 (1980).
[100] *La Nación*, international ed., no. 1017 (17 March 1980).
[101] Personal interview with two MPM members, London, 26 August 1980.
[102] 'Condecoración', *Estrella Federal*, no. 5 (September 1978), p. 12.

thereby created the conditions for a successful counter-offensive in 1979. *Evita Montonera* then announced the advent of the latter amid images of uniformed Montoneros, photographs of the Montonero Army High Command, and shots of each *comandante* having his hand shaken by Commander Firmenich in front of huge maps of Argentina, the others standing to attention in the background. And a sample of the text: 'The brilliant performance of Commander Mendizábal while heading the General Staff of the Montonero Army was praised by Commander Firmenich, who congratulated him and expressed thanks on behalf of the whole Party for the role played by the military forces under his command in detaining the enemy offensive.'[103] It would all have been somewhat more convincing had the photographs been taken in Argentina.

Behind all the militarism lay a Montonero chief's readiness to sacrifice dozens of lives, including those of several prominent colleagues, in a counter-offensive from which any eventual political benefits would be reaped by few survivors, led by non-participants Firmenich and Vaca Narvaja. It was a readiness already apparent in the case of Tulio Valenzuela, 'the unforgettable "Tucho", who died so heroically'.[104] Valenzuela was kidnapped along with his wife and son by the Army in January 1978, having been betrayed by members of the Rosario Regional Secretariat which he headed. With his family held as hostages, he was obliged to accompany officers of the 2nd Army Corps and Naval Intelligence agents to Mexico, where his orders were to facilitate the abduction or assassination of Montonero leaders, including Ricardo Obregón Cano. Having arrived there, however, he denounced the plot at a press conference, causing great embarrassment to General Galtieri, commander of the Army corps concerned, and future Army C-in-C. Valenzuela then wrote to Galtieri on a 'General-to-General' basis, promising a 'Normandy Landing' by the Montoneros within two years and requesting that, if the Army had not already shot his wife and son, the latter be

---

[103] *Evita Montonera*, no. 23, pp. 13–18. At the same time, the tactical and strategic leadership organs of the PM and EM were merged, simplifying the organizational structure but also increasing the differentiation between the leadership and the rank-and-file.

[104] *Noticias*, no. 23 (1–7 December 1979), pp. 5–8.

told of how proud the Montoneros were of their heroism before they were killed. Apart from eulogies of Valenzuela and references to his 'heroic' death, that was as far as the official Montonero version of *Operación México* went.[105] What it did not say was that the Montoneros were not 100 per cent sure that Valenzuela's collaboration with the Army had been simulated and had ended; that they therefore reduced him to the rank of *aspirante* and ordered him back into Argentina; and that he was shot as he attempted to cross the frontier.[106]

A DISASTROUS ATTEMPTED RETURN

The 1979 'Counter-Offensive' was a disaster from start to finish: yet another display of militarism despite guerrilla protestations that what was underway was a 'popular' counter-offensive. Encouraged by more strikes in 1978 and even a 5,000-strong demonstration on the 4th anniversary of Perón's death, the Montoneros attempted their promised 'Normandy Landing'. According to their analyses, there was now a real possibility of the workers taking to the streets, of recovering trade union rights, bringing down Martínez de Hoz, and of splitting the Armed Forces, obliging them to undertake a disorderly retreat. Perhaps more important than consideration of the mood of the Argentine masses, though, was an age-old fear of all political exiles: that unless they returned soon, they would be forgotten; they would, as they put it, 'disappear politically in the eyes of the masses'.[107] Maybe this was what blinded Montonero strategists to the reality of a divided labour movement — divided in part because the military had not 'intervened' all the unions, rendering their situation heterogeneous; divided too because, in the absence of a confederation to mediate, personal, political, and bureaucratic rivalries became more entrenched. As was seen when a general strike was attempted on 27 April 1979, the working class was not yet ready, either organizationally or politically, for a united militant counter-

[105] Ibid. See also *The Guardian*, 26 January 1978.
[106] Personal interview with a former Montonero, England, January 1981.
[107] 'Balance de la Campaña "Carlos Hobert" de Lanzamiento de la Contraofensiva Popular', *Boletín Interno*, no. 12 (January 1980).

offensive.[108] Many workers held back for fear of the consequences of participating, and possibly too because of signs of a minor recovery in the level of real wages. Towards the end of 1979, a couple of important industrial conflicts arose in Greater Buenos Aires and General Menéndez rose in token rebellion against his military superiors, but such developments fell far short of Montonero expectations. What was programmed as a popular counter-offensive thus remained primarily a military one, and a very costly one at that.

In intention, the plan of campaign emphasized trade-union mobilization as the key to success. While a quarter of the returning Montoneros regrouped as members of the Special Infantry Troops (TEI, led by Yäger), entrusted with military tasks, the remaining three-quarters returned as members of the Special Agitational Troops (TEA, commanded by Mendizábal), responsible for political and labour activities. And though the former bore instructions to annihilate the junta's economic team,[109] their orders were to synchronize their death blows with the expected explosion of labour combativity, coming at the end of months of agitation, *Radio Liberación* transmissions, and political negotiations.[110] So far as the planners were concerned the culmination of the process would see workers streaming out of their factories, especially in northern Buenos Aires, and marching on *Plaza de Mayo*. There, anything might happen. Recalling the historic 17 October 1945 workers' mobilization, the 1969 *Cordobazo*, and the 1975 *Rodrigazo*, the Montoneros immodestly decreed the initiation of the *Argentinazo*.

Quite apart from their traditional overestimation of the levels of labour's unity, Montonero identification, and

---

[108] The general strike was led, despite the arrest of twenty-one of its leaders, by the Commission of the 25, but did not receive the backing of the other union coordinating body of the period, the National Labour Commission (CNT). The Twenty-Five claimed a 75 per cent success; *Le Matin* (Paris) estimated that 60-80 per cent of the workers in the Federal Capital and Greater Buenos Aires downed tools [*Vencer*, no. 1 (1979), p. 64].

[109] Attacks on the economic team had begun in 1978, with the assassination of Miguel Padilla, an Economy Ministry advisor on wages policy, in April, and the blowing up of the home of Treasury Secretary Juan Alemann during the World Cup campaign. The number of Montonero victims in 1978 reached six by mid-August.

[110] See the replies to the 'Documento de Madrid', especially that by Eduardo Pereyra, in Partido Montonero, *Boletín Interno*, no. 13 (February 1980).

revolutionary preparedness, and underestimation of the enemy, the Montoneros again demonstrated how even their labour-orientated initiatives were incorrigibly militaristic. Here, their summarized counter-offensive plans were most revealing:

*Phase III. Attack (the battle): (Idea behind actions, without precise dates).
— Workers mobilization from Greater Buenos Aires to *Plaza de Mayo*: principal zone being the North (Idea behind the *Rodrigazo*). Adequate Column: around 5,000 workers (a large factory: Ford?).[111]

Casting aside all the rhetoric about a central commitment to labour struggles, what this clearly showed was that, far from seeing the workers as revolutionary protagonists to be mobilized as a class, the Montoneros regarded them as strategic troops to be brought into action in measured quantities, as decided by guerrilla generals. Labour was to be manipulated so as to provide the heavy brigades which would be brought up to the front, reinforcing the crack troops of the light brigade while the latter sliced through the immobilized ranks of the enemy, cutting down the foe one-by-one.

Labour, however, showed itself resistant to Montonero manipulation. The workers stayed in their factories, some as strugglers but all as spectators of the Montonero set-pieces. TEI units demolished the home of Planning and Economic Coordination Secretary, Guillermo Walter Klein, at the end of September, injuring his whole family and killing two policemen in the process; a fortnight later, they wounded two guards in an unsuccessful Belgrano shooting and bazooka attack on Treasury Secretary, Juan Alemann; and in mid-November they assassinated entrepreneur Francisco Soldati, and a guard, in busy central Buenos Aires. They hit more guards than targets, attracted general disapprobation by attacking the Kleins and labour condemnation by attacking Alemann,[112] and they failed to make Soldati's links with the

---

[111] 'Balance de la Campaña "Carlos Hobert"'.
[112] The attack on Alemann was condemned by the United Leadership of Argentine Workers (CUTA), created in an effort to unify the labour movement, and based on the CNT and the 25. Divisions however persisted and the CUTA proved incapable of organizing opposition to the new trade union law announced in November 1979, under which the CGT was formally dissolved, only unions and federations (not confederations) were permitted, and the pre-1976 right of unions to adopt political positions was eliminated.

Economy Ministry public knowledge. Their 'achievement' was negative, their losses catastrophic. So clear was the victory of the State intelligence services that the Montoneros never revealed their total number of casualties. Among them there was one member of the National Leadership (Mendizábal) and seven of the Central Committee. Of a dozen MPM Superior Councillors who returned to Argentina, six were captured and two (ex-deputy Armando Croatto and agrarian militant Carlos Píccoli) died in combat. The First Secretaries of the MPM Labour, Youth, and Feminine Branches (Croatto, Guillermo Amarilla, and Adriana Lesgart), two assistant secretaries (Píccoli and María Antonia Berger), and a talented member of the Political Branch (Julio Suárez) were all lost, and the Youth Branch left totally decapitated. Other notable casualties were CGT-R General Secretary José Dálmaso López, youth leader Jorge Gullo (brother of the former JP leader), FAR veteran Daniel Tolchinsky, and his wife Ana Weissen.[113]

Such losses were surely irreparable, yet, after the survivors had withdrawn from Argentina at the end of the year, the marshals of the defeat, consistent with their previous judgements, declared that their decision to launch the counter-offensive had been 'correct and opportune'.[114] Mario Firmenich, who along with Fernando Vaca Narvaja had spent mid-1979 in Managua, posing alongside Sandinista commanders and being photographed in full battle dress in front of captured Argentine supplies to Somoza, claimed: 'Obviously, the political outcome would have been different if the trade union mobilization towards *Plaza de Mayo* had come off. Nevertheless, it was a triumph.' Thousands of workers, he contended, had identified themselves with Montonero policies; only a twenty-day Army occupation of the Santa Rosa metalworks and the concession of all the demands made by Peugeot workers had prevented a workers' march on the *Plaza*.[115] In other words, the Montoneros did very well, and would have been totally successful if their opponents had not opposed them.

[113] 'El Documento de Madrid: Ante la crisis del Partido. Reflexiones críticas y una propuesta superadora', *Boletín Interno*, no. 13; and *Vencer*, nos. 1-4, *passim*.
[114] 'Balance de la Campaña "Carlos Hobert"'.
[115] 'Nos honraría'.

THE MONTONERO DECLINE

It was this kind of lack of realism, as much as anything else, which provoked the departure of two Montonero tendencies around the time of the counter-offensive. The first, primarily associated with the name of Rodolfo Galimberti, withdrew early in 1979, rejecting the counter-offensive as a strategic blunder; the second, which took the name Montoneros *17 de Octubre* (M-17), departed a year later, refusing to accept the Leadership's positive evaluation of the fiasco.

Galimberti's colleagues included the poet Juan Gelman, whose son and daughter-in-law were abducted in 1976, and Pablo Fernández Long, former *Auténtico* deputy for Misiones and International Affairs Secretary of the MPM Youth Branch. Both Galimberti and Fernández Long had been members of the Tactical Command originally designated to direct the counter-offensive in Buenos Aires. Gelman and Galimberti's resignation letter was critical of 'the resurgence of a militarism, *foquista* in origin, which permeates all manifestations of political life in the structures from which we resign'; of the Montoneros' 'elitist concept of a party of cadres', of the Leadership's 'recourse to conspiratorial practices' and its 'mad sectarianism'; and of 'the definitive bureaucratization of all levels of the Party leadership, whose ultimate expression is the absolute lack of internal democratic practice, which strangles all attempts at critical reflection, dismissing them as defection or treason, hiding the lack of any political response behind an irresponsible triumphalism which convinces nobody'.[116] The dissidents urged their former leaders to abandon the pretence of leading the mass movement and instead to participate in it, to abandon PM-MPM differentiation and paper organizations, and to recognize that the labour movement was still passing through a phase of resistance.

With them, the departing group took 68,750 dollars, apologizing only for not having been able to lay their hands on more! The other 30m dollars, they maintained, rather than be the sole remaining source of political power of the Montonero Leadership, should be redistributed among all the revolutionary forces, to all those resisting and protesting,

---

[116] Open letter of Galimberti and Gelman, 22 February 1979 (duplicated circular).

whether armed or not.[117] In response, the Montonero leaders pointed out that Galimberti had been preparing youth cadres for the counter-offensive right up to the moment of his *pronunciamiento*, it claimed that he had *caudillo* ambitions,[118] and it threatened to assassinate him and his colleagues. Clearly many of the dissident criticisms hit raw nerves, even if some of Galimberti's claims at press conferences ('We should never have killed Mugica') were probably mischievous, concocted to embarrass Firmenich. But what the new group stood for was not immediately clear: on the one hand, they christened their tendency 'Peronism in the Resistance', implying less emphasis upon *montonerismo*, and devoted their subsequent efforts in exile to reaching a *rapprochement* with the Peronist Movement; on the other, they spoke about building an 'Authentic Montonero Peronist Alternative', committed to internal democracy and reconquering the political territory surrendered by their parent organization as a result of its militarism. In practical terms their main positive contribution to the reorientation of Peronist Left activists may turn out to be their publication of the critical reports intelligently written by Rodolfo Walsh in 1976-7, to which his superiors never replied. In them, Walsh had recommended that there should be 'no military action which is not directly and unequivocally linked with an immediate interest of the masses'.[119]

M-17's disaffection was initially expressed through a 'Documento de Madrid', drawn up by six Montonero lieutenants including Miguel Bonasso and Jaime Dri.[120] As in the case of Galimberti (a former leader of *Columna Norte*), their critique referred back to the internal criticism of 1976, before going on to reject the Leadership's contention that the 1979 losses were merely 'costs of war'. They criticized the *comandantes'* refusal to permit them tendency rights (though their document was circulated internally), self-criticized

[117] 'Reflexiones para la construcción', *passim*.
[118] Interview with a Montonero, England, 30 March 1980.
[119] *Los papeles de Walsh*, p. 17.
[120] Op. cit. The other signatories were Daniel Vaca Narvaja, Pablo Ramos, Olimpia Díaz, and Gerardo Bavio. When M-17 was created, its provisional council also included Eduardo Astiz, Sylvia Bermann, René Chávez, Ernesto Jauretche, Pedro Orgambide, Julio Rodríguez Anido, and Susana Sanz [*La Nación*, international ed., no. 1021 (14 April 1980)].

the *foquista* nature of the counter-offensive, and acknowledged that a genuine popular counter-offensive could only have been 'promoted' and not 'launched' by an organization such as their own. Above all, they isolated the roots of original Montonero sin in a 'Clausewitzian reductionism' which presented 'the complex social struggle as movements of conventional military forces', and which had condemned experienced leaders to be lost in a 'confrontation between two apparata and not between two social forces'. They also noted that the military attacks of the campaign had been condemned by Peronist political and labour leaders, lamented the reduction of democratic centralism in the PM to mere centralism, and called for armed struggle to be adapted to the real level and nature of mass resistance.[121] Ostensibly, they differed from Galimberti's group in appealing to the authority of Lenin and Cooke rather than Rodolfo Walsh; in practice, the difference amounted to the former group leaning more towards orthodox Peronism and seeking to re-establish some credibility there, while M-17 pursued a new variant of *montonerismo*, devoid of militarism. Although the latter group was larger, it only had Miguel Bonasso,[122] editor of the original *Noticias*, to command immediate respect in Peronist circles, whereas Galimberti, as Peronist Youth leader of the early 1970s, had stronger claims to Peronist recognition.

The Montonero leaders responded to the resignations with expulsions and to charges of militarism with death threats.[123] Weakened by the departures and their 1979 losses, they were reduced to near impotence. They promoted their 'historic' fellow-travellers, Bidegain, Obregón Cano, and Puiggrós, to a newly-formulated MPM National Leadership in 1980, but of these Puiggrós died in Havana of a heart attack at the end of the year. Abroad, they simply closed down whole continent-based departments of the organization — in Europe, the USA, and Canada — just to silence dissenting

---

[121] 'El Documento de Madrid', *passim*.

[122] Bonasso's decision to depart may have been influenced by the fact that, as former MPM Press Secretary, he had had to issue communiqué after communiqué informing the public about Montonero losses in 1979. Montonero publications were disrupted for several months as a result of his leaving.

[123] The Montoneros spoke of the 'conspiracy, desertion, and eventual treason of the Galimberti-Gelman group' in *Boletín Interno*, no. 12; and the 'expulsion' was announced in *Vencer*, no. 1, p. 23.

voices.[124] From Havana, they were still financially-viable, still of nuisance value to the regime back home, but little more than that. Their credibility had reached an all-time low.

Five years after the March 1976 military coup, the erstwhile soldiers of Perón had little to offer to the massive but divided opposition to the regime in Argentina. Militarily, they could do little to challenge the supremacy of the 130,000-strong Argentine Armed Forces,[125] while politically their proposals for a State Capitalism with heavy corporatist overtones[126] were barely known to Argentines. And those involved in the splinter groups, however refreshing their self-criticism and critiques may have been, were probably too closely identified with the Montonero past to escape the popular disenchantment with what the Montoneros had offered and continued, now feebly, to offer.

Notwithstanding the crisis of the Peronist Left, the Argentine military showed itself to be in no great hurry over returning power to civilian politicians. The generals spoke of the need for more dialogue with 'representative sectors', prior to a demarcated stage of dialogue with officially-recognized political parties, and only at a final stage some form of elections. Interior Minister Harguindeguy once hinted that the latter might come in 1999,[127] though most military figures clearly had no idea when or where their Process of National Reorganization would end. Aware that for many they had outstayed their welcome, that they had held on to the reins of power long after anything approaching a 'subversive threat' had passed, and had gone in for a massive 'overkill' in the name of a 'dirty war' against the guerrillas, fears of reprisals began to figure in the military's reluctance to relinquish power. If it was only the militaristic Left which was predicting 'war trials' for the punishment of officers implicated in illegal acts of repression, if the main parties could be relied upon to reject such proposals, there was still no guarantee that relatives of the thousands of 'disappeared' people would not in future seek revenge when cornering

---

[124] Interview with a Montonero, England, 30 March 1980.
[125] John Keegan, *World Armies* (London & Basingstoke: Macmillan, 1979), p. 24.
[126] MPM, 'Al pueblo argentino: la justicia social'.
[127] *The Times*, 25 November 1977; *La Nación*, international ed., no. 938 (11 September 1978).

military officers in the streets. Perhaps it was these considerations which Navy Chief Lambruschini had in mind when he stated that, although mistakes might have been made, to turn back would be 'suicidal'.[128]

Meanwhile, the examples of Iran and Nicaragua in their minds, surviving Montoneros continued to believe that 'no dictatorship, however strong it may appear, can withstand the explosive coordination of the insurrectional mobilization of the working masses, the rising of a whole people, and the armed guerrilla struggle of a revolutionary vanguard emanating from and nurtured by the national history and historical experience of the popular struggles of its country'.[129] But by now it was apparent, at least to many critics, that urban guerrillas — due to their class extraction, security factors, and their proximity to enemy forces — were incapable of unifying military and mass struggles. The two might co-exist, as they had in Iran and earlier in Argentina, but were unlikely to effectively coalesce except where the guerrillas had secure rural zones, within which they might organize a protected population while fighting. This had been one of the keys to the Sandinista triumph in Nicaragua, yet one which could not unlock the doors to success in highly-urbanized Argentina, where the assailed State was far more formidable anyway. If armed struggle had any future in Argentina, it depended on the emergence of greater combativity in the mass movement rather than upon the initiatives of 'professionals', whether urban or rural.

This was something which the Montonero leadership was never able to grasp. It finished the first five years of military rule devoid of a viable strategy, on the bankrupt note sounded in the introductory quotation to this chapter. Slightly earlier, it was referring to 'the casualties and crimes that the military dictatorship has caused among our people', and stating, 'This we have exposed and raised proudly as a banner — proof of our correct policies and the heroism which has placed our people behind them'.[130] If some idealism remained in the dwindling Montonero ranks, the commander-in-chief's voice was one betraying total cynicism: the sacrifice of his own

---

[128] *La Nación*, international ed., no. 1059 (5 January 1981).
[129] Editorial, *Evita Montonera*, no. 25 (August 1979), p. 5.
[130] 'Interview with Commandant Mario Eduardo Firmenich', p. 2.

troops had become a last desperate means of winning popular acclaim and recognition; the last card which he was prepared to throw away was his own organization, gambling on there being some political pay-off for the guerrilla command when Peronism eventually returned to power. But it was a voice which found no echo in Argentina.

Glossary of Spanish Terms

Agrupación	Rank-and-file group. For the Montoneros, a group of their supporters inside a trade union, in the universities, or within the Peronist Movement.
Ajusticiamiento	Guerrilla 'execution'.
Alternativismo	A Peronist Left tendency which argued that only the labour base and Left of Peronism were really revolutionary, and so should be organized independently of the leadership of the Movement.
Alternativista	One who subscribes to the ideas of *alternativismo*.
Aparatismo	Undue emphasis upon building the guerrilla apparatus, usually to the detriment of work in the mass movement.
Aramburazo	Montonero abduction and killing of ex-President Aramburu.
Aspirante	Guerrilla trainee.
Auténticos	Authentic Peronists.
Barrio Norte	Fashionable, wealthy area of Buenos Aires.
Burocracia sindical	Trade union bureaucracy/leadership.
Casa Rosada	Government House, Buenos Aires.
Cipayo	Sepoy. Somebody or something strongly influenced by a dominating foreign power.
Círculo Militar	Army Officers Club, Buenos Aires.
Clasista	Somebody who emphasizes (working) class struggle.
Colegio Nacional	National School of Buenos Aires.
Columna Norte	Northern Buenos Aires Column of the Montoneros.
Comandante	Guerrilla commander. Top Montonero rank.
Comando	Guerrilla unit.
Compañero	Comrade, companion.
Conducción Nacional	National Leadership of the Montoneros.
Consejo Nacional	National Council.
Coordinadora	Coordinating committee or organization.
Cordobazo	Popular rising in the city of Córdoba, 1969.
Descamisados	Shirtless-ones, Perón's followers; name of an urban guerrilla organization.
Ejército	Army.
Evitismo	Eva Perón cult.
Foco	Guerrilla nucleus/base.
Foquismo	The guerrilla theory associated with Guevara and Debray, according to which armed struggle can help to create revolutionary conditions.

Glossary of Spanish Terms 273

Foquista	One who subscribes to the principles of *foquismo*.
Forjista	Member of FORJA.
Golpe de Estado	Coup; military takeover.
Golpista	One who is in favour of a military coup.
Gorila	Reactionary, often an anti-Peronist military officer.
Gringo	Foreigner, foreign.
Guerra de desgaste	War with the aim of exhausting the enemy.
Guerrillero/a	Guerrilla fighter.
Ideologista	One who bases political analyses upon one's ideological preconceptions, ignoring concrete circumstances.
Intervención	The appointment of a trustee by a government or party/union leadership to take over the running of a province, university, party branch, or union section.
Interventor	A trustee appointed when there is an *intervención*.
Izquierda Nacional	National Left.
Jefe	(Guerrilla) Chief.
Justicialismo	Justicialism. Peronist doctrine.
Laborista	Member of the 1940s Labour Party.
Leales	Members of Peronist 'Loyalist' tendency.
Malvinas	Falkland Islands.
Miguelitos	Nails scattered on roads by guerrillas to prevent police pursuit.
Montonera	Band of mounted gauchos who fought in Independence wars.
Movimientismo	A Peronist Left tendency which viewed the Peronist Movement as a whole as revolutionary.
Movimientista	One who subscribes to the ideas of *movimientismo*.
Mundial	World Cup Football Championship (Argentina 1978).
Onganiato	Onganía's 1966–70 regime and political project.
Operación/ Operativo	Guerrilla action. Social or community project.
Pastilla	Cyanide capsule.
Patria	Fatherland or homeland.
Pelotón de combate	Combat platoon. Basic Montonero fighting unit.
Plaza de Mayo	Main square in Buenos Aires, in front of Government House.
Pronunciamiento	Military rebellion.
Puerta de Hierro	Madrid suburb, place of Perón's residence in exile.
Rama	Branch of the Peronist Movement, or of other movements.
Resistencia	Resistance movement; the post-1955 Peronist labour struggles against anti- and non-Peronist governments.
Revolución Libertadora	The anti-Peronist military coup of 1955, as referred to by its supporters.

274 *Glossary of Spanish Terms*

Rodrigazo	The mid-1975 general strike and labour protests against the economic measures announced by Economy Minister Rodrigo.
Rosista	Supporter of Juan Manuel de Rosas.
Salto	Leap. Move to a higher level of warfare.
Sindicalismo Nacional	National Syndicalism.
Socialismo Nacional	For the Peronist Right, National Socialism; for the Left, a national form of socialism.
Tacuarista	Member of Tacuara.
Tendencia Revolucionaria	The Peronist Left in general, or more specifically the Montoneros and their front organizations of 1973–4.
Tercermundismo	Identification with the Third World and its liberation movements.
Transvasamiento generacional	Generational rejuvenation (of the Peronist Movement).
Unidad básica	Basic political unit of the Justicialist or Peronist Party.
Vanguardismo	The tendency to see the main revolutionary task as one of developing the vanguard, while ignoring the development of the mass movement.
Vendepatria	Traitor prepared to sacrifice national interests for the sake of his or her own.
Verticalismo	Peronist principle of authority and command, according to which all Peronists are expected to obey orders emanating from the leader.
Villa miseria	Shanty town.

Appendices

A: SPLITS AND MERGERS IN MONTONERO AND PRT-ERP DEVELOPMENT

The Montoneros

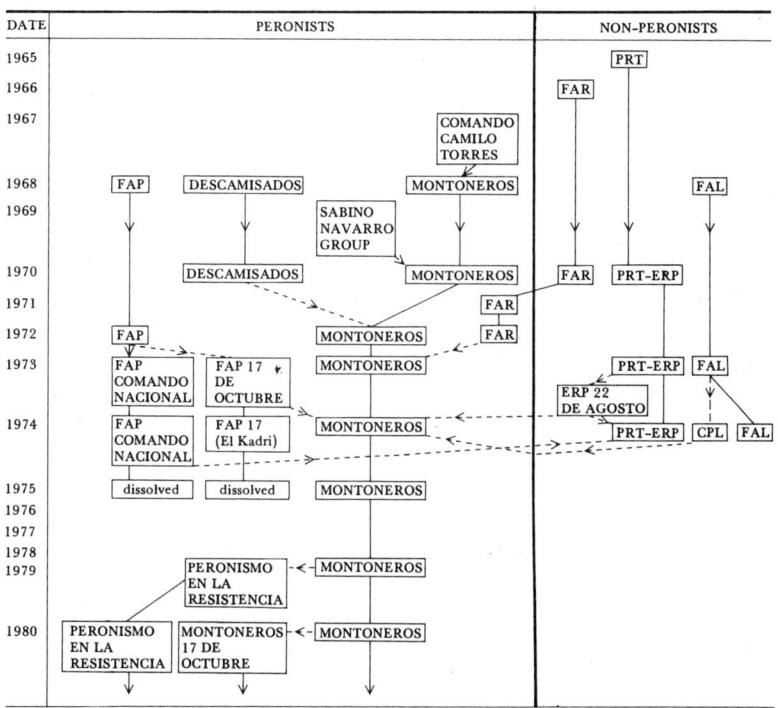

NOTE: Non-Peronist organizations are introduced here only to the extent of their relevance to Montonero development. Some therefore are excluded, while most PRT-ERP and FAL divisions are ignored.

Appendices

Genealogy of the PRT-ERP

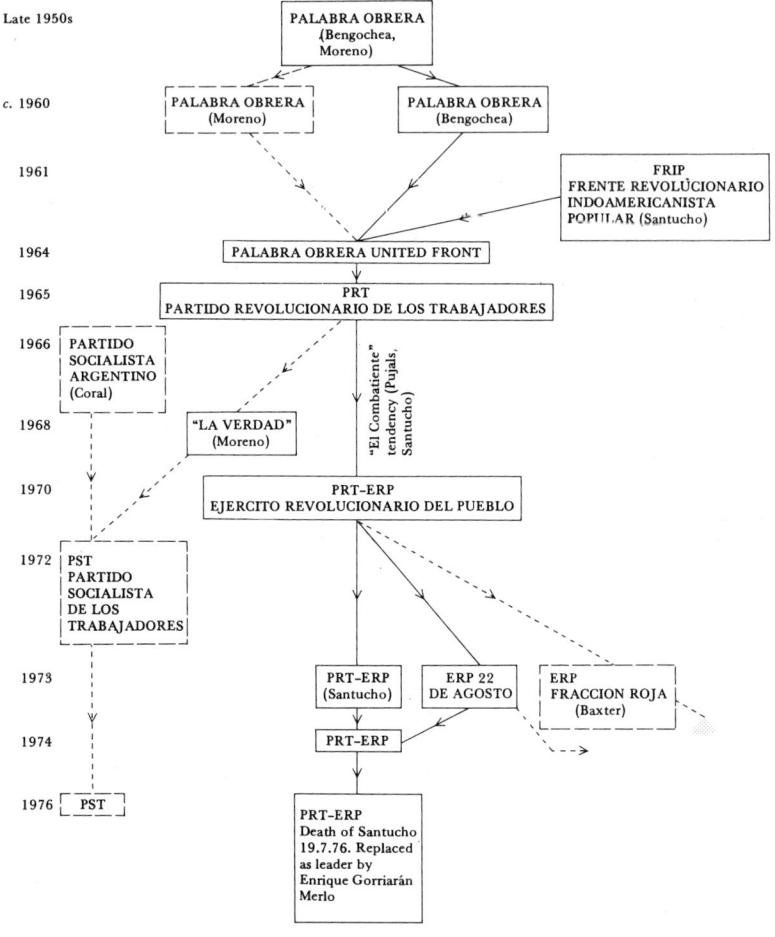

NOTE: Broken lines indicate developments tangential to the emergence of the PRT-ERP; names in brackets are leaders of organizations.

In exile, the PRT-ERP split at least twice (1978 and 1980), leaving small groups led by Gorriarán, Matini, and Roberto Guevara (brother of Che).

B: MONTONERO ORGANIZATIONAL STRUCTURES

(i) Pre-1973

1970   Comandos

1972   Unidades básicas de combate/unidades básicas combatientes

1972   Juventud Peronista (Regionales)

(ii) Tendencia revolucionaria 1973-4

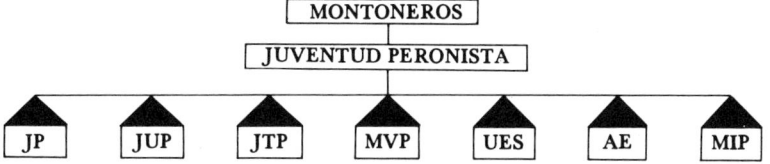

- *Juventud Peronista (Regionales)* — JP
  Peronist Youth (Regions)
  For youth and general political work, based in *barrios* (city districts)

- *Juventud Universitaria Peronista* — JUP
  Peronist University Youth
  For work among university students, in association with university employees

- *Juventud Trabajadora Peronista* — JTP
  Peronist Working Youth
  For trade union activity

- *Movimiento de Villeros Peronistas* — MVP
  Peronist Shanty-Town Dwellers Movement
  For work in the *villas miserias*

- *Unión de Estudiantes Secundarios* — UES
  Secondary Students Union
  For activity in schools

- *Agrupación Evita de la Rama Femenina* — AE
  Evita Group of the Feminine Branch
  For work in the Peronist Movement's women's section

- *Movimiento de Inquilinos Peronistas* — MIP
  Peronist Tenants Movement
  To organize tenants living in *hoteles* (slum boarding houses) and *conventillos* (single-room tenement blocks)

NOTE: *Juventud Peronista* was both a generic term applied to all of the organizations performing 'mass front' tasks and also a more specific name designating the mass political front organization based in the *barrios*. The latter was organized into seven, and later eight, regions and its executive was composed of the leader of each region. Hence *Juventud Peronista (Regionales)*.

(iii) 1975

	MONTONEROS		
	(Platoons) (Militias)		

	MOVIMIENTO PERONISTA AUTENTICO (Agrupaciones)		

POLITICAL/ ELECTORAL BRANCH	FEMININE BRANCH	YOUTH BRANCH	TRADE UNION BRANCH
Partido Peronista Auténtico	Agrupación Evita	Juventud Peronista	Bloque Sindical del Peronismo Auténtico
		Juventud Universitaria Peronista	
		Unión de Estudiantes Secundarios	

NOTE: The introduction of specialization towards the end of 1974, with the establishment of militias and their differentiation from platoons, signified an end to a 1973-4 structure of 'integrated platoons': units to undertake both mass work and military tasks. Some militias were stable, others intentionally temporary.

(iv) 1977-9

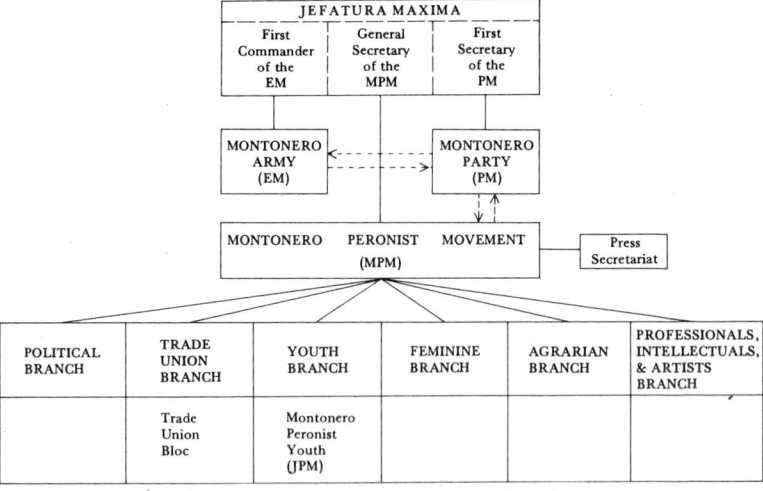

NOTE: Except for the trade union and youth branches of the MPM, there were no specific front organizations for mass activity, this being generally conducted in the name of the branch (*Rama*). The Trade Union Bloc launched the General Confederation of Labour in the Resistance (*CGT en la Resistencia*) in 1976, in theory but not in practice an organization including non-MPM militants as well as Montonero supporters.

This structure replaced a brief 1976 attempt to launch a Montonero Movement led by a Montonero Party.

Appendices 279

In the 1977 structure, all members of the EM are members of the PM. The PM also provides most of the members of the branch leaderships (composed of a 1st Secretary, an Assistant Secretary, an Organization Secretary, and an International Affairs Secretary).
Mario Eduardo Firmenich fills the *Jefatura Máxima*, signifying leadership of the PM, EM and MPM. The composition of the National Leadership of the PM is identical to that of the EM High Command (Mario Firmenich, Roberto Perdía, Raúl Yäger, Horacio Mendizábal).

(v) 1979

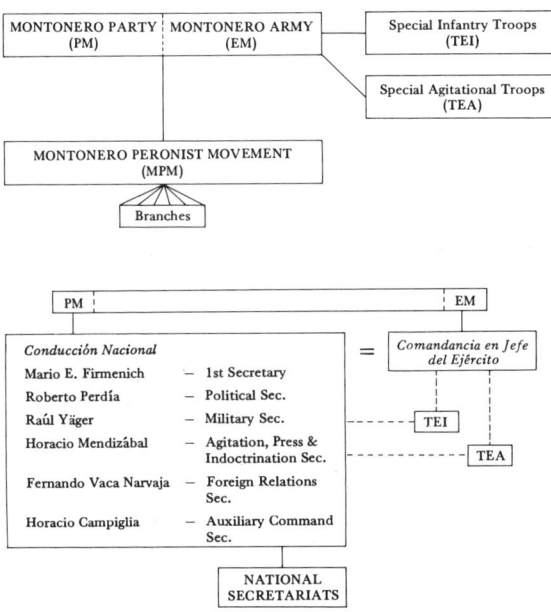

NOTES: The reorganization in preparation for the 1979 counter-offensive involved the dissolution of the National Secretariat and EM general staff, previously the tactical leaderships of the PM and EM respectively. Now, strategic and tactical command structures were unified, and the National Leadership expanded to six members: the 1st Secretary and the heads of five national secretariats. The membership of this *Conducción Nacional* is identical to that of the Army High Command (*Comandancia en Jefe del Ejército*). However, now the EM became structurally part of the PM, even though the name Montonero Army was retained for propagandistic purposes. Overall, the 1979 changes signified a drastic but much-needed simplification of organizational structures: previously there had been a duplication of work by strategic and tactical or functional commands in both the PM and EM, as well as a duplication of tasks by the political and military structures. Of the units used in the 1979 counter-offensive, the TEI came under the command of Military Secretary Yäger and the TEA under Agitation, Press & Indoctrination Secretary Mendizábal.

Bibliography

Note: This bibliography only contains items which are cited in the text and does not include background material. The documentary entries consist of: political programmes and statements issued by organizations; texts of speeches; published interviews; letters; and official reports. Unsigned items, mainly articles which appeared in Argentine political periodicals, are listed separately. The bibliography is arranged alphabetically and falls into four sections:
I. NEWSPAPERS
II. PERIODICALS
III. BOOKS, DOCUMENTS, & SIGNED ARTICLES
IV. UNSIGNED ITEMS

I. NEWSPAPERS

Buenos Aires
Buenos Aires Herald, January 1966-October 1976, and numerous editions 1955-66
La Nación, numerous editions 1955-76
La Nación, edición internacional, 1977-81
La Opinión, July 1975-October 1976
La Razón, numerous editions 1955-76
Noticias, 3-11 June 1974

London
The Guardian, 1970-81
The Times, 1974-81

II. PERIODICALS (Buenos Aires unless otherwise indicated)
Avanzada Socialista, May-December 1974, nos. 104-31
Carta Política, September 1974-September 1975, nos. 7-30
Che, October 1960-November 1961, nos. 1-16
Che Compañero, August 1968, no. 4
Compañero, June 1963-February 1965, nos. 1-77
Confirmado, December 1975-August 1976, nos. 401-11
Con Todo, late 1968, nos. 0-2
Cristianismo y Revolución, September 1966-September 1971, nos. 1-30
Crónica de la resistencia sindical argentina (Np), 1978-80
Cuestionario, March 1974-June 1976, nos. 11-38
De Frente (con las bases peronistas), May-July 1974, nos. 1-9
De Frente (Un testigo insobornable de la realidad mundial), March 1954-October 1955, nos. 2-85
El Auténtico, September-December 1975, nos. 1-8

El Caudillo (de la tercera posición), 15 October 1975, no. 68
El Combatiente, June 1968-February 1976, nos. 9-205
El Descamisado, May 1973-April 1974, nos. 1-46
El Montonero, April 1976, no. 11
El Peronista (lucha para la Liberación), April-May 1974, nos. 1-6
En Lucha, November 1973-September 1974, nos. 12-18
Envido, June 1971-May 1973, nos. 3-9
Estrella Federal (Np), August-September 1978, nos. 5-6
Estrella Roja, July-September 1973, nos. 22-5
Evita Montonera, March 1975-August 1979, nos. 3-25
Izquierda Nacional, October 1963-March 1976, nos. 4-44
La Causa Peronista, July-September 1974, nos. 1-9
Militancia (Peronista para la Liberación), June 1973-March 1974, nos. 1-38
Noticias (de Argentina) (Np), 3 July 1979-15 October 1980
Nuevo Hombre, (1st series) September 1971-September 1974, nos. 8-70; (2nd series) November 1975-March 1976, nos. 2-10
Palabra Obrera, 30 June 1964, no. 364
Peronismo y Liberación, August 1974, no. 1
Peronismo y Socialismo, September 1973, no. 1
Todo es Historia, April 1971-February 1976, nos. 48-105
Vencer (Panama, then Mexico), 1979-80, nos. 1-4

III. BOOKS, DOCUMENTS, & SIGNED ARTICLES

Achával, C. T., 'Córdoba: de Cabrera al Cordobazo', *Todo es Historia*, no. 75 (July 1973): 102-29
Alberti, B. M., *Peronismo, burocracia y burguesía nacional* (Buenos Aires, 1974)
Amnesty International, *Report of an Amnesty International Mission to Argentina, 6-15 November 1976* (London, 1977)
——, *Testimony on Secret Detention Camps in Argentina* (London, 1980)
Arbelos, C. A., and Roca, A. M., *Los muchachos peronistas* (Madrid, 1981)
Balvé, B., et al., *Lucha de calles, lucha de clases* (Buenos Aires, 1973)
Barnes, J., *Eva Perón* (Glasgow, 1978)
Benítez, Padre H., 'Causas y responsables de la "ejecución" de Aramburu', *Cristianismo y Revolución*, no. 25 (September 1970): 5-11
Borro, S., 'El Lisandro de la Torre del 59: bastión de Resistencia Peronista', *Peronismo y Liberación*, no. 1 (August 1974): 97-102
Braun, O., *El capitalismo argentino en crisis* (Buenos Aires, 1973)
Budeisky, C., *El retorno oligárquico 1955-1958* (Buenos Aires, 1973)
Cabo, D. M., 'Carta del director: Compañeros', *El Descamisado*, no. 13 (14 August 1973): 2-3
——, 'Compañeros', *El Descamisado*, no. 26 (13 November 1973): 2-3
——, 'La lucha interna en el movimiento peronista, 1945-1955', *Nuevo Hombre*, no. 8 (8-14 September 1971): 8-9
——, 'La milicia peronista', *La Causa Peronista*, no. 4 (30 July 1974): 29
Cairo, A., *Peronismo claves* (Buenos Aires, 1975)

Cámpora, H. J., *El mandato de Perón* (Argentina, 1975)
——, *La revolución peronista* (Buenos Aires, 1973)
Canton, D., *Elecciones y partidos políticos en la Argentina* (Buenos Aires, 1973)
CGT and 62 Organizations, 'El movimiento obrero argentino ante la situación nacional', *La Razón*, 22 July 1975
CGTA, 'Mensaje a los trabajadores y al pueblo', 1 May 1968, in Ongaro (1970): 27–40
CICSO, *Los asalariados. Composición social y orientaciones organizativas* (Buenos Aires, nd)
Clausewitz, C. von, *On War*, ed. and trans. by M. Howard and P. Paret (New Jersey, 1976)
Codovilla, V., *Batir al nazi-peronismo para abrir una era de libertad y progreso* (Buenos Aires, 1946)
Cooke, J. W., *Apuntes para la militancia* (Buenos Aires, 1973)
——, *El peronismo y el golpe de estado. Informe a las bases del movimiento* (Buenos Aires, 1966); also published as *Peronismo y revolución* (Buenos Aires, 1971)
——, *La lucha por la liberación nacional* (Buenos Aires, 1971)
Coordinadora de Gremios en Lucha, 'La guerrilla industrial, un nuevo cuento para perseguir a los trabajadores', *El Auténtico*, no. 8 (24 December 1975): 6
Corbière, E., Series of articles on Socialist Party, *Cuestionario*, 1975–6
Cornblit, O., 'European Immigrants in Argentine Industry and Politics', in C. Veliz (ed), *The Politics of Conformity in Latin America* (USA, 1970): 221–48
Correa, J., *Los jerarcas sindicales* (Buenos Aires, 1972; extended ed. 1974)
Day, D., ed., *Camilo Torres: Priest and Revolutionary* (London, 1968)
Debray, R., *A Critique of Arms* (2 vols., Harmondsworth, 1978)
——, *Revolution in the Revolution?* (Harmondsworth, 1968)
Delich, F. J., *Crisis y protesta social. Córdoba 1969–1973* (Buenos Aires, 1974)
Díaz Alejandro, C. F., *Essays in the Economic History of the Argentine Republic* (Yale, 1970)
——, *Exchange-Rate Devaluation in a Semi-Industrialized Country. The Experience of Argentina 1955–61* (Massachusetts, 1965)
Di Tella, G., and Zymelman, M., *Las etapas del desarrollo económico argentino* (Buenos Aires, 1967)
Dobson, C., and Payne, R., *The Weapons of Terror* (London, 1979)
Ejército Montonero, *600 Operaciones en 1977* (Np, 1978)
Ellis, J., *A Short History of Guerrilla Warfare* (London, 1975)
Eloy Martínez, T., 'El asenso, triunfo, decadencia y derrota de José López Rega', *La Opinión*, 22 July 1975
——, *La pasión según Trelew* (Buenos Aires, 1973)
ENR, 'Declaración del ENR con motivo del ajusticiamiento de Augusto T. Vandor', *Cristianismo y Revolución*, no. 28 (April 1971): 52–3
FAP, 'Con las armas en la mano', *Cristianismo y Revolución*, no. 28 (April 1971): 77–80

—, 'Nuestros errores pueden servir de lección y ejemplo, pero no de negación de la única salida del pueblo ante la violencia gorila', *Con Todo*, no. 2 (December 1968): 4
Fayt, C. S., *La naturaleza del peronismo* (Buenos Aires, 1967)
Feinmann, J. P., *El peronismo y la primacia de la política* (Buenos Aires, 1974)
Ferla, S., *Mártires y verdugos* (Buenos Aires, 1964)
Fernández Alvariño, P. G., *Z.-Argentina. El crimen del siglo* (Buenos Aires, 1973)
Ferrer, A., ed., *Los planes de estabilización en la Argentina* (Buenos Aires, 1969)
Firmenich, M. E., 'Acerca de la unidad del peronismo' (Np, June 1978)
—, 'A Political Analysis', *NACLA Report*, vol. 11, no. 1 (January 1977): 17-22
—, 'Atlanta', text of speech of 22 August 1973, *Militancia*, no. 12 (30 August 1973): 26-9
—, 'Etapa y conjuntura', text of talk given at JP School, January 1974
—, 'Interview with Commandant Mario Eduardo Firmenich', 16 March 1979 (London, 1979)
—, 'La base del triunfo está siempre en la masa', *Bohemia* (Havana), 9 January 1981
—, 'La provocación de derecha no puede dividirnos'; 'Mi afecto y agradecimiento al Padre Carlos Mugica'; 'Nuestras diferencias políticas', *El Peronista*, no. 5 (21 May 1974): 4-8
—, 'Nos honraría haber matado a Somoza', *Noticias (de Argentina)*, 1-15 September 1980
—, 'Palabras de Firmenich', text of speech of 11 March 1974, *Militancia*, no. 37 (14 March 1974): 37-42
—, 'Por qué Videla perdió el Mundial', *Resistencia Socialista* (Great Britain), 1978: 3-5
Framini, A., 'Hacia la unidad que nos marcaba Perón', *La Causa Peronista*, no. 1 (9 July 1974): 46
Franco, J. P., 'Notas para una historia del peronismo', supplement to *Envido*, no. 3 (June 1971)
—, and Alvarez, F., 'Peronismo: antecedentes y gobierno', *Cuadernos de Antropología 3$^{er.}$ Mundo*, no. 1 (June 1972)
Galimberti, R., 'Unidad Nacional o "Gran Acuerdo Nacional"', *La Causa Peronista*, no. 3 (23 July 1974): 2-3
—, and Gelman, J., Open letter of 22 February 1979 (duplicated circular)
García Lupo, R., 'Diálogo con los jóvenes fascistas', in García Lupo, *La rebelión de los generales* (Buenos Aires, 1962): 71-8
Gastiazoro, E., *Argentina hoy. Latifundio, dependencia y estructura de clases* (Buenos Aires, 1971)
Gerassi, J., ed., *Revolutionary Priest* (Harmondsworth, 1973)
Gillespie, R. H. C., 'A Critique of the Urban Guerrilla: Argentina, Uruguay, and Brazil', *Conflict Quarterly* (New Brunswick), no. 2 (Fall 1980): 39-53
—, 'The Peronist Left' (University of Liverpool PhD thesis, 1979)

Godio, J., *La caída de Perón* (Buenos Aires, 1973)
Goldar, E., *Jauretche* (Buenos Aires, 1975)
González, A. M., and Mendizábal, H., Interview in *Cambio 16* (Madrid), no. 245 (16 August 1976)
González, E., *Qué fue y qué es el peronismo* (Buenos Aires, 1974)
González Janzen, I., *Argentina: 20 años de luchas peronistas* (Mexico, 1975)
González Trejo, H., *Argentina: tiempo de violencia* (Buenos Aires, 1969)
Gott, R., *Guerrilla Movements in Latin America* (London, 1970)
Graham-Yooll, A., *The Press in Argentina 1973-8* (London, 1979)
——, *Tiempo de tragedia* (Buenos Aires, 1972)
——, *Tiempo de violencia* (Buenos Aires, 1973)
Guevara, Che, *Guerrilla Warfare* (Harmondsworth, 1969)
Guillén, A., *Teoría de la violencia* (Buenos Aires, 1965)
Gullo, J. C. D., 'El país se pregunta: ¿qué es la Juventud Peronista?', *El Descamisado*, no. 8 (10 July 1973): 10-13
Halperin Donghi, T., *El revisionismo histórico argentino* (Buenos Aires, 1971)
Hernández Arregui, J. J., *Imperialismo y cultura* (Buenos Aires, 1957)
——, *La formación de la conciencia nacional* (Buenos Aires, 1960)
——, *Nacionalismo y liberación* (Buenos Aires, 1969)
——, *¿Qué es el ser nacional?* (Buenos Aires, 1963)
Hodges, D. C., *Argentina, 1943-1976* (New Mexico, 1976)
——, ed., *Philosophy of the Urban Guerrilla: The Revolutionary Writings of Abraham Guillén* (New York, 1973)
Irazusta, J., *Perón y la crisis argentina* (Buenos Aires, 1966)
Islas, A., and Ferreira, C., 'Apuntes para una historia crítica del MLN (tupamaros)', *Combate* (Sweden), nos. 31-7 (March-September 1978)
James, D., 'Power and Politics in Peronist Trade Unions', *Journal of Interamerican Studies and World Affairs*, vol. 20, no. 1 (February 1978): 3-36
——, 'The Peronist Left, 1955-1975', *Journal of Latin American Studies*, vol. 8, no. 2 (1976): 273-96
Jauretche, A., *FORJA y la década infame* (Buenos Aires, 1962)
Jorge, E. F., *Industria y concentración económica* (Buenos Aires, 1971)
Josephs, R., *Argentine Diary* (London, 1945)
JP, 'Habla Juventud Peronista', *El Descamisado*, no. 36 (22 January 1974): 4-5
JTP Agrupación Metalúrgica 17 de Octubre, communiqué, *El Descamisado*, no. 43 (12 March 1974): 15
JUP, 'El peronismo y la universidad', *Envido*, no. 9 (May 1973): 54-61
Kandel, P., and Monteverde, M., *Entorno y caída* (Buenos Aires, 1976)
Keegan, J., *World Armies* (London & Basingstoke, 1979)
Kendell, J., 'I cannot imagine what would happen if the police left', *Times Higher Education Supplement*, 7 January 1977: 9
Kestelboim, M., 'Una experiencia de militancia: la Asociación Gremial de Abogados', *Peronismo y Socialismo*, no. 1 (September 1973): 87-9

Kohl, J., and Litt, J., *Urban Guerrilla Warfare in Latin America* (Massachusetts, 1974)
Labrousse, A., *The Tupamaros* (Harmondsworth, 1973)
Laclau, E., 'Argentina — Imperialist Strategy and the May Crisis', *New Left Review*, no. 62 (July-August 1970): 3-21
——, 'Peronism and Revolution', *Latin American Review of Books*, no. 1 (1973): 117-30
Lanusse, A. A., *Mi testimonio* (Buenos Aires, 1977)
Laqueur, W., *Terrorism* (London, 1978)
——, *The Guerrilla Reader* (Philadelphia, 1977)
Lenin, V. I., *Imperialism, the Highest Stage of Capitalism* (1916), 15th printing (Moscow, 1970)
Lesseps, M., and Traveler, L., *Argentina: un país entregado* (Madrid, 1978)
Little, W., 'Party and State in Peronist Argentina, 1945-1955', *Hispanic American Historical Review*, vol. 53, no. 4 (November 1973): 644-62
——, 'The Popular Origins of Peronism', in Rock (ed), *Argentina in the Twentieth Century* (1975): 162-78
Lizaso, M., 'General, el peronismo no está de acuerdo', *El Peronista*, no. 3 (4 May 1974): 2-4
——, '1 de mayo: ¿quién ganó? ¿qué cambió?', *El Peronista*, no. 4 (14 May 1974): 2-3
Luna, F., *De Perón a Lanusse 1943/1973* (Buenos Aires, 1973)
——, *El 45*, 7th ed. (Buenos Aires, 1975)
Main, M., *Evita: The Woman with the Whip* (USA, 1952)
Marín, E., 'El 25 de mayo de 1973: Cámpora al gobierno', *Transformaciones en el Tercer Mundo*, no. 24 (1974)
Masetti, J. R., *Los que luchan y los que lloran* (Buenos Aires, 1969)
Mendizábal, H., 'Comunicación oficial del Ejército Montonero al Vaticano', special supplement to *Estrella Federal*, no. 5 (August 1978): 2-4
Mercier Vega, L., *Las guerrillas en América Latina* (Buenos Aires, 1969)
Milenky, E. S., *Argentina's Foreign Policies* (USA, 1978)
Military Junta, Proclamation of 24 March 1976, in Kandel and Monteverde (1976): 223-6
MLN Tupamaros, *Actas tupamaras* (Buenos Aires, 1971)
MNRT, 'Reportaje al Movimiento N. Revolucionario Tacuara', *Compañero*, no. 63 (8 September 1964): 4
——, 'Violencia revolucionaria', 1 May 1964, *Militancia*, no. 6 (19 July 1973): 35-8
Monahan, J., 'Fallen star who guided Señora Perón', *The Times*, 23 July 1975
——, 'I agreed to teach but not to be a gaoler', *Times Higher Education Supplement*, 11 February 1977: 10
Montoneros, 'Argentina: la guerra continúa', *Marka* (Peru), c. June 1976
——, *Argentina '78* (Np, 1978)
——, 'Carta a la policía', *Evita Montonera*, no. 3 (March 1975): 47
——, Communiqué concerning the abduction and assassination of J. P. Egan, *Evita Montonera*, no. 3 (March 1975): 48

——, Communiqué concerning the kidnapping of E. Metz, *Evita Montonera*, no. 11 (January 1976): 22
——, Communiqué concerning the attack on Juan Ramón Morales, Appendix to González Janzen (1975): 243-54
——, 'Construir el poder popular', *El Descamisado*, no. 4 (12 June 1973): 2-4
——, 'El llanto del enemigo', *Cristianismo y Revolución*, no. 28 (April 1971): 70-3
——, 'Hablan los Montoneros', *Cristianismo y Revolución*, no. 26 (November–December 1970): 11-14
——, 'Las armas de la Independencia hoy están apuntadas hacia el Pueblo', *Cristianismo y Revolución*, no. 30 (September 1971): 13-15
——, *Lettre a l'Episcopat d'Argentine du Commandemant National du Parti Montonero* (France, December 1976)
—— and FAR, 'La unidad de FAR y Montoneros', *El Descamisado*, no. 22 (16 October 1973): 6-7
Montoneros José Sabino Navarro, 'Cartilla para militantes no. 4', *Militancia*, no. 30 (3 January 1974): 20-2
Montoneros 17 de Octubre, 'El Documento de Madrid: "Ante la crisis del Partido. Reflexiones críticas y una propuesta superadora"', PM *Boletín Interno*, no. 13 (February 1980)
Montonero Tendency, 'Un documento para la Liberación', supplement to *El Peronista*, no. 1 (19 April 1974)
Morales, E., *Uturunco y las guerrillas en la Argentina* (Montevideo, 1964)
Moreno, O., *Contradicciones, conflictos y movimientos sociales en la problemática urbano-regional* (Caracas, 1979)
MPA, Consejo Superior, 'Emprendemos la histórica transformación del Movimiento', *El Auténtico*, no. 2 (1 October 1975): 5
MPM, 'Al pueblo argentino: la justicia social y la soberanía popular son el camino hacia la democracia y la paz' (Np, April 1980); English trans., *Vencer*, no. 4 (1980)
——, Montonero correspondence concerning the composition of the Argentine delegation to the 1978 World Youth Festival in Havana (photocopies)
——, *Victory is Born with People's Unity* (Np, 1978)
——, *With the People of the World* (Np, 1978)
——, Secretaría de Prensa, Testimony of Horacio Maggio (Np, 1978)
Mugica, Padre C., *Peronismo y cristianismo* (Buenos Aires, 1973)
Munck, R., 'The Crisis of late Peronism and the Working Class, 1973-1976', *SLAS*, Bulletin of the Society for Latin American Studies (UK), no. 30 (April 1979): 5-34
Murmis, M., and Portantiero, J. C., *Estudios sobre los orígenes del peronismo* (Buenos Aires, 1971)
Nadra, F., *Perón hoy y ayer, 1971-1943* (Buenos Aires, 1972)
Navarro Gerassi, M., *Los nacionalistas* (Buenos Aires, 1968)
Niosi, J., *Los empresarios y el estado argentino, 1955-1969* (Buenos Aires, 1974)
North American Congress on Latin America, *Argentina in the Hour of the Furnaces* (USA, 1975)

Ongaro, R., *Sólo el pueblo salvará al pueblo* (Buenos Aires, 1970)
Organization of American States, Inter-American Commission on Human Rights, *Report on the Situation of Human Rights in Argentina* (Washington, 1980)
Partido Justicialista, 'Primeras jornadas de economía social: declaración final' (Buenos Aires, 16 December 1980)
Partido Montonero, 'Balance de la Campaña "Carlos Hobert" de Lanzamiento de la Contraofensiva Popular', *Boletín Interno*, no. 12 (January 1980)
——, 'Hacia una nueva política para la conquista del poder por los trabajadores y el pueblo peronista' (Buenos Aires, August 1976)
——, 'Informe del Consejo Nacional del Partido Montonero, septiembre de 1977', *Boletín Interno*, no. 4 (nd)
——, Untitled internal document of October 1977
Pavón Pereyra, E., *Perón tal como es* (Buenos Aires, 1973)
PCA, 'El Partido Comunista apoya la decisión de la CGT y reclama la formación de un gabinete cívico-militar de amplia coalición democrática, *La Opinión*, 6 July 1975
Peña, M., *El peronismo, selección de documentos para la historia* (Buenos Aires, 1973)
Peralta Ramos, M., *Etapas de acumulación y alianzas de clases en la Argentina (1930-1970)* (Buenos Aires, 1972)
Perón, E., *Historia del peronismo* (Buenos Aires, 1971)
——, *La razón de mi vida* (Buenos Aires, 1973)
Perón, J. D., *Doctrina peronista*, 2nd ed. (Buenos Aires, 1973)
——, Interview in *Primera Plana* (Buenos Aires), 7 September 1971
——, Interview of November 1972, *Peronismo y Socialismo*, no. 1 (September 1973): 33-4
——, *La comunidad organizada* (Buenos Aires, 1974)
——, *La hora de los pueblos* (Buenos Aires, 1968)
——, Letter of 10 December 1969 to J. J. Hernández Arregui, *Peronismo y Socialismo*, no. 1 (September 1973): 31-2
——, 'Mensaje a la Juventud', *Militancia*, no. 11 (23 August 1973): 49
——, 'Perón a los Montoneros', 20 February 1971, *La Causa Peronista*, no. 9 (3 September 1974): 28-9
——, 'Perón habla a la juventud', *Cristianismo y Revolución*, no. 29 (June 1971): 8-10
—— and Cooke, J. W., *Correspondencia Perón-Cooke* (2 vols., Buenos Aires, 1973)
Peronismo en la Resistencia, *Reflexiones para la construcción de una alternativa peronista montonera auténtica* (Np, 1979)
Pinedo, J., *Consignas y lucha popular en el proceso revolucionario argentino, 1955-1973* (Buenos Aires, 1974)
Portnoy, L., *Análisis crítico de la economía* (Buenos Aires, 1961)
Poulantzas, N., *Classes in Contemporary Capitalism* (London, 1978)
Puiggrós, R., *El peronismo: sus causas* (Buenos Aires, 1969)
——, *El proletariado en la revolución nacional* (Buenos Aires, 1968)
——, *Las izquierdas y el problema nacional* (Buenos Aires, 1973)
——, *La universidad del pueblo* (Buenos Aires, 1974)

——, 'Puiggrós y el avance del pueblo', interview, *Militancia*, no. 5 (12 July 1973): 16-20
Quieto, R., 'Hablan los Montoneros', text of speech in La Plata, *La Causa Peronista*, no. 4 (30 July 1974): 6-8
——, 'Under the Shadow of a Gunman', Quieto interviewed by Richard Gott, *The Guardian*, 18 October 1974
Ramos, J. A., *Historia del stalinismo en la Argentina* (Buenos Aires, 1974)
——, *Revolución y contrarevolución en la Argentina* (5 vols., Buenos Aires, 1973)
Rearte, G., 'La única respuesta válida', *Compañero*, no. 77 (February 1965): 3
——, 'Por que fracasó el MRP', supplement to *En Lucha*, no. 18 (September 1974): 3
República Argentina, Poder Ejecutivo Nacional, *Terrorism in Argentina* (Buenos Aires, 1980)
Rivera, E., *Peronismo y frondizismo* (Buenos Aires, 1958)
Rock, D., 'Lucha civil en la Argentina Semana Trágica de enero de 1919', *Desarrollo Económico*, vol. 11, no. 42 (July 1971): 165-215
——, 'Machine Politics in Buenos Aires and the Argentine Radical Party, 1912-1930', *Journal of Latin American Studies*, vol. 4, no. 2 (November 1972): 233-74
——, 'Radical Populism and the Conservative Elite, 1912-1930', and 'The Survival of Peronism', in Rock (ed), *Argentina in the Twentieth Century* (London, 1975)
Rojo, R., *My Friend Che* (New York, 1968)
Romero, J. L., *A History of Argentine Political Thought* (Stanford, 1963)
Roqué, J., *Cuadernos Políticos* interview, 'Argentina: un país en guerra', republished in *Revolución* (Np, December 1977)
Roth, R., *Los años de Onganía* (Buenos Aires, 1980)
Salas, H., 'La ideología de la violencia', *Discusión*, no. 15 (April 1975): 14-17
Santucho, M. R., *Argentina: Bourgeois Power, Revolutionary Power* (California, nd)
Scenna, M. A., *FORJA: una aventura argentina* (2 vols., Buenos Aires, 1972)
Scobie, J., *Argentina: A City and a Nation* (USA, 1964)
Sebreli, J. J., *Eva Perón: ¿aventurera o militante?* (Buenos Aires, 1966)
Selser, G., *El onganiato* (2 vols., Buenos Aires, 1973)
Senén González, *El poder sindical* (Buenos Aires, 1978)
——, *El sindicalismo después de Perón* (Buenos Aires, 1971)
Smith, P. H., 'Los radicales argentinos y la defensa de los intereses ganaderos, 1916-30', *Desarrollo Económico*, vol. 7, no. 35 (April-June 1967): 795-829
Snow, P. G., *Political Forces in Argentina* (USA, 1979)
Spilimbergo, J. E., *El socialismo en la Argentina* (2 vols., Buenos Aires, 1969)
Strafford, P., 'The Church of Change', *The Times*, 2 December 1977

Terragno, R., *Los 400 días de Perón* (Buenos Aires, 1974)
Torre, J. C., 'La CGT y el 17 de octubre de 1945', *Todo es Historia*, no. 105 (February 1976): 70-90
Torres Molina, R., 'La etapa actual de las guerrillas argentinas', *Cristianismo y Revolución*, no. 29 (June 1971): 17-19
Troxler, J., 'Los asesinatos de junio del 56 en el testimonio de un militante', *Peronismo y Socialismo*, no. 1 (September 1973): 94-7
Urondo, F., *La patria fusilada* (Buenos Aires, 1973)
Vigo, J. M., *¡La vida por Perón!* (Buenos Aires, 1973)
Viñas, D., *De los montoneros a los anarquistas*, vol. 1 of Viñas, *Rebeliones populares argentinas* (2 vols., Buenos Aires, 1971)
Walsh, R., 'A Letter to my Friends', *Vencer*, no. 4 (1980): 37
——, 'Carta abierta de un escritor a la Junta Militar' (24 March 1977)
——, *Los papeles de Walsh* (Np, 1979)
——, *Operación Masacre* (Buenos Aires, 1972)
Walter, R. J., *Student Politics in Argentina* (USA, 1968)
——, *The Socialist Party of Argentina, 1890-1930* (Texas, 1977)
Wilkinson, P., *Political Terrorism* (London, 1974)
——, *Terrorism and the Liberal State* (London, 1977)

IV. UNSIGNED ITEMS

'Ante la muerte de José Rucci', *El Descamisado*, no. 20 (2 October 1973): 2-3
'Apuntes para una historia de la resistencia y del peronismo revolucionario', six supplements to *En Lucha*, nos. 13-18 (December 1973-September 1974)
'Así se mató a Somoza', *El Socialista* (Madrid), no. 172 (September 1980): 50
'A tres años de La Calera', *Militancia*, no. 4 (5 July 1973): 8-9
'Balance de Operativo Dorrego: la Juventud Peronista fue a trabajar', *El Descamisado*, no. 25 (6 November 1973): 27
'Bendix: patrón que colabore con la represión irá al paredón', *Evita Montonera*, no. 12 (February-March 1976): 18-20
'Carlos Capuano Martínez, por compañero, por peronista, por montonero, ya sos entraña de tu pueblo', *La Causa Peronista*, no. 7 (20 August 1974): 22-3
'5 de agosto: jornada histórica', *Compañero*, no. 59 (11 August 1964): 1
'Como murió Aramburu', *La Causa Peronista*, no. 9 (3 September 1974): 25-31
'Compañeros presos: la aurora de la libertad', *El Descamisado*, no. 1 (22 May 1973): back cover
'Condecoración', *Estrella Federal*, no. 5 (September 1978): 12
'Con el pueblo hacia Perón', *El Descamisado*, no. 16 (4 September 1973): 2-3
'Congreso Nacional del PPA', *El Auténtico*, no. 4 (29 October 1975): 6
'Con Perón era otra cosa', *El Auténtico*, no. 1 (17 September 1975): 6
'Contra el ejército represor de Sierra Grande', *Evita Montonera*, no. 11 (January 1976): 9-11
'Córdoba: a cinco años del 29 de mayo, un montonero cuenta el

Cordobazo', *El Peronista*, no. 6 (28 May 1974): 26-9
'Córdoba: el porqué del conflicto de SMATA', *La Causa Peronista*, no. 4 (30 June 1974): 30-1
'Córdoba rebelde', *Trasformaciones en la historia presente*, no. 23 (September 1974)
'Córdoba: si es necesario aquí pondremos sangre montonera', *La Causa Peronista*, no. 6 (13 August 1974): 26-31
'Crónica de la resistencia', *Evita Montonera*, no. 15 (February 1977): 27
'Definiciones del general Perón', *El Peronista*, no. 6 (28 May 1974): 8
'El Cordobazo', *Polémica*, no. 15 (July 1972)
'El final de una batalla: Perón Presidente; El comienzo de otra: Liberación', *El Descamisado*, no. 19 (26 September 1973): 2-3
'El heroismo y el individualismo en las guerras populares', *Evita Montonera*, no. 12 (February–March 1976): additional unnumbered pages
'El mandato político de Fernando Abal Medina', *Militancia*, no. 13 (6 September 1973): 10-13
'En nuestro movimiento decide el pueblo, aquí deciden ustedes', *La Causa Peronista*, no. 7 (20 August 1974): 16-19
'Entre el tiempo y la sangre', *Carta Política*, no. 21 (April 1975): 4-6 and 8
'Este gobierno traicionó al pueblo y a Perón', *El Auténtico*, no. 5 (12 November 1975): 6
'Falsa opción', *Compañero*, no. 1 (7 June 1963): 1
'Formosa: el ejército gorila oculta su derrota', *Evita Montonera*, no. 8 (October 1975): 2-8
'Fuiste hija de Evita', *El Descamisado*, no. 36 (22 January 1974): 15
'Guardaespaldas: imagen de la Argentina', *Cuestionario*, no. 32 (December 1975): 17
'Guerrilla: ¿ahora está en el Paraná?', *Cuestionario*, April 1975: 7
'Hacia la construcción del Ejército Montonero', *Evita Montonera*, no. 8 (October 1975): 25-6
'Hacia la toma de la batuta', *El Descamisado*, no. 17 (11 September 1973): 11
'Informe especial', *El Descamisado*, no. 3 (5 June 1973): 12-13
'José Sabino Navarro: un trabajador, un montonero, un peronista', *El Descamisado*, no. 12 (7 August 1973): 30
'Juan García Elorrio', *Cristianismo y Revolución*, no. 28 (April 1971): 23
'Juicio revolucionario a Roberto Quieto', *Evita Montonera*, no. 12 (February–March 1976): 13-14
'Juicio revolucionario a un delator', *Evita Montonera*, no. 8 (October 1975): 21
'La clase obrera y el movimiento peronista', *Evita Montonera*, no. 7 (September 1975): 14-15
'La conducción del MPA: hombres y mujeres con trayectoria de lucha en defensa de los intereses populares', *El Auténtico*, no. 2 (1 October 1975): 4
'La conducta revolucionaria', *Evita Montonera*, no. 12 (February–March 1976): 36
'La federación gráfica es de los gráficos', *De Frente*, no. 1 (2 May 1974): 50

'La historia de la Triple A', three parts, *El Auténtico*, nos. 6 (26 November 1975), 7 (10 December 1975), and 8 (24 December 1975)
'La JP y la Reconstrucción Nacional', *El Descamisado*, no. 20 (2 October 1973): 25
'La muerte de Mor Roig', *La Causa Peronista*, no. 3 (23 July 1974): 20-3
'La Universidad al borde de la opción: liberación o continuismo gorila', *El Descamisado*, no. 43 (12 March 1974): 7-8
'Las armas montoneras en nuestro accionar militar', *Estrella Federal*, no. 5 (September 1978): 13
'Las milicias peronistas son posibles', *Evita Montonera*, no. 3 (March 1975): 22-3
'Las revelaciones de Paino', *La Opinión, segunda sección*, 12 February 1976
'Las villas triunfarán', *El Descamisado*, no. 43 (12 March 1974): 12-14
'Los guerrilleros', *Confirmado*, no. 402 (December 1975): 20-5
'Los militares cipayos: una nueva etapa de la guerra', *Evita Montonera*, no. 11 (January 1976): 12-15
'Los trabajadores hundiremos al régimen, porque queremos el poder para el pueblo', *Evita Montonera*, no. 12 (February-March 1976): 2-5
'Mayo 69: Cordobazo', *En Lucha*, no. 16 (June 1974): 6
'Memorandum I: Explicitación política de la experiencia mantenida por militantes montoneros con la Marina de Guerra, en calidad de detenidos y bajo condiciones de secuestro' (Geneva, July 1979)
'Militancia entre el ahogo y la clausura', *Militancia*, no. 38 (28 March 1974): 3
'Monte Chingolo: equivocarse conduce a la derrota', *Evita Montonera*, no. 11 (January 1976): 18-19
'Montonero Emilio Maza: La Calera', *La Causa Peronista*, no. 2 (16 June 1974): 22-3
'Montonero José Sabino Navarro. Volverás en brazos de tu pueblo', *La Causa Peronista*, no. 4 (30 July 1974): 9-11
'Operativo Dorrego', *El Descamisado*, no. 22 (16 October 1973): 28-30
'Organizarse para vencer', *Evita Montonera*, no. 23 (January 1979): 3-10
'Otra vez el poder militar', *Evita Montonera*, no. 7 (September 1975): 2-4
'Paco: dió la vida por Perón', *El Descamisado*, no. 40 (19 February 1974): 23
'Parar a los milicos cipayos, preparar el avance popular', *Evita Montonera*, no. 12 (February-March 1976): 7-8
'Por qué murió Coria', *El Descamisado*, no. 45 (26 March 1974): 2-3 and 8
'Qué votamos el 11 de marzo', *El Descamisado*, no. 43 (12 March 1974): 2-3
'¿Quién votó a Isabel, López Rega?', *La Causa Peronista*, no. 8 (27 August 1974): 2-3
'Quiénes, cómo y por qué lo ejecutaron. La muerte de José Alonso', *La Causa Peronista*, no. 8 (27 August 1974): 25-9
'Respuesta socialista al llamamiento montonero', *Avanzada Socialista*,

no. 120 (9 September 1974): 8-9
'Righi: el nuevo orden revolucionario', *Militancia*, no. 5 (12 July 1973): 7
'Semana política: entre la definición y la violencia', *Militancia*, no. 35 (21 February 1974): 4-9
'7 de setiembre — Día del Montonero', *El Descamisado*, no. 17 (11 September 1973): 5-8
'Soy leal, total, incondicional a Perón', *El Descamisado*, no. 9 (17 July 1973): 12
Survey on Argentina, *The Financial Times* (London), 1 December 1980
Survey on Argentina, *The Economist* (London), 26 January 1980
'Tacuara juega a la milicia revolucionaria', *Che*, no. 15 (2 June 1961): 10-11
'Tercer Campaña Militar Nacional Montonera', *Evita Montonera*, no. 12 (February–March 1976): 32-5
'Terrorismo y antiterrorismo', *Confirmado*, no. 411 (August 1976): 14-19
'30 Meses de camino descendente', *Confirmado*, no. 400 (December 1975): 52-4
'Tucumán: golpe a las fuerzas de ocupación', *Evita Montonera*, no. 7 (September 1975): 16-18
'Un balance de 1976', *Evita Montonera*, no. 15 (February 1977): 2-11
'Universidad: o del pueblo o de nadie', *El Descamisado*, no. 45 (26 March 1974): 22-4
'Volvemos para triunfar o morir junto a Isabel', *El Caudillo*, no. 68 (15 October 1975): 3
'Y esto, ¿qué es?', *El Descamisado*, no. 21 (9 October 1973): 2-3

Index

Note: Names of Latin American organizations appear here in English translation, with Spanish initials provided in parenthesis. For Spanish names, see pp. xi-xvi.

Abal Medina, Fernando Luis: early militancy, 48, 52, 84-6; visits Cuba 83; in *Aramburazo* 89-90, 94, 96; death 97-8, 99 (n. 17), 138; remembered 84, 116, 149, 177
Abal Medina, Juan Manuel 120, 132 (n. 19)
Acosta, Captain 249
Acuña, Hipólito 170
Adur, Father Jorge 254, 257 (n. 89)
Agosti, Bri. Gen. Orlando Ramón 228
Agrarian Leagues 207 (n. 126), 224
Aguirre, Mario 209 (n. 136), 255
Ahumada, Captain Ciro 153
Alac, Diana 209 (n. 136)
Alberte, Bernardo 44
Alcaracito, Battle of 2
Alemán, Francisco 125
Alemann, Juan 263 (n. 109), 264
Alende, Oscar 211-12
Alfonsín, Raúl 140 (n. 40)
Algañaraz de Román, Elsa Calia 156
Algeria, liberation struggle 50, 79, 248, 254
Allende, Salvador 117, 123, 150 (n. 61), 155
Almirón, Inspector Rodolfo Eduardo 153
Alonso, José 35, 43, 108, 171-2
Alsogaray, Juan Carlos 224 (n. 177)
Alsogaray, General Julio Rodolfo 224 (n. 177)
alternativismo and *alternativistas* 45, 127, 129, 168 (n. 14), 272; *see also* Peronist Armed Forces *and* Rank-and-File Peronism
Alvarez, Fernando 68-9, 71
Amarilla, Guillermo 265
Amnesty International 213 (n. 148), 216 (n. 156), 236, 245 (n. 46), 251 (n. 66)
Amodio Pérez, Héctor 222 (n. 172)
anarchism 3-4, 185
Anchorena, Manuel de 121
Añon, Juan 151

anti-Semitism 49, 156
anti-subversion legislation 32-3, 143, 145, 184-5, 210-11, 230; 1974 law 190, 203-4
Aramburu, General Pedro Eugenio: as President (1955-8) 22-3, 29-30, 91, 94; political evolution 33, 66, 92; assassination (the *Aramburazo*) 89-96, 98-9, 121, 160 (n. 86); body seized 183
Araya, Jorge Ernesto 186 (n. 67)
Argentine Anti-Communist Alliance (AAA): see Triple A
Argentine Engineering Centre 69
Argentine Industrial Union 12 (n. 29)
Argentine Liberation Organization (OLA) 241, 243
Argentine Patriotic League (*Liga Patriótica Argentina*) 5, 48
Argentine Plastic Arts Association 69
Argentine Political Youth (JPA) 160-1
Argentine Psychiatry Federation 69
Argentine Psycho-analytical Association 69
'Argentine Revolution' (of 1966) 61, 95, 116
Argentine Revolutionary Current (CAR) 211
Argentine Socialist Party (PSA): traditional PSA founded by Justo 7 (n. 15), 9-10, 12; PSA of Jorge Selser 104; PSA led by Coral 60 (n. 39), 104 (n. 22), 276
Argentine University Federation (FUA) 68, 215
Argentine University Teachers Confederation 157
Argentine Youth for National Emancipation (JAEN) 68, 120
Armed Liberation Forces (FAL) 220 (n. 166), 275
Arrostito, Nélida Esther ('Norma') 236; breaks with Communist Party 86; visits Cuba 83; and *Aramburazo* 90, 93 (n. 9), 96, 99, 99 (n. 17),

Index

Arrostito, Nélida Esther (*cont.*) 160 (n. 86); death 249
Association of Pharmaceutical Workers 35, 168 (n. 14)
Astiz, Eduardo 267 (n. 120)
Auténticos 205-15, 226, 244, 255, 266, 272, 278; *El Auténtico* newspaper 177 (n. 41), 190-1, 209-12; *Auténtico* Trade Union Bloc 213-14; Authentic Party (PA) 206-12; Authentic Peronist Group (APA) 206; Authentic Peronist Movement (MPA) 207, 209-10; Authentic Peronist Party (PPA) 177 (n. 41), 205
Avellaneda Congress 43

Baffi, Juan 110
Balbín, Ricardo 95, 104, 115, 188, 231 (n. 15)
Bank Employees Association (AB) 51, 139, 160
Bárbaro, Julio 68 (n. 55)
Baretta, Hugo 188
Barry, Alejandro 257 (n. 89)
Basque Homeland and Freedom (ETA) 255
Batista, Fulgencio 35
Bavio, Gerardo 267 (n. 120)
Baxter, José Luis ('Joe') 50-1, 153 (n. 67), 276
Beauvoir, Simone de 218
Beckerman, Eduardo 155, 165
Beltrán, Horacio José 246
Bengochea, Angel 38, 60 (n. 39), 276
Benítez, Antonio 190
Benítez, Father Hernán 47 (n. 1), 98
Berger, María Antonia 125, 126 (n. 6), 265
Berisso, Rear Admiral Emilio 166 (n. 10)
Bermann, Sylvia 267 (n. 120)
Bettanín, Cristina 177 (n. 41)
Bettanín, Guillermo Juan 177 (n. 41)
Bettanín, Leonardo 146, 151, 176, 177 (n. 41)
Bidegain, Dr Oscar: Governor of Buenos Aires 132, 155 (n. 73), 174; and *Auténticos* 206, 209 (n. 136), 211; and Montoneros 244, 268
Binstock, Susana 257 (n. 89)
Bolivia 257 (n. 89)
Bonasso, Miguel 127 (n. 9), 267-8
Borda, Guillermo 66

Born, Jorge 180-2, 252
Born, Juan 180-1, 252
Borro, Sebastián 32, 36, 206
Bosch, Alberto 180
Braden, Spruille 7
Brandazza, Carlos 165
Bravo, Lieutenant Roberto Guillermo 117
Brazil 74 (n. 71), 249, 257 (n. 89)
Britain 1-2, 4, 15 (n. 34), 196, 249
Brito Lima, Alberto 134 (n. 25), 153, 187 (n. 74)
Buenos Aires, as capital 1-2
Buenos Aires Herald, 190
Buenos Aires Lawyers Association 69
Buenos Aires Press Association 156
Buenos Aires Printers Federation (FGB) 65, 69, 159, 168 (n. 14)
Bunge y Born, Montonero operation 180-2, 203, 212 (n. 148), 252
Burgos, Gerardo 117

Cabo, Armando 74, 108, 206
Cabo, Dardo Manuel 74, 206 (n. 123); early militancy 48, 108, 147; as Montonero 144-5, 212; death 212-13 (n. 148), 235
Cabral, Juan José 65
Cáceres Monié, General Jorge Esteban 185, 201, 210
Caffatti, Jorge 51-2
Cafiero, Antonio 173 (n. 32), 231 (n. 15)
Caggiano, Cardinal 98
Calabró, Victorio 174
Camilo Torres Command 57, 275
Campiglia, Horacio 239 (n. 34), 257 (n. 89), 279
Cámpora, Héctor J.: prison escape 36; delegate of Perón 105; uses Left 105, 120, 132; as President 115, 123-33 *passim*, 141 (n. 41), 143, 158 (n. 82), 167, 206; resignation 130, 143-4; post-1973 activity 208, 212, 260; as seen by Lanusse and Cooke 105 (n. 26); as seen by Videla 229; death 208 (n. 130)
Camps, Alberto 118, 125, 126 (n. 6), 260
Camus, Albert 59
Capellini, Brigadier Jesús Orlando 224
Capuano Martínez, Carlos: Catholic militant 59; in Montoneros 90, 96, 99 (n. 17); death 117; tributes to

118, 122; father murdered 187 (n. 76)
Car Workers Union (SMATA), 86, 139-40, 155, 155 (n. 73), 158-9, 164, 168 (n. 14), 174
Carbone, Father Alberto 98
Carcagno, General Jorge Raúl 161
Cardozo, Brig. Gen. Cesario Angel 185, 233-4
Cardozo, Tomás Roberto 168 (n. 12)
Caride, Carlos 19 (n. 49), 67, 107, 109, 151-2, 245
Carral, José Enrique 103, 106, 117-18
Carrizo, Manuel 195 (n. 98)
Carter, James 255
Carvalli, Adolfo 43
Caseros, Battle of 1
Castelazzi, Delia 209 (n. 136)
Castro, Fidel 35, 37-9, 221, 256
Catholic organizations: Catholic Action (AC) 47, 56, 59, 98; Catholic Student Youth (JEC) 56, 59, 116; Catholic Working Youth (JOC) 59, 106; others 48-50, 59
Catholic radicalism 52-60, 64, 70, 91, 94, 96, 98, 100, 107, 118, 154, 170, 191 (n. 85), 212, 250, 254
caudillo tradition 2, 6, 13, 23-4, 152, 267
El Caudillo 156, 186
La Causa Peronista 159-60, 190
Cepernic, Jorge 132, 177, 206, 209 (n. 136)
Cesaris, Ramón 98-9
Chávez, Gonzalo 209 (n. 136), 213
Chávez, Horacio 154
Chávez, René 209 (n. 136), 267 (n. 120)
Chejolán, Alberto 152 (n. 66)
Chiappe, François 153 (n. 69)
Chile 160, 182 (n. 56), 212; relations with Argentina 117, 123, 130, 150, 220, 249; refugees persecuted 155, 257 (n. 89)
China (PRC) 51, 79, 130 (n. 16), 255-6
Church, Roman Catholic: and Marxism 53, 55; and Peronism 8, 21, 53, 55; and social change 52-5, 57-8; and violence 54-5, 254
Civic Front of National Liberation (FRECILINA) 104 (n. 23)
Civic Legion (*Legión Cívica*) 5, 48
clasismo 75
Clausewitz, Carl von 80-2, 175, 191, 202

College of Lawyers (*Colegio de Abogados*) 69
Colombo, Lt. Col. 185 (n. 66)
Commission of the 25, 263 (n. 108), 264 (n. 112)
communism 3-4, 40
Communist Party of Argentina (PCA) 86, 133, 167, 170, 184-5, 207 (n. 127), 212, 220; opposition to Peronism 7 (n. 15), 9-12, 10 (n. 22); student support 67, 140 (n. 40), 215; backs Videla 255-6
Communist Vanguard (VC) 126
Compañero 30, 34, 43
Construction Workers Union of the Argentine Republic (UOCRA) 165, 167, 172 (n. 30)
Conte Grande, Raúl Héctor Guzzo 96, 99 (n. 17)
Conti, Jorge 186 (n. 68)
Cooke, John William: early political life 29, 35-6; resistance leader 32, 35-6; in Cuba 36-7; political views 23, 24 (n. 60), 36-8, 44, 105 (n. 26); as revolutionary Peronist 57, 87, 268; death 45 (n. 115)
Coordinación Federal 233-5
Coral, Juan Carlos 60 (n. 39), 104 (n. 22), 276
Corbat, Brig. Major Aly Luis Ipres 133 (n. 21), 197 (n. 103)
Corbetta, General Arturo 235
Córdoba: centre of militancy 59, 64-6, 75, 103, 155, 158-9, 168 (n. 14), 187 (n. 76), 214; the *Cordobazo* 65-6, 68, 75, 84, 90, 94, 120, 154, 161, 263, 272; the *Cordobacito* 113
Coria, Rogelio 165-7, 169-70, 172
Coronel, José Carlos 246
Costa-Gavras 189 (n. 80)
Cristianismo y Revolución 57-9, 100
Croatto, Armando 131, 132 (n. 19), 257-8, 265
Cuba: impact of revolution 35-8, 50, 74, 78-9, 155 (n. 73), 195 (n. 98); Montonero-Cuban connection 57, 83, 117, 220-1, 252-3, 256, 260, 268-9; relations with Argentina 123, 130-1, 132 (n. 20)
Cuesta, Marcela 176
Curutchet, Alfredo 154-5

Dagnino Pastore, José María 66

298 Index

Dálmaso López, José 265
D'Amico, Col. Leonardo 236
De Frente: original 29; of 1974, 127 (n. 9)
De Gregorio, Oscar 257 (n. 89)
De Luca, Ricardo 87, 171-2
death squads 69-70, 115, 131, 152-6, 166, 185, 187 (n. 76), 216 (n. 156), 233, 235, 257, 261; *see also* Liberators of America Command *and* Triple A
Debray, Régis 48 (n. 3), 78, 227
Deleroni, José Antonio Pastor 70
Dellepiane, Luis 8 (n. 16)
El Descamisado 108, 127 (n. 9), 144-5, 152, 190
Descamisados, guerrilla organization 106, 108-9
Devotazo 125-6
'Devoto Massacre' 250
Di Pasquale, Jorge 35, 44, 87, 168
Díaz, 'el Negro' 116
Díaz, Olimpia 267 (n. 120)
Díaz Bessone, General Ramón 228
Díaz Ortiz, Santiago 131
Dibatista, Adolfo 186
Dickmann, Enrique 10
Domínico, Rubén 187
Dorrego, Colonel Manuel, National Reconstruction Operation 161-2
Dórticos, Osvaldo 123
Dri, Jaime 249 (n. 58), 257 (n. 89), 267
Duarte, María Eva ('Evita'): see Perón, Evita
Duhalde, Eduardo L. 70, 127 (n. 9)

Echeverría, Ramón 201
economy: agrarian sector 15, 26-9; economic crises 4, 16, 18, 22, 26-7, 31, 128-9, 227-8, 231-2; economic strategy 21-2, 33, 61-2, 141-2, 173, 226, 229-31; economic structure 1-4, 17, 27, 79; foreign involvement 1-2, 4, 15-16, 18, 20, 32-3, 61-2, 83, 112, 130-1, 161, 230, 240; income distribution 7, 10, 15, 22-3, 30-1, 62, 78, 141, 170 (n. 19), 230; industrialization 3-4, 6, 14-15, 26-8, 230; inflation 128, 142, 227, 231; trade 4, 130-1, 255-6
Egan, John Patrick 188-9
El Kadri, Envar 19 (n. 49), 67, 107, 275

elections: State 4, 7, 11 (n. 26), 19 (n. 48), 30, 32-4, 52, 61, 114-15, 120-1, 143, 205-8, 206 (n. 123), 210, 212 (n. 146), 269; student 139-40, 215; trade union 159, 168 (n. 14), 169 (n. 17), 170
Escribano, Jorge 117
Espina, Héctor 19 (n. 49), 51 (n. 14)
Estevez, Adriana 186 (n. 67)
Estrella, Miguel 257 (n. 89)
European Economic Community (EEC) 128, 130
Evita Group (AE) 134, 164, 277-8
Evita Montonera 191, 214, 221, 261
Ezcurra, Alberto 49-50
Ezeiza Massacre 106, 135, 152-3, 166

falangismo, influence in Argentina 47-50
Falcón, Ramón 185
Falkland (*Malvinas*) Islands 108, 196, 249
Fanon, Frantz 86
Farrell, General Edelmiro J. 7
fascism in Argentina 148, 155-8, 186-7, 245; *see also* National University Concentration, Organizational Command, *and* Restorationist Nationalist Guard
Federation of Soap and Perfume Workers 35
Federation of Tucumán Sugar Industry Workers (FOTIA) 172 (n. 30)
Feinmann, José Pablo 71
Fernández, Avelino 206
Fernández, Florencio 176
Fernández, Orlando 165
Fernández, Alvariño, Próspero 93
Fernández Long, Pablo 207, 266
Ferrari, Gerardo 107
Ferré Gadea, Arturo 107
Ferreyra, gunbattle of 110
fidelismo 35, 50, 67, 256
Fierro, José 96, 99 (n. 17)
Figueredo, Juan 207
Figueroa, Hugo 188
Filler, Silvia 168 (n. 12)
Firmenich, Mario Eduardo 134 (n. 25), 154, 187 (n. 76), 267; President of JEC 56-7; Montonero original 11 (n. 26), 84; in *Aramburazo* 90-6 *passim*, 99 (n. 17), 160 (n. 86); Montonero leader 116, 127 (n. 10), 151-2, 181, 222, 239 (n. 34), 241,

244, 246, 279; declarations 128, 163 (n. 94), 164, 171, 254, 259, 265; speeches 142, 146-8, 158, 168, 184; in exile 253, 256, 261, 265; and casualties 227, 270-1
Firmenich, Mario Norberto 187 (n. 76)
foquismo and *foquistas* 48, 76, 78, 87, 195, 266, 268, 272-3 *see also* rural guerrillas
Formosa, Montonero operation 197-200, 204 (n. 119), 210, 245 (n. 47)
Framini, Andrés 34-5, 206, 209 (n. 136), 210
Franco, Francisco 73-4, 255
Franco, Juan Pablo 68, 71
Franja Morada (FM) 140 (n. 40), 215
Frondizi, Arturo: as President (1958-62) 26, 29-30, 32-4, 36, 60-1, 154, 187 (n. 76); since 1962, 104 (n. 23), 231 (n. 15)
Frondizi, Silvio 154, 184

Galimberti, Rodolfo: early activity 48, 50, 68, 120; Peronist Youth leader 120-1, 140-1, 161; editor of *La Causa Peronista* 151, 160 (n. 86); leading Montonero 148, 209 (n. 136), 246; expelled 268 (n. 123); founds new tendency 266-8
Galtieri, Lt. Gen. Leopoldo Fortunato 261-2
García Elorrio, Juan 53, 55, 57-9
García Rey, Héctor 186
Garín, occupied by FAR 107-8
Gazzera, Miguel 98
Gelbard, José Ber 130, 173
Gelín, Raquel Liliana 107, 118-19
Gelman, Juan 255, 257, 266, 268 (n. 123)
General Economic Confederation (CGE) 20-1, 141
General Labour Confederation (CGT): pre-1955, 19, 21; 1955-73, 23, 32, 32, (n. 79), 34, 44, 75, 114, 172, 206 (n. 123), 209 (n. 136); 1973-76, 21, 135-6, 139-41, 143-4, 147, 159, 168 (n. 14), 173-4; 1976-81, 225-6, 228, 238, 241, 264 (n. 112); condemns *Aramburazo* 121
General Labour Confederation in the Resistance (CGT-R) 238-9, 241, 243, 253 (n. 73), 265, 278 (n.)
General Labour Confederation of the Argentines (CGTA) 44, 64-6, 68-70, 75, 87, 107, 172
General University Confederation (CGU) 67
Giannotti de Molfino, Noemí Esther 257 (n. 89)
Giovenco, Alejandro 147
Glellel, Jorge 131
Gómez, Juan Carlos 168 (n. 12)
González, Ana María 233-4
Gorriarán Merlo, Enrique 117, 276 (and n.)
Grabois, Roberto 68, 68 (n. 55)
Graiver, David 252
Gras, Martín 248
Great National Agreement (GAN) 92, 114-15, 167
Grecco, Guillermo 251-2
Greene, Graham 106 (n. 28)
Grynberg, Enrique 165 (n. 4)
Guerrero, Luis 121
guerrilla warfare: appeal of 75, 84; definition 79-80 (n. 86), 147 (n. 56), 192-3 (n. 90); elitism of 59-60, 138, 171, 194, 264, 266, 270; guerrilla coordination 108-10, 116-17, 182 (n. 56), 194-5; social base 76-8; theory 48 (n. 3), 78-80, 192, 202 *see also* rural guerrillas
Guevara, Ernesto 'Che': and guerrilla warfare 48, 58, 76, 78, 107, 126 (n. 8); influence in Argentina 60 (n. 39), 111; 'New Man' theory 221-2
Guevara, Roberto 276 (n.)
Guevarism and Guevarists 47-8, 60 (n. 39), 106, 111, 125-6, 129, 172, 195, 231
Guido, José M. 29
Guillén, Abraham 78-82, 191, 193 (n. 90)
Gullo, Jorge 265
Gullo, Juan Carlos Dante 124, 141 (n. 41), 151, 164, 212
Gutiérrez Ruiz, Héctor 257 (n. 89)
Guzzetti, Ana 156
Guzzetti, Admiral César 229, 237

Habegger, Norberto 108, 257, 257 (n. 89)
Haidar, Adriana 257
Haidar, Ricardo 117, 125, 126 (n. 6)
Harguindeguy, General Albano 162 (n. 91), 225, 269
Haya de la Torre, Víctor Raúl 9

300 *Index*

Haymal, Fernando 197 (n. 102), 217-18, 220 (n. 164)
Hernández, Mario 70, 80, 145
Hernández Arregui, Juan José 5 (n. 9), 8, 10-12, 11 (n. 26), 14, 16 (n. 38), 80
Herreras, Casildo 225
historical revisionism 4-6, 12-13, 25, 100-1
Hobert, Carlos 239 (n.34), 245
Hour of the People, political pact 104

Iaccuzzi, Father Rafael 254
Ibañez, Paco 218
Ibarra, Ricardo 51 (n. 14)
Illia, Arturo 29, 34, 36, 60-1, 64
Imaz, Brig. Gen. Francisco 66, 93 (n. 8)
immigration 3
imperialism and anti-imperialism 15-18, 20, 33-7, 66, 71, 82-3, 100-3, 109, 127, 145-7, 150-1, 160-1, 171, 175, 196, 209, 232
Indo-American Popular Revolutionary Front (FRIP) 60 (n. 39), 276
industrialists, attitudes of 16, 20-2, 33-4, 64 (n. 49), 100, 129, 141, 230, 260
Iñíguez, General Miguel Angel 154
International Commission of Jurists 70 (n. 59)
International Labour Organization 254
Intransigent Party (PI) 104 (n. 23), 207 (n. 127), 211-12
Intransigent Radicals (UCRI) 30, 32-4
Iranian Revolution 270
Iraq 256
Irazusta, Julio 8
Iriart, Carlos 166
Iribarren, Colonel Héctor 113
Italian Socialist Party 218
Italy 3, 258 (n. 92)
Iturbe, Alberto 43
Iturrieta, Aníbal 131
Ivanissevich, Oscar 156-7, 176
Ivanoff, Liliana 187

Jaime, Armando 30, 44, 168
Jáuregui, Emilio 66
Jauretche, Arturo, 8-9, 11 (n. 26), 98
Jauretche, Ernesto 11 (n. 26), 260, 267 (n. 120)
Jozami, Eduardo 220 (n. 166)

Juárez, Enrique 151, 164
Justicialism 8, 17-19, 25, 38-40, 71, 140, 146, 157 (n. 78), 208, 240
Justicialist Liberation Front (FREJULI) 127, 170 (n. 22); in Congress 131-2, 145-6, 176-7; in elections 115, 121, 167, 207-8; origins 104; 1973 programme 127, 132 (n. 20), 206
Justicialist Party (PJ) 19, 43, 104 (n. 23), 105 (n. 26), 114, 120, 151, 167, 184, 205-8, 214, 231 (n. 15)
Justo, Agustín P. 4
Justo, Juan B. 12

Kennedy, Norma 153
Kestelboim, Mario 176
Klein, Guillermo Walter 264
Kloosterman, Dirk Henry 86, 155 (n. 73), 172
Korea (DPRK), relations with Argentina 130, 132 (n. 20)
Kraiselburd, David 165-6
Krieger Vasena, Adalbert 61-2, 64, 66
Kunkel, Carlos 131, 132 (n. 19)

laboristas 7, 24, 273
labour movement: attacks on trade union leaders 108, 121, 144, 150, 155 (n. 73), 165-74, 251 (n. 68), 251-2; and guerrilla warfare 76-7, 103, 106, 121, 171-4, 203-5, 213-14, 224, 264; heterogeneity 31, 170 (n. 19), 262; leadership (*burocracia sindical*) 33 (n. 81), 34-5, 64 (n. 49), 65, 73, 143, 158-9, 165-74, 203-4, 214, 225; militancy 22-3, 31-2, 42, 61-2, 64-6, 75, 169 (n. 18), 187 (n. 76), 213, 226, 230-1; and Peronism 7, 10, 15, 19-26, 31, 43, 124, 135-6, 148-50, 159, 167-74; rank-and-file activity 22, 64, 75, 109, 168 (n. 14), 204 (n. 121), 213; strikes 21-2, 32 (n. 78), 32-3, 36, 65-6, 114, 129, 136, 139, 142, 158, 168 (n. 14), 173, 187 (n. 76), 194, 201, 203-5, 213-14, 226, 228, 230, 262-3; *see also* General Labour Confederation, General Labour Confederation of the Argentines, *and* Vandorism
Lacabanne, Brig. Maj. Raúl 174 (n. 35)
Laguzzi, Pablo 156 (n. 74)
Laguzzi, Raúl 156 (n. 74), 158, 208 (n. 130)

Lambruschini, Rear Admiral Armando 248, 270
land ownership: *see* economy, agrarian sector
Lanusse, General Alejandro: on Cámpora 105 (n. 26); political plan 66, 92, 95, 109, 114-15, 167; as President 29, 99, 113, 124, 150 (n. 61), 154, 165, 259
Laplane, General Alberto Numa 204 (n. 119)
Lastiri, Raúl 74 (n. 71)
Law of Professional Associations 32, 143, 158, 264 (n. 112)
Lawyers Trade Union Association (*Asociación Gremial de Abogados*) 69-70
legal profession, militancy within 69-70, 115
Lenin, Vladimir Ilyich 2, 268
Leninism 84, 239, 241, 260
Lesgart, Adriana 164, 265
Lesgart, Susana 99 (n. 17), 113, 117
Levingston, General Roberto 29, 94-5, 113
Lewinger, Arturo 196
'Liberating Revolution' (*Revolución Libertadora*) of 1955, 15, 35, 169, 273
Liberators of America Command 185, 187 (n. 76), 210
Licastro, Francisco Julián 119-20
Liendo, General Horacio Tomás 237
Liprandi de Vélez, María C. 99 (n. 17)
Lizaso, Arnaldo 206
Lizaso, Carlos Alberto 152 (n. 66)
Lizaso, Miguel 151, 152 (n. 66)
Lombardich, Dr Antonio 210
Lonardi, General Eduardo 22, 29
López, Atilio 133, 154
López Jordán, Ricardo 2
López Rega, José: Perón's secretary 74 (n. 71); Social Welfare Minister 130, 138 (n. 32), 145, 152 (n. 66), 159, 164, 166, 173, 183, 186, 208, 232, 240; and the occult 173 (n. 31); Triple A organizer 153-4, 186 (n. 68), 216 (n. 156); downfall 173, 188
Losada, Luis 41, 96, 99 (n. 17), 138
Lovey, Osvaldo 224
'Loyalist' (*Leal*) tendency of Peronism 52, 138-9
Lysak, Oscar 126

Maestre, Juan Pablo 108
Maggio, Horacio 249 (n. 58)
Maguid, Carlos 86, 96-9, 125, 257 (n. 89)
Malvinas (Falkland) Islands 108, 196, 249
Mansilla, Marcelino 172
Marcha 63
Margaride, Luis 63, 184-5
Marighela, Carlos 193 (n. 90)
Martínez, María Estela ('Isabel'): see Perón, Isabel
Martínez Baca, Alberto 132, 206
Martínez Borelli, Holver 191 (n. 85)
Martínez de Hoz, José Alfredo 228-32, 255, 259-60, 262
Martins, Néstor 69
Marxism and Marxists 10, 28, 50, 53, 57, 68 (n. 55), 75, 109, 144, 154, 157 (n. 78), 167, 172, 206, 239, 259
Mascardi, Enrique 164-5
Masetti, Jorge Ricardo 38, 60 (n. 39), 76
Massaferro, Sub-Lieutenant Ricardo Eduardo 200
Massera, Admiral Emilio Eduardo 132 (n. 19), 197 (n. 101), 228, 248-9
Maurras, Charles 4
Mayol, Roberto 199 (n. 106)
Maza, Emilio Angel: as Catholic militant 59; Montonero commander 84, 86; in *Aramburazo* 89-90, 94; death 95-8, 99 (n. 17), 188
Medellín, Conference of the Latin American Episcopate 54-5
Melena, Norma 67
Mendizabál, Horacio: founds Descamisados 108; leading Montonero 124, 234 (n. 21), 239 (n. 34), 253-4, 256, 261, 263, 279 (and n.); capture and escape 217 (n. 160), 221 (n. 168); death 265
Mendozazo 114
Menéndez, Brig. Gen. Luciano Benjamín 195 (n. 98), 228, 263
Menna, Domingo 117, 241
Metalworkers Union (UOM) 121, 130, 139, 159, 168 (n. 14), 170 (n. 19), 171, 173-4, 206 (n. 123)
Metz, Enrique 182
Mexico, exiles in 131, 158 (n. 82), 208 (n. 130), 252, 257 (n. 89), 259-62
Michelini, Zelmar 257 (n. 89)

302 Index

middle classes, attitudes of 3, 13, 20, 61-9, 83, 162, 223, 232
Miguel, Lorenzo 171, 174, 206 (n. 123)
Militancia 127 (n. 9), 154, 190
military: 1930 coup 4, 49; 1943 coup 6, 169; 1955 coup 15, 48, 89, 100, 166, 169, 178-9, 196; 1962 coup 33-4, 61; 1966 coup 30, 47, 52, 61, 68, 81, 228; 1976 coup 70, 193, 204-5, 223-9, 250; 1956 military revolt 67, 91-2, 94, 111, 152, 152 (n. 66), 154, 161, 200; 1960 military revolt 154; failure in office 228-32; and Peronism 21; and 1973-6 Peronist governments 161-2, 224; repressive role 66, 188, 195 (n. 96), 201, 204-5, 228-30, 232-3, 244-52, 257, 261-2
Minimax supermarkets, bombed by FAR 66, 107
Misetich, Mirta 108
Misiones election 205-8, 210
Mitrione, Dan 189
Mitterand, François 218
Molina, Alberto 147, 150, 246
Mondelli, Emilio 173, 226
Monte Chingolo, ERP defeat 211
Montonero Army (EM) 174-8, 183 (n. 58), 198, 204, 221 (n. 168), 232-3, 239 (n. 34), 241, 244, 253-4, 258, 260-1, 278-9 (and nn.)
Montonero Movement 240, 243, 278 (n.)
Montonero Party (PM) 239-44, 253, 257 (n. 89), 261, 266, 268, 278-9 (and nn.)
Montonero Peronist Movement (MPM) 191 (n. 85), 243-4, 253-4, 259-60, 265-6, 268, 278-9 (and nn.)
Montonero Peronist Youth (JPM) 253 (n. 73), 266, 278
Montoneros: apparatus 178-9, 183, 242, 247, 259; appeal to the police 179-80; and the Army 161-2, 195, 223; attacks on the Air Force 133 (n. 21), 197, 237, 251 (n. 68); attacks on the Army 195, 197-201, 211, 225, 236-7, 251 (n. 68), 258; attacks against entrepreneurs 224, 236-8, 242, 251 (n. 68), 264; attacks on the Navy 196-7, 248, 251 (n. 68), 258; attacks on the police 109, 112, 165, 180, 184-5, 189 (n. 79), 193-4, 196 (n. 99), 201, 224-5, 233-6, 251 (n. 68); attacks against trade union leaders 121, 144, 165-74, 225, 251 (n. 68); backgrounds of founders 47-8, 52, 56-7, 59; bomb attacks 99, 111-12, 164, 181, 194, 196-7, 225-6, 233-4, 236-7, 248, 264; breakaway tendencies 52, 138-9, 163, 165 (n. 4), 266-8, 275 (*see also* names of tendencies); casualties 96-7, 113, 116-18, 152, 153 (n. 67), 155, 166, 176, 177 (n. 41), 186 (n. 67), 188 (n. 78), 189 (n. 79), 194, 196 (n. 99), 197-200, 212-13, 215-19, 227, 235-6, 238, 244-7, 251, 254-5, 257, 261-2, 265, 267; Catholic influence 52-9, 91, 98 (*see also* Catholic radicalism); 1979 counter-offensive 261-5; and 1976 military coup 223, 232-3; creation of 47-8, 53, 56-7, 71, 82-3; and death 58-9, 118-19, 149 (n. 59), 227, 246, 270; decline of 266-70; documents of 90-1, 100-3, 127-8, 148 (n. 57), 239-40, 259-60; electoral activity of 119-21, 134, 136, 205-8; in exile 244, 252-62; finance 166 (n. 8), 180-2, 211, 242, 244, 252-3, 256, 266, 269 (*see also* kidnappings and raids); and Great National Agreement (GAN) 92, 109; hijackings 198-9, 225; ideological orientation 70-1, 90-1, 100-3, 162, 209, 239-40, 259-60; impact of operations 91, 111, 112 (n. 33), 113-14, 122, 184-7, 200, 203-5, 223, 234-5, 248, 258; influence in trade unions 139-40, 213; influence in universities 130-1, 133-4, 156-8, 215; intelligence service 179-80, 188, 233, 245 (n. 47); internal bureaucratism 85, 137-9, 223, 266; internal discipline 216-23, 243-4, 245 (n. 48), 268 (n. 123); internal divisions 210, 242-3, 267; kidnappings 112 (n. 33), 113, 133 (n. 21), 164-5, 180-2, 188-9; labour-orientated operations 112, 164-5, 180-2, 214, 224, 237-8, 242, 263; leadership 86, 89-90, 106, 116, 197 (n. 102), 220-3, 239 (n. 34), 243, 247, 252-3, 261 (n. 103), 265, 267, 279 (and nn.); and

Marxism 109, 239, 259; mass front organizations and activity 98-9, 119-26, 134-63 *passim*, 176-7, 205-15 (*see also* names of organizations); membership estimated 99, 178, 252; militarism of 138-9, 158, 163, 171-4, 178-9, 191-2, 194-205, 210, 214, 223, 241-2, 248, 259-64, 266-8; mobilization tactics and capacity 98, 121, 123-6, 134-6, 139-40, 145, 148-50; as *movimientistas* 46, 129-30, 159-60, 192; munitions workshops 183, 236-7; name chosen 82-3, 121; occupy State positions 131-3, 141 (n. 41), 146-7; occupations of towns and neighbourhoods 95-6, 110, 193-4, 203; organizational mergers 106, 109, 144, 171, 220 (n. 166), 275; organizational structures 84-5, 106, 176-9, 239-41, 246 (n. 49), 261 (n. 103), 277-9 (and nn.); original *montoneros* 1-4, 13, 100, 273; outlawed 210-11; and Perón 41-2, 46, 72, 74, 85, 102-5, 128, 141, 143-52, 209-10, 239-40; and Peronism 71-5, 92, 100-2, 150-1, 173-5, 239-40; and 1973-76 Peronist administrations 127-8, 163-4, 175, 194, 209-11, 232; press and publications 108, 127 (n. 9), 144-5, 151-2, 159-60, 190-1, 214, 221, 245 (n. 47), 253, 261 (*see also* titles); in prison 217, 245, 247-51; prison escapes 116-17; propaganda operations 95-6, 110-13, 164, 181, 193, 202-3, 237 (n. 29), 257-8; radio broadcasts 190, 253, 263; raids 84, 95, 97, 99, 110, 112; relations with other guerrilla organizations 102, 106-10, 116-17, 160, 162-3, 194-5, 241-3; relations with labour movement 121-2, 165-74, 194, 200, 203-5, 213-14, 224, 226, 237-8, 242-3, 251-2, 264, 268; relations with non-Peronist Left 160, 162-3, 207 (n. 127), 238, 241; rural and mountain units 224, 236; self-criticism 129-30, 146, 192, 214, 222-3, 239, 267-8; social base and composition 61, 77, 86, 96, 103, 117, 121-2, 139-40, 162, 209, 213, 222, 237-8; strategic influences upon 78-82; strategy 47-8, 81, 92, 102-3, 109-13, 119, 126-7, 145-6, 157, 160-4, 174-5, 193, 195, 201-5, 210, 223-6, 232-3, 260-4, 270; Third World orientation 58, 102-3, 256-7; and Triple A, 185-9; and urban guerrilla warfare 41, 75-8, 79-80 (n. 86), 84, 110-13, 192; vacillating behaviour of 140-8, 151, 157-9, 206; vengeance killings 89-95, 164-8, 184-9, 192-3, 201, 248; view of Argentine history 100-1; weaponry 83, 94, 96, 99, 110, 165, 178, 182-3, 198, 200 (n. 106), 225, 236-7, 252, 258

Montoneros, José Sabino Navarro Column 138, 163, 165 (n. 4)
Montoneros *17 de Octobre* (M-17) 266-8, 275
Mor Roig, Arturo 114, 165-7
Morales, Juan Ramón 153, 185, 186 (n. 68)
Moreno, Nahuel 60 (n. 39), 276
Moro, Aldo 258 (n. 92)
Mosse, Miguel Angel 212, 213 (n. 148), 235
'Mothers of Plaza de Mayo' 254
Mott, Hugo 204 (n. 119)
Movement of Integration and Development (MID) 104 (n. 23), 231 (n. 15)
Movement of Reformist Orientation (MOR) 140 (n. 40), 215
Movement of the Revolutionary Left (MIR, Chile) 182 (n. 56)
movimientismo and *movimientistas* 46, 69, 126-7, 129-30, 132-3, 138, 159-60, 192, 273
Mugica, Father Carlos: and liberation theology 53, 56-7; and violence 55, 57; becomes a Peronist 55, 59; and early Montoneros 56-7, 98; assassinated 154, 267
El Mundo 156, 190
Muñiz Barreto, Diego 131, 132 (n. 19)
Mussolini, Benito 13

Nasif, Col. Jacobo 125
National Council of Federations and Centres (CNFC) 215
National Labour Commission (CNT) 263 (n. 108), 264 (n. 112)
National Law Students Association (ANDE) 67

304 Index

National Left: ideological current 10-17; political parties 10, 11 (n. 26), 14 (n. 32)
National Liberation Army (ELN, Bolivia) 58, 182 (n. 56)
'National Reconstruction' 128-9, 137, 161-2
National Reformist Movement (MNR) 215
National Revolutionary Army (ENR) 108, 170-1
National School of Buenos Aires (*Colegio Nacional*) 56, 99, 134 (n. 25), 272
National Student Front (FEN) 68
National Union of Students (UNE) 68, 68 (n. 55)
National University Concentration (CNU) 147, 156, 165, 168 (n. 12)
nationalism: evolution of 2, 4-17, 48-52; national bourgeoisie 14-17, 21-3, 34, 62, 130, 141-2, 232; national liberation fronts 141-2, 161, 175, 209; national question 6, 12, 25
Navazo, Félix 165-6
Navy Engineering School (ESMA) 123-4, 247-9, 257 (n. 89), 258
Nell, José Luis 50-2, 153 (n. 67)
neo-Peronists 26, 33
New Argentina Movement (MNA) 48, 108
Nicaraguan Revolution 254, 256-7, 270
'Night of the Long Sticks' 63
Nixon, Richard M. 124
Noticias 127 (n. 9), 159-60, 190, 245 (n. 47), 268

Obeid, Jorge 139
Obregón Cano, Ricardo: Governor of Córdoba 132-3, 174 (n. 35); as leading *Auténtico* 206; in exile 208 (n. 130); leading Montonero 244, 260-1, 268
October 17, 1945, events of 7, 21, 23, 72; commemorated 135 (n. 27), 236
oligarchy 3, 7 (n. 15), 27-9, 160-1, 240, 260
Olmedo, Carlos Enrique 99 (n. 15), 107, 110, 116, 260
Onganía, General Juan Carlos: seizes power 30, 47; 1966-70 presidency 26, 29, 33, 43, 57-8, 60-6, 68, 132 (n. 19), 224 (n. 177); and *Aramburazo* 92-4; downfall 66, 75, 94
Ongaro, Raimundo: and CGT of the Argentines 64-5, 66 (n. 52), 69; and Printers Union 159, 168 (n. 14); radical Catholic 105, 170 (n. 20); revolutionary Peronist 44, 75
La Opinión 190
Orgambide, Pedro 267 (n. 120)
Organization of American States (OAS) 130, 251
Organizational Command (C de O) 134 (n. 25), 147, 153, 156, 187 (n. 74)
Organized Community, in Peronist ideology 18
Ortega Peña, Rodolfo 70, 127, (n. 9), 154, 184
Osatinsky, Marcos 84, 117, 197, 217, 217 (n. 160), 248, 259
Osinde, Lt. Col. Jorge 106, 153
Otero, Ricardo 130, 159
Ottalango, Alberto 156-7

Pacem in terris 53
Padilla, Miguel 263 (n. 109)
Paino, Héctor 186 (n. 68)
Palacio, Ernesto 8
Paladino, Jorge Daniel 92, 104-5
Palestine Liberation Organization (PLO) 256
Pampillón, Santiago 64
Panama 74 (n. 71), 130
Parodi, Delia 43
'participationist' tendency of Peronism 26, 34, 44, 64
Pedreira, Manuel 238 (n. 33)
Penal Code reform 143, 145, 155 (n. 73)
Peñaloza, Angel Vicente 2
Peñaloza, Comando Chaco 111
People's Guerrilla Army (EGP) 38, 60 (n. 39), 76
People's Revolutionary Army (ERP) 190; background 60, 276; casualties 116-17, 154, 195 (n. 96), 211 (n. 144), 241; decline and defeat 211, 224, 231, 241, 246; and Peronism 125-6, 129; press 156, 190; relations with Montoneros 116-17, 160, 162-3, 194-5, 241; in Revolutionary Coordinating Council 182 (n. 56); and Rucci

assassination 165 (n. 4); rural guerrilla activity 155 (n. 73), 195 (nn. 96 and 98), 197 (n. 103), 204 (n. 119); social composition 162 (n. 93); and Somoza assassination 254; splits and mergers 155, 275-6; urban activity 51, 106, 116-17, 122, 125-6, 129, 155 (n. 73), 166, 172 (n. 30), 185, 211 (n. 144)
Perdía, Roberto C. 239 (n. 34), 253, 279 (and n.)
Perdini, Lt. Col. 124
Peressini, Juan Carlos 110
Pérez, Juan Carlos 180
Pérez Esquivel, Adolfo 251
Pérez Jiménez, Marcos 74
Perón, Evita: and 17 October 1945, 72 (n. 63); and women 19; writings 72-3, 86; *Fundación Eva Perón* 72; death 24; body seized 23, 91, 94; body brought back 183; cult of 72-5, 84, 89, 95, 101, 111-12, 118, 134 (n. 25), 145-6, 149, 164 (n. 1), 165 (n. 4), 180-1
Perón, Isabel: meets Perón 74 (n. 71); 1965-6 visit to Argentina 108; vice-presidential candidate 143-4; Montonero criticism of 143-4, 149, 163, 164 (n. 1), 209-10, 232; as President 21, 153, 159, 173-4, 183, 186, 205-6, 209-10, 215 (n. 155), 227, 240
Perón, Juan Domingo 86, 181, 259; rise to power 7, 23; as President (1946-55) 9-10, 23-4, 111; in exile (1955-73) 23-4, 37, 74; 1972 visit to Argentina 115, 119, 121; 1973 return to Argentina 135, 152-3; as President (1973-4) 136, 144-53; death 151, 206; bourgeois appeal 39-40, 100, 172; and Chilean coup 150 (n. 61); doctrine 17-19, 38-40, 102, 146; and Great National Agreement 92, 95, 114; and guerrillas 40-1, 74, 98, 103-5, 122, 172; and Hour of the People 104; and labour bureaucracy 144, 149-50, 239-40; and the Left 38-46, 122, 136, 144-51; and Onganía coup 64 (n. 49); quoted 1, 18, 24, 34, 38-41, 52, 56, 61, 64 (n. 49), 91, 105, 122, 136, 149-51, 153; and the Right 13, 38-9, 74, 144, 150, 152-3, 156, 240; strategy in opposition 42-5, 80, 103-5, 119-22; addresses Youth 40-1
Peronism, interpretations of 9, 13-25, 17 (n. 39)
Peronism in the Resistance tendency 266-8, 275
Peronist Armed Organizations (OAP) 109-10
Peronist Left: origins and development 11, 29-46, 207; internal differentiation 44-6; attitude to Perón 40-6; *see also* Montoneros and Rank-and-File Peronism
Peronist Movement 48, 53; emergence of 6-7; social base 20-1, 70, 78, 100; special (guerrilla) formations of 30, 92, 103, 106-10, 114, 122; structure of 19-21, 209 (n. 136); *see also* labour movement
Peronist Party 19, 24, 32, 34; *see also* Justicialist Party
Peronist Revolutionary Youth (JRP) 19 (n. 49), 30, 66
Peronist Right: view of Peronism 38-9; political activity 130, 132-3, 144, 173; press 156; support for 134 (n. 25), 135; in universities 67, 156-8, 176; and violence 67, 147, 152-6, 176, 186-7, 190 (n. 83), 216 (n. 156)
Peronist Shanty-Town Dwellers Movement (MVP) 134, 138 (n. 32), 152 (n. 66), 277
Peronist Tenants Movement (MIP) 134, 277
Peronist Trade Union Youth (JSP) 135 (n. 27)
Peronist University Youth (JUP): original JUP 67; pro-Montonero JUP 67, 134, 137, 139-40, 155, 157, 164, 176, 215, 277-8
Peronist Working Youth (JTP) 134, 137, 149, 151, 164, 277; assaults upon 155, 159, 184; replaced 176, 213; and trade unions 139-40, 159, 168 (n. 14), 170; vacillations 143, 158
Peronist Youth (JP): original JP 19 (n. 49), 50, 67, 107. JP of early 1970s 19, 30, 98-9, 106, 119-22, 126, 136, 140, 147. JP *Regionales*: 120, 139, 164, 165 (n. 4), 206, 268, 277 (and n.), 278; activity 124-6, 134, 145, 148-50, 160-2; attacks

Peronist Youth (cont.)
  on 155-6, 167-8, 184, 187, 212;
  and Perón 136, 145-6, 151-2;
  structure 137, 176-7; undemocratic 137 (n. 31)
Peronist Youth Movement (MJP) 19 (n. 49)
Peronist Youth of the Argentine Republic 135 (n. 27), 186 (n. 68)
El Peronista 151-2
'peronization' (in 1960s) 29, 49-60
Peru 130, 257 (n. 89)
Piccinini, Alberto 168
Píccoli, Carlos 265
Pinochet, General Augusto 150, 212 (n. 148)
Piriz, Mario 222 (n. 172)
Pita, Colonel Juan Alberto 241
Ponce, Teodoro 170
Popular Advance Union (UDELPA) 104 (n. 23), 212 (n. 146)
Popular Christian Party 191 (n. 85)
Popular Conservative Party 104
Popular Conservative (Party) Youth 160
Popular Left Front (FIP) 11 (n. 26), 14 (n. 32), 184, 207 (n. 127)
Popular Liberation Commands (CPL) 220 (n. 166), 275
Popular Radicals (UCRP) 34
Popular Socialist Party 215
population 3 (n. 7), 6, 76
Populorum progressio 53-4
Portantiero, Juan Carlos 220 (n. 166)
Posse, Gustavo 51 (n. 14)
Poulantzas, Nicos 162 (n. 92)
Power Workers Union (Luz y Fuerza) 140, 168 (n. 14), 230
Prats, General Carlos 155
press: commercial 165-6, 189-90, 191 (n. 85), 217 (n. 159), 234; left-wing 29 (n. 71), 30 (n. 73), 57-8, 127 (n. 9), 138, 152, 159-60, 177 (n. 41), 190-1, 245 (n. 47), 253
Press Workers Union 66, 220 (n. 166)
Primera Plana 177 (n. 41), 196 (n. 99)
professional bodies 67-70
Progressive Democratic Party 104
Publicity Workers Union 168 (n. 14)
Puch, Ramón 209 (n. 136)
Puig, Juan Carlos 130
Puiggrós, Rodolfo: political evolution 10, 11 (n. 26); writings 14-15; university rector 133-4, 158; in exile 208 (n. 130); son 245 (n. 47); and Montoneros 244, 260, 268; death 268
Puiggrós, Sergio 245
Pujadas, Mariano 99 (n. 17), 113, 117, 119, 187 (n. 76)
Pujals, Luis 60 (n. 39), 116, 276
Puro Pueblo 138

Quieto, Roberto Jorge: early activity 220; 1971 abduction 69, 108; as FAR leader 107, 127 (n. 10), 220; in Rawson escape 117, 220; leading Montonero 151, 259; 1974 arrest 152; interviewed 195; abduction and trial 218-23, 239; character 220, 222 (n. 171)
Quijada, Rear Admiral Hermes 166 (n. 10)
Quispe, Antonio 152

Radical Orientation Force of the Argentine Youth (FORJA) 8-9, 206 (n. 123), 273
Radical Party (UCR): pre-1946, 3-4, 7 (n. 15), 7-8, 37; of Balbín 95, 104, 115, 154, 167, 188, 207-8, 231 (n. 15)
Radical (Party) Youth 160
radicalization (in 1960s) 30-9, 60-70
Radio Liberación 253, 263
Radio Noticias del Continente 253 (n. 74)
Radowitzky, Simón 185
Ragone, Miguel 132-3, 177
Railway Workers Union (UF) 140
Ramírez, Julio César 257 (n. 89)
Ramírez, General Pedro P. 7
Ramos, Jorge Abelardo 10, 11 (n. 26), 14-16
Ramos, Pablo 267 (n. 120)
Ramus, Carlos Gustavo: in Tacuara 48, 52; founding Montonero 56-7, 84-5; in Aramburazo 90, 94, 96; death 97, 99 (n. 17), 106, 138; remembered 84, 98, 149
Ranier, Jesús 211 (n. 144)
Rank-and File Peronism (PB) 52, 70, 75, 107, 129, 168 (n. 14)
Raverta, María Inés 257 (n. 89)
Rawson, General Arturo 7
Rawson Prison escape 110, 116-17, 187 (n. 76), 197 (n. 102), 220
Rearte, Gustavo 19 (n. 49), 30, 35, 44-

Index 307

5, 45 (n. 115), 87
Redundancy Law 143, 158
Remorino, Jerónimo 44
Resistencia, the 32, 35-6, 101, 154, 206, 273
Restorationist Nationalist Guard (GNR) 50
Revolutionary Armed Forces (FAR) 69-70, 89, 120, 124, 197 (n. 102), 220 (n. 166), 265; casualties 110, 116, 118, 152; guerrilla activity 66, 107-10, 116-17, 166; merge with Montoneros 106, 109-10, 127-8, 144, 259, 275; origins 99 (n. 15), 107
Revolutionary Christian Party (PRC) 104 (n. 23), 212
Revolutionary Communist Party (PCR) 220 (n. 166)
Revolutionary Coordinating Council (JCR) 182 (n. 56)
Revolutionary Peronist Movement (MRP) 30, 34, 38, 42-5, 101
Revolutionary Popular Alliance (APR) 212 (n. 146)
Revolutionary Vanguard (VR) 220 (n. 166)
Reyes, Cipriano 24
Righi, Esteban 131, 208 (n. 130)
Rivera, Enrique 10
Roca, General Julio 2
Roca-Runciman Pact 4
Rocazo, the 114
Rockefeller, Nelson 66, 107
Rodeiro, Luis 97, 99 (n. 17), 138
Rodrigo, Celestino 173, 226; the *Rodrigazo* 173, 263-4, 274
Rodríguez, José 86
Rodríguez Anido, Julio 267 (n. 120)
Rogers, William 124
Rojas, Admiral Isaac 35
Romeo, Felipe 156, 186 (n. 68)
Roqué, Julio 125, 126 (n. 6), 239 (n. 34), 241, 246, 259
Rosas, Police Insp. 218
Rosas, Juan Manuel de 1, 5, 23-4, 49
rosistas 5-6, 274
Rossi, Jorge Gustavo 59, 103, 113
Roth, Carlos 217 (n. 160)
Rucci, José 169 (n. 17); CGT leader 147, 167-8, 172; killed 144, 150, 165-6, 170, 172, 252
Rulli, Jorge 19 (n. 49)
rural guerrillas 38, 76, 107, 155 (n. 73),

195, 233; *see also foquismo* and *foquistas*
Russo, José Mario 185
Russo, Vicenzo 113

Sabattinistas 8
Sabelli, María Angélica 99 (n. 15)
Sabino Navarro, José: Catholic militancy 59, 87; creates guerrilla group 86, 275; joins Montoneros 87, 97, 99 (n. 17), 103; as Montonero leader 106, 112; death 116; remembered 84, 138, 149, 183
Sáenz Peña Law 3
Saint-Jean, General Ibérico 250
Salamanca, René 158, 168, 174 (n. 35)
Salame, Ismael 209 (n. 136), 246
Salas, Martín 165-6
Salas, Samuel 224
Salato, Leando 165-6
Sallustro, Oberdan 51, 106 (n. 28)
San Juan, Rubén 165
San Martín, General José de 84, 95, 100
Sandinistas (FSLN) 256-7, 265, 270
Sandler, Héctor 211
Sanmartino, Major Julio Ricardo 109
Santillán, Atilio 172
Santucho, Mario Roberto: studies 195 (n. 98); PRT leader 60 (n. 39), 276; on PRT-ERP composition 162 (n. 93); quoted 129; escapes from Rawson 117; wife executed 117, 184; death 241
Sanz de Llorente, Susana 209 (n. 136), 267 (n. 120)
Sapag, Felipe 133
Sapag, Ricardo Omar 133
Sartre, Jean-Paul 218
Sbédico, Luis 195 (n. 98)
Secondary Students Nationalist Union (UNES) 48
Secondary Students Union (UES) 134, 137, 138 (n. 32), 176, 277-8
Selser, Jorge 104 (n. 22)
Semana Trágica (of 1919) 13
62 De Pie Junto a Perón 34, 43
62 Organizations 19, 35, 167, 170 (n. 22), 171, 228
Sfeir, Carlos 126
Silvesti, Roberto 176
Simone, Horacio Beto 152
sindicalismo de liberación 64-5
sindicalismo nacional 50, 274

SITRAC-SITRAM 75, 109
Slemenson, Claudio 209 (n. 136)
Soares, Eduardo 196 (n. 99)
Social Pact 141-2, 148, 158, 164, 168, 172
social structure 77-8
socialism 3-4
socialismo nacional 274; advocated 68 (n. 55), 71; and Montoneros 46, 101-2, 128, 142, 146, 151; used by Perón 25, 38-9, 146
Socialist International 254-5
Socialist Party: see Argentine Socialist Party
Socialist Party of the National Revolution (PSRN) 10
Socialist Workers Party (PST): creation of 60 (n. 39), 276; relations with other forces 160, 168 (n. 14), 207 (n. 127); and repression 184, 229; statement on Formosa attack 200
Solano Lima, Vicente 120, 158 (n. 82), 167
Solari Yrigoyen, Hipólito 154
Solarz, Sara 248
Soldati, Francisco 264
Somoza, Anastasio 254, 256, 265
Soratti Martínez 99 (n. 17)
Sosa, Captain Luis Emilio 117
Soviet Union 18, 102, 130 (n. 16), 255-6
Spain 1, 3, 73, 74 (n. 71), 78, 191, 255, 257 (n. 89)
Span, Benito Miguel 168 (n. 12)
Spanish Socialist Workers Party (PSOE) 255
Stalin, Joseph 14 (n. 32)
Starita, Carlos 166
State Gas Union (*Gas del Estado*) 139
State Workers Association (ATE) 139, 206, 209 (n. 136), 255
Stenfer, Gustavo Natalio 185 (n. 66), 189 (n. 79)
Stroessner, Alfredo 74, 167
students: and guerrilla warfare 61, 77, 215; political sympathies of 20-1, 55, 67-8, 139-40, 215; protests by 63-6, 131; and university reforms 133-4 *see also* elections
Suárez, Julio 265
Suárez Masón, General Carlos Guillermo 228
Sueldo, Horacio 211, 212 (n. 146)
Sun Yat-sen 9 (n. 20)

Susini, Grassi 67
Sylvester, Stanley 106 (n. 28)
syndicalism 3

Taco Ralo, FAP venture 76, 107
Tacuara 47-50, 52, 56, 67, 274
Tacuara Revolutionary Nationalist Movement (MNRT) 49-52, 67, 78, 153 (n. 67)
Taiana, Jorge 130-1, 156
Talento, Miguel 176
Tanzania 256
Tapia, Roberto 209 (n. 136)
Tarquini, José Miguel 186
Tendencia Revolucionaria 134-53, 176, 206, 274
terrorism: condemned 215; data 215-16 (n. 156); military view of 229; and Montoneros 79-80 (n. 86), 111, 189, 201, 224-5, 235, 258 (n. 92); and Peronist Right 147, 187; 'State terrorism' 244-52, 257 (n. 89); and urban guerrilla warfare 11 (n. 26), 79-80, 147 (n. 56), 187-8, 192; in Venezuela 113
Third Position: in Peronist doctrine 18-19, 38, 102, 146; political party 207
Third World, identification with (*tercermundismo*) 38, 54, 58, 83, 102-3
Third World Priests Movement 54-5, 58, 98
Tía Vicenta 63
Tolchinsky, Daniel 265
Torres, Father Camilo 53, 55-8
Torres, Heriberto 209 (n. 136)
Torres, General Juan 257 (n. 89)
Torres Molina, Ramón 122 (n. 49)
torture 107, 115, 131-2, 147 (n. 56), 154, 217, 233, 245, 247
Tosco, Agustín 168
Touraine, Alain 218
trade unions: see labour movement and under names of unions
Transport Workers Union (UTA) 139, 149, 209 (n. 136)
Trelew Massacre 116-17, 126 (n. 6), 160, 166, 184, 187 (n. 76), 196
Triple A (AAA): activity 154-6, 212-13, 233; guerrilla responses to 179, 184-9; origins of 74 (n. 71), 152-4; and the State 153, 156, 186, 190 (n. 83); structure of 185, 186 (n. 68)

Trotsky, Leon 14 (n. 32)
Trotskyism in Argentina 9-10, 14 (n. 32), 29 (n. 70), 50, 60 (n. 39), 106
Trotz, Colonel 233-4
Troxler, Julio 152 (n. 66), 154
Trujillo, Rafael 74
Tucumán Province: and guerrilla activity 76, 107, 155 (n. 73), 195-7, 203, 204 (n. 119), 224 (n. 177), 233, 236; and sugar workers 58, 172 (n. 30), 195 (n. 96)
Tupamaros (MLN-T) 79-80 (n. 86), 81-2, 96, 113, 189; Argentine connection 51, 155, 182 (n. 56); in JCR 182 (n. 56); structure 84, 177 (n. 43); and traitors 222 (n. 172)

Ugarte, Manuel 9
United Leadership of Argentine Workers (CUTA) 264 (n. 112)
United States of America: economic interests 15-16, 66, 83, 130 (n. 16), 131, 161, 240, 255; relations with Argentina 18, 102, 124, 150 (n. 61), 188-9
universities 3, 229; attitudes of academics 63-4, 68-9, 134; autonomy of 63-4, 77, 157; and *cátedras nacionales* 68-9; Peronist Left influence in 67-9, 133-4, 215; Peronist Right takeover of 156-8; University of Buenos Aires 57, 63, 67-9, 133-4, 139-40, 156-8, 176, 215; 1974 University Law 157-8; *see also* students
University Law Union (SUD) 49, 67
Uriburu, José Camilo 113
Uriburu, General José F. 4-5, 49
Uriz, Rufino 212-13 (n. 148), 235
Urondo, Francisco 117 (n. 41), 125-6, 245, 259
Urquiza, General Justo José de 1
Urteaga, José Benito 241
Uruguay 51, 77-8, 96, 182 (n. 56), 203, 204 (n. 119), 222 (n. 172), 257 (n. 89)
Uturuncos 38, 76, 84, 95, 101
Uzal, Roberto 113

Vaca Narvaja, Daniel 267 (n. 120)
Vaca Narvaja, Fernando: escapes from Rawson 117; Montonero spokesman 150; member of National Leadership 239 (n. 34), 253, 261, 279 (and n.); in Nicaragua 256-7, 265; reprisal against family 187 (n. 76); wife executed 117
Vaca Narvaja, Dr. Hugo 187 (n. 76)
Vaca Narvaja Jr., Hugo 235
Valenzuela, Tulio 261-2
Valladares, Carlos 257 (n. 89)
Valle, Gen. Juan José 90-2, 101, 112, 154, 200
Vallese, Felipe 84
Valotta, Mario 30
Van Lierde, Pablo 155, 165
Vandor, Augusto T.: as union leader 34-5, 42-5, 64; assassination of 44, 66, 108, 150, 165 (n. 4), 170-2; Vandorism 34-5, 42-5, 61, 64-5, 73, 168-70, 173
Varela, Felipe 2
Vázquez, Jorge Alberto 130
Vélez, Ignacio 86, 96, 99, 99 (n. 17)
Ventura, Juan Pablo 157, 164, 176
Verd, Marcelo Aburnio 107-8
Verdinelli, Néstor Raúl 107
Vidaña, Roberto 132
Videla, Lt. Gen. Jorge Rafael: as C-in-C 204 (n. 119); on democracy 231 (n. 12); escapes assassination attempts 225, 236-7; as President 63, 116, 124, 162 (n. 91), 185, 227-32, 238, 255, 258; on terrorism 229
Viel, Dante 206
Vietnam (SRV) 51, 130, 132 (n. 20)
Vilar, Pierre 218
Vilas, General Acdel Eduardo 229
Villa Devoto: prison revolt 125-6, 189 (n. 79); alleged massacre 250
Villagra, Agustín 110
Villalón, Héctor 38, 42-3
Villanueva, Ernesto 158
Villar, Alberto 154, 184-5, 187
Villarreal de Santucho, Ana María 117, 184
Villegas, General Osiris Guillermo 99
Villone, Carlos 186 (n. 68)
Villot, Cardinal Jean 254
Viola, Captain Humberto Antonio 195 (n. 96)
Viola, General Roberto 228, 231
violence, political: data 70 (n. 59), 112 (n. 33), 113, 116, 155, 194 (n. 93), 195 (n. 96), 211 (n. 144), 215-16, 223, 235-6, 238, 247, 250-1
Vittar, Rodolfo 132

Walsh, María Victoria 246
Walsh, Rodolfo 65, 91 (n. 5), 132 (n. 19), 245-6, 267-8
Weissen, Ana 265
William Morris, gun-fight of 97
women 19, 134 (n. 25)
Workers Power Communist Organization (OCPO) 241
Workers Revolutionary Party (PRT) 60 (n. 39), 168 (n. 14), 182 (n. 56), 195 (nn. 96 and 98), 275-6
Workers' Word (*Palabra Obrera*) 29 (n. 70), 38, 60 (n. 39), 276
working class: see labour movement
World Cup Football Championship (1978) 238, 257-8, 260, 263 (n. 109), 273
World Youth Festival (1978) 256, 260

Yäger, Raúl 239 (n. 34), 263, 279 (and nn.)
Yessi, Julio 186 (n. 68)
Yrigoyen, Hipólito 4-5, 9, 13
Yrigoyenism 68 (n. 55), 100-1

Zavala Rodríguez, Miguel Domingo 146, 151, 176, 177 (n. 41), 209 (n. 136), 245, 260
Zimbabwe African National Union (ZANU) 256

DATE DUE